TOTAL
BASIC SKILLS
Grade 4

Crocodile Tears & other stories

Copyright © 2004 by School Specialty Children's Publishing. Published by American Education Publishing, an imprint of School Specialty Children's Publishing, a member of the School Specialty Family.

Printed in the United States of America. All rights reserved. Except as permitted under the United States Copyright Act, no part of this publication may be reproduced or distributed in any form or by any means, or stored in a database or retrieval system, without prior written permission from the publisher, unless otherwise indicated.

Send all inquiries to:
School Specialty Children's Publishing
8720 Orion Place
Columbus, OH 43240-2111

ISBN 0-7696-3644-6

1 2 3 4 5 6 7 8 9 10 VHJ 09 08 07 06 05 04

GRADE 4

Table of Contents

Math

READING

Crocodile
Tears
& other
stories

Name _____

Spelling: Short Vowels

Vowels are the letters **a, e, i, o, u** and sometimes **y**. There are five short vowels: **ă** as in **a**pple, **ě** as in **e**gg and br**ea**th, **ĭ** as in s**i**ck, **ŏ** as in t**o**p and **ŭ** as in **u**p.

Directions: Complete the exercises using words from the box.

blend	insist	health	pump	crop
fact	pinch	pond	hatch	plug

1. Write each word under its vowel sound.

ă	**ě**	**ĭ**	**ŏ**	**ŭ**
_____	_____	_____	_____	_____
_____	_____	_____	_____	_____

2. Complete these sentences, using a word with the vowel sound given. Use each word from the box only once.

Here's an interesting (**ă**) _____ about your (**ě**) _____.

Henry was very pleased with his corn (**ŏ**) _____.

The boys enjoyed fishing in the (**ŏ**) _____.

They (**ĭ**) _____ on watching the egg (**ă**) _____.

(**ě**) _____ in a (**ĭ**) _____ of salt.

The farmer had to (**ŭ**) _____ water from the lake for his cows to drink.

Did you put the (**ŭ**) _____ in the bathtub this time?

Name _____

Spelling: Short Vowels

Directions: Read the words. After each, write the correct vowel sound. Underline the letter or letters that spell the sound in the word. The first one has been done for you.

Word	Vowel		Word	Vowel
1. str<u>u</u>ck	U	9. breath	____
2. scramble	____	10. edge	____
3. strong	____	11. kick	____
4. chill	____	12. stop	____
5. thud	____	13. quiz	____
6. dread	____	14. brush	____
7. plunge	____	15. crash	____
8. mask	____	16. dodge	____

Directions: List four words (nouns and verbs) with short vowel sounds. Then write two sentences using the words.

Example: Ann, can, hand, Pam
Ann can give Pam a hand.

_____

_____

_____

_____

1. _____

_____

2. _____

_____

Name _____

Spelling: Long e and a

Long **ē** can be spelled **ea** as in **real** or **ee** as in **deer**. Long **ā** can be spelled **a** as in **apron**, **ai** as in **pail**, **ay** as in **pay** or **a-e** as in **lake**.

Directions: Complete the exercises with words from the box.

deal	clay	grade	weave	stream
pain	tape	sneeze	claim	treat

1. Write each word in the row with the matching vowel sound.

   ā _____ _____ _____ _____ _____

   ē _____ _____ _____ _____ _____

2. Complete each sentence, using a word with the vowel sound given. Use each word from the word box only once.

   Everyone in (**ā**) _____ four ate an ice-cream (**ē**) _____.

   Every time I (**ē**) _____, I feel (**ā**) _____ in my chest.

   When I (**ē**) _____ with yarn, I put a piece of (**ā**) _____ on the loose ends so they won't come undone.

   You (**ā**) _____ you got a good (**ē**) _____ on your new bike, but I still think you paid too much.

   We camped beside a (**ē**) _____.

   We forgot to wrap up our (**ā**) _____ and it dried out.

Spelling: Long e and a

When a vowel is long, it sounds the same as its letter name.

Examples: Long ē as in **treat**, **eel**, **complete**.
Long ā as in **ape**, **trail**, **say**, **apron**.

Directions: Read the words. After each word, write the correct vowel sound. Underline the letter or letters that spell the sound in the word. The first one has been done for you.

Word	Vowel		Word	Vowel
1. sp<u>ee</u>ch	e	9. plate	_____
2. grain	_____	10. breeze	_____
3. deal	_____	11. whale	_____
4. baste	_____	12. clay	_____
5. teach	_____	13. veal	_____
6. waiting	_____	14. apron	_____
7. cleaning	_____	15. raining	_____
8. crane	_____	16. freezer	_____

Directions: Choose one long vowel sound. On another sheet of paper, list six words (nouns and verbs) that have that sound. Below, write two sentences using the words.

Example: freeze, teaches, breeze, speech, keep, Eve

Eve teaches speech in the breeze.

_____

_____

Name _____

Spelling: Long i and o

Long **ī** can be spelled **i** as in **wild**, **igh** as in **night**, **i-e** as in **wipe** or **y** as in **try**. Long **ō** can be spelled **o** as in **most**, **oa** as in **toast**, **ow** as in **throw** or **o-e** as in **hope**.

| stripe | groan | glow | toast | grind | fry | sight | stove | toads | flight |

Directions: Complete the exercises with words from the box.

1. Write each word from the box with its vowel sound.

ī _____

ō _____

2. Complete these sentences, using a word with the given vowel sound. Use each word from the box only once.

We will (ī) _____ potatoes on the (ō) _____.

I thought I heard a low (ō) _____, but when I looked, there was nothing

in (ī) _____.

The airplane for our (ī) _____ had a (ī) _____ painted on its side.

I saw a strange (ō) _____ coming from the toaster while

making (ō) _____.

Do (ō) _____ live in the water like frogs?

We need to (ī) _____ up the nuts before we put them in the cookie dough.

Name _____

Spelling: Long i and o

Directions: Read the words. After each word, write the correct vowel sound. Underline the letter or letters that spell the sound. The first one has been done for you.

Word	Vowel		Word	Vowel
1. br<u>i</u>ght	i		9. white	_____
2. globe	_____		10. roast	_____
3. plywood	_____		11. light	_____
4. mankind	_____		12. shallow	_____
5. coaching	_____		13. myself	_____
6. prize	_____		14. throne	_____
7. grind	_____		15. cold	_____
8. withhold	_____		16. snow	_____

Directions: Below are words written as they are pronounced. Write the words that sound like:

1. thrōn	_____	5. brīt	_____
2. skōld	_____	6. grīnd	_____
3. prīz	_____	7. plīwood	_____
4. rōst	_____	8. mīself	_____

Name _____

Spelling: Long u

Long **ū** can be spelled, **u-e** as in **cube** or **ew** as in **few**. Some sounds are similar in sound to **u** but are not true **u** sounds, such as the **oo** in **tooth**, the **o-e** in **move** and the **ue** in **blue**.

Directions: Complete each sentence using a word from the box. Do not use the same word more than once.

blew
tune
flute
cute
stew
June
glue

1. Yesterday, the wind _____ so hard it knocked down a tree on our street.

2. My favorite instrument is the _____.

3. The little puppy in the window is so _____.

4. I love _____ because it's so warm, and we get out of school.

5. For that project, you will need scissors, construction paper and _____.

6. I recognize that song because it has a familiar _____.

7. My grandmother's beef _____ is the best I've ever tasted.

Name _____

Spelling: The k Sound

The **k** sound can be spelled with **k** as in **peek**, **c** as in **cousin**, **ck** as in **sick**, **ch** as in **Chris** and **cc** as in **accuse**. In some words, however, one **c** may be pronounced **k** and the other **s** as in **accident**.

Directions: Answer the questions with words from the box.

Christmas	freckles	command	cork	jacket
accused	castle	stomach	rake	accident

1. Which two words spell **k** with a **k**?

   _____   _____

2. Which two words spell **k** with **ck**?

   _____   _____

3. Which two words spell **k** with **ch**?

   _____   _____

4. Which five words spell **k** with **c** or **cc**? _____

   _____   _____

   _____   _____

5. Complete these sentences, using a word with **k** spelled as shown. Use each word from the box only once.

   Dad gave Mom a garden (**k**) _____ for (**ch**) _____.

   There are (**ck**) _____ on my face and (**ch**) _____.

   The people (**cc**) _____ her of taking a (**ck**) _____.

   The police took (**c**) _____ after the (**cc**) _____.

   The model of the (**c**) _____ was made out of

   (**c and k**) _____.

Name _____

Spelling: The f Sound

The **f** sound can be spelled with **f** as in **fun**, **gh** as in **laugh** or **ph** as in **phone**.

Directions: Answer the questions with words from the box.

fuss	paragraph	phone	friendship	freedom
defend	flood	alphabet	rough	laughter

1. Which three words spell **f** with **ph**?

   _____ _____ _____

2. Which two words spell **f** with **gh**?

   _____ _____

3. Which five words spell **f** with an **f**?

   _____ _____ _____

   _____ _____

4. Complete these sentences, using a word with **f** spelled as shown. Use each word from the box only once.

   I don't know why my teacher makes so much (**f**) _____ over writing

   a (**ph**) _____.

   A (**f**) _____ can help you through (**gh**) _____ times.

   The soldiers will (**f**) _____ our (**f**) _____.

   Can you say the (**ph**) _____ backwards?

   When I answered the (**ph**) _____, all I could

   hear was (**gh**) _____.

   If it keeps raining, we'll have a (**f**) _____.

GRADE 4

Name _____

Spelling: The s Sound

The **s** sound can be spelled with **s** as in **super** or **ss** as in **assign**, **c** as in **city**, **ce** as in **fence** or **sc** as in **scene**. In some words, though, **sc** is pronounced **sk**, as in **scare**.

Directions: Answer the questions using words from the box.

exciting	medicine	lettuce	peace	scissors
slice	scientist	sauce	bracelet	distance

1. Which five words spell **s** with just an **s** or **ss**?

   _____ _____ _____

   _____ _____

2. Which two words spell **s** with just a **c**?

   _____ _____

3. Which six words spell **s** with a **ce**?

   _____ _____ _____

   _____ _____ _____

4. Which two words spell **s** with **sc**?

   _____ _____

5. Complete these sentences, using a word with **s** spelled as shown. Use each word from the box only once.

   My (**ce**) _____ fell off my wrist into the tomato

   _____ (**s and ce**).

   My salad was just a (**s and ce**) _____ of (**ce**) _____.

   It was (**c**) _____ to see the lions, even though they were a long

   (**s and ce**) _____ away.

   The (**sc and s**) _____ invented a new (**c**) _____.

   If I lend you my (**sc**) _____, will you leave me in

   (**ce**) _____?

Name _____

Spelling: Syllables

A **syllable** is a word—or part of a word—with only one vowel sound. Some words have just one syllable, such as **cat**, **dog** and **house**. Some words have two syllables, such as **in-sist** and **be-fore**. Some words have three syllables, such as **re-mem-ber**; four syllables, such as **un-der-stand-ing**; or more. Often words are easier to spell if you know how many syllables they have.

Syl-la-bles

Directions: Write the number of syllables in each word below.

Word	Syllables		Word	Syllables
1. amphibian	_____		11. want	_____
2. liter	_____		12. communication	_____
3. guild	_____		13. pedestrian	_____
4. chili	_____		14. kilo	_____
5. vegetarian	_____		15. autumn	_____
6. comedian	_____		16. dinosaur	_____
7. warm	_____		17. grammar	_____
8. piano	_____		18. dry	_____
9. barbarian	_____		19. solar	_____
10. chef	_____		20. wild	_____

Directions: Next to each number, write words with the same number of syllables.

1 _____ _____ _____ _____

2 _____ _____ _____ _____

3 _____ _____ _____ _____

4 _____ _____ _____ _____

5 _____ _____ _____ _____

Name _____

Spelling: Syllables

Directions: Write each word from the box next to the number that shows how many syllables it has.

fuss	paragraph	phone	friendship	freedom
defend	flood	alphabet	rough	laughter

One: _____ _____ _____ _____

Two: _____ _____ _____ _____

Three: _____ _____

How many syllables are there in the word **friendship**?

Directions: Circle the two words in each row that have the same number of syllables as the first word.

Example: fact   (clay)   happy   (phone)   command

rough	freckle	pump	accuse	ghost
jacket	flood	laughter	defend	paragraph
accident	paragraph	carpenter	stomach	castle
comfort	agree	friend	friendship	health
fuss	collect	blend	freedom	hatch
alphabet	thankful	Christmas	enemy	unhappy
glowing	midnight	defending	grading	telephone

Reading

17

Basic Total Skills Grade 4

Vocabulary: Synonyms

A **synonym** is a word that means the same, or nearly the same, as another word.
Example: quick and **fast**

Directions: Draw lines to match the words in Column A with their synonyms in Column B.

Column A	Column B
plain	unusual
career	vocation
rare	disappear
vanish	greedy
beautiful	finish
selfish	simple
complete	lovely

Directions: Choose a word from Column A or Column B to complete each sentence below.

1. Dad was very excited when he discovered the _____ coin for sale on the display counter.

2. My dog is a real magician; he can _____ into thin air when he sees me getting his bath ready!

3. Many of my classmates joined the discussion about _____ choices we had considered.

4. "You will need to _____ your report on ancient Greece before you sign up for computer time," said Mr. Rastetter.

5. Your _____ painting will be on display in the art show.

Name _____

Vocabulary: Synonyms

| tired | greedy | easy | rough | minute | melted | friend | smart |

Directions: For each sentence, choose a word from the box that is a synonym for the bold word. Write the synonym above the word.

1. Boy, this road is really **bumpy**!

2. The operator said politely, "One **moment**, please."

3. My parents are usually **exhausted** when they get home from work.

4. "Don't be so **selfish**! Can't you share with us?" asked Rob.

5. That puzzle was actually quite **simple**.

6. "Who's your **buddy**?" Dad asked as we walked onto the porch.

7. When it comes to animals, my Uncle Steve is quite **intelligent**.

8. The frozen treat **thawed** while I stood in line for the bus.

Name _____

Vocabulary: Antonyms

An **antonym** is a word that means the opposite of another word.
Example: difficult and **easy**

Directions: Choose words from the box to complete the crossword puzzle.

| friend | vanish | quit | safety | liquids | scatter | help | noisy |

ACROSS:

2. Opposite of **gather**

3. Opposite of **enemy**

4. Opposite of **prevent**

6. Opposite of **begin**

7. Opposite of **silent**

DOWN:

1. Opposite of **appear**

2. Opposite of **danger**

5. Opposite of **solids**

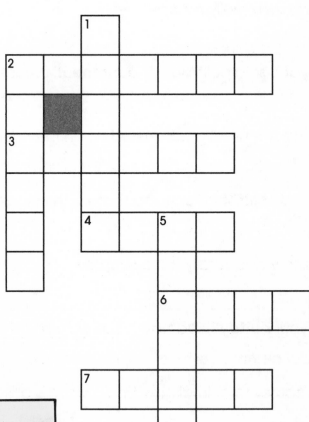

Name _____

Vocabulary: Antonyms

Directions: Each bold word below has an antonym in the box. Use these words to write new sentences. The first one is done for you.

friend	vanish	quit	safety	liquids	help	scatter	worse

1. I'll help you **gather** all the papers on the lawn.

   <u>The strong winds will scatter the leaves.</u>

2. The fourth graders were learning about the many **solids** in their classroom.

   _____

   _____

3. "It's time to **begin** our lesson on the continents," said Ms. Haynes.

   _____

   _____

4. "That's strange. The stapler decided to **appear** all of a sudden," said Mr. Jonson.

   _____

   _____

5. The doctor said this new medicine should **prevent** colds.

   _____

   _____

6. "She is our **enemy**, boys, we can't let her in our clubhouse!" cried Paul.

   _____

   _____

7. I'm certain that dark cave is full of **danger**!

   _____

   _____

8. Give me a chance to make the situation **better**.

   _____

   _____

Name _____

Vocabulary: Homophones

Homophones are two words that sound the same, have different meanings and are usually spelled differently.
Example: write and **right**

Directions: Write the correct homophone in each sentence below.

weight — how heavy something is
wait — to be patient

threw — tossed
through — passing between

steal — to take something that doesn't belong to you
steel — a heavy metal

1. The bands marched _____ the streets lined with many cheering people.

2. _____ for me by the flagpole.

3. One of our strict rules at school is: Never _____ from another person.

4. Could you estimate the _____ of this bowling ball?

5. The bleachers have _____ rods on both ends and in the middle.

6. He walked in the door and _____ his jacket down.

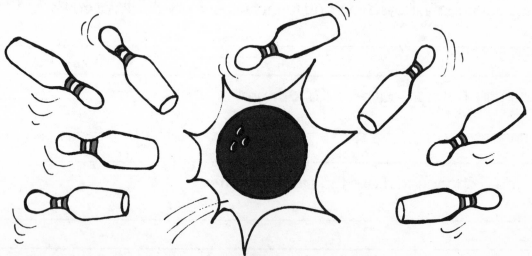

Vocabulary: Homophones

Directions: Write the correct homophone in each sentence below.

cent — a coin having the value of one penny
scent — odor or aroma

chews — grinds with the teeth
choose — to select

course — the path along which something moves
coarse — rough in texture

heard — received sounds in the ear
herd — a group of animals

1. My uncle Mike always _____

   each bite of his food 20 times!

2. As we walked through her garden, we detected

   the _____ of roses.

3. It was very peaceful sitting on the hillside watching

   the _____ of cattle grazing.

4. Which flavor of ice cream did you _____ ?

5. The friendly clerk let me buy the jacket even though I was one _____ short.

6. You will need _____ sandpaper to make the wood smoother.

Vocabulary: Prefixes

A **prefix** is a syllable at the beginning of a word that changes its meaning.

Directions: Add a prefix to the beginning of each word in the box to make a word with the meaning given in each sentence below. The first one is done for you.

PREFIX	MEANING
bi	two or twice
en	to make
in	within
mis	wrong
non	not or without
pre	before
re	again
un	not

grown	write	information	large	cycle	usual	school	sense

1. Jimmy's foot hurt because his toenail was (growing within). __*ingrown*__

2. If you want to see what is in the background, you will have to (make bigger) the

   photograph. _____

3. I didn't do a very good job on my homework, so I will have to (write it again)

   it. _____

4. The newspaper article about the event has some (wrong facts). _____

5. I hope I get a (vehicle with two wheels) for my birthday. _____

6. The story he told was complete (words without meaning)! _____

7. Did you go to (school that comes before kindergarten) before you went to

   kindergarten? _____

8. The ability to read words upside down is most (not usual). _____

Vocabulary: Prefixes

Directions: Circle the correct word for each sentence.

1. You will need to _____ the directions before you complete this page.

   reset   reread   repair

2. Since she is allergic to milk products she has to

   use _____ products.

   nondairy   nonsense   nonmetallic

3. That certainly was an _____ costume he selected for the Halloween party.

   untied   unusual   unable

4. The directions on the box said to _____ the oven before baking the brownies.

   preheat   preschool   prevent

5. "I'm sorry if I _____ you as to the cost of the trip," explained the travel agent.

   misdialed   misread   misinformed

6. You may use the overhead projector to _____ the picture so the whole class can see it.

   enlarge   enable   endanger

Name _____

Vocabulary: Suffixes

A **suffix** is a syllable at the end of a word that changes its meaning. In most cases, when adding a suffix that begins with a vowel, drop the final **e** of the root word. For example, **fame** becomes **famous**. Also, change a final **y** in the root word to **i** before adding any suffix except **ing**. For example, **silly** becomes **silliness**.

Directions: Add a suffix to the end of each word in the box to make a word with the meaning given (in parentheses) in each sentence below. The first one is done for you.

SUFFIX	MEANING
ful	full of
ity	quality or degree
ive	have or tend to be
less	without or lacking
able	able to be
ness	state of
ment	act of
or	person that does something
ward	in the direction of

effect	like	thought	pay	beauty	thank	back	act	happy

1. Mike was (full of thanks) for a hot meal. _____**thankful**_____

2. I was (without thinking) for forgetting your birthday. _____

3. The mouse trap we put out doesn't seem to be (have an effect). _____

4. In spring, the flower garden is (full of beauty). _____

5. Sally is such a (able to be liked) girl! _____

6. Tim fell over (in the direction of the back) because he wasn't watching where he was going. _____

7. Jill's wedding day was one of great (the state of being happy). _____

8. The (person who performs) was very good in the play. _____

9. I have to make a (act of paying) for the stereo I bought. _____

Name _____

Vocabulary: Suffixes

Directions: Read the story. Choose the correct word from the box to complete the sentences.

beautiful	colorful	payment
breakable	careful	backward
careless	director	agreement
basement	forward	firmness

Colleen and Marj carried the boxes down to the _____ apartment. "Be _____ with those," cautioned Colleen's mother. "All the things in that box are _____ ." As soon as the two girls helped carry all the boxes from the moving van down the stairs, they would be able to go to school for the play tryouts. That was the _____ made with Colleen's mother earlier that day.

"It won't do any good to get _____ with your work. Just keep at it and the job will be done quickly," she spoke with a _____ in her voice.

"It's hard to see where I'm going when I have to walk _____ ," groaned Marj. "Can we switch places with the next box?"

Colleen agreed to switch places, but they soon discovered that the last two boxes were lightweight. Each girl had her own box to carry, so each of them got to walk looking _____ . "These are so light," remarked Marj. "What's in them?"

"These have the _____ , _____ hats I was telling you about. We can take them to the play tryouts with us," answered Colleen. "I bet we'll impress the _____ . Even if we don't get parts in the play, I bet our hats will!"

Colleen's mother handed each of the girls a 5-dollar bill. "I really appreciate your help. Will this be enough?"

"Thanks, Mom. You bet!" Colleen shouted as the girls ran down the sidewalk.

Reading Skills: Classifying

Classifying is placing similar things into categories.

Directions: Classify each group by crossing out the word that does not belong.

1. factory   hotel   lodge   pattern

2. Thursday   September   December   October

3. cottage   hut   carpenter   castle

4. cupboard   orchard   refrigerator   stove

5. Christmas   Thanksgiving   Easter   spring

6. brass   copper   coal   tin

7. stomach   breathe   liver   brain

8. teacher   mother   dentist   office

9. musket   faucet   bathtub   sink

10. basement   attic   kitchen   neighborhood

Name _____

Reading Skills: Classifying

Directions: Complete each idea by crossing out the word or phrase that does not belong.

1. If the main idea is **things that are green**, I don't need:

    the sun   apples   grass   leaves in summer

2. If the idea is **musical instruments**, I don't need a:

    piano   trombone   beach ball   tuba

3. If the idea is **months of the year**, I don't need:

    Friday   January   July   October

4. If the idea is **colors on the U.S. flag**, I don't need:

    white   blue   black   red

5. If the idea is **types of weather**, I don't need:

    sleet   stormy   roses   sunny

6. If the idea is **fruits**, I don't need:

    kiwi   orange   spinach   banana

7. If the idea is **U.S. presidents**, I don't need:

    Lincoln   Jordan   Washington   Adams

8. If the idea is **flowers**, I don't need:

    oak   daisy   tulip   daffodil

9. If the idea is **sports**, I don't need:

    pears   soccer   wrestling   baseball

Name _____

Reading Skills: Analogies

An **analogy** indicates how different items go together or are similar in some way.

Examples:
   Petal is to **flower** as **leaf** is to **tree**.
   Book is to **library** as **food** is to **grocery**.

If you study the examples, you will see how the second set of objects is related to the first set. A petal is part of a flower, and a leaf is part of a tree. A book can be found in a library, and food can be found in a grocery store.

Directions: Fill in the blanks to complete the analogies. The first one has been done for you.

1. Cup is to saucer as glass is to _____coaster_____.

2. Paris is to France as London is to _____.

3. Clothes are to hangers as _____ are to boxes.

4. California is to _____ as Ohio is to Lake Erie.

5. _____ is to table as blanket is to bed.

6. Pencil is to paper as _____ is to canvas.

7. Cow is to _____ as child is to house.

8. State is to country as _____ is to state.

9. Governor is to state as _____ is to country.

10. _____ is to ocean as sand is to desert.

11. Engine is to car as hard drive is to _____.

12. Beginning is to _____ as stop is to end.

Directions: Write three analogies of your own.

_____

_____

_____

Name _____

Reading Skills: Analogies

Directions: Write a word from the box to complete the following analogies.

fence	club	glove	saw	father
blanket	dish	rug	snow	ten
compass	hat	brake	finger	blue

1. Racket is to tennis as _____ is to golf.

2. Glass is to drink as _____ is to eat.

3. Wheel is to steer as _____ is to stop.

4. Roof is to house as _____ is to floor.

5. Rain is to storm as _____ is to blizzard.

6. Clock is to time as _____ is to directions.

7. Lid is to pan as _____ is to head.

8. Hammer is to pound as _____ is to cut.

9. Mother is to daughter as _____ is to son.

10. Shoe is to foot as _____ is to hand.

11. Five is to ten as _____ is to twenty.

12. Shade is to lamp as _____ is to bed.

13. Toe is to foot as _____ is to hand.

14. Frame is to picture as _____ is to yard.

15. Green is to grass as _____ is to sky.

Name _____

Following Directions: Maps

Directions: Follow the directions below to reach a "mystery" location on the map.

1. Begin at home.
2. Drive east on River Road.
3. Turn south on Broadway.
4. Drive to Central Street and turn west.
5. When you get to City Street, turn south.
6. Turn east on Main Street and drive one block to Park Avenue; turn north.
7. At Central Street turn east, then turn southeast on Through Way.
8. Drive to the end of Through Way. Your "mystery" location is to the east.

You are at the _____ .

Can you write an easier way to get back home?

_____

_____

Following Directions: Recipes

Sequencing is putting items or events in logical order.

Directions: Read the recipe. Then number the steps in order for making brownies.

Preheat the oven to 350 degrees. Grease an 8-inch square baking dish.

In a mixing bowl, place two squares (2 ounces) of unsweetened chocolate and 1/3 cup butter. Place the bowl in a pan of hot water and heat it to melt the chocolate and the butter.

When the chocolate is melted, remove the pan from the heat. Add 1 cup sugar and two eggs to the melted chocolate and beat it. Next, stir in 3/4 cup sifted flour, 1/2 teaspoon baking powder and 1/2 teaspoon salt. Finally, mix in 1/2 cup chopped nuts.

Spread the mixture in the greased baking dish. Bake for 30 to 35 minutes. The brownies are done when a toothpick stuck in the center comes out clean. Let the brownies cool. Cut them into squares.

_____ Stick a toothpick in the center of the brownies to make sure they are done.

_____ Mix in chopped nuts.

_____ Melt chocolate and butter in a mixing bowl over a pan of hot water.

_____ Cool brownies and cut into squares.

_____ Beat in sugar and eggs.

_____ Spread mixture in a baking dish.

_____ Stir in flour, baking powder and salt.

_____ Bake for 30 to 35 minutes.

_____ Turn oven to 350 degrees and grease pan.

Reading Skills: Bus Schedules

Schedules are important to our daily lives. Your parents' jobs, school, even watching television—all are based on schedules. When you travel, you probably follow a schedule, too. Most forms of public transportation, such as subways, buses and trains, run on schedules. These "timetables" tell passengers when they will leave each stop or station.

Directions: Use the following city bus schedule to answer the questions.

No. 2 Cross-Town Bus Schedule

State St. at Park Way	Oak St. at Green Ave.	Fourth St. at Ninth Ave.	Buyall Shopping Center
5:00 a.m.	5:14 a.m.	5:23 a.m.	5:30 a.m.
6:38	6:52	7:01	7:08
7:50	8:05	8:14	8:21
9:04	9:18	9:27	9:34
10:15	10:29	10:38	10:47
12:20 p.m.	12:34 p.m.	12:43 p.m.	12:50 p.m.
1:46	2:00	2:09	2:16
3:30	3:44	3:53	4:00
5:20	5:34	5:43	5:50
6:02	6:16	6:25	6:32

1. The first bus of the day leaves the State St./Park Way stop at 5 a.m. What time does the last bus of the day leave this stop? _____

2. The bus that leaves the Oak St./Green Ave. stop at 8:05 a.m. leaves the Buyall Shopping Center at what time? _____

3. What time does the first afternoon bus leave the Fourth St./Ninth Ave. stop? _____

4. How many buses each day run between the State St./Park Way stop and the Buyall Shopping Center? _____

Name _____

Reading Skills: Labels

Directions: You should never take any medicine without your parents' permission, but it is good to know how to read the label of a medicine bottle. Read the label to answer the questions.

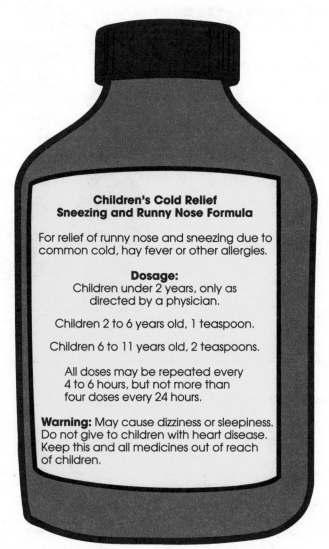

**Children's Cold Relief
Sneezing and Runny Nose Formula**

For relief of runny nose and sneezing due to common cold, hay fever or other allergies.

Dosage:
Children under 2 years, only as directed by a physician.

Children 2 to 6 years old, 1 teaspoon.

Children 6 to 11 years old, 2 teaspoons.

All doses may be repeated every 4 to 6 hours, but not more than four doses every 24 hours.

Warning: May cause dizziness or sleepiness. Do not give to children with heart disease. Keep this and all medicines out of reach of children.

1. How much medicine should a 5 year old take? _____

2. How often can this medicine be taken? _____

3. How do you know how much medicine to give a 1 year old? _____

4. Who should not take this medicine? _____

Reading Skills: Advertisements

Directions: Use the following newspaper ad to answer the questions.

New-Look Fashions

Final Week!
Spring Suit Sale

Buy one suit at the regular price and get a second one for only $50!

Suits: From $75 to $150

New-Look Fashions

5290 Main Street

Hours: Monday–Friday 10–7; Saturday 10–6; Closed Sunday

1. What is the regular price for a suit? _____

2. If you buy one suit at the regular price, what is the price for a second one?

   _____

3. What day is the store closed? _____

4. What hours is the store open on Wednesday? _____

5. When is the sale? _____

Name _____

Facts and Opinions

Facts are statements or events that have happened and can be proven to be true.

Example: George Washington was the first president of the United States.
This statement is a fact. It can be proven to be true by researching the history of our country.

Opinions are statements that express how someone thinks or feels.

Example: George Washington was the greatest president the United States has ever had. This statement is an opinion. Many people agree that George Washington was a great president, but not everyone agrees he was the greatest president. In some people's opinion, Abraham Lincoln was our greatest president.

Directions: Read each sentence. Write **F** for fact or **O** for opinion.

_____ 1. There is three feet of snow on the ground.

_____ 2. A lot of snow makes the winter enjoyable.

_____ 3. Chris has a better swing set than Mary.

_____ 4. Both Chris and Mary have swing sets.

_____ 5. California is a state.

_____ 6. California is the best state in the west.

Directions: Write three facts and three opinions.

Facts:

1) _____

2) _____

3) _____

Opinions:

1) _____

2) _____

3) _____

Name _____

Facts and Opinions

Directions: Write **F** before the facts and **O** before the opinions.

_____ 1. Our school football team has a winning season this year.

_____ 2. Mom's spaghetti is the best in the world!

_____ 3. Autumn is the nicest season of the year.

_____ 4. Mrs. Burns took her class on a field trip last Thursday.

_____ 5. The library always puts 30 books in our classroom book collection.

_____ 6. They should put only books about horses in the collection.

_____ 7. Our new art teacher is very strict.

_____ 8. Everyone should keep take-home papers in a folder so they don't have to look for them when it is time to go home.

_____ 9. The bus to the mall goes right by her house at 7:45 a.m.

_____10. Our new superintendent, Mr. Willeke, is very nice.

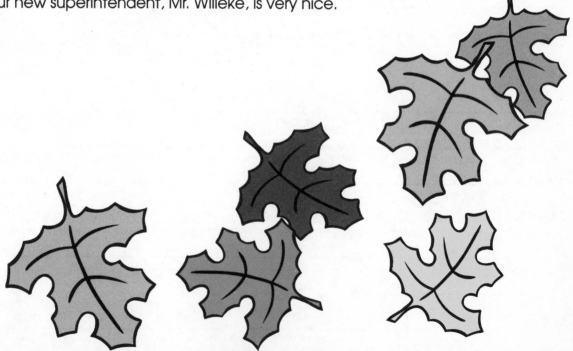

38

Name _____

Reading Skills: Context Clues

When you read, you may confuse words that look alike. You can tell when you read a word incorrectly because it doesn't make sense. You can tell from the **context** (the other words in the sentence or the sentences before or after) what the word should be. These **context clues** can help you figure out the meaning of a word by relating it to other words in the sentence.

Directions: Circle the correct word for each sentence below. Use the context to help you.

1. We knew we were in trouble as soon as we heard the crash.

   The baseball had gone (through, thought) the picture window!

2. She was not able to answer my question because her (month, mouth) was full of pizza.

3. Asia is the largest continent in the (world, word).

4. I'm not sure I heard the teacher correctly. Did he say what I (through, thought) he said?

5. I was not with them on vacation so I don't know a (think, thing) about what happened.

6. My favorite (month, mouth) of the year is July because I love fireworks and parades!

7. You will do better on your book report if you (think, thing) about what you are going

   to say.

Reading Skills: Context Clues

Directions: Read each sentence carefully and circle the word that makes sense.

1. We didn't (except, expect) you to arrive so early.

2. "I can't hear a (word, world) you are saying. Wait until I turn down the stereo," said Val.

3. I couldn't sleep last night because of the (noise, nose) from the apartment below us.

4. Did Peggy say (weather, whether) or not we needed our binoculars for the game?

5. He broke his (noise, nose) when he fell off the bicycle.

6. All the students (except, expect) the four in the front row are excused to leave.

7. The teacher said we should have good (whether, weather) for our field trip.

Directions: Choose a word pair from the sentences above to write two sentences of your own.

1. _____

_____

2. _____

_____

Name _____

Reading Skills: Context Clues

Directions: Use context clues to help you choose the correct word for each sentence below.

designs	studying	collection

Our fourth-grade class will be _____ castles for the next four weeks.

Mrs. Oswalt will be helping with our study. She plans to share her _____

of castle models with the class. We are all looking forward to our morning in the sand at

the school's volleyball court. We all get to try our own _____ to see

how they work.

breath	excited	quietly

Michelle was very _____ the other day when she came into the classroom.

We all noticed that she had trouble sitting _____ in her seat until it was

her turn to share with us. When her turn finally came, she took a deep _____

and told us that her mom was going to have a baby!

responsibility	chooses	messages

Each week, our teacher _____ classroom helpers. They get to be part

of the Job Squad. Some helpers have the _____ of watering the plants.

Everyone's favorite job is when they get to take _____ to the office or to

another teacher's room.

41

Name _____

Reading Skills: Sequencing

Directions: Read each set of events. Then number them in the correct order.

_____ Get dressed for school and hurry downstairs for breakfast.

_____ Roll over, sleepy-eyed, and turn off the alarm clock.

_____ Meet your friends at the corner to walk to school.

_____ The fourth-grade class walked quietly to a safe area away from the building.

_____ The teacher reminded the last student to shut the classroom door.

_____ The loud clanging of the fire alarm startled everyone in the room.

_____ Barb's dad watched from the seat of the tractor as the boys and girls climbed into the wagon.

_____ By the time they returned to the barn, there wasn't much straw left.

_____ As the wagon bumped along the trail, the boys and girls sang songs they learned in music class.

_____ The referee blew his whistle and held up the hand of the winner of the match.

_____ Each wrestler worked hard, trying to outmaneuver his opponent.

_____ The referee said, "Shake hands, boys, and wrestle a fair match."

Name _____

Reading Skills: Sequencing

Directions: In each group below, one event in the sequence is missing. Write the correct sentence from the box where it belongs.

- Paul put his bait on the hook and cast out into the pond.

- "Sorry," he said, "but the TV repairman can't get here until Friday."

- Everyone pitched in and helped.

- Corey put the ladder up against the trunk of the tree.

1. "All the housework has to be done before anyone goes to the game," said Mom.

2. _____

3. We all agreed that "many hands make light work."

1. _____

2. It wasn't long until he felt a tug on the line, and we watched the bobber go under.

3. He was the only one to go home with something other than bait!

1. The little girl cried as she stood looking up into the maple tree.

2. Between her tears, she managed to say, "My kitten is up in the tree and can't get down."

3. _____

1. Dad hung up the phone and turned to look at us.

2. _____

3. "This would be a good time to get out those old board games in the hall closet," he said.

Name _____

Reading Skills: Main Idea in Sentences

The **main idea** is the most important idea, or main point, in a sentence, paragraph or story.

Directions: Circle the main idea for each sentence.

1. Emily knew she would be late if she watched the end of the TV show.
   a. Emily likes watching TV.
   b. Emily is always running late.
   c. If Emily didn't leave, she would be late.

2. The dog was too strong and pulled Jason across the park on his leash.
   a. The dog is stronger than Jason.
   b. Jason is not very strong.
   c. Jason took the dog for a walk.

3. Jennifer took the book home so she could read it over and over.
   a. Jennifer loves to read.
   b. Jennifer loves the book.
   c. Jennifer is a good reader.

4. Jerome threw the baseball so hard it broke the window.
   a. Jerome throws baseballs very hard.
   b. Jerome was mad at the window.
   c. Jerome can't throw very straight.

5. Lori came home and decided to clean the kitchen for her parents.
   a. Lori is a very nice person.
   b. Lori did a favor for her parents.
   c. Lori likes to cook.

6. It was raining so hard that it was hard to see the road through the windshield.
   a. It always rains hard in April.
   b. The rain blurred our vision.
   c. It's hard to drive in the rain.

Reading Skills: Main Idea in Paragraphs

Directions: Read each paragraph below. Then circle the sentence that tells the main idea.

It looked as if our class field day would have to be cancelled due to the weather. We tried not to show our disappointment, but Mr. Wade knew that it was hard to keep our minds on the math lesson. We noticed that even he had been sneaking glances out the window. All morning the classroom had been buzzing with plans. Each team met to plan team strategies for winning the events. Then, it happened! Clouds began to cover the sky, and soon the thunder and lightning confirmed what we were afraid of—field day was cancelled. Mr. Wade explained that we could still keep our same teams. We could put all of our plans into motion, but we would have to get busy and come up with some inside games and competitions. I guess the day would not be a total disaster!

a. Many storms occur in the late afternoon.

b. Our class field day had to be cancelled due to the weather.

c. Each team came up with its own strategies.

Allison and Emma had to work quietly and quickly to get Mom's birthday cake baked before she got home from work. Each of the girls had certain jobs to do—Allison set the oven temperature and got the cake pans prepared, while Emma got out all the ingredients. As they stirred and mixed, the two girls talked about the surprise party Dad had planned for Mom. Even Dad didn't know that the girls were baking this special cake. The cake was delicious. "It shows you what teamwork can do!" said the girls in unison.

a. Dad worked with the girls to bake the cake.

b. Mom's favorite frosting is chocolate cream.

c. Allison and Emma baked a birthday cake for Mom.

Name _____

Main Idea: Busy Beavers

Directions: Read about busy beavers. Then answer the questions.

> Has anyone ever told you that you are as busy as a beaver? If they have, then they mean that you are very busy. Beavers swim easily in streams, picking up rocks and sticks to build their dams. They gnaw at trees with their big front teeth to cut them down. Then they use parts of the trees to build their houses.
>
> Beavers are clever builders. They know exactly what they need to build their beaver dams. They use mud from the stream to make their dams stay together. They use their tails to pat down the mud.
>
> Beavers put a snug room at the top of their dams for their babies. They store their food underwater. Beavers eat the bark from the trees that they cut down!

1. What is the main idea of the first paragraph? _____

_____

2. What is the main idea of the second paragraph? _____

_____

3. What is the main idea of the third paragraph? _____

_____

_____

4. What do beavers use for their dams? _____

5. What parts of their bodies do beavers use to build their homes? _____

_____

_____

Name _____

Main Idea: Bats

Directions: Read about bats. Then answer the questions.

> Bats are unusual animals. Even though they fly, they are not birds. A bat's body is covered with fur. Its wings are made of skin. Bats do not have any feathers.
>
> Bats are the only mammals that fly. A mammal is an animal that has hair and feeds its babies with its own milk. Humans are mammals, too. Mother bats have one or two babies each spring. Baby bats hang onto their mothers until they learn to fly by themselves.
>
> Bats can be many different colors. Most are brown, but some are black, orange, gray or even green.
>
> Even though many people do not like bats, bats don't usually bother people. Only vampire bats, which live in hot jungles, are very dangerous. Bats in the United States help people. Every year they eat billions and billions of harmful insects! Some bats also eat fruit or pollen from flowers.

1. What is the main idea?

   _____ Bats are mammals.

   _____ Bats are unusual animals.

   _____ Some people are afraid of bats.

2. What covers a bat's body? _____

3. How do bats in the United States help people? _____

_____

Directions: Read the clues. Find the answers in the story.

Across:
  2. Vampire bats live
     in hot _____.
  4. What do bats eat?
  5. Most bats are what
     color?

Down:
  1. Bats are not ____.
  3. What are bats' wings
     made of?

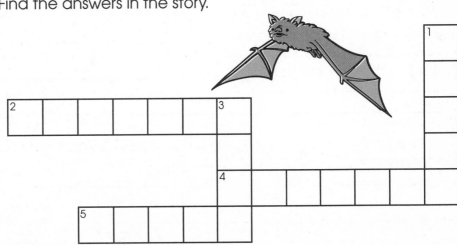

Recognizing Details: Blind Bats

Directions: Read about bats. Then answer the questions.

Bats sleep all day because they cannot see well in the bright sunlight. They hang upside down in dark places such as barns, caves or hollow trees. As soon as darkness begins to fall, bats wake up. They fly around easily and quickly at night.

Bats make sounds that help them fly, since they cannot see well. People cannot hear these sounds. When bats make sounds, the sounds hit objects in front of them and bounce back at them. Bats can tell if something is in their way because there is an echo. Some people say this is like a radar system!

There are many different kinds of bats. Some bats fly all night, while others fly only in the evening or the early morning.

Most bats eat mosquitoes and moths, but there are some bats that will catch fish swimming in water and eat them. Still other kinds of bats eat birds or mice. Bats that live in very hot areas eat only some parts of flowers.

Bats that live in cold areas of the country sometimes sleep all winter. That means they hibernate. Other bats that live in cold areas fly to warmer places for the winter. We call this migration.

1. Who cannot hear the sounds bats make? _____

2. Why do bats sleep all day? _____

3. When do bats eat? _____

4. Where do bats that eat only parts of flowers live? _____

5. Why do bats make sounds? _____

6. What does **hibernate** mean? _____

7. What is the main idea of this selection? _____

_____

8. Do you think a bat would make a good pet? Why or why not? _____

_____

_____

Name _____

Reading Skills: Class Field Trip

Directions: Read this story about a class field trip. Pay careful attention to the details. As you read, think about the beginning, middle and end of the story.

Megan was very excited on her way to school. This was the day her fourth-grade class was going on its field trip to the town historical museum. As she looked out the bus window, she noticed that the bus was stopping at her friend Emily's house. She watched as Emily and her little sister climbed aboard the bus.

"I see you remembered your sack lunch," said Megan as her friend plopped down into the seat next to her.

"Remember? How could I forget?" said Emily breathlessly. "That's all we've talked about in class for the last two days."

The girls knew everyone was looking forward to the trip. Some children in the class were looking forward to the trip because they usually didn't get to ride a bus to school. Others in the class had been enjoying the study of their town's history and learning about what early life had been like for their ancestors. The girls laughed as they remembered what their classmate Paul had said, "I can't wait for the field trip—a day out of school!"

Soon they were at school and joined the rest of the fourth graders in homeroom. Obviously, by the chatter around them, their classmates were just as excited as they were.

Reading Skills: Class Field Trip

"Take your seats, class," said Miss Haynes. "No one gets on the bus for the trip until we take care of some business first. After I check attendance and all of you have your name tags, we can think about getting lined up. While I check attendance, Ms. Diehl and Mrs. Denes will collect your lunch sacks and put them in the cooler. Make sure your names are on your lunch sacks, please!"

All heads turned and looked at the back of the room as Paul let out a loud moan. "Oh, no! I left my lunch at home on the table by the door!"

Miss Haynes said, "Fortunately, the cafeteria will be able to put together a sack lunch for you." She wrote a note to the kitchen staff to explain the problem and sent a much happier Paul on his way down the hall. "Hurry, Paul, we load the bus for our trip in 10 minutes."

"Don't worry, Miss Haynes, I'll be there in time!" replied Paul as he hurried out the door.

True to his word, Paul returned, sack lunch in hand, with plenty of time to spare. Business was soon taken care of and the children and adults were on the bus, heading for their exciting day at the museum.

Reading Skills: Sequencing

Directions: Reread the story, if necessary. Then choose an important event from the beginning, middle and end of the story, and write it below.

Beginning: _____

_____

Middle: _____

_____

End: _____

_____

Directions: Number these story events in the order in which they happened.

_____ Paul moaned, "Oh, no! I left my lunch on the table at home!"

_____ Megan watched as the bus stopped at Emily's house to pick up Emily and her little sister.

_____ Miss Haynes sent Paul to the cafeteria with a note explaining the problem.

_____ The teacher said they had some business to take care of before they could leave on the trip.

_____ Paul quickly returned with a sack lunch packed by the cafeteria helpers.

_____ Megan told Emily, "I see you remembered your sack lunch."

_____ The fourth graders finally loaded onto the bus for the field trip.

Name _____

Reading Skills: Recalling Details

Directions: Answer the questions below about "Class Field Trip."

1. Who were the two adult helpers that would be going on the trip with Miss Haynes'

   class? _____

2. The students in Miss Haynes' class were excited about the field trip for different reasons.

   What were the three different reasons mentioned in the story?

   a. _____

   b. _____

   c. _____

3. What business did Miss Haynes need to take care of before the class could leave on

   its trip? _____

Directions: Write the letter of the definition beside the word it defines. If you need help,
use a dictionary or check the context of the story.

a. sat down, not very gently
b. easy to understand; without doubt
c. family members that lived in the past,
   such as grandparents
d. in a favorable way

_____ ancestors

_____ fortunately

_____ plopped

_____ obviously

READING COMPREHENSION

Name _____

Comprehension: "The Princess and the Pea"

Fairy tales are short stories written for children involving magical characters.

Directions: Read the story. Then answer the questions.

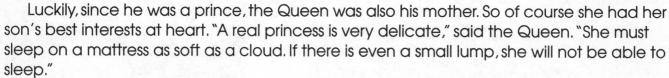

Once there was a prince who wanted to get married. The catch was, he had to marry a *real* princess. The Prince knew that real princesses were few and far between. When they heard he was looking for a bride, many young women came to the palace. All claimed to be real princesses.

"Hmmm," thought the Prince. "I must think of a way to sort out the real princesses from the fake ones. I will ask the Queen for advice."

Luckily, since he was a prince, the Queen was also his mother. So of course she had her son's best interests at heart. "A real princess is very delicate," said the Queen. "She must sleep on a mattress as soft as a cloud. If there is even a small lump, she will not be able to sleep."

"Why not?" asked the Prince. He was a nice man but not as smart as his mother.

"Because she is so delicate!" said the Queen impatiently. "Let's figure out a way to test her. Better still, let me figure out a test. You go down and pick a girl to try out my plan."

The Prince went down to the lobby of the castle. A very pretty but humble-looking girl caught his eye. He brought her back to his mother, who welcomed her.

"Please be our guest at the castle tonight," said the Queen. "Tomorrow we will talk with you about whether you are a real princess."

The pretty but humble girl was shown to her room. In it was a pile of five mattresses, all fluffy and clean. "A princess is delicate," said the Queen. "Sweet dreams!"

The girl climbed to the top of the pile and laid down, but she could not sleep. She tossed and turned and was quite cross the next morning.

"I found this under the fourth mattress when I got up this morning," she said. She handed a small green pea to the Queen. "No wonder I couldn't sleep!"

The Queen clapped her hands. The Prince looked confused. "A real princess is delicate. If this pea I put under the mattress kept you awake, you are definitely a princess."

"Of course I am," said the Princess. "Now may I please take a nap?"

1. Why does the Prince worry about finding a bride? _____

_____

2. According to the Queen, how can the Prince tell who is a real princess? _____

_____

3. Who hides something under the girl's mattress? _____

Name _____

Comprehension: "The Princess and the Pea"

Directions: Review the story "The Princess and the Pea." Then answer the questions.

1. Why does the Prince need a test to see who is a real princess?

_____

_____

2. Why does the Princess have trouble sleeping? _____

_____

3. In this story, the Queen puts a small pea under a pile of mattresses to see if the girl is delicate. What else could be done to test a princess for delicacy? _____

_____

_____

_____

The story does not tell whether or not the Prince and Princess get married and live happily ever after, only that the Princess wants to take a nap.

Directions: Write a new ending to the story.

4. What do you think happens after the Princess wakes up?

_____

_____

_____

_____

_____

_____

_____

Name _____

Comprehension: "The Frog Prince"

Directions: Read the story "The Frog Prince." Then answer the questions.

Once upon a time, there lived a beautiful princess who liked to play alone in the woods. One day, as she was playing with her golden ball, it rolled into a lake. The water was so deep she could not see the ball. The Princess was very sad. She cried out, "I would give anything to have my golden ball back!"

Suddenly, a large ugly frog popped out of the water. "Anything?" he croaked. The Princess looked at him with distaste. "Yes," she said, "I would give anything."

"I will get your golden ball," said the frog. "In return, you must take me back to the castle. You must let me live with you and eat from your golden plate."

"Whatever you want," said the Princess. She thought the frog was very ugly, but she wanted her golden ball.

The frog dove down and brought the ball to the Princess. She put the frog in her pocket and took him home. "He is ugly," the Princess said. "But a promise is a promise. And a princess always keeps her word."

The Princess changed her clothes and forgot all about the frog. That evening, she heard a tapping at her door. She ran to the door to open it and a handsome prince stepped in.

"Who are you?" asked the Princess, already half in love.

"I am the prince you rescued at the lake," said the handsome Prince. "I was turned into a frog one hundred years ago today by a wicked lady. Because they always keep their promises, only a beautiful princess could break the spell. You are a little forgetful, but you did keep your word!"

Can you guess what happened next? Of course, they were married and lived happily ever after.

1. What does the frog ask the Princess to promise? _____

_____

2. Where does the Princess put the frog when she leaves the lake? _____

_____

3. Why could only a princess break the spell? _____

_____

_____

Comprehension: "The Frog Prince"

Directions: Review the story "The Frog Prince." Then answer the questions.

1. What does the Princess lose in the lake? _____

2. How does she get it back? _____

_____

_____

3. How does the frog turn back into a prince? _____

_____

4. What phrases are used to begin and end this story? _____

_____

5. Are these words used frequently to begin and end fairy tales? _____

There is more than one version of most fairy tales. In another version of this story, the Princess has to kiss the frog in order for him to change back into a prince.

Directions: Write your answers.

6. What do you think would happen in a story where the Princess kisses the frog, but he remains a frog?

_____

_____

7. What kinds of problems would a princess have with a bossy frog in the castle? Brainstorm ideas and write them here.

_____

_____

8. Rewrite the ending to "The Frog Prince" so that the frog remains a frog and does not turn into a handsome prince. Continue your story on another sheet of paper.

_____

Name _____

Main Idea: "The Hare and the Tortoise"

The story of "The Hare and the Tortoise" is called a **fable.** Fables are usually short stories. As you read this story and the other fables on the next few pages, look for two characteristics the fables have in common.

Directions: Read the fable "The Hare and the Tortoise." Then answer the questions.

One day the hare and the tortoise were talking. Or rather, the hare was bragging and the tortoise was listening.

"I am faster than the wind," bragged the hare. "I feel sorry for you because you are so slow! Why, you are the slowest fellow I have ever seen."

"Do you think so?" asked the tortoise with a smile. "I will race you to that big tree across the field."

Slowly, he lifted a leg. Slowly, he pointed toward the tree.

"Ha!" scoffed the hare. "You must be kidding! You will most certainly be the loser! But, if you insist, we will race."

The tortoise nodded politely. "I'll be off," he said. Slowly and steadily, the tortoise moved across the field.

The hare stood back and laughed. "How sad that he should compete with me!" he said. His chest puffed up with pride. "I will take a little nap while the poor old tortoise lumbers along. When I wake up, he will still be only halfway across the field."

The tortoise kept on, slow and steady, across the field. Some time later, the hare awoke. He discovered that while he slept, the tortoise had won the race.

1. What is the main idea? (Check one.)

_____ Tortoises are faster than hares.

_____ Hares need more sleep than tortoises.

_____ Slow and steady wins the race.

2. The hare brags that he is faster than what? (Check one.)

_____ a bullet

_____ a greyhound

_____ the wind

3. Who is modest, the tortoise or the hare? _____

Name _____

Cause and Effect: "The Hare and the Tortoise"

Another important skill in reading is recognizing cause and effect. The **cause** is the reason something happens. The **effect** is what happens or the situation that results from the cause. In the story, the hare falling asleep is a cause. It causes the hare to lose the race. Losing the race is the effect.

Directions: Identify the underlined words or phrases by writing **cause** or **effect** in the blanks.

1. The hare and tortoise had a race because the hare bragged about being faster.

_____

2. The tortoise won the race because he continued on, slowly, but steadily.

_____

Directions: Review the fable "The Hare and the Tortoise." Then answer the questions.

1. Who are the two main characters? _____

2. Where does the story take place? _____

3. What lessons can be learned from this story? _____

_____

4. The lesson that is learned at the end of a fable has a special name. What is that special name?

_____

5. Why did the tortoise want to race the hare? _____

_____

6. How do you think the hare felt at the end of the story? _____

_____

7. How do you think the tortoise felt at the end of the story? _____

_____

_____

_____

Sequencing: "The Fox and the Crow"

Directions: Read the fable "The Fox and the Crow." Then number the events in order.

Once upon a time, a crow found a piece of cheese on the ground. "Aha!" he said to himself. "This dropped from a workman's sandwich. It will make a fine lunch for me."

The crow picked up the cheese in his beak. He flew to a tree to eat it. Just as he began to chew it, a fox trotted by.

"Hello, crow!" he said slyly, for he wanted the cheese. The fox knew if the crow answered, the cheese would fall from its mouth. Then the fox would have cheese for lunch!

The crow just nodded.

"It's a wonderful day, isn't it?" asked the fox.

The crow nodded again and held onto the cheese.

"You are the most beautiful bird I have ever seen," added the fox.

The crow spread his feathers. Everyone likes a compliment. Still, the crow held firmly to the cheese.

"There is something I have heard," said the fox, "and I wonder if it is true. I heard that you sing more sweetly than any of the other birds."

The crow was eager to show off his talents. He opened his beak to sing. The cheese dropped to the ground.

"I said you were beautiful," said the fox as he ran away with the cheese. "I did not say you were smart!"

_____ The crow drops the cheese.

_____ The crow flies to a tree with the cheese.

_____ The fox tells the crow he is beautiful.

_____ The fox runs off with the cheese.

_____ A workman loses the cheese from his sandwich.

_____ The fox comes along.

_____ The fox tells the crow he has heard that crows sing beautifully.

_____ The crow picks up the cheese.

Predicting: "The Fox and the Crow"

Directions: Review the fable "The Fox and the Crow." Then answer the questions.

1. With what words does the story begin? _____

2. What other type of story often begins with these same words? _____

3. Although it is not stated, where do you think the story takes place?

_____

4. How does the fox get what he wants from the crow? _____

_____

_____

5. How is the crow in this story like the hare in the last fable? _____

_____

_____

Predicting is telling or guessing what you think might happen in a story or situation based on what you already know.

Directions: Write predictions to answer these questions.

6. Based on what you read, what do you think the crow will do the next time he finds a piece of cheese?

_____

_____

7. What do you think the fox will do the next time he wants to trick the crow? _____

_____

_____

_____

Name _____

Following Directions: "The Boy Who Cried Wolf"

Directions: Read the fable "The Boy Who Cried Wolf." Then complete the puzzle.

Once there was a shepherd boy who tended his sheep alone. Sheep are gentle animals. They are easy to take care of. The boy grew bored.

"I can't stand another minute alone with these sheep," he said crossly. He knew only one thing would bring people quickly to him. If he cried, "Wolf!" the men in the village would run up the mountain. They would come to help save the sheep from the wolf.

"Wolf!" he yelled loudly, and he blew on his horn.

Quick as a wink, a dozen men came running. When they realized it was a joke, they were very angry. The boy promised never to do it again. But a week later, he grew bored and cried, "Wolf!" again. Again, the men ran to him. This time they were very, very angry.

Soon afterwards, a wolf really came. The boy was scared. "Wolf!" he cried. "Wolf! Wolf! Wolf!"

He blew his horn, but no one came, and the wolf ate all his sheep.

Across:

2. This is where the boy tends sheep.

4. When no one came, the wolf _____ all the sheep.

5. Sheep are _____ and easy to take care of.

Down:

1. The people who come are from here.

2. At first, when the boy cries, "Wolf!" the _____ come running.

3. When a wolf really comes, this is how the boy feels.

Cause and Effect: "The Boy Who Cried Wolf"

Directions: Identify the underlined words as a cause or an effect.

1. <u>The boy cries wolf</u> because he is bored.   _____

2. <u>The boy blows his horn</u> and the men come running.   _____

3. No one comes, and <u>the wolf eats all the sheep</u>.   _____

Directions: Answer the questions.

4. What lesson can be learned from this story? _____

_____

_____

_____

5. How is this story like the two other fables you read? _____

_____

_____

_____

6. Is the boy in the story more like the fox or the hare? How so? _____

_____

_____

_____

_____

_____

_____

Name _____

Reading Comprehension: Paul Bunyan

There is a certain kind of fable called a "tall tale." In these stories, each storyteller tries to "top" the other. The stories get more and more unbelievable. A popular hero of American tall tales is Paul Bunyan—a giant of a man. Here are some of the stories that have been told about him.

Even as a baby, Paul was very big. One night, he rolled over in his sleep and knocked down a mile of trees. Of course, Paul's father wanted to find some way to keep Paul from getting hurt in his sleep and to keep him from knocking down all the forests. So he cut down some tall trees and made a boat for Paul to use as a cradle. He tied a long rope to the boat and let it drift out a little way into the sea to rock Paul to sleep.

One night, Paul had trouble sleeping. He kept turning over in his bed. Each time he turned, the cradle rocked. And each time the cradle rocked, it sent up waves as big as buildings. The waves got bigger and bigger until the people on the land were afraid they would all be drowned. They told Paul's parents that Paul was a danger to the whole state! So Paul and his parents had to move away.

After that, Paul didn't get into much trouble when he was growing up. His father taught him some very important lessons, such as, "If there are any towns or farms in your way, be sure to step around them!"

Directions: Answer these questions about Paul Bunyan.

1. What kind of fable is the story of Paul Bunyan? _____

2. What did Paul's father make for Paul to use as a cradle? _____

3. What happened when Paul rolled over in his cradle? _____

_____

4. What did Paul's father tell Paul to do to towns and farms that were in his way?

_____

Reading Comprehension: Paul Bunyan

When Paul Bunyan grew up, he was taller than other men—by about 50 feet or so! Because of his size, he could do almost anything. One of the things he did best was to cut down trees and turn them into lumber. With only four strokes of his axe, he could cut off all the branches and bark. After he turned all the trees for miles into these tall square posts, he tied a long rope to an axe head. Then he yelled, "T-I-M-B-E-R-R-R!" and swung the rope around in a huge circle. With every swing, 100 trees fell to the ground.

One cold winter day, Paul found a huge blue ox stuck in the snow. It was nearly frozen. Although it was only a baby, even Paul could hardly lift it. Paul took the ox home and cared for it. He named it Babe, and they became best friends. Babe was a big help to Paul when he was cutting down trees.

When Babe was full grown, it was hard to tell how big he was. There were no scales big enough to weigh him. Paul once measured the distance between Babe's eyes. It was the length of 42 axe handles!

Once Paul and Babe were working with other men to cut lumber. The job was very hard because the road was so long and winding. It was said that the road was so crooked that men starting home for camp would meet themselves coming back! Well, Paul hitched Babe to the end of that crooked road. Babe pulled and pulled. He pulled so hard that his eyes nearly turned pink. There was a loud snap. The first curve came out of the road and Babe pulled harder. Finally the whole road started to move. Babe pulled it completely straight!

Directions: Answer these questions about Paul Bunyan and Babe.

1. What was Paul Bunyan particularly good at doing? _____

2. What did Paul find in the snow? _____

3. How big was the distance between Babe's eyes? _____

4. What did Babe do to the crooked road? _____

Sequencing: "Kanati's Son"

A **legend** is a story or group of stories handed down through generations. Legends are usually about an actual person.

Directions: Read about Kanati's son. Then number the events in order.

This legend is told by a tribe called the Cherokee (chair-oh-key).

Long ago, soon after the world was made, a hunter and his wife lived on a big mountain with their son. The father's name was Kanati (kah-na-tee), which means "lucky hunter." The mother's name was Selu (see-loo), which means "corn." No one remembers the son's name.

The little boy used to play alone by the river each day. One day, elders of the tribe told the boy's parents they had heard two children playing. Since their boy was the only child around, the parents were puzzled. They told their son what the elders had said.

"I do have a playmate," the boy said. "He comes out of the water. He says he is the brother that mother threw in the river."

Then Selu knew what had happened.

"He is formed from the blood of the animals I washed in the river," she told Kanati. "After you kill them, I wash them in the river before I cook them."

Here is what Kanati told his boy: "Tomorrow when the other boy comes, wrestle with him. Hold him to the ground and call for us."

The boy did as his parents told him. When he called, they came running and grabbed the wild boy. They took him home and tried to tame him. The boy grew up with magic powers. The Cherokee called this "adawehi" (ad-da-we-hi). He was always getting into mischief! But he saved himself with his magic.

_____ Selu and Kanati try to tame the boy from the river.

_____ The little boy tells Selu and Kanati about the other boy.

_____ The little boy's parents are puzzled.

_____ The new boy grows up with magic powers.

_____ The elders tell Selu and Kanati they heard two children playing.

_____ The little boy wrestles his new playmate to the ground.

Name _____

Recognizing Details:
"Why Bear Has a Short Tail"

Some stories try to explain the reasons why certain things occur in nature.

Directions: Read the legend "Why Bear Has a Short Tail." Then answer the questions.

Long ago, Bear had a long tail like Fox. One winter day, Bear met Fox coming out of the woods. Fox was carrying a long string of fish. He had stolen the fish, but that is not what he told Bear.

"Where did you get those fish?" asked Bear, rubbing his paws together. Bear loved fish. It was his favorite food.

"I was out fishing and caught them," replied Fox.

Bear did not know how to fish. He had only tasted fish that others gave him. He was eager to learn to catch his own.

"Please Fox, will you tell me how to fish?" asked Bear.

So, the mean old Fox said to Bear, "Cut a hole in the ice and stick your tail in the hole. It will get cold, but soon the fish will begin to bite. When you can stand it no longer, pull your tail out. It will be covered with fish!"

"Will it hurt?" asked Bear, patting his tail.

"It will hurt some," admitted Fox. "But the longer you leave your tail in the water, the more fish you will catch."

Bear did as Fox told him. He loved fish, so he left his tail in the icy water a very, very long time. The ice froze around Bear's tail. When he pulled free, his tail remained stuck in the ice. That is why bears today have short tails.

1. How does Fox get his string of fish? _____

2. What does he tell Bear to do? _____

_____

3. Why does Bear do as Fox told him? _____

_____

4. How many fish does Bear catch? _____

5. What happens when Bear tries to pull his tail out? _____

_____

Name _____

Recognizing Details: "Why Bear Has a Short Tail"

Directions: Review the legend "Why Bear Has a Short Tail." Then answer the questions.

1. When Bear asks Fox where he got his fish, is Fox truthful in his response? Why or why not?

_____

_____

2. Why does Bear want to know how to fish? _____

_____

3. In reality, are bears able to catch their own fish? How? _____

_____

4. Is Bear very smart to believe Fox? Why or why not? _____

_____

5. How would you have told Bear to catch his own fish? _____

_____

6. What is one word you would use to describe Fox? _____

Explain your answer. _____

_____

7. What is one word you would use to describe Bear? _____

Explain your answer. _____

_____

8. Is this story realistic? _____

9. Could it have really happened? Explain your answer. _____

_____

Predicting: "How the Donkey Got Long Ears"

Directions: Write your predictions to answer these questions.

1. How do you think animals got their names? _____

_____

2. Why would it be confusing if animals did not have names? _____

_____

Directions: Read the legend "How the Donkey Got Long Ears." Then answer the questions.

In the beginning when the world was young, animals had no names. It was very confusing! A woman would say, "Tell the thingamajig to bring in the paper." The man would say, "What thingamajig?" She was talking about the dog, of course, but the man didn't know that.

Together, they decided to name the animals on their farm. First, they named their pet thingamajig Dog. They named the pink thingamajig that oinked Pig. They named the red thingamajig that crowed Rooster. They named the white thingamajig that laid eggs Hen. They named the little yellow thingamajigs that cheeped Chicks. They named the big brown thingamajig they rode Horse.

Then they came to another thingamajig. It looked like Horse, but was smaller. It would be confusing to call the smaller thingamajig Horse, they decided.

"Let's name it Donkey," said the woman. So they did.

Soon all the animals knew their names. All but Donkey, that is. Donkey kept forgetting.

"What kind of a thingamajig am I again?" he would ask the man.

"You are Donkey!" the man would answer. Each time Donkey forgot, the man tugged on Donkey's ears to help him remember.

Soon, however, Donkey would forget his name again.

"Uh, what's my name?" he would ask the woman.

She would answer, "Donkey! Donkey! Donkey!" and pull his ears each time. She was a clever woman but not very patient.

At first, the man and woman did not notice that Donkey's ears grew longer each time they were pulled. Donkey was patient but not very clever. It took him a long time to learn his name. By the time he remembered his name was Donkey, his ears were much longer than Horse's ears. That is why donkeys have long ears.

3. What words could you use to describe Donkey? _____

Explain your choice. _____

Name _____

Comprehension: "How the Donkey Got Long Ears"

Directions: Review the legend "How the Donkey Got Long Ears." Then answer the questions.

1. What do the man and woman call the animals before they have names?

_____

2. Why do they decide to name the animals? _____

_____

3. What is the first animal they name? _____

4. Besides being impatient, what else is the woman? _____

5. What did the people do each time they reminded Donkey of his name? _____

_____

6. Which thingamajigs are yellow? _____

7. Which thingamajig is pink? _____

8. What is the thingamajig they ride? _____

9. Why don't they call the donkey Horse? _____

Directions: Imagine that you are the one who gets to name the animals. Write names for these new "animals."

10. A thingamajig with yellow spots that swims _____

11. A thingamajig with large ears, a short tail and six legs _____

12. A thingamajig with purple wings that flies and sings sweet melodies

_____

13. A thingamajig that gives chocolate milk _____

_____

Name _____

Following Directions: Early Native Americans

Directions: Read about the early Native Americans. Then work the puzzle.

There were about 300 Native American tribes in North America when the first white settlers came to New England in the 1500s. These Native Americans loved and respected the earth. They hunted buffalo on the plains. They fished in the clear rivers. They planted corn and beans on the rich land. They gathered roots and herbs. Before the white settlers drove them out, the Native Americans were masters of the land and all its riches.

The Native Americans grew crops, hunted for food, made clothing and built their homes from what they found on the land in the area where they lived. That is why each tribe of Native Americans was different. Some Native Americans lived in special tents called "tepees." Some lived in adobe pueblos. Some lived in simple huts called "hogans."

Across:

2. Native American homes made of adobe

3. Native Americans hunted this animal.

4. Tents some Native Americans lived in

Down:

1. Huts some Native Americans lived in

4. There were this many hundred tribes of Native Americans when settlers came.

5. All the tribes loved the _____.

Name _____

Comprehension: The Pueblo People

Directions: Read about the Pueblo people. Then answer the questions.

Long ago, Native Americans occupied all the land that is now Arizona, New Mexico, Utah and parts of California and Colorado. Twenty-five different tribes lived in this southwestern area. Several of the tribes lived in villages called "pueblos." The Hopi (hope-ee) Indians lived in pueblos. So did the Zuñi (zoo-nee) and the Laguna (lah-goon-nah). These and other tribes who lived in villages were called the "Pueblo people."

When it was time for the Pueblo people to plant crops, everyone helped. The men kept the weeds pulled. Native Americans prayed for rain to make their crops grow. As part of their worship, they also had special dances called rain dances. When it was time for harvest, the women helped.

The land was bountiful to the Pueblo people. They grew many different crops. They planted beans, squash and 19 different kinds of corn. They gathered wild nuts and berries. They hunted for deer and rabbits. They also traded with other tribes for things they could not grow or hunt.

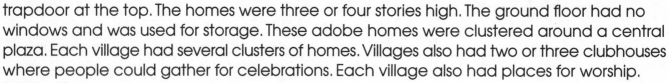

The Pueblo people lived in unusual houses. Their homes were made of adobe brick. Adobe is a type of mud. They shaped the mud into bricks, dried them, then built with them. Many adobe homes exist today in the Southwest.

The adobe homes of long ago had no doors. The Pueblo people entered through a type of trapdoor at the top. The homes were three or four stories high. The ground floor had no windows and was used for storage. These adobe homes were clustered around a central plaza. Each village had several clusters of homes. Villages also had two or three clubhouses where people could gather for celebrations. Each village also had places for worship.

1. What were the five states where the Pueblo people lived? _____

_____

2. What were three crops the Pueblo people grew? _____

_____

3. The early pueblo houses had no

☐ yards.   ☐ windows.   ☐ doors.

Recognizing Details: The Pueblo People

"At the edge of the world
It grows light.
The trees stand shining."
(Pueblo poem)

Directions: Read more about the Pueblo people. Then answer the questions.

The Pueblo people were peaceful. They loved nature, and they seldom fought in wars. When they did fight, it was to protect their people or their land. Their dances, too, were gentle. The Pueblo people danced to ask the gods to bring rain or sunshine. Sometimes they asked the gods to help the women have children.

Some Native Americans wore masks when they danced. The masks were called kachinas (ka-chee-nas). They represented the faces of dead ancestors. (Ancestors are all the family members who have lived and died before.)

The Pueblo people were talented at crafts. The men of many tribes made beautiful jewelry. The women made pottery and painted it with beautiful colors. They traded some of the things they made with people from other tribes.

Both boys and girls needed their parents' permission to marry. After they married, they were given a room next to the bride's mother. If the marriage did not work out, sometimes the groom moved back home again.

1. Among the Pueblo people, who made jewelry? _____

2. Who made pottery? _____

3. What did some of the Pueblo people wear when they danced? _____

_____

4. Why did the Pueblo people dance for the gods? _____

_____

5. Where did newly married couples live? _____

_____

6. Why would a man move back home after marriage? _____

_____

Recognizing Details: The Pueblo People

Directions: Review what you learned about the Pueblo people. Then answer the questions.

1. How many different tribes lived in the Southwestern part of the United States? _____

2. The article specifically names three of the Pueblo tribes. Where could you find the names of the other Pueblo tribes?

_____

_____

3. How did the Pueblo people build their adobe homes? _____

_____

4. How did the location and climate affect their lifestyle? _____

_____

_____

_____

5. How were the jobs of the men and women of a Pueblo tribe alike? _____

_____

_____

6. How were their jobs different? _____

_____

7. How do the responsibilities of the Pueblo men and women discussed differ from those of men and women today?

_____

_____

_____

_____

Comprehension: A California Tribe

Directions: Read about the Yuma. Then answer the questions.

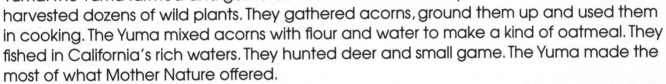

California was home to many Native Americans. The weather was warm, and food was plentiful. California was an ideal place to live.

One California tribe that made good use of the land was the Yuma. The Yuma farmed and gathered roots and berries. They harvested dozens of wild plants. They gathered acorns, ground them up and used them in cooking. The Yuma mixed acorns with flour and water to make a kind of oatmeal. They fished in California's rich waters. They hunted deer and small game. The Yuma made the most of what Mother Nature offered.

The Yuma lived in huts. The roofs were made of dirt. The walls were made of grass. Some Yuma lived together in big round buildings made with poles and woven grasses. As many as 50 people lived in these large homes.

Like other tribes, the Yuma made crafts. Their woven baskets were especially beautiful. The women also wove cradles, hats, bowls and other useful items for the tribe.

When it was time to marry, a boy's parents chose a 15-year-old girl for him. The girl was a Yuma, too, but from another village. Except for the chief, each man took only one wife.

When a Yuma died, a big ceremony was held. The Yumas had great respect for death. After someone died, his or her name was never spoken again.

1. What were two reasons why California was an ideal place to live?

_____

_____

2. What did the Yuma use acorns for? _____

_____

3. What was a beautiful craft made by the Yuma? _____

4. How old was a Yuma bride? _____

5. What types of homes did the Yuma live in? _____

6. How did the Yuma feel about death? _____

_____

Name _____

Recognizing Details: The Yuma

Directions: Review what you read about the Yuma. Write the answers.

1. How did the Yuma make good use of the land?

_____

_____

2. How were the Yuma like the Pueblo people? _____

_____

_____

3. How were they different? _____

_____

_____

4. Why did the Yuma have homes different than those of the Pueblo tribes?

_____

_____

5. When it was time for a young Yuma man to marry, his parents selected a fifteen-year-old bride for him from another tribe. Do you think this is a good idea? Why or why not?

_____

_____

6. Why do you suppose the Yuma never spoke a person's name after he/she died?

_____

_____

7. Do you think this would be an easy thing to do? Explain your answer. _____

_____

Name _____

Following Directions: Sailor Native Americans

Directions: Read about the Sailor Native Americans of Puget Sound. Then work the puzzle.

Three tribes lived on Puget (pew-jit) Sound in Washington state. They made their living from the sea. People later called them the "Sailor" Indians.

These Native Americans fished for salmon. They trapped the salmon in large baskets. Sometimes they used large nets. The sea was filled with fish. Their nets rarely came up empty.

The Sailor Native Americans also gathered roots and berries. They hunted deer, black bear and ducks.

Their homes were amazing! They built big wooden buildings without nails. They did not use saws to cut the wood. The walls and roofs were tied together. Each building had different homes inside. As many as 50 families lived in each big building.

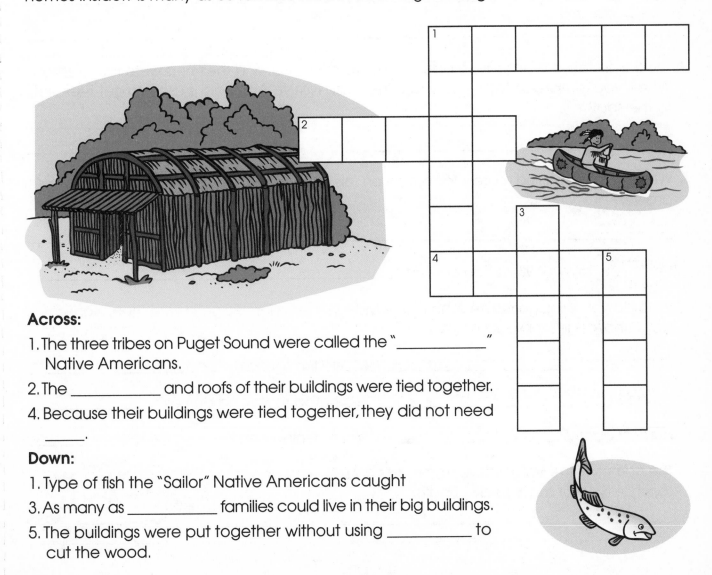

Across:

1. The three tribes on Puget Sound were called the "_____" Native Americans.

2. The _____ and roofs of their buildings were tied together.

4. Because their buildings were tied together, they did not need _____.

Down:

1. Type of fish the "Sailor" Native Americans caught

3. As many as _____ families could live in their big buildings.

5. The buildings were put together without using _____ to cut the wood.

77

Following Directions: Sailor Native Americans

Directions: Review what you read about the Sailor Native Americans. Write your answers.

1. How were the housing arrangements of the Puget Sound Native Americans similar to those of the Yuma?

   _____

2. How was the diet of the Sailor Native Americans like those of the Yuma and Pueblo?

   _____

3. How was it different? _____

   _____

4. The Sailor Native Americans made a living from the sea, and their nets were rarely empty. What type of transportation do you think these Native Americans used to get their nets to the sea?

   _____

5. Where could you find more information on this group of Native Americans to check your answer?

   _____

6. Verify your answer. Were you correct?_____

7. Who do you think performed the many tasks in the Sailor village? Write men, women, boys and/or girls for your answers.

   Built homes? _____   Made fishing baskets? _____

   Fished?_____   Gathered roots and berries? _____

   Hunted game?_____   Made fishing nets? _____

8. The homes of the Sailor Native Americans could be compared to what type of modern dwelling?

   _____

Name _____

Reading Comprehension: Hummingbirds

Hummingbirds are very small birds. This tiny bird is quite an acrobat. Only a few birds, such as kingfishers and sunbirds, can hover, which means to stay in one place in the air. But no other bird can match the flying skills of the hummingbird. The hummingbird can hover, fly backward and fly upside down!

Hummingbirds got their name because their wings move very quickly when they fly. This causes a humming sound. Their wings move so fast that you can't see them at all. This takes a lot of energy. These little birds must have food about every 20 minutes to have enough strength to fly. Their favorite foods are insects and nectar. Nectar is the sweet water deep inside a flower. Hummingbirds use their long, thin bills to drink from flowers. When a hummingbird sips nectar, it hovers in front of a flower. It never touches the flower with its wings or feet.

Besides being the best at flying, the hummingbird is also one of the prettiest birds. Of all the birds in the world, the hummingbird's colors are among the brightest. Some are bright green with red and white markings. Some are purple. One kind of hummingbird can change its color from reddish-brown to purple to red!

The hummingbird's nest is special, too. It looks like a tiny cup. The inside of the nest is very soft. This is because one of the things the mother bird uses to build the nest is the silk from a spider's web.

Directions: Answer these questions about hummingbirds.

1. How did hummingbirds get their name? _____

_____

2. What does **hover** mean? _____

3. How often do hummingbirds need to eat? _____

4. Name two things that hummingbirds eat. _____

5. What is one of the things a mother hummingbird uses to build her nest?

_____

Name _____

Reading Comprehension: Bats

Bats are the only mammals that can fly. They have wings made of thin skin stretched between long fingers. Bats can fly amazing distances. Some small bats have been known to fly more than 25 miles in one night.

Most bats eat insects or fruit. But some eat only fish, others only blood and still others the nectar and pollen of flowers that bloom at night. Bats are active only at night. They sleep during the day in caves or other dark places. At rest, they always hang with their heads down.

You may have heard the expression "blind as a bat." But bats are not blind. They don't, however, use their eyes to guide their flight or to find the insects they eat. A bat makes a high-pitched squeak, then waits for the echo to return to it. This echo tells it how far away an object is. This is often called the bat's sonar system. Using this system, a bat can fly through a dark cave without bumping into anything. Hundreds of bats can fly about in the dark without ever running into each other. They do not get confused by the squeaks of the other bats. They always recognize their own echoes.

Directions: Answer these questions about bats.

1. Bats are the only mammals that
   ☐ eat insects.   ☐ fly.   ☐ live in caves.

2. Most bats eat
   ☐ plants.   ☐ other animals.   ☐ fruits and insects.

3. Bats always sleep
   ☐ with their heads down.   ☐ lying down.   ☐ during the night.

4. Bats are blind.   True   False

5. Bats use a built-in sonar system to guide them.   True   False

6. Bats are confused by the squeaks of other bats.   True   False

Name _____

Review: Venn Diagram

Directions: Make a Venn diagram comparing hummingbirds (see page 79) and bats (see page 80). Write at least three characteristics for each section of the diagram.

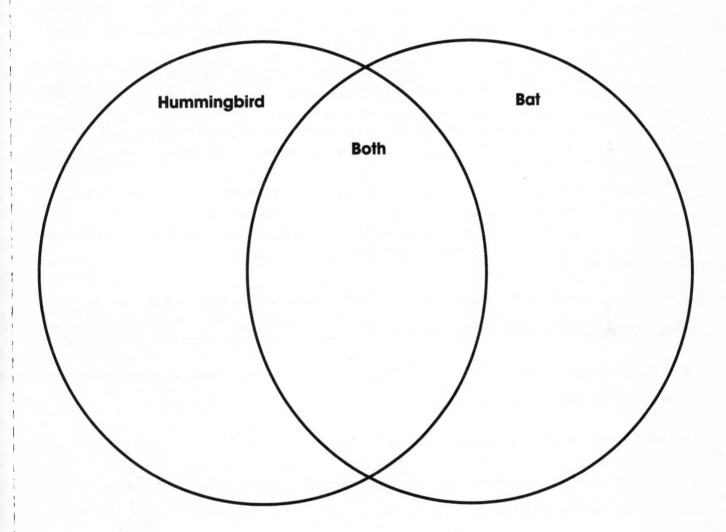

Name _____

Recognizing Details: Giraffes

Directions: Read about giraffes. Then answer the questions.

Giraffes are tall, beautiful, graceful animals that live in Africa. When they are grown, male giraffes are about 18 feet tall. Adult females are about 14 feet tall.

Giraffes are not fat animals, but because they are so big, they weigh a lot. The average male weighs 2,800 pounds. Females weigh about 400 pounds less. Giraffes reach their full height when they are four years old. They continue to gain weight until they are about eight years old.

If you have ever seen giraffes, you know their necks and legs are very long. They are not awkward, though! Giraffes can move very quickly. They like to jump over fences and streams. They do this gracefully. They do not trip over their long legs.

If they are frightened, they can run 35 miles an hour. When giraffes gallop, all four feet are sometimes off the ground! Usually, young and old giraffes pace along at about 10 miles an hour.

Giraffes are strong. They can use their back legs as weapons. A lion can run faster than a giraffe, but a giraffe can kill a lion with one quick kick from its back legs.

Giraffes do not look scary. Their long eyelashes make them look gentle. They usually have a curious look on their faces. Many people think they are cute. Do you?

1. What is the weight of a full-grown male giraffe? _____

2. What is the weight of an adult female? _____

3. When does a giraffe run 35 miles an hour? _____

4. What do giraffes use as weapons? _____

5. For how long do giraffes continue to gain weight?

_____

6. When do giraffes reach their full height?

_____

7. Use a dictionary. What does **gallop** mean?

_____

_____

Name _____

Comprehension: More About Giraffes

Directions: Read more about giraffes. Then answer the questions.

Most people don't notice, but giraffes have different patterns of spots. Certain species of giraffes have small spots. Other species have large spots. Some species have spots that are very regular. You can tell where one spot ends and another begins. Other species have spots that are kind of blotchy. This means the spots are not set off from each other as clearly. There are many other kinds of spot patterns. The pattern of a giraffe's spots is called "markings." No two giraffes have exactly the same markings.

There is one very rare type of giraffe. It is totally black! Have you ever seen one? This kind of giraffe is called a "melanistic" (mell-an-iss-tick) giraffe. The name comes from the word "melanin," which is the substance in cells that gives them color. Giraffes' spots help them blend in with their surroundings. A black giraffe would not blend in well with tree trunks and leaves. Maybe that is why they are so rare.

Being able to blend with surroundings helps animals survive. If a lion can't see a giraffe, he certainly can't eat it. This is called "protective coloration." The animal's color helps protect it.

Another protection giraffes have is their keen eyesight. Their large eyes are on the sides of their heads. Giraffes see anything that moves. They can see another animal a mile away! It is very hard to sneak up on a giraffe. Those who try usually get a quick kick with a powerful back leg.

1. What are markings? _____

2. How far away can a giraffe see another animal? _____

3. Where are a giraffe's eyes? _____

4. What is protective coloration? _____

5. What color is the very rare type of giraffe? _____

6. How do giraffes protect themselves? _____

7. How many kinds of spot patterns do giraffes have? ☐ two ☐ four ☐ many

8. Use a dictionary. What does **species** mean? _____

_____

_____

Name _____

Following Directions: Puzzling Out Giraffes

Directions: Review what you read about giraffes. Read more about giraffes below. Then work the puzzle.

Have you noticed that giraffes have a curious look? That is because they are always paying attention. Their lives depend upon it! Giraffes cannot save themselves from a lion if they don't see it. Giraffes look around a lot. Even when they are chewing their food, they are checking to see if danger is near.

By nature, giraffes are gentle. They do not attack unless they are in danger. A giraffe will lower its head when it is angry. It will open its nostrils and its mouth. Then watch out!

Across:

2. How a giraffe feels when it lowers its head and opens its nose and mouth

4. Giraffes look this way because they are always paying attention.

6. By nature, giraffes are _____.

7. The continent where giraffes live

9. Another name for a black giraffe is _____.

Down:

1. The patterns of a giraffe's spots

3. An animal's ability to blend with surroundings is called protective _____.

5. _____ means a certain kind of animal.

8. Giraffes' eyes are so keen they can see another animal a mile _____.

10. Are giraffes often mean?

Name _____

Recognizing Details: Giraffes

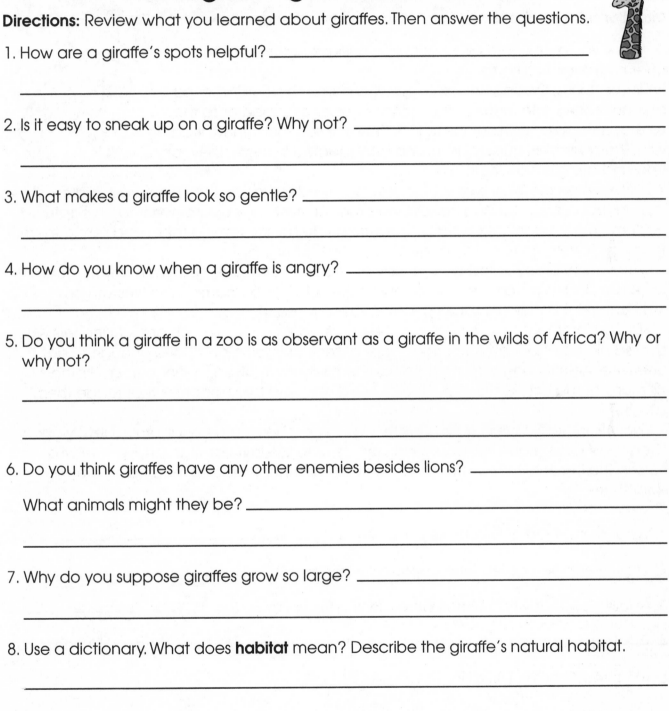

Directions: Review what you learned about giraffes. Then answer the questions.

1. How are a giraffe's spots helpful? _____

_____

2. Is it easy to sneak up on a giraffe? Why not? _____

_____

3. What makes a giraffe look so gentle? _____

_____

4. How do you know when a giraffe is angry? _____

_____

5. Do you think a giraffe in a zoo is as observant as a giraffe in the wilds of Africa? Why or why not?

_____

_____

6. Do you think giraffes have any other enemies besides lions? _____

What animals might they be? _____

_____

7. Why do you suppose giraffes grow so large? _____

_____

8. Use a dictionary. What does **habitat** mean? Describe the giraffe's natural habitat.

_____

_____

_____

Name _____

Comprehension: Wild Horses

Directions: Read about wild horses. Then answer the questions.

Have you ever heard of a car called a Mustang? It is named after a type of wild horse.

In the 1600s, the Spanish explorers who came to North America brought horses with them. Some of these horses escaped onto the prairies and plains. With no one to feed them or ride them, they became wild. Their numbers quickly grew, and they roamed in herds. They ran free and ate grass on the prairie.

Later, when the West was settled, people needed horses. They captured wild ones. This was not easy to do. Wild horses could run very fast. They did not want to be captured!

Some men made their living by capturing wild horses, taming them and selling them. These men were called "mustangers." Can you guess why?

After cars were invented, people did not need as many horses. Not as many mustangers were needed to catch them. More and more wild horses roamed the western prairies. In 1925, about a million mustangs were running loose.

The government was worried that the herds would eat too much grass. Ranchers who owned big herds of cattle complained that their animals didn't have enough to eat because the mustangs ate all the grass. Permission was given to ranchers and others to kill many of the horses. Thousands were killed and sold to companies that made them into pet food.

Now, wild horses live in only 12 states. The largest herds are in California, New Mexico, Oregon, Wyoming and Nevada. Most people who live in these states never see wild horses. The herds live away from people in the distant plains and mountains. They are safer there.

1. What is one type of wild horse called? _____

2. What were men called who captured wild horses? _____

3. About how many wild horses were running free in the U.S. in 1925? _____

4. The wild mustangs were killed and turned into ☐ cars. ☐ pet food. ☐ lunch meat.

5. The largest herds of wild horses are now in

☐ Oregon.   ☐ Ohio.   ☐ New Mexico.   ☐ Wyoming.

☐ California.   ☐ Nevada.   ☐ Kansas.   ☐ Arkansas.

Name _____

Main Idea: More About Wild Horses

Directions: Read more about wild horses. Then answer the questions.

Have you noticed that in any large group, one person seems to be the leader? This is true for wild horses, too. The leader of a band of wild horses is a stallion. Stallions are adult male horses.

The stallion's job is important. He watches out for danger. If a bear or other animal comes close, he lets out a warning cry. This helps keep the other horses safe. Sometimes they all run away together. Other times, the stallion protects the other horses. He shows his teeth. He rears up on his back legs. Often, he scares the other animal away. Then the horses can safely continue eating grass.

Much of the grass on the prairies is gone now. Wild horses must move around a lot to find new grass. They spend about half their time eating and looking for food. If they cannot find prairie grass, wild horses will eat tree bark. They will eat flowers. If they can't find these either, wild horses will eat anything that grows!

Wild horses also need plenty of water. It is often hot in the places where they roam. At least twice a day, they find streams and take long, long drinks. Like people, wild horses lose water when they sweat. They run and sweat a lot in hot weather. To survive, they need as much water as they can get.

Wild horses also use water another way. When they find deep water, they wade into it. It feels good! It cools their skin.

1. What is the main idea? (Check one.)

_____ Wild horses need plenty of water.

_____ Wild horses move in bands protected by a stallion.

_____ Wild horses eat grass.

2. What are two reasons why wild horses need water? _____

_____

3. Why do wild horses move around so much? _____

4. What do wild horses most like to eat? _____

5. What do wild horses spend half their time doing? _____

_____

Name _____

Recognizing Details: Wild Horses

Directions: Review what you read about wild horses. Then answer the questions.

1. How did horses come to North America and become wild? _____

_____

2. Why is it so difficult to capture, tame and train wild horses? _____

_____

3. Do you think it was right of the government to allow the killing of wild horses? _____

Explain your answer. _____

_____

4. Do you think the remaining wild horses should be protected? _____

Explain your answer. _____

_____

5. What is the role of the lead stallion in a wild horse herd? _____

_____

6. What are some things wild horses have in common with giraffes? _____

_____

_____

7. What do you think will happen to wild horses as the prairie lands continue to disappear as a result of developments for homes and businesses?

_____

_____

_____

ENGLISH

highest

higher

high

Writing: Sentences

A **sentence** is a group of words that expresses a complete thought.

Directions: Write **S** by each group of words that is a sentence and **NS** by those that are not a complete sentence.

Examples:

<u>NS</u> A pinch of salt in the soup.

<u>S</u> Grandmother was fond of her flower garden.

_____ 1. Tigers blend in with their surroundings.

_____ 2. Our crop of vegetables for this summer.

_____ 3. Don't forget to put the plug in the sink.

_____ 4. Usually older people in good health.

_____ 5. Fond of lying in the sun for hours.

_____ 6. Will ducks hatch a swan egg?

_____ 7. I hope he won't insist on coming with us.

_____ 8. Regular exercise will pump up your muscles.

_____ 9. A fact printed in all the newspapers.

_____10. Did you pinch the baby?

_____11. Plug the hole with your finger.

_____12. A new teacher today in health class.

_____13. I insist on giving you some of my candy.

_____14. A blend of peanut butter and honey.

_____15. As many facts as possible in your report.

Kinds of Sentences: Statements and Questions

A **statement** tells some kind of information. It is followed by a period (.).

Examples: It is a rainy day. We are going to the beach next summer.

A **question** asks for a specific piece of information. It is followed by a question mark (?).

Examples: What is the weather like today? When are you going to the beach?

Directions: Write whether each sentence is a statement or question. The first one has been done for you.

1. Jamie went for a walk at the zoo.   ____statement____

2. The leaves turn bright colors in the fall.   _____

3. When does the Easter Bunny arrive?   _____

4. Madeleine went to the new art school.   _____

5. Is school over at 3:30?   _____

6. Grandma and Grandpa are moving.   _____

7. Anthony went home.   _____

8. Did Mary go to Amy's house?   _____

9. Who went to work late?   _____

10. Ms. McDaniel is a good teacher.   _____

Directions: Write two statements and two questions below.

Statements:

_____

_____

Questions:

_____

_____

Name _____

Kinds of Sentences: Commands and Exclamations

A **command** tells someone to do something. It is followed by a period (.).

Examples: Get your math book. Do your homework.

An **exclamation** shows strong feeling or excitement. It is followed by an exclamation mark (!).

Examples: Watch out for that car! Oh, no! There's a snake!

Directions: Write whether each sentence is a command or exclamation. The first one has been done for you.

1. Please clean your room. _____command_____

2. Wow! Those fireworks are beautiful! _____

3. Come to dinner now. _____

4. Color the sky and water blue. _____

5. Trim the paper carefully. _____

6. Hurry, here comes the bus! _____

7. Isn't that a lovely picture! _____

8. Time to stop playing and clean up. _____

9. Brush your teeth before bedtime. _____

10. Wash your hands before you eat! _____

Directions: Write two commands and two exclamations below.

Commands:

_____

_____

Exclamations:

_____

_____

Name _____

Sentences: Subjects

The **subject** of a sentence tells you who or what the sentence is about. A subject is either a common noun, a proper noun or a pronoun.

Examples: Sue went to the store.

Sue is the subject of the sentence.

The tired boys and girls walked home slowly.

The tired boys and girls is the subject of the sentence.

Directions: Underline the subject of each sentence. The first one has been done for you.

1. <u>The birthday cake</u> was pink and white.
2. Anthony celebrated his fourth birthday.
3. The tower of building blocks fell over.
4. On Saturday, our family will go to a movie.
5. The busy editor was writing sentences.
6. Seven children painted pictures.
7. Two happy dolphins played cheerfully on the surf.
8. A sand crab buried itself in the dunes.
9. Blue waves ran peacefully ashore.
10. Sleepily, she went to bed.

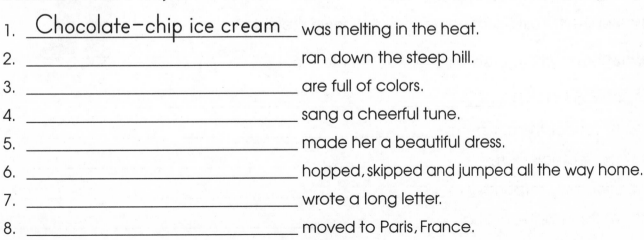

Directions: Write a subject for each sentence.

1. _Chocolate-chip ice cream_ was melting in the heat.
2. _____ ran down the steep hill.
3. _____ are full of colors.
4. _____ sang a cheerful tune.
5. _____ made her a beautiful dress.
6. _____ hopped, skipped and jumped all the way home.
7. _____ wrote a long letter.
8. _____ moved to Paris, France.

Name _____

Sentences: Predicates

The **predicate** of a sentence tells what the subject is doing. The predicate contains the action, linking and/or helping verb.

Examples: Sue went to the store.

Went to the store is the predicate.

The tired boys and girls walked home slowly.

Walked home slowly is the predicate.

Hint: When identifying the predicate, look for the verb. The verb is usually the first word of the predicate.

Directions: Underline the predicate in each sentence with two lines. The first one has been done for you.

1. The choir sang joyfully.
2. Their song had both high and low notes.
3. Sal played the piano while they sang.
4. This Sunday the orchestra will have a concert in the park.
5. John is working hard on his homework.
6. He will write a report on electricity.
7. The report will tell about Ben Franklin's kite experiment.
8. Jackie, Mary and Amy played on the swings.
9. They also climbed the rope ladder.
10. Before the girls went home, they slid down the slide.

Directions: Write a predicate for each sentence.

1. Sam and Libby _____.
2. At school, the children _____.
3. The football team _____.
4. Seven silly serpents _____.
5. At the zoo, the animals _____.

Subjects and Predicates

The **subject** tells who or what the sentence is about. The **predicate** tells what the subject does, did, is doing or will do. A complete sentence must have a subject and a predicate.

Examples:

Subject	Predicate
Sharon	writes to her grandmother every week.
The horse	ran around the track quickly.
My mom's car	is bright green.
Denise	will be here after lunch.

Directions: Circle the subject of each sentence. Underline the predicate.

1. My sister is a very happy person.

2. I wish we had more holidays in the year.

3. Laura is one of the nicest girls in our class.

4. John is fun to have as a friend.

5. The rain nearly ruined our picnic!

6. My birthday present was exactly what I wanted.

7. Your bicycle is parked beside my skateboard.

8. The printer will need to be filled with paper before you use it.

9. Six dogs chased my cat home yesterday!

10. Anthony likes to read anything he can get his hands on.

11. Twelve students signed up for the dance committee.

12. Your teacher seems to be a reasonable person.

Name _____

Subjects and Predicates

Directions: Write subjects to complete the following sentences.

1. _____ went to school last Wednesday.

2. _____ did not understand the joke.

3. _____ barked so loudly that no one could sleep a wink.

4. _____ felt unhappy when the ball game was rained out.

5. _____ wonder what happened at the end of the book.

6. _____ jumped for joy when she won the contest.

Directions: Write predicates to complete the following sentences.

7. Everyone _____.

8. Dogs _____.

9. I _____.

10. Justin _____.

11. Jokes _____.

12. Twelve people _____.

Name _____

Compound Subjects

A **compound subject** is a subject with two parts joined by the word **and** or another conjunction. Compound subjects share the same predicate.

Example:

Her shoes were covered with mud. Her ankles were covered with mud, too.

Compound subject: Her shoes and ankles were covered with mud.

The predicate in both sentences is **were covered with mud**.

Directions: Combine each pair of sentences into one sentence with a compound subject.

1. Bill sneezed. Kassie sneezed.

_____

2. Kristin made cookies. Joey made cookies.

_____

3. Fruit flies are insects. Ladybugs are insects.

_____

4. The girls are planning a dance. The boys are planning a dance.

_____

5. Our dog ran after the ducks. Our cat ran after the ducks.

_____

6. Joshua got lost in the parking lot. Daniel got lost in the parking lot.

_____

Name _____

Compound Subjects

If sentences do not share the same predicate, they cannot be combined to write a sentence with a compound subject.

Example: Mary laughed at the story.
Tanya laughed at the television show.

Directions: Combine the pairs of sentences that share the same predicate. Write new sentences with compound subjects.

1. Pete loves swimming. Jake loves swimming.

_____

2. A bee stung Elizabeth. A hornet stung Elizabeth.

_____

3. Sharon is smiling. Susan is frowning.

_____

4. The boys have great suntans. The girls have great suntans.

_____

5. Six squirrels chased the kitten. Ten dogs chased the kitten.

_____

6. The trees were covered with insects. The roads were covered with ice.

_____

Compound Predicates

A **compound predicate** is a predicate with two parts joined by the word **and** or another conjunction. Compound predicates share the same subject.

Example: The baby grabbed the ball. The baby threw the ball.

> **Compound predicate:** The baby grabbed the ball and threw it.
> The subject in both sentences is **the baby**.

Directions: Combine each pair of sentences into one sentence to make a compound predicate.

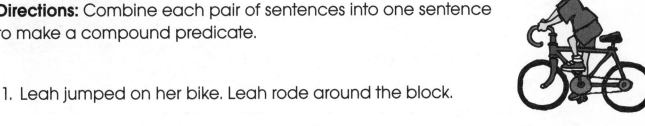

1. Leah jumped on her bike. Leah rode around the block.

   _____

2. Father rolled out the pie crust. Father put the pie crust in the pan.

   _____

3. Anthony slipped on the snow. Anthony nearly fell down.

   _____

4. My friend lives in a green house. My friend rides a red bicycle.

   _____

5. I opened the magazine. I began to read it quietly.

   _____

6. My father bought a new plaid shirt. My father wore his new red tie.

   _____

Name _____

Compound Predicates

Directions: Combine the pairs of sentences that share the same subject. Write new sentences with compound predicates.

1. Jenny picked a bouquet of flowers. Jenny put the flowers in a vase.

   _____

   _____

2. I really enjoy ice cream. She really enjoys ice cream.

   _____

   _____

3. Everyone had a great time at the pep rally. Then everyone went out for a pizza.

   _____

   _____

4. Cassandra built a model airplane.
   She painted the airplane bright yellow.

   _____

   _____

5. Her brother was really a hard person to get to know. Her sister was very shy, too.

   _____

   _____

Name _____

Writing: Nouns

A **noun** names a person, place or thing.

Examples: **Persons** — boy, girl, Mom, Dad
                Places — park, pool, house, office
                Things — bike, swing, desk, book

Directions: Read the following sentences.
Underline the nouns. The first one has been done for you.

1. The girl went to school.

2. Grandma and Grandpa will visit us soon.

3. The bike is in the garage.

4. Dad went to his office.

5. Mom is at her desk in the den.

6. John's house is near the park.

7. Her brothers are at school.

8. We took the books to the library.

Directions: Read the following words. Underline the nouns. Then categorize the nouns on another sheet of paper into groups of people, places and things.

tree	Mrs. Smith	Dad	cards	Grandma	skip	sell
house	car	truck	Mom	office	grass	sign
boy	run	Sam	stove	greet	grade	school
girl	camp	jump	weave	free	driver	room
salesperson	sad	teach	treat	stripe	paint	Jane
clay	man	leave	happy	play	desk	tape
watch	lives	painter	brother	rain	window	hop

Nouns

Directions: Write nouns that name persons.

1. Could you please give this report to my _____ ?

2. The _____ works many long hours to plant crops.

3. I had to help my little _____ when he wrecked his bike yesterday.

Directions: Write nouns that name places.

4. I always keep my library books on top of the _____ so I can find them.

5. We enjoyed watching the kites flying high in the _____ .

6. Dad built a nice fire in the _____ to keep us warm.

Directions: Write nouns that name things.

7. The little _____ purred softly as I held it.

8. Wouldn't you think a _____ would get tired of carrying its house around all day?

9. The _____ scurried into its hole with the piece of cheese.

10. I can tell by the writing that this _____ is mine.

11. Look at the _____ I made in art.

12. His _____ blew away because of the strong wind.

Name _____

Writing: Common and Proper Nouns

Common nouns name general people, places and things.

Examples: boy, girl, cat, dog, park, city, building

Proper nouns name specific persons, places and things.

Examples: John, Mary, Fluffy, Rover, Central Park, Chicago, Empire State Building

Proper nouns begin with capital letters.

Directions: Read the following nouns. On the blanks, indicate whether the nouns are common or proper. The first two have been done for you.

1. New York City	_proper_	9. Dr. DiCarlo	_____
2. house	_common_	10. man	_____
3. car	_____	11. Rock River	_____
4. Ohio	_____	12. building	_____
5. river	_____	13. lawyer	_____
6. Rocky Mountains	_____	14. Grand Canyon	_____
7. Mrs. Jones	_____	15. city	_____
8. nurse	_____	16. state	_____

On another sheet of paper, write proper nouns for the above common nouns.

Directions: Read the following sentences. Underline the common nouns. Circle the proper nouns.

1. Mary's birthday is Friday, October 7.

2. She likes having her birthday in a fall month.

3. Her friends will meet her at the Video Arcade for a party.

4. Ms. McCarthy and Mr. Landry will help with the birthday party games.

5. Mary's friends will play video games all afternoon.

6. Amy and John will bring refreshments and games to the party.

Name _____

Proper Nouns: Capitalization

Proper nouns always begin with a capital letter.

Examples:

    Monday

    Texas

    Karen

    Mr. Logan

    Hamburger Avenue

    Rover

Directions: Cross out the lower-case letters at the beginning of the proper nouns. Write capital letters above them. The first one has been done for you

1. My teddy bear's name is ̶c̶ocoa.

2. ms. bernhard does an excellent job at crestview elementary school.

3. emily, elizabeth and megan live on main street.

4. I am sure our teacher said the book report is due on monday.

5. I believe you can find lake street if you turn left at the next light.

6. Will your family be able join our family for dinner at burger barn?

7. The weather forecasters think the storm will hit the coast of louisiana friday afternoon.

8. My family went to washington, d.c. this summer.

9. Remember, we don't have school on tuesday because of the teachers' meeting.

10. Who do you think will win the game, the cougars or the arrows?

Name _____

Spelling: Plurals

Nouns come in two forms: singular and plural. When a noun is **singular**, it means there is only one person, place or thing.

Examples: car, swing, box, truck, slide, bus

When a noun is **plural**, it means there is more than one person, place or thing.

Examples: two cars, four trucks, three swings, five slides, six boxes, three buses

Usually an **s** is added to most nouns to make them plural. However, if the noun ends in **s**, **x**, **ch** or **sh**, then **es** is added to make it plural.

Directions: Write the singular or plural form of each word.

Singular	Plural		Singular	Plural
1. car	_____	9. _____	tricks
2. bush	_____	10. mess	_____
3. wish	_____	11. box	_____
4. _____	foxes	12. dish	_____
5. _____	rules	13. _____	boats
6. stitch	_____	14. path	_____
7. _____	switches	15. _____	arms
8. barn	_____	16. _____	sticks

Directions: Rewrite the following sentences and change the bold nouns from singular to plural or from plural to singular. The first one has been done for you.

1. She took a **book** to school.
   She took books to school. _____

2. Tommy made **wishes** at his birthday party.

   _____

3. The **fox** ran away from the hunters.

   _____

4. The **houses** were painted white.

   _____

Name _____

Spelling: Plurals

When a word ends with a consonant before **y**, to make it plural, drop the **y** and add **ies**.

Examples:

party	parties
cherry	cherries
daisy	daisies

However, if the word ends with a vowel before **y**, just add **s**.

Examples:

boy	boys
toy	toys
monkey	monkeys

Directions: Write the singular or plural form of each word.

	Singular	Plural		Singular	Plural
1.	fly	_____	7.	_____	decoys
2.	_____	boys	8.	candy	_____
3.	_____	joys	9.	toy	_____
4.	spy	_____	10.	_____	cries
5.	_____	keys	11.	monkey	_____
6.	_____	dries	12.	daisy	_____

Directions: Write six sentences of your own using any of the plurals above.

_____

_____

_____

_____

_____

_____

Spelling: Plurals

Some words in the English language do not follow any of the plural rules discussed earlier. These words may not change at all from singular to plural, or they may completely change spellings.

No Change	Examples:		Complete Change	Examples:

Singular	Plural		Singular	Plural
deer	deer		goose	geese
pants	pants		ox	oxen
scissors	scissors		man	men
moose	moose		child	children
sheep	sheep		leaf	leaves

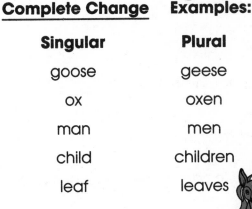

Directions: Write the singular or plural form of each word. Use a dictionary to help if necessary.

	Singular	Plural		Singular	Plural
1.	moose	_____	6.	leaf	_____
2.	woman	_____	7.	_____	sheep
3.	_____	deer	8.	scissors	_____
4.	_____	children	9.	tooth	_____
5.	_____	hooves	10.	wharf	_____

Directions: Write four sentences of your own using two singular and two plural words from above.

_____

_____

_____

_____

Pronouns

A **pronoun** is a word that takes the place of a noun in a sentence.

Examples:

I, my, mine, me

we, our, ours, us

you, your, yours

he, his, him

she, her, hers

it, its

they, their, theirs, them

Directions: Underline the pronouns in each sentence.

1. Bring them to us as soon as you are finished.

2. She has been my best friend for many years.

3. They should be here soon.

4. We enjoyed our trip to the Mustard Museum.

5. Would you be able to help us with the project on Saturday?

6. Our homeroom teacher will not be here tomorrow.

7. My uncle said that he will be leaving soon for Australia.

8. Hurry! Could you please open the door for him?

9. She dropped her gloves when she got off the bus.

10. I can't figure out who the mystery writer is today.

Name _____

Writing: Verbs

Verbs are the action words in a sentence. There are three kinds of verbs: action verbs, linking verbs and helping verbs.

An **action verb** tells the action of a sentence.

Examples: run, hop, skip, sleep, jump, talk, snore
Michael **ran** to the store. **Ran** is the action verb.

A **linking verb** joins the subject and predicate of a sentence.

Examples: am, is, are, was, were
Michael **was** at the store. **Was** is the linking verb.

A **helping verb** is used with an action verb to "help" the action of the sentence.

Examples: am, is, are, was, were
Matthew **was** helping Michael. **Was** helps the action verb **helping**.

Directions: Read the following sentences. Underline the verbs. Above each, write **A** for action verb, **L** for linking verb and **H** for helping verb. The first one has been done for you.

1. Amy <u>jumps</u> rope. [A]

2. Paul was jumping rope, too.

3. They were working on their homework.

4. The math problem requires a lot of thinking.

5. Addition problems are fun to do.

6. The baby sleeps in the afternoon.

7. Grandma is napping also.

8. Sam is going to bed.

9. John paints a lovely picture of the sea.

10. The colors in the picture are soft and pale.

Name _____

Writing: Verb Tense

Not only do verbs tell the action of a sentence, but they also tell when the action takes place. This is called the **verb tense**. There are three verb tenses: past, present and future tense.

Present-tense verbs tell what is happening now.

Example: Jane **spells** words with long vowel sounds.

Past-tense verbs tell about action that has already happened. Past-tense verbs are usually formed by adding **ed** to the verb.

Example: stay — stayed
John **stayed** home yesterday.

Past-tense verbs can also be made by adding helping verbs **was** or **were** before the verb and adding **ing** to the verb.

Example: talk — was talking
Sally **was talking** to her mom.

Future-tense verbs tell what will happen in the future. Future-tense verbs are made by putting the word **will** before the verb.

Example: paint — will paint
Susie and Sherry **will paint** the house.

Directions: Read the following verbs. Write whether the verb tense is past, present or future.

Verb	Tense	Verb	Tense
1. watches	present	8. writes	_____
2. wanted	_____	9. vaulted	_____
3. will eat	_____	10. were sleeping	_____
4. was squawking	_____	11. will sing	_____
5. yawns	_____	12. is speaking	_____
6. crawled	_____	13. will cook	_____
7. will hunt	_____	14. likes	_____

Name _____

Verbs: Present, Past and Future Tense

Directions: Read the following sentences. Write **PRES** if the sentence is in present tense. Write **PAST** if the sentence is in past tense. Write **FUT** if the sentence is in future tense. The first one has been done for you.

<u>FUT</u>   1. I will be thrilled to accept the award.

_____ 2. Will you go with me to the dentist?

_____ 3. I thought he looked familiar!

_____ 4. They ate every single slice of pizza.

_____ 5. I run myself ragged sometimes.

_____ 6. Do you think this project is worthwhile?

_____ 7. No one has been able to repair the broken plate.

_____ 8. Thoughtful gifts are always appreciated.

_____ 9. I liked the way he sang!

_____ 10. With a voice like that, he will go a long way.

_____ 11. It's my fondest hope that they visit soon.

_____ 12. I wanted that coat very much.

_____ 13. She'll be happy to take your place.

_____ 14. Everyone thinks the test is easy.

_____ 15. Collecting stamps is her favorite hobby.

Name _____

Writing: Using ing Verbs

Remember, use **is** and **are** when describing something happening right now. Use **was** and **were** when describing something that already happened.

Directions: Use the verb in bold to complete each sentence. Add **ing** to the verb and use **is**, **are**, **was** or **were**.

Examples:

When it started to rain, we <u>were raking</u> the leaves.　　**rake**

When the soldiers marched up that hill,

Captain Stevens <u>was commanding</u> them.
　　　　　　　command

1. Now, the police _____ them of stealing the money.
　　　　　　accuse

2. Look! The eggs _____.
　　　　　hatch

3. A minute ago, the sky _____.
　　　　　　glow

4. My dad says he _____ us to ice cream!
　　　　　treat

5. She _____ the whole time we were at the mall.
　　　sneeze

6. While we were playing outside at recess, he _____ our tests.
　　　　　　　　　　grade

7. I hear something. Who _____?
　　　　　groan

8. As I watched, the workers _____ the wood into little chips.
　　　　　　grind

Name _____

Writing: Present-Tense Verbs

Directions: Write two sentences for each verb below. Tell about something that is happening now and write the verb as both simple present tense and present tense with a helping verb.

Example: run

Mia runs to the store. Mia is running to the store.

1. hatch

_____

_____

2. check

_____

_____

3. spell

_____

_____

4. blend

_____

_____

5. lick

_____

_____

6. cry

_____

_____

7. write

_____

_____

8. dream

_____

_____

Name _____

Writing: Verb Tense

Directions: Read the following sentences. Underline the verbs. Above each verb, write whether it is past, present or future tense.

         past

1. The crowd <u>was booing</u> the referee.

2. Sally will compete on the balance beam.

3. Matt marches with the band.

4. Nick is marching, too.

5. The geese swooped down to the pond.

6. Dad will fly home tomorrow.

7. They were looking for a new book.

8. Presently, they are going to the garden.

9. The children will pick the ripe vegetables.

10. Grandmother canned the green beans.

Directions: Write six sentences of your own using the correct verb tense.

Past tense:

_____

_____

Present tense:

_____

_____

Future tense:

_____

_____

Adding "ed" to Make Verbs Past Tense

To make many verbs past tense, add **ed**.

Examples:

cook + ed = cooked   wish + ed = wished   play + ed = played

When a verb ends in a **silent e**, drop the **e** and add **ed**.

Examples:

hope + ed = hoped   hate + ed = hated

When a verb ends in **y** after a consonant, change the **y** to **i** and add **ed**.

Examples:

hurry + ed = hurried   marry + ed = married

When a verb ends in a single consonant after a single short vowel, double the final consonant before adding **ed**.

Examples:

stop + ed = stopped   hop + ed = hopped

Directions: Write the past tense of the verb correctly. The first one has been done for you.

1. call   _____called_____
2. copy   _____
3. frown   _____
4. smile   _____
5. live   _____
6. talk   _____
7. name   _____
8. list   _____
9. spy   _____
10. phone   _____

11. reply   _____
12. top   _____
13. clean   _____
14. scream   _____
15. clap   _____
16. mop   _____
17. soap   _____
18. choke   _____
19. scurry   _____
20. drop   _____

Name _____

Writing: Past-Tense Verbs

To write about something that already happened, you can add **ed** to the verb.

Example: Yesterday, we **talked**.

You can also use **was** and **were** and add **ing** to the verb.

Example: Yesterday, we **were talking**.

When a verb ends with **e**, you usually drop the **e** before adding **ing**.

Examples: grade — was grading   weave — were weaving
tape — was taping   sneeze — were sneezing

Directions: Write two sentences for each verb below. Tell about something that has already happened and write the verb both ways.
(Watch the spelling of the verbs that end with **e**.)

Example: stream

The rain streamed down the window.

The rain was streaming down the window.

1. grade

_____

_____

2. tape

_____

_____

3. weave

_____

_____

4. sneeze

_____

_____

Name _____

Irregular Verbs: Past Tense

Irregular verbs change completely in the past tense. Unlike regular verbs, past-tense forms of irregular verbs are not formed by adding **ed**.

Example: The past tense of **go** is **went**.

Other verbs change some letters to form the past tense.
Example: The past tense of **break** is **broke**.

A **helping verb** helps to tell about the past. **Has**, **have** and **had** are helping verbs used with action verbs to show the action occurred in the past. The past-tense form of the irregular verb sometimes changes when a helping verb is added.

Present Tense Irregular Verb	Past Tense Irregular Verb	Past Tense Irregular Verb With Helper
go	went	have/has/had gone
see	saw	have/has/had seen
do	did	have/has/had done
bring	brought	have/has/had brought
sing	sang	have/has/had sung
drive	drove	have/has/had driven
swim	swam	have/has/had swum
sleep	slept	have/has/had slept

Directions: Choose four words from the chart. Write one sentence using the past-tense form of the verb without a helping verb. Write another sentence using the past-tense form with a helping verb.

1. _____

_____

2. _____

_____

3. _____

_____

4. _____

_____

Name _____

The Irregular Verb "Be"

Be is an irregular verb. The present-tense forms of **be** are **be**, **am**, **is** and **are**. The past-tense forms of **be** are **was** and **were**.

Directions: Write the correct form of **be** in the blanks. The first one has been done for you.

1. I _____ am _____ so happy for you!

2. Jared _____ unfriendly yesterday.

3. English can _____ a lot of fun to learn.

4. They _____ among the nicest people I know.

5. They _____ late yesterday.

6. She promises she _____ going to arrive on time.

7. I _____ nervous right now about the test.

8. If you _____ satisfied now, so am I.

9. He _____ as nice to me last week as I had hoped.

10. He can _____ very gracious.

11. Would you _____ offended if I moved your desk?

12. He _____ watching at the window for me yesterday.

Name _____

Verbs: "Was" and "Were"

Singular	Plural
I was	we were
you were	you were
he, she, it was	they were

Directions: Write the correct form of the verb in the blanks. Circle the subject of each sentence. The first one has been done for you.

_____**was**_____ 1. (He) was/were so happy that we all smiled, too.

_____ 2. Was/Were you at the party?

_____ 3. She was/were going to the store.

_____ 4. He was/were always forgetting his hat.

_____ 5. Was/Were she there?

_____ 6. Was/Were you sure of your answers?

_____ 7. She was/were glad to help.

_____ 8. They was/were excited.

_____ 9. Exactly what was/were you planning to do?

_____ 10. It was/were wet outside.

_____ 11. They was/were scared by the noise.

_____ 12. Was/Were they expected before noon?

_____ 13. It was/were too early to get up!

_____ 14. She was/were always early.

_____ 15. You were/was the first person I asked.

Verbs: "Went" and "Gone"

The word **went** is used without a helping verb.

Examples:

    Correct: Susan **went** to the store.

    Incorrect: Susan **has went** to the store.

Gone is used with a helping verb.

Examples:

    Correct: Susan **has gone** to the store.

    Incorrect: Susan **gone** to the store.

Directions: Write **C** in the blank if the verb is used correctly. Draw an **X** in the blank if the verb is not used correctly.

_____C_____ 1. She has gone to my school since last year.

_____ 2. Has he been gone a long time?

_____ 3. He has went to the same class all year.

_____ 4. I have went to that doctor since I was born.

_____ 5. She is long gone!

_____ 6. Who among us has not gone to get a drink yet?

_____ 7. The class has gone on three field trips this year.

_____ 8. The class went on three field trips this year.

_____ 9. Who has not went to the board with the right answer?

_____ 10. We have not went on our vacation yet.

_____ 11. Who is went for the pizza?

_____ 12. The train has been gone for 2 hours.

_____ 13. The family had gone to the movies.

_____ 14. Have you went to visit the new bookstore?

_____ 15. He has gone on and on about how smart you are!

Name _____

Writing: Adjectives

Adjectives tell more about nouns. Adjectives are describing words.

Examples: scary animals   **bright** glow   **wet** frog

Directions: Add at least two adjectives to each sentence below. Use your own words or words from the box.

pale faint	soft shivering	sticky slippery	burning gleaming	furry gentle	glistening foggy	peaceful tangled

Example: The stripe was blue.
The wide stripe was light blue.

1. The frog had eyes.

   _____

2. The house was a sight.

   _____

3. A boy heard a noise.

   _____

4. The girl tripped over a toad.

   _____

5. A tiger ran through the room.

   _____

6. They saw a glow in the window.

   _____

7. A pan was sitting on the stove.

   _____

8. The boys were eating French fries.

   _____

Writing: Adjectives

Adjectives tell a noun's size, color, shape, texture, brightness, darkness, personality, sound, taste, and so on.

Examples: color — red, yellow, green, black
          size — small, large, huge, tiny
          shape — round, square, rectangular, oval
          texture — rough, smooth, soft, scaly
          brightness — glistening, shimmering, dull, pale
          personality — gentle, grumpy, happy, sad

Directions: Follow the instructions below.

1. Get an apple, orange or other piece of fruit. Look at it very carefully and write adjectives that describe its size, color, shape and texture.

   _____

   _____

2. Take a bite of your fruit. Write adjectives that describe its taste, texture, smell, and so on.

   _____

   _____

3. Using all the adjectives from above, write a cinquain about your fruit. A **cinquain** is a five-line poem. See the form and sample poem below.

Form: Line 1 — noun   **Example:**   Apple
        Line 2 — two adjectives   red, smooth
        Line 3 — three sounds   cracking, smacking, slurping
        Line 4 — four-word phrase   drippy, sticky, sour juice
        Line 5 — noun   Apple

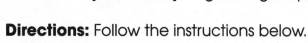

            _____

         _____ , _____

      _____ , _____ , _____

            _____

               _____

Adjectives That Add "er"

The suffix **er** is often added to adjectives to compare two things.

Example:

My feet are **large**.

Your feet are **larger** than my feet.

When a one-syllable adjective ends in a single consonant and the vowel is short, double the final consonant before adding **er**. When a word ends in two or more consonants, add **er**.

Examples:

big — bigger (single consonant)

bold — bolder (two consonants)

When an adjective ends in **y**, change the **y** to **i** before adding **er**.

Examples:

easy — easier

greasy — greasier

breezy — breezier

Directions: Use the correct rule to add **er** to the words below. The first one has been done for you.

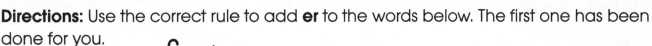

1. fast _____faster_____   11. skinny _____

2. thin _____   12. fat _____

3. long _____   13. poor _____

4. few _____   14. juicy _____

5. ugly _____   15. early _____

6. silly _____   16. clean _____

7. busy _____   17. thick _____

8. grand _____   18. creamy _____

9. lean _____   19. deep _____

10. young _____   20. lazy _____

Name _____

Adjectives That Add "est"

The suffix **est** is often added to adjectives to compare more than two things.

Example:

My glass is **full**.

Your glass is **fuller**.

His glass is **fullest**.

When a one-syllable adjective ends in a single consonant and the vowel sound is short, you usually double the final consonant before adding **est**.

Examples:

big — biggest (short vowel)

steep — steepest (long vowel)

When an adjective ends in **y**, change the **y** to **i** before adding **est**.

Example:

easy — easiest

Directions: Use the correct rule to add **est** to the words below. The first one has been done for you.

1. thin   thinnest

2. skinny _____

3. cheap _____

4. busy _____

5. loud _____

6. kind _____

7. dreamy _____

8. ugly _____

9. pretty _____

10. early _____

11. quick _____

12. trim _____

13. silly _____

14. tall _____

15. glum _____

16. red _____

17. happy _____

18. high _____

19. wet _____

20. clean _____

Adjectives Preceded by "More"

Most adjectives of two or more syllables are preceded by the word **more** as a way to show comparison between two things.

Examples:

    Correct: intelligent, more intelligent

    Incorrect: intelligenter

    Correct: famous, more famous

    Incorrect: famouser

Directions: Write **more** before the adjectives that fit the rule. Draw an **X** in the blanks of the adjectives that do not fit the rule. To test yourself, say the words aloud using **more** and adding **er** to hear which way sounds correct. The first two have been done for you.

_____X_____ 1. cheap	_____ 11. awful
___more___ 2. beautiful	_____ 12. delicious
_____ 3. quick	_____ 13. embarrassing
_____ 4. terrible	_____ 14. nice
_____ 5. difficult	_____ 15. often
_____ 6. interesting	_____ 16. hard
_____ 7. polite	_____ 17. valuable
_____ 8. cute	_____ 18. close
_____ 9. dark	_____ 19. fast
_____ 10. sad	_____ 20. important

Name _____

Adjectives Using "er" or "More"

Directions: Add the word or words needed in each sentence. The first one has been done for you.

1. I thought the book was <u>**more interesting**</u> than the movie. (interesting)

2. Do you want to carry this box? It is _____ than the one you have now. (light)

3. I noticed you are moving _____ this morning. Does your ankle still bother you? (slow)

4. Thomas Edison is probably _____ for his invention of the electric light bulb than of the phonograph. (famous)

5. She stuck out her lower lip and whined, "Your ice-cream cone is _____ than mine!" (big)

6. Mom said my room was _____ than it has been in a long time. (clean)

Adjectives Preceded by "Most"

Most adjectives of two or more syllables are preceded by the word **most** as a way to show comparison between more than two things.

Examples:

Correct: intelligent, most intelligent
Incorrect: intelligentest
Correct: famous, most famous
Incorrect: famousest

Directions: Read the following groups of sentences. In the last sentence for each group, write the adjective preceded by **most**. The first one has been done for you.

1. My uncle is intelligent.
   My aunt is more intelligent.
   My cousin is the _____ most intelligent _____.

2. I am thankful.
   My brother is more thankful.
   My parents are the _____.

3. Your sister is polite.
   Your brother is more polite.
   You are the _____.

4. The blouse was expensive.
   The sweater was more expensive.
   The coat was the _____.

5. The class was fortunate.
   The teacher was more fortunate.
   The principal was the _____.

6. The cookies were delicious.
   The cake was even more delicious.
   The brownies were the _____.

7. That painting is elaborate.
   The sculpture is more elaborate.
   The finger painting is the _____.

Name _____

Adjectives Using "est" or "Most"

Directions: Add the word or words needed to complete each sentence. The first one has been done for you.

1. The star over there is the ___brightest___ of all! (bright)

2. "I believe this is the _____ time I have ever had," said Mackenzie. (delightful)

3. That game was the _____ one of the whole year! (exciting)

4. I think this tree has the _____ leaves. (green)

5. We will need the _____ knife you have to cut the face for the jack-o-lantern. (sharp)

6. Everyone agreed that your chocolate chip cookies were the _____ of all. (delicious)

Name _____

Writing: Adverbs

Like adjectives, **adverbs** are describing words. They describe verbs. Adverbs tell how, when or where action takes place.

Examples:

How	When	Where
slowly	yesterday	here
gracefully	today	there
swiftly	tomorrow	everywhere
quickly	soon	

Hint: To identify an adverb, locate the verb, then ask yourself if there are any words that tell how, when or where action takes place.

Directions: Read the following sentences. Underline the adverbs, then write whether they tell how, when or where. The first one has been done for you.

1. At the end of the day, the children ran <u>quickly</u> home from school. _____how_____

2. They will have a spelling test tomorrow. _____

3. Slowly, the children filed to their seats. _____

4. The teacher sat here at her desk. _____

5. She will pass the tests back later. _____

6. The students received their grades happily. _____

Directions: Write four sentences of your own using any of the adverbs above.

_____

_____

_____

_____

Adverbs

Adverbs are words that tell when, where or how.

Adverbs of time tell when.

Example:

The train left yesterday.

Yesterday is an adverb of time. It tells when the train left.

Adverbs of place tell where.

Example:

The girl walked away.

Away is an adverb of place. It tells where the girl walked.

Adverbs of manner tell how.

Example:

The boy walked quickly.

Quickly is an adverb of manner. It tells how the boy walked.

Directions: Write the adverb for each sentence in the first blank. In the second blank, write whether it is an adverb of time, place or manner. The first one has been done for you.

1. The family ate downstairs. <u>downstairs</u> <u>place</u>

2. The relatives laughed loudly. _____ _____

3. We will finish tomorrow. _____ _____

4. The snowstorm will stop soon. _____ _____

5. She sings beautifully! _____ _____

6. The baby slept soundly. _____ _____

7. The elevator stopped suddenly. _____ _____

8. Does the plane leave today? _____ _____

9. The phone call came yesterday. _____ _____

10. She ran outside. _____ _____

Adverbs of Time

Directions: Choose a word or group of words from the box to complete each sentence. Make sure the adverb you choose makes sense with the rest of the sentence.

in 2 weeks	last winter
next week	at the end of the day
soon	right now
2 days ago	tonight

1. We had a surprise birthday party for him _____ .

2. Our science projects are due _____ .

3. My best friend will be moving _____ .

4. Justin and Ronnie need our help _____ !

5. We will find out who the winners are _____ .

6. Can you take me to ball practice _____ ?

7. She said we will be getting a letter _____ .

8. Diane made the quilt _____ .

Name _____

Adverbs of Place

Directions: Choose one word from the box to complete each sentence. Make sure the adverb you choose makes sense with the rest of the sentence.

inside	upstairs	below	everywhere
home	somewhere	outside	there

1. Each child took a new library book _____ .

2. We looked _____ for his jacket.

3. We will have recess _____ because it is raining.

4. From the top of the mountain we could see the village far
_____ .

5. My sister and I share a bedroom _____ .

6. The teacher warned the children, "You must play with the ball
_____ ."

7. Mother said, "I know that recipe is _____
in this file box!"

8. You can put the chair _____ .

Name _____

Adverbs of Manner

Directions: Choose a word from the box to complete each sentence. Make sure the adverb you choose makes sense with the rest of the sentence. One word will be used twice.

quickly	carefully	loudly	easily	carelessly	slowly

1. The scouts crossed the old bridge _____ .

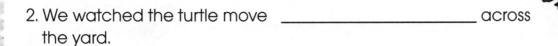

2. We watched the turtle move _____ across the yard.

3. Everyone completed the math test _____ .

4. The quarterback scampered _____ down the sideline.

5. The mother _____ cleaned the child's sore knee.

6. The fire was caused by someone _____ tossing a match.

7. The alarm rang _____ while we were eating.

Adjectives and Adverbs

Directions: Write **ADJ** on the line if the bold word is an adjective. Write **ADV** if the bold word is an adverb. The first one has been done for you.

_____ADV_____ 1. That road leads **nowhere**.

_____ 2. The squirrel was **nearby**.

_____ 3. Her **delicious** cookies were all eaten.

_____ 4. Everyone rushed **indoors**.

_____ 5. He **quickly** zipped his jacket.

_____ 6. She hummed a **popular** tune.

_____ 7. Her **sunny** smile warmed my heart.

_____ 8. I hung your coat **there**.

_____ 9. Bring that **here** this minute!

_____ 10. We all walked **back** to school.

_____ 11. The **skinniest** boy ate the most food!

_____ 12. She acts like a **famous** person.

_____ 13. The **silliest** jokes always make me laugh.

_____ 14. She must have parked her car **somewhere**!

_____ 15. Did you take the test **today**?

Name _____

Writing: Using Conjunctions

Conjunctions are joining words that can be used to combine sentences. Words such as **and**, **but**, **or**, **when** and **after** are conjunctions.

Examples:
Sally went to the mall. She went to the movies.
Sally went to the mall, and she went to the movies.

We can have our vacation at home. We can vacation at the beach.
We can have our vacation at home, or we can vacation at the beach.

Mary fell on the playground. She did not hurt herself.
Mary fell on the playground, but she did not hurt herself.

Note: The conjunctions **after** or **when** are usually placed at the beginning of the sentence.

Example: Marge went to the store. She went to the gas station.
After Marge went to the store, she went to the gas station.

Directions: Combine the following sentences using a conjunction.

1. Peter fell down the steps. He broke his foot. (and)

   _____

2. I visited New York. I would like to see Chicago. (but)

   _____

3. Amy can edit books. She can write stories. (or)

   _____

4. He played in the barn. John started to sneeze. (when)

   _____

5. The team won the playoffs. They went to the championships. (after)

   _____

Directions: Write three sentences of your own using the conjunctions **and**, **but**, **or**, **when** or **after**.

_____

_____

_____

_____

Name _____

"And," "But," "Or"

Directions: Write **and**, **but** or **or** to complete the sentences.

1. I thought we might try that new hamburger place, _____ Mom wants to eat at the Spaghetti Shop.

2. We could stay home, _____ would you rather go to the game?

3. She went right home after school, _____ he stopped at the store.

4. Mother held the piece of paneling, _____ Father nailed it in place.

5. She babysat last weekend, _____ her big sister went with her.

6. She likes raisins in her oatmeal, _____ I would rather have mine with brown sugar.

7. She was planning on coming over tomorrow, _____ I asked her if she could wait until the weekend.

8. Tomato soup with crackers sounds good to me, _____ would you rather have vegetable beef soup?

"Because" and "So"

Directions: Write **because** or **so** to complete the sentences.

1. She cleaned the paint brushes _____ they would be ready in the morning.

2. Father called home complaining of a sore throat _____ Mom stopped by the pharmacy.

3. His bus will be running late _____ it has a flat tire.

4. We all worked together _____ we could get the job done sooner.

5. We took a variety of sandwiches on the picnic _____ we knew not everyone liked cheese and olives with mayonnaise.

6. All the school children were sent home _____ the electricity went off at school.

7. My brother wants us to meet his girlfriend _____ she will be coming to dinner with us on Friday.

8. He forgot to take his umbrella along this morning _____ now his clothes are very wet.

"When" and "After"

Directions: Write **when** or **after** to complete the sentences.

1. I knew we were in trouble _____ I heard the thunder in the distance.

2. We carried the baskets of cherries to the car _____ we were finished picking them.

3. Mother took off her apron _____ I reminded her that our dinner guests would be here any minute.

4. I wondered if we would have school tomorrow _____ I noticed the snow begin to fall.

5. The boys and girls all clapped _____ the magician pulled the colored scarves out of his sleeve.

6. I was startled _____ the phone rang so late last night.

7. You will need to get the film developed _____ you have taken all the pictures.

8. The children began to run _____ the snake started to move!

Name _____

Conjunctions

Directions: Choose the best conjunction from the box to combine the pairs of sentences. Then rewrite the sentences.

and	but	or	because	when	after	so

1. I like Leah. I like Ben.

_____

2. Should I eat the orange? Should I eat the apple?

_____

3. You will get a reward. You turned in the lost item.

_____

4. I really mean what I say! You had better listen!

_____

5. I like you. You're nice, friendly, helpful and kind.

_____

6. You can have dessert. You ate all your peas.

_____

7. I like your shirt better. You should decide for yourself.

_____

8. We walked out of the building. We heard the fire alarm.

_____

9. I like to sing folk songs. I like to play the guitar.

_____

"Good" and "Well"

Use the word **good** to describe a noun. Good is an adjective.

Example: She is a **good** teacher.

Use the word **well** to tell or ask how something is done or to describe someone's health. Well is an adverb. It describes a verb.

Example: She is not feeling **well**.

Directions: Write **good** or **well** in the blanks to complete the sentences correctly. The first one has been done for you.

__good__ 1. Our team could use a good/well captain.

_____ 2. The puny kitten doesn't look good/well.

_____ 3. He did his job so good/well that everyone praised him.

_____ 4. Whining isn't a good/well habit.

_____ 5. I might just as good/well do it myself.

_____ 6. She was one of the most well-/good- liked girls at school.

_____ 7. I did the book report as good/well as I could.

_____ 8. The television works very good/well.

_____ 9. You did a good/well job repairing the TV!

_____ 10. Thanks for a job good/well done!

_____ 11. You did a good/well job fixing the computer.

_____ 12. You had better treat your friends good/well.

_____ 13. Can your grandmother hear good/well?

_____ 14. Your brother will be well/good soon.

Name _____

"Your" and "You're"

The word **your** shows possession.

Examples:

    Is that **your** book?

    I visited **your** class.

The word **you're** is a contraction for **you are**. A **contraction** is two words joined together as one. An apostrophe shows where letters have been left out.

Examples:

    You're doing well on that painting.

    If **you're** going to pass the test, you should study.

Directions: Write **your** or **you're** in the blanks to complete the sentences correctly. The first one has been done for you.

You're   1. Your/You're the best friend I have!

_____ 2. Your/You're going to drop that!

_____ 3. Your/You're brother came to see me.

_____ 4. Is that your/you're cat?

_____ 5. If your/you're going, you'd better hurry!

_____ 6. Why are your/you're fingers so red?

_____ 7. It's none of your/you're business!

_____ 8. Your/You're bike's front tire is low.

_____ 9. Your/You're kidding!

_____ 10. Have it your/you're way.

_____ 11. I thought your/you're report was great!

_____ 12. He thinks your/you're wonderful!

_____ 13. What is your/you're first choice?

_____ 14. What's your/you're opinion?

_____ 15. If your/you're going, so am I!

_____ 16. Your/You're welcome.

Name _____

"Its" and "It's"

The word **its** shows ownership.

Examples:

> **Its** leaves have all turned red.
> **Its** paw was injured.

The word **it's** is a contraction for **it is**.

Examples:

> **It's** better to be early than late.
> **It's** not fair!

Directions: Write **its** or **it's** to complete the sentences correctly. The first one has been done for you.

___It's___   1. Its/It's never too late for ice cream!

_____ 2. Its/It's eyes are already open.

_____ 3. Its/It's your turn to wash the dishes!

_____ 4. Its/It's cage was left open.

_____ 5. Its/It's engine was beyond repair.

_____ 6. Its/It's teeth were long and pointed.

_____ 7. Did you see its/it's hind legs?

_____ 8. Why do you think its/it's mine?

_____ 9. Do you think its/it's the right color?

_____ 10. Don't pet its/it's fur too hard!

_____ 11. Its/It's from my Uncle Harry.

_____ 12. Can you tell its/it's a surprise?

_____ 13. Is its/it's stall always this clean?

_____ 14. Its/It's not time to eat yet.

_____ 15. She says its/it's working now.

Name _____

"Can" and "May"

The word **can** means am able to or to be able to.

Examples:

> I **can** do that for you.
> **Can** you do that for me?

The word **may** means be allowed to or permitted to. May is used to ask or give permission. **May** can also mean **might** or **perhaps**.

Examples:

> **May** I be excused?
> You **may** sit here.

Directions: Write **can** or **may** in the blanks to complete the sentences correctly. The first one has been done for you.

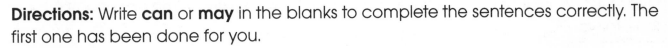

__May__ 1. Can/May I help you?

_____ 2. He's smart. He can/may do it himself.

_____ 3. When can/may I have my dessert?

_____ 4. I can/may tell you exactly what she said.

_____ 5. He can/may speak French fluently.

_____ 6. You can/may use my pencil.

_____ 7. I can/may be allowed to attend the concert.

_____ 8. It's bright. I can/may see you!

_____ 9. Can/May my friend stay for dinner?

_____ 10. You can/may leave when your report is finished.

_____ 11. I can/may see your point!

_____ 12. She can/may dance well.

_____ 13. Can/May you hear the dog barking?

_____ 14. Can/May you help me button this sweater?

_____ 15. Mother, can/may I go to the movies?

"Sit" and "Set"

The word **sit** means to rest.

Examples:

    Please **sit** here!

    Will you **sit** by me?

The word **set** means to put or place something.

Examples:

    Set your purse there.

    Set the dishes on the table.

Directions: Write **sit** or **set** to complete the sentences correctly. The first one has been done for you.

_____sit_____ 1. Would you please sit/set down here?

_____ 2. You can sit/set the groceries there.

_____ 3. She sit/set her suitcase in the closet.

_____ 4. He sit/set his watch for half past three.

_____ 5. She's a person who can't sit/set still.

_____ 6. Sit/set the baby on the couch beside me.

_____ 7. Where did you sit/set your new shoes?

_____ 8. They decided to sit/set together during the movie.

_____ 9. Let me sit/set you straight on that!

_____ 10. Instead of swimming, he decided to sit/set in the water.

_____ 11. He sit/set the greasy pan in the sink.

_____ 12. She sit/set the file folder on her desk.

_____ 13. Don't ever sit/set on the refrigerator!

_____ 14. She sit/set the candles on the cake.

"They're," "Their," "There"

The word **they're** is a contraction for **they are**.

Examples:

> **They're** our very best friends!
>
> Ask them if **they're** coming over tomorrow.

The word **their** shows ownership.

Examples:

> **Their** dog is friendly.
>
> It's **their** bicycle.

The word **there** shows place or direction.

Examples:

> Look over **there**.
>
> **There** it is.

Directions: Write **they're**, **their** or **there** to complete the sentences correctly. The first one has been done for you.

__There__ 1. They're/Their/There is the sweater I want!

_____ 2. Do you believe they're/their/there stories?

_____ 3. Be they're/their/there by one o'clock.

_____ 4. Were you they're/their/there last night?

_____ 5. I know they're/their/there going to attend.

_____ 6. Have you met they're/their/there mother?

_____ 7. I can go they're/their/there with you.

_____ 8. Do you like they're/their/there new car?

_____ 9. They're/Their/There friendly to everyone.

_____ 10. Did she say they're/their/there ready to go?

_____ 11. She said she'd walk by they're/their/there house.

_____ 12. Is anyone they're/their/there?

_____ 13. I put it right over they're/their/there!

Name _____

"This" and "These"

The word **this** is an adjective that refers to things that are near. **This** always describes a singular noun. Singular means one.

Example:

I'll buy **this** coat.

(Coat is singular.)

The word **these** is also an adjective that refers to things that are near. **These** always describes a plural noun. A plural refers to more than one thing.

Example:

I will buy **these** flowers.

(Flowers is a plural noun.)

Directions: Write **this** or **these** to complete the sentences correctly. The first one has been done for you.

these 1. I will take this/these cookies with me.

_____ 2. Do you want this/these seeds?

_____ 3. Did you try this/these nuts?

_____ 4. Do it this/these way!

_____ 5. What do you know about this/these situation?

_____ 6. Did you open this/these doors?

_____ 7. Did you open this/these window?

_____ 8. What is the meaning of this/these letters?

_____ 9. Will you carry this/these books for me?

_____ 10. This/These pans are hot!

_____ 11. Do you think this/these light is too bright?

_____ 12. Are this/these boots yours?

_____ 13. Do you like this/these rainy weather?

Capital Letters and Periods

The first letter of a person's first, last and middle name is always capitalized.

Example: **E**lizabeth **J**ane **M**arks is my best friend.

The first letter of a person's title is always capitalized.
If the title is abbreviated, the title is followed by a period.

Examples: Her mother is **Dr**. Susan Jones Marks.
Ms. Jessica Joseph was a visitor.

Directions: Write **C** if the sentence is punctuated and capitalized correctly. Draw an **X** if the sentence is not punctuated and capitalized correctly. The first one has been done for you.

__X__ 1. I asked Elizabeth if I should call her mother Mrs. marks or dr. Marks.

_____ 2. Mr. and Mrs. Francesco were friends of the DeVuonos.

_____ 3. Dr. Daniel Long and Dr Holly Barrows both spoke with the patient.

_____ 4. Did you get Mr. MacMillan for English next year?

_____ 5. Mr. Sweet and Ms. Ellison were both at the concert.

_____ 6. When did the doctor. tell you about this illness?

_____ 7. Dr. Donovan is the doctor that Mr. Winham trusted.

_____ 8. Why don't you ask Doctor. Williams her opinion?

_____ 9. All three of the doctors diagnosed Ms. Twelp.

_____ 10. Will Ms. Davis and Ms Simpson be at school today?

_____ 11. Did Dr Samuels see your father last week?

_____ 12. Is Judy a medical doctor or another kind of specialist?

_____ 13. We are pleased to introduce Ms King and Mr. Graham.

Punctuation: Commas

Use a comma to separate the number of the day of a month and the year. Do not use a comma to separate the month and year if no day is given.

Examples:

> June 14, 1999
>
> June 1999

Use a comma after **yes** or **no** when it is the first word in a sentence.

Examples:

> Yes, I will do it right now.
>
> No, I don't want any.

Directions: Write **C** if the sentence is punctuated correctly. Draw an **X** if the sentence is not punctuated correctly. The first one has been done for you.

__C__ 1. No, I don't plan to attend.

_____ 2. I told them, oh yes, I would go.

_____ 3. Her birthday is March 13, 1995.

_____ 4. He was born in May, 1997.

_____ 5. Yes, of course I like you!

_____ 6. No I will not be there.

_____ 7. They left for vacation on February, 14.

_____ 8. No, today is Monday.

_____ 9. The program was first shown on August 12, 1991.

_____ 10. In September, 2007 how old will you be?

_____ 11. He turned 12 years old on November, 13.

_____ 12. I said no, I will not come no matter what!

_____ 13. Yes, she is a friend of mine.

_____ 14. His birthday is June 12, 1992, and mine is June 12, 1993.

_____ 15. No I would not like more dessert.

Name _____

Punctuation: Commas

Use a comma to separate words in a series. A comma is used after each word in a series but is not needed before the last word. Both ways are correct. In your own writing, be consistent about which style you use.

Examples:

We ate apples, oranges, and pears.
We ate apples, oranges and pears.

Always use a comma between the name of a city and a state.

Example:

She lives in Fresno, California.
He lives in Wilmington, Delaware.

Directions: Write **C** if the sentence is punctuated correctly. Draw an **X** if the sentence is not punctuated correctly. The first one has been done for you.

__X__ 1. She ordered shoes, dresses and shirts to be sent to her home in Oakland California.

_____ 2. No one knew her pets' names were Fido, Spot and Tiger.

_____ 3. He likes green beans lima beans, and corn on the cob.

_____ 4. Typing paper, pens and pencils are all needed for school.

_____ 5. Send your letters to her in College Park, Maryland.

_____ 6. Orlando Florida is the home of Disney World.

_____ 7. Mickey, Minnie, Goofy and Daisy are all favorites of mine.

_____ 8. Send your letter to her in Reno, Nevada.

_____ 9. Before he lived in New York, City he lived in San Diego, California.

_____ 10. She mailed postcards, and letters to him in Lexington, Kentucky.

_____ 11. Teacups, saucers, napkins, and silverware were piled high.

_____ 12. Can someone give me a ride to Indianapolis, Indiana?

_____ 13. He took a train a car, then a boat to visit his old friend.

_____ 14. Why can't I go to Disney World to see Mickey, and Minnie?

Name _____

Book Titles

All words in the title of a book are underlined. Underlined words also mean italics.

Examples:

The Hunt for Red October was a best-seller!
(*The Hunt for Red October*)

Have you read Lost in Space? (*Lost in Space*)

Directions: Underline the book titles in these sentences. The first one has been done for you.

1. The Dinosaur Poster Book is for eight year olds.

2. Have you read Lion Dancer by Kate Waters?

3. Baby Dinosaurs and Giant Dinosaurs were both written by Peter Dodson.

4. Have you heard of the book That's What Friends Are For by Carol Adorjan?

5. J.B. Stamper wrote a book called The Totally Terrific Valentine Party Book.

6. The teacher read Almost Ten and a Half aloud to our class.

7. Marrying Off Mom is about a girl who tries to get her widowed mother to start dating.

8. The Snow and The Fire are the second and third books by author Caroline Cooney.

9. The title sounds silly, but Goofbang Value Daze really is the name of a book!

10. A book about space exploration is The Day We Walked on the Moon by George Sullivan.

11. Alice and the Birthday Giant tells about a giant who came to a girl's birthday party.

12. A book about a girl who is sad about her father's death is called Rachel and the Upside Down Heart by Eileen Douglas.

13. Two books about baseball are Baseball Bloopers and Oddball Baseball.

14. Katharine Ross wrote Teenage Mutant Ninja Turtles: The Movie Storybook.

Name _____

Book Titles

Capitalize the first and last word of book titles. Capitalize all other words of book titles except short prepositions, such as **of, at** and **in**; conjunctions, such as **and, or** and **but**; and articles, such as **a, an** and **the**.

Examples:

Have you read <u>War and Peace</u>?

Pippi Longstocking in Moscow is her favorite book.

Directions: Underline the book titles. Circle the words that should be capitalized. The first one has been done for you.

1. (murder) in the (blue room) by Elliot Roosevelt

2. growing up in a divided society by Sandra Burnham

3. the corn king and the spring queen by Naomi Mitchison

4. new kids on the block by Grace Catalano

5. best friends don't tell lies by Linda Barr

6. turn your kid into a computer genius by Carole Gerber

7. 50 simple things you can do to save the earth by Earth Works Press

8. garfield goes to waist by Jim Davis

9. the hunt for red october by Tom Clancy

10. fall into darkness by Christopher Pike

11. oh the places you'll go! by Dr. Seuss

12. amy the dancing bear by Carly Simon

13. the great waldo search by Martin Handford

14. the time and space of uncle albert by Russel Stannard

15. true stories about abraham lincoln by Ruth Gross

Punctuation: Quotation Marks

Use quotation marks (" ") before and after the exact words of a speaker.

Examples:

I asked Aunt Martha, "How do you feel?"

"I feel awful," Aunt Martha replied.

Do not put quotation marks around words that report what the speaker said.

Examples:

Aunt Martha said she felt awful.

I asked Aunt Martha how she felt.

Directions: Write **C** if the sentence is punctuated correctly. Draw an **X** if the sentence is not punctuated correctly. The first one has been done for you.

__C__ 1. "I want it right now!" she demanded angrily.

_____ 2 "Do you want it now? I asked."

_____ 3. She said "she felt better" now.

_____ 4. Her exact words were, "I feel much better now!"

_____ 5. "I am so thrilled to be here!" he shouted.

_____ 6. "Yes, I will attend," she replied.

_____ 7. Elizabeth said "she was unhappy."

_____ 8. "I'm unhappy," Elizabeth reported.

_____ 9. "Did you know her mother?" I asked.

_____ 10. I asked "whether you knew her mother."

_____ 11. I wondered, "What will dessert be?"

_____ 12. "Which will it be, salt or pepper?" the waiter asked.

_____ 13. "No, I don't know the answer!" he snapped.

_____ 14. He said "yes he'd take her on the trip.

_____ 15. Be patient, he said. "it will soon be over."

Name _____

Punctuation: Quotation Marks

Use quotation marks around the titles of songs and poems.

Examples:

Have you heard "Still Cruising" by the Beach Boys?

"Ode To a Nightingale" is a famous poem.

Directions: Write **C** if the sentence is punctuated correctly. Draw an **X** if the sentence is not punctuated correctly. The first one has been done for you.

__C__ 1. Do you know "My Bonnie Lies Over the Ocean"?

_____ 2. We sang The Stars and Stripes Forever" at school.

_____ 3. Her favorite song is "The Eensy Weensy Spider."

_____ 4. Turn the music up when "A Hard Day's "Night comes on!

_____ 5. "Yesterday" was one of Paul McCartney's most famous songs.

_____ 6. "Mary Had a Little Lamb" is a very silly poem!

_____ 7. A song everyone knows is "Happy Birthday."

_____ 8. "Swing Low, Sweet Chariot" was first sung by slaves.

_____ 9. Do you know the words to Home on "the Range"?

_____ 10. "Hiawatha" is a poem many older people had to memorize.

_____ 11. "Happy Days Are Here Again! is an upbeat tune.

_____ 12. Frankie Valli and the Four Seasons sang "Sherry."

_____ 13. The words to "Rain, Rain" Go Away are easy to learn.

_____ 14. A slow song I know is called "Summertime."

_____ 15. Little children like to hear "The Night Before Christmas."

Name _____

Proofreading

Proofreading means searching for and correcting errors by carefully reading and rereading what has been written. Use the proofreading marks below when correcting your writing or someone else's.

To insert a word or a punctuation mark that has been left out, use this mark: ∧. It is called a caret.

Example: We∧to the dance together.

To show that a letter should be capitalized, put three lines under it.

Example: Mrs. jones drove us to school.

To show that a capital letter should be small or lowercase, draw a diagonal line through it.

Example: Mrs. Jones Drove us to school.

To show that a word is spelled incorrectly, draw a horizontal line through it and write the correct spelling above it.

Example: The wolros is an amazing animal.

Directions: Proofread the two paragraphs using the proofreading marks you learned. The author's last name, Towne, is spelled correctly.

The Modern ark

My book report is on the modern ark by Cecilia Fitzsimmons. The book tells abut 80 of worlds endangered animals. The book also an arc and animals inside for kids put together.

Their House

there house is a Great book! The arthur's name is Mary Towne. they're house tells about a girl name Molly. Molly's Family bys an old house from some people named warren. Then there big problems begin!

Proofreading

Directions: Proofread the sentences. Write **C** if the sentence has no errors. Draw an **X** if the sentence contains missing words or other errors. The first one has been done for you.

_C_ 1. The new Ship Wreck Museum in Key West is exciting!

_____ 2. Another thing I liked was the litehouse.

_____ 3. Do you remember Hemingway's address in Key West?

_____ 4. The Key West semetery is on 21 acres of ground.

_____ 5. Ponce de eon discovered Key West.

_____ 6. The cemetery in Key West is on Francis Street.

_____ 7. My favorete tombstone was the sailor's.

_____ 8. His wife wrote the words on it. Remember?

_____ 9. The words said, "at least I know where to find him now!"

_____ 10. That sailor must have been away at sea all the time.

_____ 11. The troley ride around Key West is very interesting.

_____ 12. Do you why it is called Key West?

_____ 13. Can you imagine a lighthouse in the middle of your town?

_____ 14. It's interesting to no that Key West is our southernmost city.

_____ 15. Besides Harry Truman and Hemingway, did other famous people live there?

Name _____

Proofreading

Directions: Proofread the paragraphs, using the proofreading marks you learned. There are seven capitalization errors, three missing words and eleven errors in spelling or word usage.

Key West

key West has been tropical paradise ever since Ponce de Leon first saw the set of islands called the keys in 1513. Two famus streets in Key West are named duval and whitehead. You will find the city semetery on Francis Street. The tombstones are funny!

The message on one is, "I told you I was sick!" On sailor's tombston is this mesage his widow: "At lease I no where to find him now."

The cemetery is on 21 akres in the midle of town. The most famous home in key west is that of the authur, Ernest Hemingway. Heminway's home was at 907 whitehead Street. He lived their for 30 years.

Proofreading

Directions: Read more about Key West. Proofread and correct the errors. There are eight errors in capitalization, seven misspelled words and three missing words.

More About Key West

a good way to lern more about key West is to ride the trolley. Key West has a great troley system. The trolley will take on a tour of the salt ponds. You can also three red brick forts. The troley tour goes by a 110-foot high lighthouse. It is rite in the middle of the city. Key west is the only city with a Lighthouse in the midle of it! It is also the southernmost city in the United States.

If you have time, the new Ship Wreck Museum. Key west was also the hom of former president Harry truman. During his presidency, Trueman spent many vacations on key west.

Run-On Sentences

A **run-on sentence** occurs when two or more sentences are joined together without punctuation.

Examples:

Run-on sentence: I lost my way once did you?
Two sentences with correct punctuation: I lost my way once. Did you?
Run-on sentence: I found the recipe it was not hard to follow.
Two sentences with correct punctuation: I found the recipe. It was not hard to follow.

Directions: Rewrite the run-on sentences correctly with periods, exclamation points and question marks. The first one has been done for you.

1. Did you take my umbrella I can't find it anywhere!

Did you take my umbrella? I can't find it anywhere!

2. How can you stand that noise I can't!

_____

3. The cookies are gone I see only crumbs.

_____

4. The dogs were barking they were hungry.

_____

5. She is quite ill please call a doctor immediately!

_____

6. The clouds came up we knew the storm would hit soon.

_____

7. You weren't home he stopped by this morning.

_____

Writing: Punctuation

Directions: In the paragraphs below, use periods, question marks or exclamation marks to show where one sentence ends and the next begins. Circle the first letter of each new sentence to show the capital.

Example: ⓜy sister accused me of not helping her rake the leaves. ⓣhat's silly! ⓘhelped at least a hundred times.

1. I always tie on my fishing line when it moves up and down, I know a fish is there after waiting a minute or two, I pull up the fish it's fun

2. I tried putting lemon juice on my freckles to make them go away did you ever do that it didn't work my skin just got sticky now, I'm slowly getting used to my freckles

3. once, I had an accident on my bike I was on my way home from school what do you think happened my wheel slipped in the loose dirt at the side of the road my bike slid into the road

4. one night, I dreamed I lived in a castle in my dream, I was the king or maybe the queen everyone listened to my commands then Mom woke me up for school I tried commanding her to let me sleep it didn't work

5. what's your favorite holiday Christmas is mine for months before Christmas, I save my money, so I can give a present to everyone in my family last year, I gave my big sister earrings they cost me five dollars

6. my dad does exercises every night to make his stomach flat he says he doesn't want to grow old I think it's too late don't tell him I said that

Name _____

Writing: Putting Ideas Together

Directions: Make each pair of sentences into one sentence. (You may have to change the verbs for some sentences—from **is** to **are**, for example.)

Example: Our house was flooded. Our car was flooded.

Our house and car were flooded.

1. Kenny sees a glow.   Carrie sees a glow.

_____

2. Our new stove came today.   Our new refrigerator came today.

_____

3. The pond is full of toads.   The field is full of toads.

_____

4. Stripes are on the flag.   Stars are on the flag.

_____

5. The ducks took flight.   The geese took flight.

_____

6. Joe reads stories.   Dana reads stories.

_____

7. French fries will make you fat.   Milkshakes will make you fat.

_____

8. Justine heard someone groan.   Kevin heard someone groan.

_____

Name _____

Writing: Putting Ideas Together

Directions: Write each pair of sentences as one sentence.

Example: Jim will deal the cards one at a time. Jim will give four cards to everyone.

Jim will deal the cards one at a time and give four cards to everyone.

1. Amy won the contest.   Amy claimed the prize.

   _____

2. We need to find the scissors.   We need to buy some tape.

   _____

3. The stream runs through the woods.   The stream empties into the East River.

   _____

   _____

4. Katie tripped on the steps.   Katie has a pain in her left foot.

   _____

   _____

5. Grandpa took me to the store.   Grandpa bought me a treat.

   _____

6. Charity ran 2 miles.   She walked 1 mile to cool down afterwards.

   _____

   _____

Name _____

Writing: Using Fewer Words

Writing can be more interesting when fewer words are used. Combining sentences is easy when the subjects are the same. Notice how the comma is used.

Example: Sally woke up. Sally ate breakfast. Sally brushed her teeth.

Sally woke up, ate breakfast and brushed her teeth.

Combining sentences with more than one subject is a little more complicated. Notice how commas are used to "set off" information.

Examples: Jane went to the store. Jane is Sally's sister.

Jane went to the store with Sally, her sister.

Eddie likes to play with cars. Eddie is my younger brother.

Eddie, my younger brother, likes to play with cars.

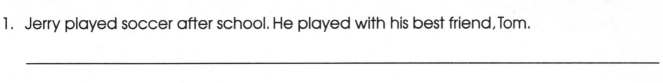

Directions: Write each pair of sentences as one sentence.

1. Jerry played soccer after school. He played with his best friend, Tom.

   _____

2. Spot likes to chase cats. Spot is my dog.

   _____

3. Lori and Janice both love ice cream. Janice is Lori's cousin.

   _____

4. Jayna is my cousin. Jayna helped me move into my new apartment.

   _____

5. Romeo is a big tomcat. Romeo loves to hunt mice.

   _____

Name _____

Combining Sentences

Some simple sentences can be easily combined into one sentence.

Examples:

Simple sentences: The bird sang. The bird was tiny. The bird was in the tree.
Combined sentence: The tiny bird sang in the tree.

Directions: Combine each set of simple sentences into one sentence. The first one has been done for you.

1. The big girls laughed. They were friendly. They helped the little girls.

<u>The big, friendly girls laughed as they helped the little girls.</u>

2. The dog was hungry. The dog whimpered. The dog looked at its bowl.

_____

3. Be quiet now. I want you to listen. You listen to my joke!

_____

4. I lost my pencil. My pencil was stubby. I lost it on the bus.

_____

5. I see my mother. My mother is walking. My mother is walking down the street.

_____

6. Do you like ice cream? Do you like hot dogs? Do you like mustard?

_____

7. Tell me you'll do it! Tell me you will! Tell me right now!

_____

Name _____

Combining Sentences in Paragraph Form

A **paragraph** is a group of sentences that share the same idea.

Directions: Rewrite the paragraph by combining the simple sentences into larger sentences.

Jason awoke early. He threw off his covers. He ran to his window. He looked outside. He saw snow. It was white and fluffy. Jason thought of something. He thought of his sled. His sled was in the garage. He quickly ate breakfast. He dressed warmly. He got his sled. He went outside. He went to play in the snow.

_____

_____

_____

_____

_____

_____

_____

_____

_____

_____

_____

Name _____

Nouns and Pronouns

To make a story or report more interesting, pronouns can be substituted for "overused" nouns.

Example:

Mother made the beds. Then Mother started the laundry.

The noun **Mother** is used in both sentences. The pronoun **she** could be used in place of **Mother** the second time to make the second sentence more interesting.

Directions: Cross out nouns when they appear a second and/or third time. Write a pronoun that could be used instead. The first one has been done for you.

__we__ 1. My friends and I like to go ice skating in the winter. ~~My friends and I~~ usually fall down a lot, but ~~my friends and I~~ have fun!

_____ 2. All the children in the fourth-grade class next to us must have been having a party. All the children were very loud. All the children were happy it was Friday.

_____ 3. I try to help my father with work around the house on the weekends. My father works many hours during the week and would not be able to get everything done.

_____ 4. Can I share my birthday treat with the secretary and the principal? The secretary and the principal could probably use a snack right now!

_____ 5. I know Mr. Jones needs a copy of this history report. Please take it to Mr. Jones when you finish.

Name _____

Nouns and Pronouns

Directions: Cross out nouns when they appear a second and/or third time. Write a pronoun that could be used instead.

_____ 1. The merry-go-round is one of my favorite rides at the county fair. I ride the merry-go-round so many times that I sometimes get sick.

_____ 2. My parents and I are planning a 2-week vacation next year. My parents and I will be driving across the country to see the Grand Canyon. My parents and I hope to have a great time.

_____ 3. The new art teacher brought many ideas from the city school where the art teacher worked before.

_____ 4. Green beans, corn and potatoes are my favorite vegetables. I could eat green beans, corn and potatoes for every meal. I especially like green beans, corn and potatoes in stew.

_____ 5. I think I left my pen in the library when I was looking up reference materials earlier today. Did you find my pen when you cleaned?

_____ 6. My grandmother makes very good apple pie. My grandmother said I could learn how to make one the next time we visit.

_____ 7. My brothers and I could take care of your pets while you are away if you show my brothers and me what you want done.

Name _____

Pronoun Referents

A **pronoun referent** is the noun or nouns a pronoun refers to.

Example:

Green beans, corn and potatoes are my favorite vegetables. I could eat them for every meal.

The pronoun **them** refers to the nouns green beans, corn and potatoes.

Directions: Find the pronoun in each sentence, and write it in the blank below. Underline the word or words the pronoun refers to. The first one has been done for you.

1. The fruit trees look so beautiful in the spring when they are covered with blossoms.

   _____they_____

2. Tori is a high school cheerleader. She spends many hours at practice.

   _____

3. The football must have been slippery because of the rain. The quarterback could not hold on to it.

   _____

4. Aunt Donna needs a babysitter for her three year old tonight.

   _____

5. The art projects are on the table. Could you please put them on the top shelf along the wall?

   _____

Name _____

Pronoun Referents

Directions: Find the pronoun in each sentence, and write it in the blank below. Underline the word or words the pronoun refers to.

1. Did Aaron see the movie *Titanic*? Jay thought it was a very good movie.

   _____

2. Maysie can help you with the spelling words now, Tasha.

   _____

3. The new tennis coach said to call him after 6:00 tonight.

   _____

4. Jim, John and Jason called to say they would be later than planned.

   _____

5. Mrs. Burns enjoyed the cake her class had for the surprise party.

   _____

6. The children are waiting outside. Ask Josh to take the pinwheels out to them.

   _____

7. Mrs. Taylor said to go on ahead because she will be late.

   _____

8. The whole team must sit on the bus until the driver gives us permission to get off.

   _____

9. Dad said the umbrella did a poor job of keeping the rain off him.

   _____

10. The umbrella was blowing around too much. That's probably why it didn't do a good job.

    _____

Name _____

Writing: Topic Sentences

A **paragraph** is a group of sentences that tells about one main idea. A **topic sentence** tells the main idea of a paragraph.

Many topic sentences come first in the paragraph. The topic sentence in the paragraph below is underlined. Do you see how it tells the reader what the whole paragraph is about?

    <u>Friendships can make you happy or make you sad.</u> You feel happy to do things and go places with your friends. You get to know each other so well that you can almost read each others' minds. But friendships can be sad when your friend moves away—or decides to be best friends with someone else.

Directions: Underline the topic sentence in the paragraph below.

    We have two rules about using the phone at our house. Our whole family agreed on them. The first rule is not to talk longer than 10 minutes. The second rule is to take good messages if you answer the phone for someone else.

Directions: After you read the paragraph below, write a topic sentence for it.

_____

_____

_____

_____

    For one thing, you could ask your neighbors if they need any help. They might be willing to pay you for walking their dog or mowing their grass or weeding their garden. Maybe your older brothers or sisters would pay you to do some of their chores. You also could ask your parents if there's an extra job you could do around the house to make money.

Directions: Write a topic sentence for a paragraph on each of these subjects.

Homework: _____

_____

Television: _____

_____

Writing: Supporting Sentences

Supporting sentences provide details about the topic sentence of a paragraph.

Directions: In the paragraph below, underline the topic sentence. Then cross out the supporting sentence that does not belong in the paragraph.

One spring it started to rain and didn't stop for 2 weeks. All the rivers flooded. Some people living near the rivers had to leave their homes. Farmers couldn't plant their crops because the fields were so wet. Plants need water to grow. The sky was dark and gloomy all the time.

Directions: Write three supporting sentences to go with each topic sentence below. Make sure each supporting sentence stays on the same subject as the topic sentence.

Not everyone should have a pet.

_____

_____

_____

I like to go on field trips with my class.

_____

_____

_____

I've been thinking about what I want to be when I get older.

_____

_____

_____

Writing:
Topic Sentences and Supporting Details

Directions: For each topic below, write a topic sentence and four supporting details.

Example:

Playing with friends: (topic sentence) <u>Playing with my friends can be lots of fun.</u>

(details)

1. We like to ride our bikes together.

2. We play fun games like "dress up" and "animal hospital."

3. Sometimes, we swing on the swings or slide down the slides on our swingsets.

4. We like to pretend we are having tea with our stuffed animals.

Recess at school: _____

_____

_____

_____

_____

Summer vacation: _____

_____

_____

_____

_____

Brothers or sisters: _____

_____

_____

_____

_____

Writing: Paragraphs

Each paragraph should have one main idea. If you have a lot of ideas, you need to write several paragraphs.

Directions: Read the ideas below and number them:
   1. If the idea tells about Jill herself.
   2. If the idea tells what she did.
   3. If the idea tells why she did it.

_____ found a bird caught in a kite string

_____ plays outside a lot

_____ in grade four at Center School

_____ knew the bird was wild

_____ untangled the bird

_____ likes pets

_____ wouldn't want to live in a cage

_____ gave the bird its freedom

Now, use the ideas to write three paragraphs. Use your own paper if necessary. Write paragraph 1 about Jill. Write paragraph 2 about what she did. Write paragraph 3 about why she did it.

_____

_____

_____

_____

_____

_____

_____

_____

Writing: Paragraphs

When you have many good ideas about a subject, you need to organize your writing into more than one paragraph. It is easy to organize your thoughts about a topic if you use a "cluster of ideas" chart.

Example:

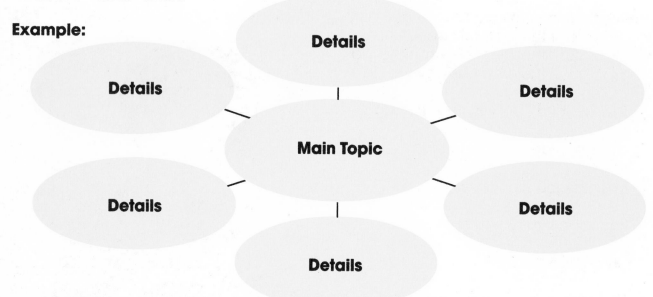

The main topic of your story is stated in the middle circle. Details about the main topic are listed in the outer circles.

Study the following "cluster of ideas" and note how the thoughts are organized in paragraph form on the following page.

1. **Introduction:** working in yard, autumn—cool weather

2. **Pants:** blue jeans, old, cotton, good for yard work, comfortable

3. **Shirt:** yellow, short-sleeved, matches slacks and sweater, not too hot

Clothes for Saturday

4. **Sweater:** red with yellow and blue designs, white buttons, warmth for cold day, cotton, long sleeves

5. **Shoes:** white sneakers, comfortable, good for walking and standing

6. **Closing:** busy, but ready

Writing: Paragraphs

Once your ideas are "clustered," go back and decide which ideas should be the first, second, third, and so on. These numbers will be the order of the paragraph in the finished story.

Directions: Read the story paragraphs below.

Clothes for Saturday

This Saturday, my family and I will be working in the yard. We will be mowing grass, raking leaves and pulling weeds. When I get up that day, I know I will need to wear clothes that will keep me warm in the autumn air. My clothes will also need to be ones that will not be ruined if they get muddy or dirty.

The best choice of pants for our busy day will be my jeans. They are nicely faded and well worn, which means they are quite comfortable. They will be good for yard work since mud and grass stains wash out of them easily.

My shirt will be my yellow golf shirt. It will match the blue of my jeans. Also, its short sleeves will be fine if the weather is warm.

For warmth on Saturday, if the day is cool, will be my yellow and red sweater. It is made from cotton and has long sleeves and high buttons to keep out frosty air.

Yard work means lots of walking, so I will need comfortable shoes. The best choice will be my white sneakers. They aren't too tight or too loose and keep my feet strong.

Saturday will be a busy day, but I'll be ready!

When "Clothes for Saturday" was written, the author added both an introductory and concluding paragraph. This helps the reader with the flow of the story.

Directions: Now, it's your turn. Select a topic from the list below or choose one of your own. Complete the "cluster of ideas" chart on page 176 and write a brief story. (You may or may not use all the clusters.)

Topics:

chores	holidays	all about me	sports
homework	family	pets	vacation

Writing: Cluster of Ideas

Details

Details

Details

Main Topic

Details

Details

Details

_____

_____

_____

_____

_____

_____

_____

_____

_____

_____

Taking Notes

Taking notes effectively can help you in many ways with schoolwork. It will help you better understand and remember what you read and hear. It will also help you keep track of important facts needed for reports, essays and tests.

Each person develops his/her own way of taking notes. While developing your style, keep in mind the following:

► Write notes in short phrases instead of whole sentences.

► Abbreviate words to save time.

    Examples: pres for president or **&** for and

► If you use the same name often in your notes, use initials.

    Examples: GW for George Washington   **AL** for Abraham Lincoln.

► Be brief, but make sure you understand what you write.

► Number your notes, so you can understand where each note starts and stops.

► When taking notes from a long article or book, write down one or two important points per paragraph or chapter.

Directions: Reread the article "Bats" on page 80. As you read the first three paragraphs, fill in the note-taking format below with your notes.

Title of Article or Story _____

Important Points

Paragraph 1 _____

_____

_____

Paragraph 2 _____

_____

_____

Paragraph 3 _____

_____

_____

Taking Notes

Directions: Use this guide for taking notes on the articles in the next two pages. Set up your own paper in a similar way, or make several photocopies, for note-taking on future pages.

Penguins Are Unusual Birds
(Title)

Paragraph or Chapter numbers	Important Points
1	_____
	_____
2	_____
	_____
3	_____
	_____
	_____

From Grapes to Raisins
(Title)

Paragraph or Chapter numbers	Important Points
1	_____
	_____
2	_____
	_____
3	_____
	_____
	_____

Name _____

Taking Notes: Penguins Are Unusual Birds

Directions: Use a sheet of paper to cover up the story about penguins. Then read the questions.

1. Why are penguins unusual?

2. Do penguins swim?

3. Where do penguins live?

4. Do penguins lay eggs like other birds?

Directions: Read about penguins. While reading, make notes on the note-taking sheet on the previous page.

Penguins may be the most unusual birds. They cannot fly, but they can swim very fast through ice-cold water. They can dive deep into the water, and they can jump high out of it. Sometimes they make their nests out of rocks instead of twigs and grass. Some penguins live in very cold parts of the world. Others live in warmer climates. All penguins live south of the equator.

Unlike other birds, penguins lay only one egg at a time. Right after a mother penguin lays her egg, she waddles back to the ocean. The father penguin holds the egg on his feet, covering it with part of his stomach to keep it warm. When the egg is ready to hatch, the mother penguin returns. Then the father penguin takes a turn looking for food.

When a penguin swims, its white belly and dark back help it hide from enemies. From under the water, predators cannot see it. From on top of the water, large birds cannot see it either. This is how the penguin stays safe!

Directions: Use your notes to complete these sentences.

1. Penguins cannot fly, but _____ .

2. Penguins can dive deep and _____ .

3. Penguins lay only _____ .

4. Father penguins keep the egg _____ .

5. Mother penguins return when the egg _____ .

Name _____

Taking Notes: From Grapes to Raisins

Directions: Use a piece of paper to cover up the story about how grapes become raisins. Then read the questions.

1. How do grapes become raisins?

2. What happens after the grapes become raisins?

3. Why are raisins brown?

4. In what countries do grapes grow?

Directions: Read about how grapes become raisins.
While reading, make notes on the note-taking sheet on page 178.

Grapes grow well in places that have lots of sun. In the United States, California is a big producer of grapes and raisins. When grapes are plump and round, they can be picked from their vines to be made into raisins. After the grapes are picked, they are put on big wooden or paper trays. They sit in the sun for many days.

Slowly, the grapes begin to dry and turn into wrinkled raisins. The sun causes them to change colors. Grapes turn brown as they become raisins. Machines take off the stems. Then the raisins are washed. After being dried again, they are put into boxes.

Some places use machines to make raisins dry faster. The grapes are put into ovens that have hot air blowing around inside. These ovens make the grapes shrivel and dry.

Raisins are made in many countries that grow grapes. Besides the United States, countries such as Greece, Turkey, Iran, Spain and Australia produce a lot of raisins.

Directions: Use your notes to answer the four questions at the top of the page. Write your answers on the lines below.

1. _____

_____

2. _____

_____

_____

3. _____

4. _____

Taking Notes: Graham Crackers

Directions: Use a piece of paper to cover up the story about Graham crackers. Then read the questions.

1. Where did Graham crackers come from?

2. Who invented Graham crackers?

3. What are Graham crackers made of?

4. Why were Graham crackers made?

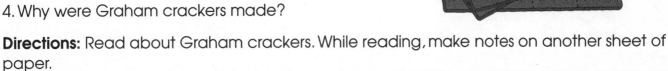

Directions: Read about Graham crackers. While reading, make notes on another sheet of paper.

> Graham crackers were invented around 1830. A minister named Sylvester Graham wanted people to eat healthier foods. He did not think that people should eat meat or white bread. He wanted people to eat more fruits and vegetables and wheat breads that were brown instead of white.
>
> Graham crackers were named after Sylvester Graham. He liked them because they were made of whole-wheat flour. There are many other kinds of crackers, but not all of them are as good for you as Graham crackers. Graham crackers are still considered a healthy snack!

Directions: Use your notes to answer the four questions at the top of the page. Write your answers on the lines below.

1. _____

_____

2. _____

_____

3. _____

_____

4. _____

_____

Name _____

Compare and Contrast

To **compare** means to look for ways two items are alike. To **contrast** means to look for ways two items are different.

Directions: Use the Venn diagram to compare and contrast penguins (page 179) with most birds you see where you live.

Penguins
only

Other Birds
only

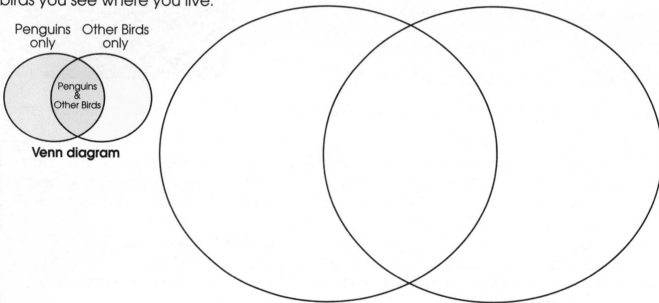

Penguins
&
Other Birds

Venn diagram

To write a comparison paragraph, begin with a topic sentence which states your main idea. Write sentences that provide supporting details. End your paragraph with a conclusion sentence. A conclusion sentence often restates the topic sentence.

Directions: Use the information from your Venn diagram to write a short comparison paragraph.

_____

_____

_____

_____

_____

_____

_____

Name _____

Outlining

Outlines are plans that help you organize your thoughts. If you are writing an essay, an outline helps you decide what to write. An outline should look similar to this:

I. First main idea
  A. A smaller idea
    1. An example
    2. An example
II. Second main idea
  A. A smaller idea
  B. Another smaller idea
III. Third main idea
  A. A smaller idea
  B. Another smaller idea
    1. An example

I. Planting a garden
  A. Choosing seeds
    1. Tomatoes
    2. Lettuce
II. Taking care of the garden
  A. Pulling the weeds
  B. Watering the garden
III. Harvesting
  A. Are they ripe?
  B. How to pick them
    1. Pick only the tomato off the vine

Directions: Use the outline for planting a garden to answer the questions.

1. What are the three main ideas?

  1) _____

  2) _____

  3) _____

2. What are the two smaller ideas listed under "Taking care of the garden"?

  1) _____

  2) _____

3. What are the smaller ideas listed under "Harvesting"?

  1) _____

  2) _____

4. What is listed under the smaller idea "How to pick them"?

_____

Name _____

Outlining: Building a Tree House

Directions: Study the sample outline for building a house. Then use words and phrases from the box to fill in the missing parts of the outline on how to build a tree house.

I. Find land
   A. On a hill
   B. By a lake
   C. In the city
II. Gather materials
   A. Buy wood
   B. Buy nails
   C. Buy tools
      1. Hammer
      2. Screwdriver
      3. Drill
      4. Saw
III. Build the house
   A. Who will use the tools?
   B. Who will carry the wood?

> Collect wood scraps
> Who will hold the boards?
> Who will use the hammer?
> Gather tools
> Can we climb it easily?
> Saw
> How will we get things off the ground?

I. Find a tree
   A. Is it sturdy?

   B. _____

II. Gather supplies

   A. _____

   B. _____

      1. Hammer and nails

      2. _____

III. Build the tree house

   A. _____

   B. _____

   C. _____

Name _____

Outlining: Finishing the Tree House

Directions: Use words and phrases from the box to fill in the missing parts of the outline of what to do once your tree house is built.

Sisters and brothers	When can they visit?
Parents	Spray paint
Tables	Choose a kind of paint
Chairs	Who can visit?

I. Painting the tree house

   A. Choose a color of paint

   B. _____

      1. Cans of paint

      2. _____

II. Putting furniture in the tree house

   A. _____

   B. _____

III. Making a visitors' policy

   A. _____

      1. Friends

      2. _____

      3. _____

   B. _____

Name _____

Outlining: The *Mayflower*'s Voyage

Directions: Read about the *Mayflower*. Then complete the outline for an essay.

The *Mayflower* left England in 1620. It carried 101 passengers. Some of those passengers were called Pilgrims. Pilgrims were people who had wandered from country to country looking for a place to make their home.

It took 66 days to cross the Atlantic Ocean. The ship was crowded. There were some accidents on board. The *Mayflower* landed at the tip of Cape Cod in Massachusetts. Several men searched the area to find the best place to start a colony. They finally settled on Plymouth.

The Pilgrims lived on the *Mayflower* through the winter. The *Mayflower* returned to England in April 1621. None of the Pilgrims went back with it.

I. The *Mayflower* leaves England

   A. _____

   B. _____

II. The journey

   A. _____

   B. _____

   C. _____

III. Landing in America

   A. _____

   B. _____

Outlining: The First Thanksgiving

Directions: Read about the first Thanksgiving. Then complete the outline.

The Pilgrims arrived at Plymouth Rock just as winter set in. Many people died that winter from cold and hunger. The following spring, the Pilgrims started planting vegetable gardens. A Native American named Squanto helped them. They planted peas, wheat, beans, corn and pumpkins.

When fall came, the Pilgrims were so glad to have enough food that they invited the Native Americans to share their first Thanksgiving. In addition to food from their garden, they also shared wild geese that they had killed and other food like sweet potatoes and fresh berries.

I. The first winter

   A. _____

   B. _____

II. Spring

   A. _____

   B. _____

III. Fall

   A. _____

   B. _____

      1. _____

      2. _____

      3. _____

Name _____

Using an Outline to Write an Essay

Outlines help you organize information and notes into a manageable form. Outlines also help you prepare to write reports and essays by keeping your thoughts in a logical order or sequence. Once you have a good outline, converting it to paragraph form is easy.

To convert an outline to an essay, add your own words to expand the words and phrases in the outline into sentence form. Information from the first main topic becomes the first paragraph.

I. Painting the tree house
  A. Choose a color of paint
  B. Choose a kind of paint
    1. Cans of paint
    2. Spray paint

Information from the second and third main topics become the second and third paragraphs of the essay.

II. Putting furniture in the tree house
  A. Tables
  B. Chairs
III. Making a visitors' policy
  A. Who can visit?
    1. Friends
    2. Sisters and brothers
    3. Parents
  B. When can they visit?

To write an essay, remember to indent each paragraph, begin each paragraph with a topic sentence and include supporting details.

Directions: Read the beginning of the essay. Then finish it on another sheet of paper using your own words and information from the outline.

Finishing Touches

Finishing a tree house takes a lot of thought and planning. First, it needs to be painted. The paint will help protect the wood from rain and snow. The best kind of paint for finishing the wood would be in cans. It would brush on easily, smoothly and quickly. Green would be a great color for the tree house because it would blend in with the green leaves of the trees.

Name _____

Summarizing: Writing an Autobiography

When you **summarize** an article, book or speech, you are simply writing a shorter article that contains only the main points. This shorter article of main points is called a **summary**.

To prepare for writing a summary of your life, you would begin with an outline. Since a summary is a brief account of main points, you will not be able to include every detail of your life. Your summary should include only basic facts.

I. Yourself
  A. Name
  B. Age and grade in school
    1. Subjects you like in school
    2. Subjects you do not like in school
  C. Looks
    1. Eye color
    2. Hair color
    3. Other features
II. Your family
  A. Parents
  B. Brothers/sisters
  C. Pets
III. Hobbies and interests
  A. Sports
  B. Clubs

Directions: Follow the format above to write an outline about your life. Feel free to add more main ideas, smaller ideas or examples.

_____

_____

_____

_____

_____

_____

_____

_____

Name _____

Summarizing: Writing an Autobiography

A summary of your life would include when you were born, who your parents are, other members of your family, your age and your grade in school. Details like your favorite joke, today's weather or how much homework you had yesterday would not be included in a summary.

Directions: Use the information from your outline to write a summary of your life.

_____

_____

_____

_____

_____

_____

_____

_____

_____

_____

_____

_____

_____

_____

_____

_____

_____

_____

_____

Summarizing: The North Pole

Directions: Read about the North Pole. Then use the main points of the article to write a paragraph summarizing conditions at the North Pole.

At the North Pole, the sun does not shine for half of the year. It stays dark outside for six months, but for the other six months of the year, the sun does not set. It is light through the night.

The North Pole is as far north as you can go. If you traveled north to the North Pole and kept going, you would start going south. You could call the North Pole the top of the Earth.

The average temperature at the North Pole is –9 degrees Fahrenheit. That is not any colder than many places in the United States get in the winter. In fact, some places get much colder than that, but at the North Pole, it stays very cold for a very long time.

The cold winds that blow off the Arctic Ocean make the North Pole a very cold place most of the time. In the summer when the sun is shining all day and all night, the temperature can rise to 38 degrees Fahrenheit in places that are sheltered from the wind. But that is still very cold.

The Arctic Ocean is at the North Pole. The area surrounding the North Pole is called the Arctic Region. Some of Canada, Alaska, Greenland, Russia and Scandinavia are in the Arctic Region. These places get very cold in the long, dark winters, too!

The main points of this article are:

1. At the North Pole, the sun is never out in the winter. It is always out in the summer.

2. The North Pole is very cold all year.

3. Winds from the Arctic Ocean make the North Pole stay very cold. The Arctic Ocean surrounds the North Pole.

4. There is some land in the Arctic Region.

_____

_____

_____

_____

_____

_____

Name _____

Summarizing: Settler Children

Directions: Read about settler children. Then complete the list of main points at the end of the article.

In the 1700s and 1800s, many children from other countries came with their parents to America. In the beginning, they had no time to go to school. They had to help their families work in the fields, care for the animals and clean the house. They also helped care for their younger brothers and sisters.

Sometimes settler children helped build houses and schools. Usually, these early school buildings were just one room. There was only one teacher for all the children. Settler children were very happy when they could attend school.

Because settler children worked so much, they had little time to play. There were not many things settler children could do just for fun. One pastime was gardening. Weeding their gardens taught them how to be orderly. Children sometimes made gifts out of the things they grew.

The settlers also encouraged their children to sing. Each one was expected to play at least one musical instrument. Parents wanted their children to walk, ride horses, visit friends and relatives and read nonfiction books.

Most settler children did not have many toys. The toys they owned were made by their parents and grandparents. They were usually made of cloth or carved from wood. The children made up games with string, like "cat's cradle." They also made things out of wood, such as seesaws. Settler children did not have all the toys we have today, but they managed to have fun anyway!

The main points of this article are:

1. Settler children worked hard.

2. Settler children had many jobs.

3. _____

4. _____

5. _____

Directions: Use the main points to write a summary of this article on a separate sheet of paper.

Name _____

Library Skills: Call Numbers

The **call number** of a book tells where it can be found among nonfiction books.

Information is presented differently on the title, subject and author card for the same book. A computer listing for this book would look quite similar.

567.91 DINOSAURS
V278 VanCleave, Janice
Dinosaurs for Every Kid
John Wiley & Sons, Inc., 1994

Author card

567.91	VanCleave, Janice
V278	Dinosaurs for Every Kid
	John Wiley & Sons, Inc., 1994

Subject card

567.91	DINOSAURS
V278	VanCleave, Janice
	Dinosaurs for Every Kid
	John Wiley & Sons, Inc., 1994

Title card

567.91	Dinosaurs for Every Kid
V278	VanCleave, Janice
	John Wiley & Sons, Inc., 1994

Directions: Answer the questions about what is shown on these cards.

1. What is written at the top of the subject card?

_____

2. What is written at the top of the title card?

_____

3. What is written at the top of the author card?

_____

4. Why do libraries have three different kinds of listings for the same book?

_____

5. What is the number listed at the top left of each card? _____

6. What other information is on the cards? _____

_____

Name _____

Library Skills: The Dewey Decimal System

Using a library catalog helps you find the books you want. All nonfiction books—except biographies and autobiographies—are filed according to their call number. **Nonfiction books** are books based on facts. **Biographies** are true books that tell about people's lives. **Autobiographies** are books that people write about their own lives.

The call numbers are part of the **Dewey Decimal System**. Each listing in a library catalog will include a book's call number.

Example:
918.8   Bringle, Mary
B85e   Eskimos
           F. Watts, 1973

All libraries using the **Dewey Decimal System** follow the same system for filing books. The system divides all nonfiction books into 10 main groups, each represented by numbers.

0–099	General works (libraries, computers, etc.)
100–199	Philosophy
200–299	Religion
300–399	Social Sciences
400–499	Language
500–599	Pure Science (math, astronomy, chemistry, etc.)
600–699	Applied Science (medicine, engineering, etc.)
700–799	Arts and Recreation
800–899	Literature
900–999	History

Each book is given a specific call number. A book about ghosts could be 133.1.

This is where some subjects fall in the Dewey Decimal System.

Pets	630	Maps	910	Cathedrals	236	Dinosaurs	560
Baseball	796	Monsters	791	Trees	580	Presidents	920
Butterflies	595	Mummies	390	Space	620	Cooking	640

Directions: Write the Dewey Decimal number for the following books.

_____ *Animals of Long Ago*   _____ *Our American Presidents*

_____ *City Leaves, City Trees*   _____ *Mummies Made in Egypt*

_____ *Easy Microwave Cooking for Kids*   _____ *Real-Life Monsters*

_____ *To Space and Back*   _____ *Great Churches in Europe*

_____ *Amazing Baseball Teams*   _____ *The Children's Atlas*

Library Skills

Some books in a library are not filed by the Dewey Decimal System. Those books include biographies, autobiographies and fiction. Biographies and autobiographies may be filed together in the 920s or be assigned a call number by subject.

Fiction books are stories that someone has made up. They are filed in alphabetical order by the author's last name in the fiction section of the library.

Directions: For each title, write **B** if it is a biography, **A** if it is an autobiography or **F** if it is fiction. Then circle the titles that would not be filed by the Dewey Decimal System.

_____ *Tales of a Fourth Grade Nothing*

_____ *The Real Tom Thumb*

_____ *Ramona the Pest*

_____ *Bill Peet: An Autobiography*

_____ *Abraham Lincoln*

_____ *Charlotte's Web*

_____ *The King and I*

_____ *My Life With Chimpanzees*

_____ *Sara Plain and Tall*

_____ *Michael Jordan, Basketball's Soaring Star*

_____ *The First Book of Presidents*

_____ *The Helen Keller Story*

Putting Library Skills to Use

You can improve your library skills by using them at your local library.

Directions: While at the library, follow the instructions and answer the questions.

1. Use the library catalog to find a book about dinosaurs. What is its title? _____

   _____

2. What is the call number for that book? _____

3. Who is the author of that book? _____

4. Go to the shelf and look for the book. Did you find it? _____

5. Use the library catalog to find the author of the book, *Mummies Made in Egypt*. Who wrote it?

   _____

6. Use the library catalog to find other books by that author. What are the names of four other books by that author?

   _____

   _____

   _____

   _____

7. Use the library catalog to find a book written by Judy Blume with the word "fudge" in the title. What is its title?

   _____

8. What is the library's most recent book by Ezra Jack Keats? _____

   _____

Encyclopedia Skills

Encyclopedias are sets of books that provide information about different subjects. If you want to know when cars were first made or who invented the phonograph, you could find the information in an encyclopedia.

Encyclopedias come in sets of books and on computer CD's. They contain many facts, illustrations, maps, graphs and tables. Encyclopedias are **reference books** found in the reference section of the library.

Each subject listed in an encyclopedia is called an **entry**. Entries are organized alphabetically.

Some good encyclopedias for students are *World Book Encyclopedia, Compton's Encyclopedia* and *Children's Britannica.*

Specialty encyclopedias, like the *McGraw-Hill Encyclopedia of Science and Technology*, contain information on one particular subject.

Directions: Number these encyclopedia entries in alphabetical order. The first one has been done for you.

_____	deep-sea diving	_____	Little League
_____	deer	_____	Little Rock
_____	Florida	_____	metric system
_____	natural fiber	_____	United Nations
_____	Death Valley	_____	poison oak
_____	flour	___1___	Air Force
_____	Gretzky, Wayne	_____	Carter, Jimmy

Name _____

Encyclopedia Skills: Using the Index

The **index** of an encyclopedia contains an alphabetical listing of all entries. To find information about a subject, decide on the best word to describe the subject. If you want to know about ducks, look up the word "duck" in the index. If you're really interested in learning about mallard ducks, then look under "mallard ducks." The index shows the page number and volume where the information is located.

Look at the index entry below about Neil Armstrong. Most index entries also tell you when a person lived and died and give a short description of the person.

> ARMSTRONG, NEIL   United States astronaut, b. 1930
> Commander of *Gemini 8*, 1966; first man to walk on the Moon, July 1969
> References in
>   Astronaut: illus. 2:56
>   Space travel 17:214

Neil Armstrong is listed under "Astronaut" and "Space travel." You can find information about him in both articles. The first entry shows there is an illustration (illus.) of Neil Armstrong in volume 2 on page 56 (2:56).

If Neil Armstrong were listed in a separate article in the encyclopedia, the index would look something like this:

> main article Armstrong, Neil
> 2:48

Directions: Answer these questions about using an encyclopedia index.

1. According to the index listing for Neil Armstrong, when was he born? _____

2. According to the index listing, who was Neil Armstrong? _____

_____

3. When did he walk on the Moon? _____

4. What are the titles of the two articles containing information about Neil Armstrong?

_____   _____

5. Where would you find the article on Space travel?

   Volume number _____ , page number _____ .

MATH

Place Value

Place value is the value of a digit, or numeral, shown by where it is in the number. For example, in 1,234, 1 has the place value of thousands, 2 is hundreds, 3 is tens and 4 is ones.

Directions: Write the numbers in the correct boxes to find how far the car has traveled.

one thousand

six hundreds

eight ones

nine ten thousands

four tens

two millions

five hundred thousands

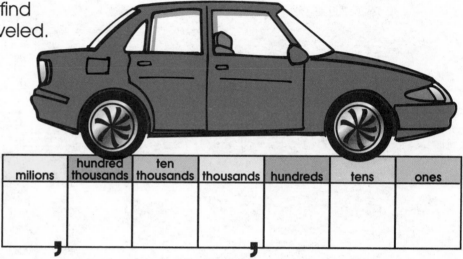

milions	hundred thousands	ten thousands	thousands	hundreds	tens	ones

How many miles has the car traveled?_____

Directions: In the number . . .

2,386 _____ is in the ones place.

4,957 _____ is in the hundreds place.

102,432 _____ is in the ten thousands place.

489,753 _____ is in the thousands place.

1,743,998 _____ is in the millions place.

9,301,671 _____ is in the hundred thousands place.

7,521,834 _____ is in the tens place.

Name _____

Place Value: Standard Form

For this activity, you will need a number spinner or number cube.

Directions: Roll the cube or spin the spinner the same number of times as there are spaces in each place value box. The first number rolled or spun goes in the ones place, the second number in the tens place, and so on.

Standard Form

4,567

Example:

thousands	hundreds	tens	ones
4	5	6	7

	hundreds	tens	ones

thousands	hundreds	tens	ones

ten thousands	thousands	hundreds	tens	ones

hundred thousands	ten thousands	thousands	hundreds	tens	ones

millions	hundred thousands	ten thousands	thousands	hundreds	tens	ones

_____

_____

_____

_____

_____

Directions: Write the number words for the numerals above.

_____

_____

_____

_____

_____

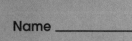

Place Value:
~~ed~~ Notation and Standard Form

Directions: Use the number cube or spinner to create numbers for the place value boxes below. Then write the number in expanded notation and standard form.

Example:

thousands	hundreds	tens	ones
8	6	2	4

Standard Form ___8,624___

Expanded Notation ___8,000 + 600 + 20 + 4___

thousands	hundreds	tens	ones

Standard Form _____

Expanded Notation _____

ten thousands	thousands	hundreds	tens	ones

Standard Form _____

Expanded Notation _____

hundred thousands	ten thousands	thousands	hundreds	tens	ones

Standard Form _____

Expanded Notation _____

Directions: Write the value of the 4 in each number below.

742,521 _____

456 _____

1,234,567 _____

65,504 _____

937,641 _____

Name _____

Add 'Em Up!

Addition is "putting together" or adding two or more numbers to find the sum.

Directions: Add the following problems as quickly and as accurately as you can.

3 + 2	6 + 4	5 + 4	2 + 9		
6 + 2	4 + 1	9 + 6	7 + 6	8 + 7	8 + 9
9 + 4	1 + 8	4 + 7	7 + 9	5 + 6	5 + 3
		6 + 6	8 + 8	7 + 7	4 + 4
		2 + 8	5 + 2	3 + 6	5 + 8

How quickly did you complete this page? _____

Name _____

Going in Circles

Directions: Where the circles meet, write the sum of the numbers from the circles on the right and left and above and below. The first row shows you what to do.

7 (16) 9 (21) 12 (20) 8

4   6   5   1

0   3   2   10

11   15   20   12

13   16   14   17

Addition Games

Directions: Play the following addition games to practice your math facts.

1. ROLL 'EM!

For one or more players.

Materials: 2 number cubes or dice or 2 number spinners per player

How to play: Each player rolls his/her number cubes (dice) or spins his/her spinners at the same time. As quickly as possible, he/she adds the two numbers rolled or spun. Whoever is first to add the numbers correctly wins the round.

Variation: Subtract the numbers.

2. FLASH 'EM!

For one or more players.

Materials: addition/subtraction flash cards

How to play: An adult shows the flash cards one at a time to each player, who solves the addition problem. Place correctly answered cards in one stack and incorrectly answered cards in another. Which stack is larger? Try again. This time try to answer all the cards correctly.

Variations: Set a time limit for play. How many flash cards can be correctly answered in 5, 4 or 3 minutes?

Name _____

Magic Squares

Directions: Some of the number squares below are "magic" and some are not. Squares that add up to the same number horizontally, vertically and diagonally are "magic." Add the numbers horizontally and vertically in each square to discover which ones are "magic."

Example:

4	9	2
3	5	7
8	1	6

15
15
15

15 15 15 15

Magic? __yes__

1.

7	2	1
3	4	8
5	9	6

___
___
___

___ ___ ___

Magic? _____

2.

6	11	4
5	7	9
10	3	8

___
___
___

___ ___ ___

Magic? _____

3.

3	8	1
2	4	6
7	0	5

___
___
___

___ ___ ___

Magic? _____

4.

2	7	0
1	3	5
6	9	4

___
___
___

___ ___ ___

Magic? _____

5.

5	10	3
4	6	8
9	2	7

___
___
___

___ ___ ___

Magic? _____

6.

7	12	5
6	8	10
11	4	9

___
___
___

___ ___ ___

Magic? _____

7.

1	2	3
4	5	6
7	8	9

___
___
___

___ ___ ___

Magic? _____

8.

6	7	4
1	5	9
8	3	2

___
___
___

___ ___ ___

Magic? _____

Challenge: Can you discover a pattern for number placement in the magic squares? Try to make a magic square of your own.

Name _____

Adding Larger Numbers

When adding two-, three- and four-digit numbers, add the ones first, then tens, hundreds, thousands, and so on.

Examples:

Tens	Ones
5	4
+2	5
	9

Tens	Ones
5	4
+2	5
7	9

Directions: Add the following numbers.

```
   81          67          34         730
  +23         +22         +82        +265
```

```
   76       1,803         523         267
  +73      +1,104        +476        + 12
```

```
                        4,254         111
                       + 545        + 82
```

```
                          164         727
                        +425        + 51
```

Addition: Regrouping

Regrouping uses 10 ones to form one 10, 10 tens to form one hundred, one 10 and 5 ones to form 15, and so on.

Directions: Add using regrouping. Color in all the boxes with a 5 in the answer to help the dog find its way home.

<table>
<tr><td></td><td>63
+ 22</td><td>5,268
4,910
+ 1,683</td><td>248
+ 463</td><td>291
+ 543</td><td>2,934
+ 112</td></tr>
<tr><td>1,736
+ 5,367</td><td>2,946
+ 7,384</td><td>3,245
1,239
+ 981</td><td>738
+ 692</td><td>896
+ 728</td><td>594
+ 738</td></tr>
<tr><td>2,603
+ 5,004</td><td>4,507
+ 289</td><td>1,483
+ 6,753</td><td>1,258
+ 6,301</td><td>27
469
+ 6,002</td><td>4,637
+ 7,531</td></tr>
<tr><td>782
+ 65</td><td>485
+ 276</td><td>3,421
+ 8,064</td><td colspan="3"></td></tr>
<tr><td>48
93
+ 26</td><td>90
263
+ 864</td><td>362
453
+ 800</td><td colspan="3"></td></tr>
</table>

Leafy Addition

Directions: Add, then color according to the code.

Code:

green — 79   orange — 35   red — 78
yellow — 87   purple — 56   brown — 94

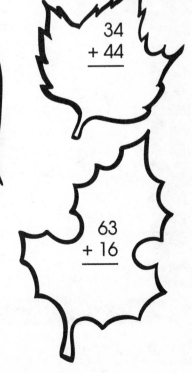

57
+ 21
___

34
+ 22
___

23
+ 12
___

35
+ 52
___

15
+ 41
___

62
+ 32
___

20
+ 74
___

34
+ 44
___

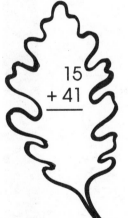

56
+ 23
___

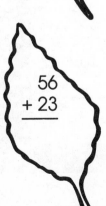

47
+ 40
___

27
+ 8
___

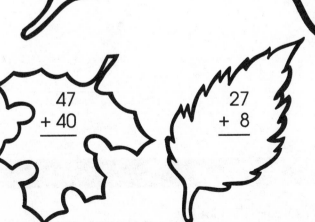

63
+ 16
___

Subtraction

Subtraction is "taking away" or subtracting one number from another.

Directions: Complete the following problems as quickly and as accurately as you can.

$$\begin{array}{r} 18 \\ -\ 9 \\ \hline \end{array} \qquad \begin{array}{r} 13 \\ -\ 6 \\ \hline \end{array} \qquad \begin{array}{r} 12 \\ -\ 5 \\ \hline \end{array} \qquad \begin{array}{r} 17 \\ -\ 8 \\ \hline \end{array} \qquad \begin{array}{r} 16 \\ -\ 8 \\ \hline \end{array}$$

$$\begin{array}{r} 12 \\ -\ 5 \\ \hline \end{array} \qquad \begin{array}{r} 10 \\ -\ 4 \\ \hline \end{array} \qquad \begin{array}{r} 5 \\ -\ 3 \\ \hline \end{array} \qquad \begin{array}{r} 14 \\ -\ 6 \\ \hline \end{array} \qquad \begin{array}{r} 15 \\ -\ 9 \\ \hline \end{array}$$

$$\begin{array}{r} 9 \\ -\ 5 \\ \hline \end{array} \qquad \begin{array}{r} 8 \\ -\ 3 \\ \hline \end{array} \qquad \begin{array}{r} 6 \\ -\ 2 \\ \hline \end{array} \qquad \begin{array}{r} 5 \\ -\ 4 \\ \hline \end{array} \qquad \begin{array}{r} 10 \\ -\ 7 \\ \hline \end{array}$$

$$\begin{array}{r} 11 \\ -\ 4 \\ \hline \end{array} \qquad \begin{array}{r} 12 \\ -\ 8 \\ \hline \end{array} \qquad \begin{array}{r} 16 \\ -\ 9 \\ \hline \end{array} \qquad \begin{array}{r} 11 \\ -\ 8 \\ \hline \end{array} \qquad \begin{array}{r} 10 \\ -10 \\ \hline \end{array}$$

How quickly did you complete this page? _____

Name _____

Subtracting Larger Numbers

When you subtract larger numbers, subtract the ones
first, then the tens, hundreds, thousands, and so on.

Example:

Tens	Ones
9	4
− 2	1
	3

Tens	Ones
9	4
− 2	1
7	3

Directions: Solve these subtraction problems.

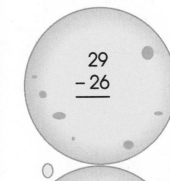

```
   29          99         359
 − 26        − 58       −  55
```

```
  735         849       7,678
 − 734       − 726     − 4,321
```

```
  865          55       9,876
 − 731        − 25     − 1,234
```

GRADE 4

Name _____

Subtraction: Regrouping

Directions: Subtract using regrouping.

Examples:

$$\begin{array}{r} 23 \\ -18 \\ \hline \end{array} \qquad \begin{array}{r} \overset{1}{\cancel{2}}\overset{1}{3} \\ -18 \\ \hline 5 \end{array}$$

$$\begin{array}{r} 243 \\ -96 \\ \hline \end{array} \qquad \begin{array}{r} \overset{1}{\cancel{2}}\overset{13}{\cancel{4}}\overset{1}{3} \\ -96 \\ \hline 147 \end{array}$$

$$\begin{array}{r} 81 \\ -53 \\ \hline \end{array} \qquad \begin{array}{r} 76 \\ -49 \\ \hline \end{array} \qquad \begin{array}{r} 94 \\ -38 \\ \hline \end{array} \qquad \begin{array}{r} 156 \\ -77 \\ \hline \end{array} \qquad \begin{array}{r} 341 \\ -83 \\ \hline \end{array} \qquad \begin{array}{r} 726 \\ -29 \\ \hline \end{array}$$

$$\begin{array}{r} 568 \\ -173 \\ \hline \end{array} \qquad \begin{array}{r} 806 \\ -738 \\ \hline \end{array} \qquad \begin{array}{r} 743 \\ -550 \\ \hline \end{array} \qquad \begin{array}{r} 903 \\ -336 \\ \hline \end{array} \qquad \begin{array}{r} 647 \\ -289 \\ \hline \end{array} \qquad \begin{array}{r} 254 \\ -69 \\ \hline \end{array}$$

$$\begin{array}{r} 730 \\ -518 \\ \hline \end{array} \qquad \begin{array}{r} 961 \\ -846 \\ \hline \end{array} \qquad \begin{array}{r} 573 \\ -76 \\ \hline \end{array} \qquad \begin{array}{r} 604 \\ -55 \\ \hline \end{array} \qquad \begin{array}{r} 265 \\ -19 \\ \hline \end{array} \qquad \begin{array}{r} 372 \\ -59 \\ \hline \end{array}$$

$$\begin{array}{r} 111 \\ -82 \\ \hline \end{array} \qquad \begin{array}{r} 358 \\ -99 \\ \hline \end{array} \qquad \begin{array}{r} 147 \\ -49 \\ \hline \end{array}$$

$$\begin{array}{r} 180 \\ -106 \\ \hline \end{array} \qquad \begin{array}{r} 325 \\ -68 \\ \hline \end{array} \qquad \begin{array}{r} 873 \\ -35 \\ \hline \end{array}$$

Addition and Subtraction

Directions: Add or subtract, using regrouping when needed.

32 68 + 43	183 246 + 89	456 398 + 597	643 – 377
1,563 – 941	3,586 + 4,218	8,711 – 4,937	9,361 – 7,452
5,734 + 6,298	293 431 + 93	743 – 529	849 250 + 82
1,227 2,431 + 5,792	9,117 – 3,828		

68 + 93 + 146 = _____   73 + 246 + 1,579 = _____

43 + 745 – 29 = _____   128 + 403 + 2,571 = _____

156 + 627 + 541 = _____   97 + 51 + 37 + 79 = _____

Tom walks 389 steps from his house to the video store. It is 149 steps to Elm Street. It is 52 steps from Maple Street to the video store. How many steps is it from Elm Street to Maple Street? _____

Addition and Subtraction

Directions: Add or subtract, using regrouping when needed.

```
   38        1,269                      629
   43        2,453       5,792          491        4,697
 + 21      + 8,219     - 4,814        + 308      - 2,988
 ____      _____     _____        _____      _____
```

```
             68          197
  5,280      27          436         7,321         456
- 3,147    + 42        + 213       - 2,789       + 974
 _____    ____        _____        _____       _____
```

```
            492
  3,932     863         9,873        4,978        6,235
+ 4,681    + 57       + 5,483      + 2,131      + 2,986
 _____    ____        _____       _____       _____
```

Sue stocked her pond with 263 bass and 187 trout. 97 fish swam away in a flood. How many fish are left?

_____

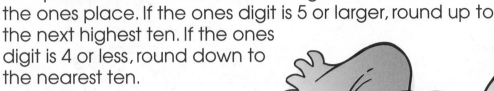

Name _____

Rounding: Tens

Rounding a number means expressing it to the nearest ten, hundred, thousand, and so on. Knowing how to round numbers makes estimating sums, differences and products easier. When rounding to the nearest ten, the key number is in the ones place. If the ones digit is 5 or larger, round up to the next highest ten. If the ones digit is 4 or less, round down to the nearest ten.

Examples:
- Round 81 to the nearest ten.
- 1 is the key digit.
- If it is less than 5, round down.
- Answer: <u>80</u>

- Round 246 to the nearest ten.
- 6 is the key digit.
- If it is more than 5, round up.
- Answer: <u>250</u>

Directions:
Round these numbers to the nearest ten.

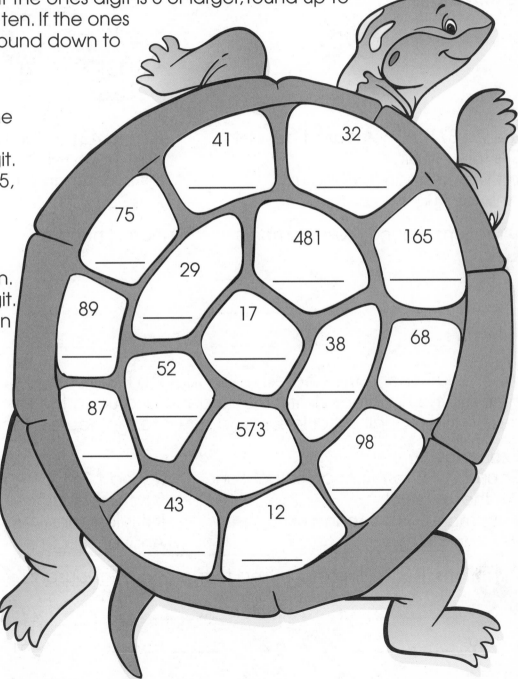

Rounding: Hundreds and Thousands

When rounding to the nearest hundred, the key number is in the tens place. If the tens digit is 5 or larger, round up to nearest hundred. If the tens digit is 4 or less, round down to the nearest hundred.

Examples:

Round 871 to the nearest hundred.
7 is the key digit.
If it is more than 5, round up.
Answer: <u>900</u>

Round 421 to the nearest hundred.
2 is the key digit.
If it is less than 4, round down.
Answer: <u>400</u>

Directions: Round these numbers to the nearest hundred.

255 _____	368 _____	443 _____	578 _____
562 _____	698 _____	99 _____	775 _____
812 _____	592 _____	124 _____	10,235 _____

When rounding to the nearest thousand, the key number is in the hundreds place. If the hundreds digit is 5 or larger, round up to the nearest thousand. If the hundreds digit is 4 or less, round down to the nearest thousand.

Examples:

Round 7,932 to the nearest thousand.
9 is the key digit.
If it is more than 5, round up.
Answer: <u>8,000</u>

Round 1,368 to the nearest thousand.
3 is the key digit.
If it is less than 4, round down.
Answer: <u>1,000</u>

Directions: Round these numbers to the nearest thousand.

8,631 _____	1,248 _____	798 _____
999 _____	6,229 _____	8,461 _____
9,654 _____	4,963 _____	99,923 _____

Name _____

Rounding

Directions: Round these numbers to the nearest ten.

18 _____ 33 _____ 82 _____ 56 _____

24 _____ 49 _____ 91 _____ 67 _____

Directions: Round these numbers to the nearest hundred.

243 _____ 689 _____ 263 _____ 162 _____

389 _____ 720 _____ 351 _____ 490 _____

463 _____ 846 _____ 928 _____ 733 _____

Directions: Round these numbers to the nearest thousand.

2,638 _____ 3,940 _____ 8,653 _____

6,238 _____ 1,429 _____ 5,061 _____

7,289 _____ 2,742 _____ 9,460 _____

3,109 _____ 4,697 _____ 8,302 _____

Directions: Round these numbers to the nearest ten thousand.

11,368 _____ 38,421 _____

75,302 _____ 67,932 _____

14,569 _____ 49,926 _____

93,694 _____ 81,648 _____

26,784 _____ 87,065 _____

57,843 _____ 29,399 _____

Name _____

Estimating

Estimating is used for certain mathematical calculations. For example, to figure the cost of several items, round their prices to the nearest dollar, then add up the approximate cost. A store clerk, on the other hand, needs to know the exact prices in order to charge the correct amount. To estimate to the nearest hundred, round up numbers over 50. **Example:** 251 is rounded up to 300. Round down numbers less than 50. **Example:** 128 is rounded down to 100.

Directions: In the following situations, write whether an exact or estimated answer should be used.

Example:

You make a deposit in your bank account. Do you want an estimated total or an exact total?

_____ Exact _____

1. Your family just ate dinner at a restaurant. Your parents are trying to calculate the tip for your server. Should they estimate by rounding or use exact numbers?

_____

2. You are at the store buying candy, and you want to know if you have enough money to pay for it. Should you estimate or use exact numbers?

_____

3. Some friends are planning a trip from New York City to Washington, D.C. They need to know about how far they will travel in miles. Should they estimate or use exact numbers?

_____

4. You plan a trip to the zoo. Beforehand, you call the zoo for the price of admission. Should the person at the zoo tell you an estimated or exact price?

_____

5. The teacher is grading your papers. Should your scores be exact or estimated?

_____

Name _____

Estimating

To **estimate** means to give an approximate, rather than an exact, answer. To find an estimated sum or difference, round the numbers of the problem, then add or subtract. If the number has 5 ones or more, round up to the nearest ten. If the number has 4 ones or less, round down to the nearest ten.

Directions: Round the numbers to the nearest ten, hundred or thousand. Then add or subtract.

Examples:

Ten		Hundred	Thousand
$\begin{array}{r} 74 \rightarrow 70 \\ +\,39 \rightarrow +\,40 \\ \hline 110 \end{array}$	$\begin{array}{r} 64 \rightarrow 60 \\ -\,25 \rightarrow -\,30 \\ \hline 30 \end{array}$	$\begin{array}{r} 352 \rightarrow 400 \\ -\,164 \rightarrow -\,200 \\ \hline 200 \end{array}$	$\begin{array}{r} 7,681 \rightarrow 8,000 \\ +\,4,321 \rightarrow +\,4,000 \\ \hline 12,000 \end{array}$

Round these numbers to the nearest ten.

$\begin{array}{r} 18 \rightarrow \\ +\,24 \rightarrow \\ \hline \end{array}$ 　　　 $\begin{array}{r} 49 \rightarrow \\ -\,33 \rightarrow \\ \hline \end{array}$ 　　　 $\begin{array}{r} 67 \rightarrow \\ -\,56 \rightarrow \\ \hline \end{array}$

Round these numbers to the nearest hundred.

$\begin{array}{r} 255 \rightarrow \\ -\,99 \rightarrow \\ \hline \end{array}$ 　　　 $\begin{array}{r} 526 \rightarrow \\ +\,145 \rightarrow \\ \hline \end{array}$ 　　　 $\begin{array}{r} 102 \rightarrow \\ -\,75 \rightarrow \\ \hline \end{array}$

Round these numbers to the nearest thousand.

$\begin{array}{r} 8,361 \rightarrow \\ +\,889 \rightarrow \\ \hline \end{array}$ 　　　 $\begin{array}{r} 9,926 \rightarrow \\ +\,3,645 \rightarrow \\ \hline \end{array}$

　　219

Name _____

Estimating

Directions: Round the numbers to the nearest hundred. Then solve the problems.

Example:

Jack and Alex were playing a computer game. Jack scored 428 points. Alex scored 132. About how many more points did Jack score than Alex?

Round Jack's 428 points down to the nearest hundred, 400.

Round Alex's 132 points down to 100. Subtract.

$$
\begin{array}{r}
400 \\
- 100 \\
\hline
\textbf{estimate} \quad 300
\end{array}
$$

258 → 300 + 117 → +100 ───── 375 ── 400	493 → + 114 →	837 → − 252 →
928 → − 437 →	700 → − 491 →	319 → + 630 →
332 → + 567 →	493 → − 162 →	1,356 → + 2,941 →

Skip Counting

Skip counting is a quick way to count by skipping numbers. For example, when you skip count by 2's, you count 2, 4, 6, 8, and so on. You can skip count by many different numbers such as 2's, 4's, 5's, 10's and 100's.

The illustration below shows skip counting by 2's to 14.

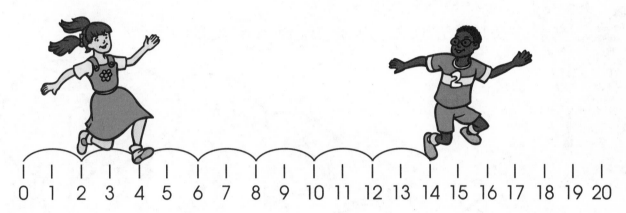

Directions: Use the number line to help you skip count by 2's from 0 to 20.

0, _____, _____, _____, 8, _____, _____, 14, _____, _____, _____

Directions: Skip count by 3's by filling in the rocks across the pond.

Name _____

Multiples

A **multiple** is the product of a specific number and any other number. For example, the multiples of 2 are 2 (2 x 1), 4 (2 x 2), 6, 8, 10, 12, and so on.

Directions: Write the missing multiples.

Example: Count by 5's.

5, 10, 15, 20, 25, 30, 35. These are multiples of 5.

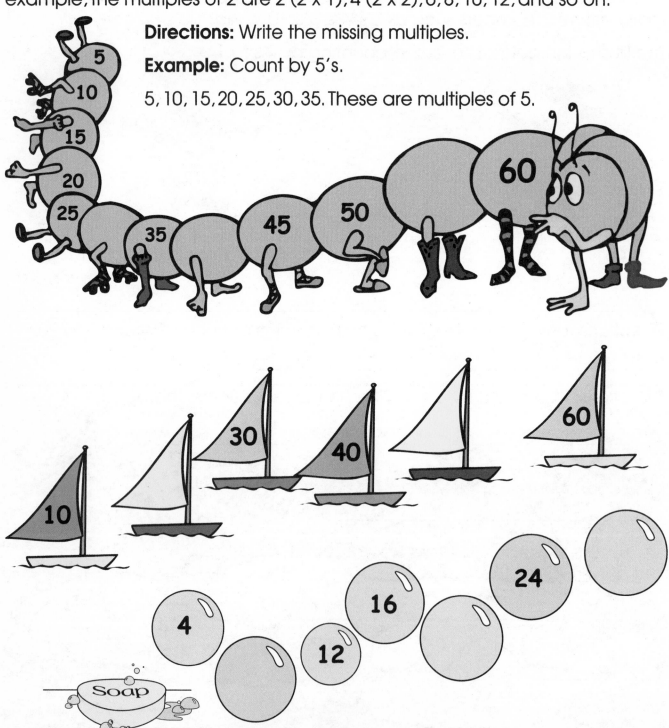

Name _____

Review

Directions: Add or subtract using regrouping.

```
   67
   93              5,029            732          2,467          8,453
 + 48            - 3,068          + 18        + 3,184        - 6,087
 ____            _____          ____        _____        _____
```

```
 5,792            7,489            463          3,567          6,342
- 3,889          + 5,938         - 209        - 2,394        + 959
 _____            _____           ____        _____        _____
```

Directions: Write the numbers in the boxes. In the blanks, write the numbers in standard form.

millions	hundred thousands	ten thousands	thousands	hundreds	tens	ones

_____

eight millions, four hundred thousands, zero ten thousands, zero thousands, nine hundreds, five tens, two ones

hundred thousands	ten thousands	thousands	hundreds	tens	ones

_____

five hundred thousands, three ten thousands, five thousands, zero hundreds, four tens, one one

Directions: Write the missing multiples in the blanks.

6, 12, 18, _____, 30, _____   3, _____, _____, 12, 15

4, _____, 12, 16, _____, 24   _____, 10, 15, _____, _____

Name _____

Multiplication

Multiplication is a short way to find the sum of adding the same number a certain amount of times, such as 7 x 4 = 28 instead of 7 + 7 + 7 + 7 = 28.

Directions: Multiply as quickly and as accurately as you can.

4 x 7	7 x 6	0 x 8	7 x 2	9 x 5	1 x 5	6 x 4
8 x 3	7 x 1	4 x 2	9 x 6	8 x 5	6 x 7	9 x 8
3 x 5	7 x 8	3 x 9	5 x 6	9 x 9	7 x 5	9 x 4

3 x 6	2 x 8	8 x 6	7 x 7
0 x 7	3 x 3	5 x 9

How quickly did you complete this page? _____

Fact Factory

Factors are the numbers multiplied together in a multiplication problem. The **product** is the answer.

Directions: Write the missing factors or products.

Name _____

X	5
1	5
5	
4	20
6	
3	
2	10
7	
9	45

X	9
8	72
3	
4	
9	
6	54
7	
2	
1	9

X	7
2	14
5	
	42
8	
7	
4	
	21
0	

X	3
7	
4	
6	
1	
3	
2	
5	
8	

X	1
1	
12	
10	
3	3
5	
7	
6	
4	

X	8
9	
8	
4	
5	
6	
7	
3	
2	

X	2
	24
2	
22	
4	
20	
6	
18	
8	

X	4
2	
4	
6	
8	
	4
	12
	20
	28

X	6
7	
6	
5	
4	
3	
2	
1	
0	

X	10
	20
3	
	40
5	
	60
7	
	80
9	

X	11
4	
7	
9	
10	
3	
5	
6	
8	

X	12
1	
2	24
3	
4	48
5	
6	
7	
8	

Multiplication: Tens, Hundreds, Thousands

When multiplying a number by 10, the answer is the number with a 0. It is like counting by tens.

Examples:

$$\begin{array}{r} 10 \\ \times\ 1 \\ \hline 10 \end{array} \qquad \begin{array}{r} 10 \\ \times\ 2 \\ \hline 20 \end{array} \qquad \begin{array}{r} 10 \\ \times\ 3 \\ \hline 30 \end{array} \qquad \begin{array}{r} 10 \\ \times\ 4 \\ \hline 40 \end{array} \qquad \begin{array}{r} 10 \\ \times\ 5 \\ \hline 50 \end{array} \qquad \begin{array}{r} 10 \\ \times\ 6 \\ \hline 60 \end{array}$$

When multiplying a number by 100, the answer is the number with two 0's. When multiplying by 1,000, the answer is the number with three 0's.

Examples:

$$\begin{array}{r} 100 \\ \times\ 1 \\ \hline 100 \end{array} \qquad \begin{array}{r} 100 \\ \times\ 2 \\ \hline 200 \end{array} \qquad \begin{array}{r} 100 \\ \times\ 3 \\ \hline 300 \end{array} \qquad \begin{array}{r} 1,000 \\ \times\ 1 \\ \hline 1,000 \end{array} \qquad \begin{array}{r} 1,000 \\ \times\ 2 \\ \hline 2,000 \end{array} \qquad \begin{array}{r} 1,000 \\ \times\ 3 \\ \hline 3,000 \end{array}$$

$$\begin{array}{r} 4 \\ \times 2 \\ \hline 8 \end{array} \qquad \begin{array}{r} 400 \\ \times\ 2 \\ \hline 800 \end{array} \qquad \begin{array}{r} 8 \\ \times 3 \\ \hline 24 \end{array} \qquad \begin{array}{r} 800 \\ \times\ 3 \\ \hline 2,400 \end{array} \qquad \begin{array}{r} 7 \\ \times 5 \\ \hline 35 \end{array} \qquad \begin{array}{r} 700 \\ \times\ 5 \\ \hline 3,500 \end{array}$$

Directions: Multiply.

$$\begin{array}{r} 10 \\ \times\ 3 \\ \hline \end{array} \qquad \begin{array}{r} 60 \\ \times\ 5 \\ \hline \end{array} \qquad \begin{array}{r} 400 \\ \times\ 5 \\ \hline \end{array} \qquad \begin{array}{r} 700 \\ \times\ 8 \\ \hline \end{array} \qquad \begin{array}{r} 50 \\ \times\ 7 \\ \hline \end{array}$$

$$\begin{array}{r} 80 \\ \times\ 9 \\ \hline \end{array} \qquad \begin{array}{r} 4,000 \\ \times\ 2 \\ \hline \end{array} \qquad \begin{array}{r} 6,000 \\ \times\ 4 \\ \hline \end{array} \qquad \begin{array}{r} 300 \\ \times\ 9 \\ \hline \end{array} \qquad \begin{array}{r} 700 \\ \times\ 6 \\ \hline \end{array}$$

Name _____

Multiplication:
One-Digit Numbers Times Two-Digit Numbers

Follow the steps for multiplying a one-digit number by a two-digit number using regrouping.

Example: **Step 1:** Multiply the ones.
Regroup.

$$\begin{array}{r} \overset{2}{5}4 \\ \times7 \\ \hline 8 \end{array}$$

Step 2: Multiply the tens.
Add two tens.

$$\begin{array}{r} \overset{2}{5}4 \\ \times7 \\ \hline 378 \end{array}$$

Directions: Multiply.

$$\begin{array}{r} 27 \\ \times3 \\ \hline \end{array} \qquad \begin{array}{r} 63 \\ \times4 \\ \hline \end{array} \qquad \begin{array}{r} 52 \\ \times5 \\ \hline \end{array} \qquad \begin{array}{r} 91 \\ \times9 \\ \hline \end{array} \qquad \begin{array}{r} 45 \\ \times7 \\ \hline \end{array} \qquad \begin{array}{r} 75 \\ \times2 \\ \hline \end{array}$$

$$\begin{array}{r} 64 \\ \times5 \\ \hline \end{array} \qquad \begin{array}{r} 76 \\ \times3 \\ \hline \end{array} \qquad \begin{array}{r} 93 \\ \times6 \\ \hline \end{array} \qquad \begin{array}{r} 87 \\ \times4 \\ \hline \end{array} \qquad \begin{array}{r} 66 \\ \times7 \\ \hline \end{array} \qquad \begin{array}{r} 38 \\ \times2 \\ \hline \end{array}$$

$$\begin{array}{r} 47 \\ \times8 \\ \hline \end{array} \qquad \begin{array}{r} 64 \\ \times9 \\ \hline \end{array} \qquad \begin{array}{r} 51 \\ \times8 \\ \hline \end{array} \qquad \begin{array}{r} 99 \\ \times3 \\ \hline \end{array}$$

$$\begin{array}{r} 13 \\ \times7 \\ \hline \end{array} \qquad \begin{array}{r} 32 \\ \times4 \\ \hline \end{array} \qquad \begin{array}{r} 25 \\ \times8 \\ \hline \end{array} \qquad \begin{array}{r} 15 \\ \times7 \\ \hline \end{array}$$

The chickens on the Smith farm produce 48 dozen eggs each day. How many dozen eggs do they produce in 7 days?

_____

Name _____

Multiplication:
Two-Digit Numbers Times Two-Digit Numbers

Follow the steps for multiplying a two-digit number by a two-digit number using regrouping.

Example:

Step 1: Multiply the ones. Regroup.

```
          2
  63      63
x 68    x 68
        ────
         504
```

Step 2: Multiply the tens. Regroup. Add.

```
   1
  63      63
x 68    x 68
────    ────
3,780    504
       +3,780
       ──────
        4,284
```

Directions: Multiply.

```
  12        27        65        19        99        35
x 55      x 15      x 27      x 39      x 13      x 14
────      ────      ────      ────      ────      ────
```

```
  43        38        53        47        57        48
x 26      x 17      x 86      x 72      x 62      x 33
────      ────      ────      ────      ────      ────
```

```
  27        93        64        53
x 54      x 45      x 16      x 23
────      ────      ────      ────
```

The Jones farm has 24 cows that each produce 52 quarts of milk a day. How many quarts are produced each day altogether? _____

Name _____

Multiplication:
Two-Digit Numbers Times Three-Digit Numbers

Follow the steps for multiplying a two-digit number by a three-digit number using regrouping.

Example: **Step 1:** Multiply the ones. **Step 2:** Multiply the tens.
Regroup. Regroup. Add.

$$
\begin{array}{r} 287 \\ \times\ 43 \\ \hline \end{array}
\qquad
\begin{array}{r} {}^{2\,2} \\ 287 \\ \times\ \ 43 \\ \hline 861 \end{array}
\qquad
\begin{array}{r} 287 \\ \times\ 43 \\ \hline 11,480 \end{array}
\qquad
\begin{array}{r} 287 \\ \times\ 43 \\ \hline 861 \\ +11,480 \\ \hline 12,341 \end{array}
$$

Directions: Multiply.

$$
\begin{array}{r} 261 \\ \times\ 36 \\ \hline \end{array}
\qquad
\begin{array}{r} 434 \\ \times\ 48 \\ \hline \end{array}
\qquad
\begin{array}{r} 357 \\ \times\ 75 \\ \hline \end{array}
$$

$$
\begin{array}{r} 231 \\ \times\ 46 \\ \hline \end{array}
\qquad
\begin{array}{r} 754 \\ \times\ 65 \\ \hline \end{array}
\qquad
\begin{array}{r} 614 \\ \times\ 59 \\ \hline \end{array}
$$

$$
\begin{array}{r} 549 \\ \times\ 89 \\ \hline \end{array}
\quad
\begin{array}{r} 372 \\ \times\ 94 \\ \hline \end{array}
\quad
\begin{array}{r} 458 \\ \times\ 85 \\ \hline \end{array}
\quad
\begin{array}{r} 368 \\ \times\ 98 \\ \hline \end{array}
$$

At the Douglas berry farm, workers pick 378 baskets
of peaches each day. Each basket holds 65 peaches.
How many peaches are picked each day? _____

Name _____

Multiplication: Two-Digit Numbers Times Two- and Three-Digit Numbers

Directions: Multiply.

25 x72	70 x66	844 x 24	124 x 15
45 x41	76 x78	74 x69	261 x 88
48 x36	263 x 57	37 x64	52 x43
321 x 78	544 x 58	797 x 24	998 x 37
249 x 33	24 x19	48 x20	817 x 59

Name _____

Multiplication:
Three-Digit Numbers Times Three-Digit Numbers

Directions: Multiply. Regroup when needed.

Example:
```
    563
  x 248
  ───────
  4,504
 22,520
+112,600
─────────
139,624
```

Hint: When multiplying by the tens, start writing the number in the tens place. When multiplying by the hundreds, start in the hundreds place.

```
  842        932        759        531
x 167      x 272      x 468      x 556
```

```
  383        523        229        738
x 476      x 349      x 189      x 513
```

James grows pumpkins on his farm. He has 362 rows of pumpkins. There are 593 pumpkins in each row. How many pumpkins does James grow?

_____

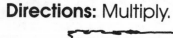
Name _____

Multiplication Drill

Directions: Multiply.

134 x 22	48 x 66	876 x 13	432 x 64

68 x 11	5,478 x 8	248 x 61	6,897 x 6

82 x 4	6,798 x 5	79 x 86	694 x 38

Directions: Color the picture by matching each number with its paintbrush.

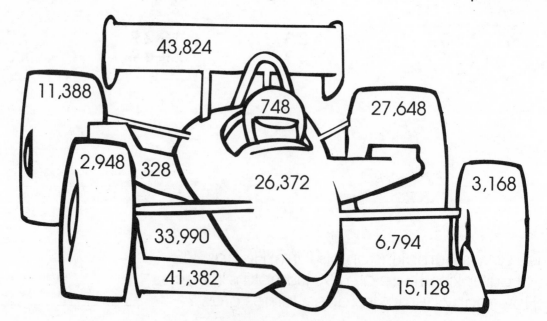

Name _____

Division

Division is a way to find out how many times one number is contained in another number. For example, $28 \div 7 = 4$ means that there are 4 groups of 7 in 28.

Division problems can be written two ways: $36 \div 6 = 6$ or $6\overline{)36}$

These are the parts of a division problem: dividend $\longrightarrow 36 \div 6 = 6 \longleftarrow$ quotient
divisor $\nearrow$

$$\text{divisor} \longrightarrow 6\overline{)36} \begin{matrix} 6 \longleftarrow \text{quotient} \\ \longleftarrow \text{dividend} \end{matrix}$$

Directions: Divide.

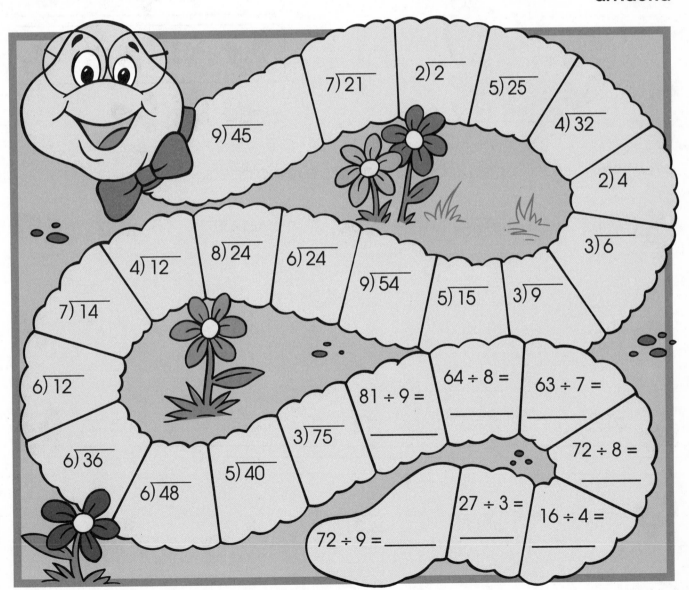

$9\overline{)45}$ $7\overline{)21}$ $2\overline{)2}$ $5\overline{)25}$ $4\overline{)32}$ $2\overline{)4}$

$4\overline{)12}$ $8\overline{)24}$ $6\overline{)24}$ $9\overline{)54}$ $5\overline{)15}$ $3\overline{)9}$ $3\overline{)6}$

$7\overline{)14}$

$6\overline{)12}$

$6\overline{)36}$ $6\overline{)48}$ $5\overline{)40}$ $3\overline{)75}$ $81 \div 9 =$ ___ $64 \div 8 =$ ___ $63 \div 7 =$ ___

$72 \div 8 =$ ___

$72 \div 9 =$ ___ $27 \div 3 =$ ___ $16 \div 4 =$ ___

Division With Remainders

Sometimes groups of objects or numbers cannot be divided into equal groups. The **remainder** is the number left over in the quotient of a division problem. The remainder must be smaller than the divisor.

Example:

Divide 18 butterflies into groups of 5.
You have 3 equal groups,
with 3 butterflies left over.

$$18 \div 5 = 3 \text{ R}3$$

or

$$
\begin{array}{r}
3 \text{ R}3 \\
5\overline{)18} \\
-15 \\
\hline
3
\end{array}
$$

Directions: Divide. Some problems may have remainders.

 $9\overline{)84}$ $7\overline{)65}$ $8\overline{)25}$ $5\overline{)35}$ $5\overline{)34}$

 $4\overline{)25}$ $6\overline{)56}$ $4\overline{)7}$ $4\overline{)16}$ $8\overline{)37}$

 $7\overline{)27}$ $2\overline{)5}$ $2\overline{)4}$ $8\overline{)73}$ $4\overline{)9}$

 $9\overline{)46}$ $5\overline{)17}$ $2\overline{)3}$ $4\overline{)13}$ $5\overline{)25}$

Name _____

Division: Larger Numbers

Follow the steps for dividing larger numbers.

Example: **Step 1:** Divide the tens first.   **Step 2:** Divide the ones next.

$$3\overline{)66}$$

$$\begin{array}{r} 2 \\ 3\overline{)66} \\ -6 \\ \hline 06 \end{array}$$

$$\begin{array}{r} 22 \\ 3\overline{)66} \\ -6 \\ \hline 06 \\ -6 \\ \hline 0 \end{array}$$

Directions: Divide.

$$4\overline{)84} \qquad 2\overline{)90} \qquad 2\overline{)64} \qquad 2\overline{)50} \qquad 3\overline{)45}$$

$$3\overline{)75} \qquad 3\overline{)36} \qquad 4\overline{)92} \qquad 2\overline{)76} \qquad 5\overline{)65}$$

In some larger numbers, the divisor goes into the first two digits of the dividend.

Example:
$$9\overline{)729}$$

$$\begin{array}{r} 8 \\ 9\overline{)729} \\ -72 \\ \hline 09 \end{array}$$

$$\begin{array}{r} 81 \\ 9\overline{)729} \\ -72 \\ \hline 09 \\ -9 \\ \hline 0 \end{array}$$

Directions: Divide.

$$7\overline{)630} \qquad 5\overline{)125} \qquad 6\overline{)486} \qquad 5\overline{)100} \qquad 6\overline{)540}$$

Name _____

Division

Directions: Divide.

7)860   6)611   8)279   4)338   6)979

3)792   5)463   6)940   4)647   3)814

7)758   5)356   4)276   8)328   9)306

4)579   8)932   3)102   2)821   6)489

The music store has 491 CD's. The store sells 8 CD's a day. How many days will it take to sell all of the CD's?

_____

Division: Checking the Answers

To check a division problem, multiply the quotient by the divisor. Add the remainder. The answer will be the dividend.

Example:

quotient
58 R1
divisor → 3) 175
          -15
dividend   25
         - 24
remainder → 1

58 ← quotient
x 3 ← divisor
174
+ 1 ← remainder
175 ← dividend

Directions: Divide each problem, then draw a line from the division problem to the correct checking problem.

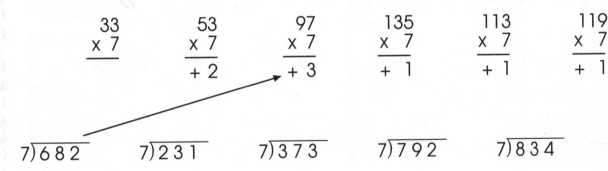

33	53	97	135	113	119
x 7	x 7	x 7	x 7	x 7	x 7
	+ 2	+ 3	+ 1	+ 1	+ 1

7)682   7)231   7)373   7)792   7)834   7)946

The toy factory puts 7 robot dogs in each box. The factory has 256 robot dogs. How many boxes will they need?

_____

Name _____

Division: Checking the Answers

Directions: Divide, then check your answers.

Example:

```
       1 8 2 R1
   4) 7 2 9
     - 4
       3 2
     - 3 2
         9
       - 8
         1
```

Check:

```
     1 8 2
   x     4
     7 2 8
   +     1
     7 2 9
```

Divide	Check	Divide	Check
35) 4 6 8	[ ] x 3 5	77) 8 1 9	[ ] x 7 7
29) 5 6 8	[ ] x 2 9	53) 2,7 9 5	[ ] x 5 3

The bookstore puts 53 books on a shelf. How many shelves will it need for 1,590 books? _____

Division: Two-Digit Divisors

Directions: Divide. Then check each answer on another sheet of paper by multiplying it by the divisor and adding the remainder.

Example:

```
      2
12)2 5 6
  -2 4
      1
```

```
     2 1 R4
12)2 5 6
  -2 4
     1 6
    -1 2
        4
```

Check:

```
      2 1
    x 1 2
    4 2
  2 1 0
  2 5 2
  +   4
  2 5 6
```

27)8 8 0   81)9 1 3   65)7 9 0   42)6 7 4   67)8 2 3

72)9 7 7   54)7 4 3   45)8 6 3   24)4 3 2   18)3 7 2

28)1 7 5   49)5 3 8   77)9 3 6   37)6 0 3   63)8 3 5

The Allen farm has 882 chickens. The chickens are kept in 21 coops. How many chickens are there in each coop? _____

Name _____

Averaging

An **average** is found by adding two or more quantities and dividing by the number of quantities.

⚾ **Example:**
Step 1: Find the sum of the numbers.
24 + 36 + 30 = 90
Step 2: Divide by the number of quantities.
90 ÷ 3 = 30
The average is 30.

Directions: Find the average of each group of numbers. Draw a line from each problem to the correct average.

12 + 14 + 29 + 1 =	410
4 + 10 + 25 =	83
33 + 17 + 14 + 20 + 16 =	40
782 + 276 + 172 =	15
81 + 82 + 91 + 78 =	13
21 + 34 + 44 =	33
14 + 24 + 10 + 31 + 5 + 6 =	14
278 + 246 =	20
48 + 32 + 18 + 62 =	262

A baseball player had 3 hits in game one, 2 hits in game two and 4 hits in game three. How many hits did she average over the three games? _____

Averaging

Directions: Find the averages.

Ted went bowling. He had scores of 112, 124 and 100. What was his average?

_____

Sue ran 3 races. Her times were 9 seconds, 10 seconds and 8 seconds. What was her average?

_____

The baseball team played 6 games. They had 12 hits, 6 hits, 18 hits, 36 hits, 11 hits and 7 hits. What is the average number of hits in a game?

_____

In 3 games of football, Chris gained 156, 268 and 176 yards running. How many yards did he average in a game?

_____

Jane scored 18, 15, 26 and 21 points in 4 basketball games. How many points did she average?

_____

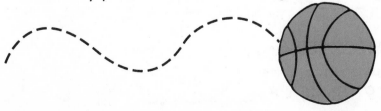

Review

Directions: Divide.

$$3\overline{)268} \qquad 15\overline{)165} \qquad 27\overline{)489} \qquad 48\overline{)695}$$

$$79\overline{)937} \qquad 49\overline{)683} \qquad 91\overline{)848} \qquad 73\overline{)592} \qquad 59\overline{)473}$$

$$23\overline{)1,268} \qquad 67\overline{)2,543} \qquad 81\overline{)3,608} \qquad 37\overline{)8,432} \qquad 97\overline{)4,528}$$

Directions: Find the averages.

22, 38 _____   105, 263, 331 _____

48, 100, 62 _____   248, 325, 250, 69 _____

17, 18, 36, 28, 6 _____   87, 91, 55, 48, 119 _____

Name _____

Fractions

A **fraction** is a number that names part of a whole, such as ½ or ⅓.

A fraction is made up of two numbers—the **numerator** (top number) and the **denominator** (bottom number). The larger the denominator, the smaller each of the equal parts: 1/16 is smaller than ½.

Directions: Study the fractions below.

1 whole.

2 equal parts or halves

One-half of the   1
circle is shaded. —
                   2

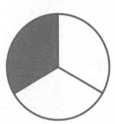

3 equal parts or thirds

One-third of the   1
circle is shaded.   —
                    3

4 equal parts or fourths

One-fourth of the   1
circle is shaded.   —
                    4

5 equal parts or fifths

One-fifth of the   1
circle is shaded.   —
                    5

6 equal parts or sixths

One-sixth of the   1
circle is shaded.   —
                    6

8 equal parts or eighths

One-eighth of the   1
circle is shaded.   —
                    8

10 equal parts or tenths

One-tenth of the   1
circle is shaded.   —
                    10

12 equal parts or twelfths

One-twelfth of the 1
circle is shaded.   —
                    12

Fractions

Directions: Name the fraction that is shaded.

Examples:

3 of 4 equal parts are shaded.

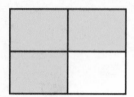

12 of 16 equal parts are shaded.

$$\frac{3}{4}$$

$$\frac{12}{16}$$

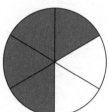

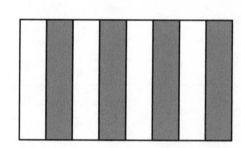

_____

_____

_____

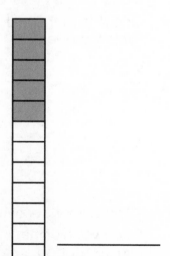

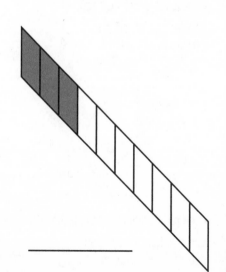

_____

_____

_____

Name _____

Fraction Pieces

Directions: Cut apart the fraction pieces below. Use them to help you work with fractions. Store the fraction sets in separate plastic bags.

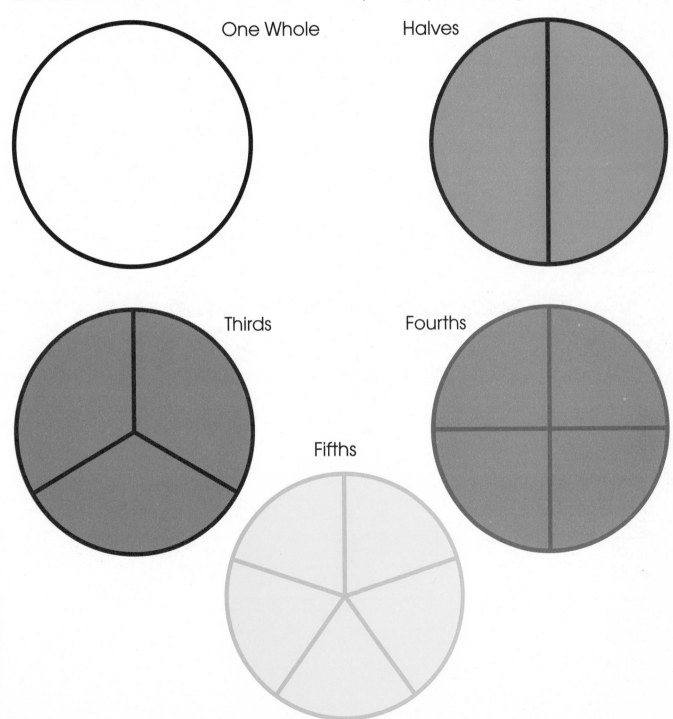

One Whole

Halves

Thirds

Fourths

Fifths

Page is blank for cutting exercise on previous page.

Fraction Pieces

Directions: Cut apart the fraction pieces below. Use them to help you work with fractions. Store the fraction sets in separate plastic bags.

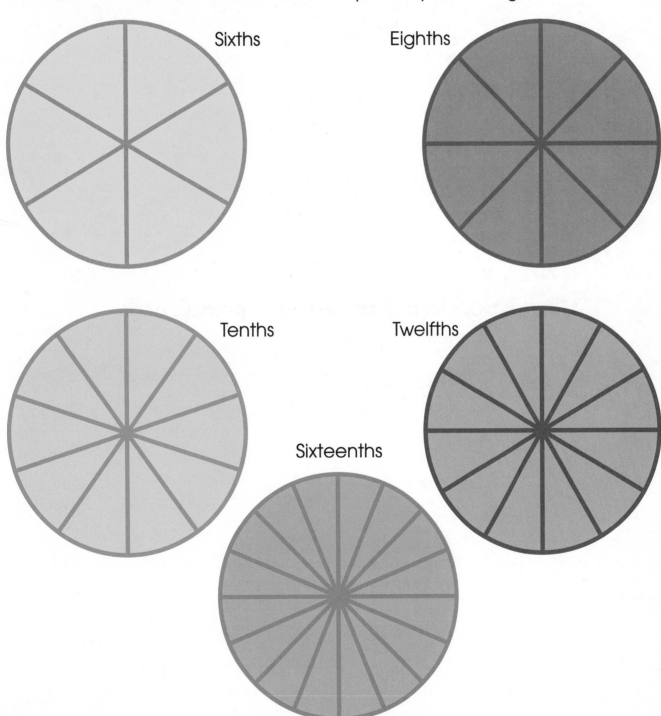

Sixths

Eighths

Tenths

Twelfths

Sixteenths

Page is blank for cutting exercise on previous page.

Name _____

Fractions: Addition

When adding fractions with the same denominator, the denominator stays the same. Add only the numerators.

Example: **numerator** **denominator** $\dfrac{1}{8}$ + $\dfrac{2}{8}$ = $\dfrac{3}{8}$

Directions: Add the fractions on the flowers. Begin in the center of each flower and add each petal. The first one is done for you.

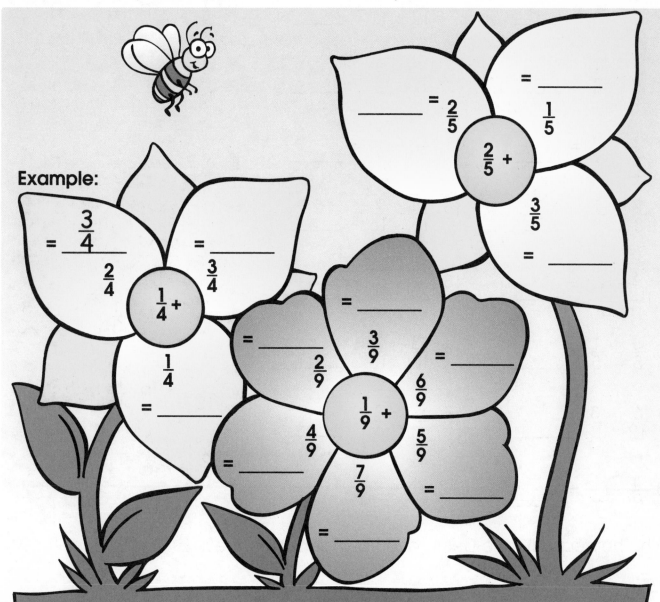

Example:

Name _____

Fractions: Subtraction

When subtracting fractions with the same denominator, the denominator stays the same. Subtract only the numerators.

Directions: Solve the problems, working from left to right. As you find each answer, copy the letter from the key into the numbered blanks. The answer is the name of a famous American. The first one is done for you.

1. $\frac{3}{8} - \frac{2}{8} = \underline{\frac{1}{8}}$

2. $\frac{2}{4} - \frac{1}{4} = \underline{\hphantom{xx}}$

3. $\frac{5}{9} - \frac{3}{9} = \underline{\hphantom{xx}}$

4. $\frac{2}{3} - \frac{1}{3} = \underline{\hphantom{xx}}$

5. $\frac{8}{12} - \frac{7}{12} = \underline{\hphantom{xx}}$

6. $\frac{4}{5} - \frac{1}{5} = \underline{\hphantom{xx}}$

7. $\frac{6}{12} - \frac{3}{12} = \underline{\hphantom{xx}}$

8. $\frac{4}{9} - \frac{1}{9} = \underline{\hphantom{xx}}$

9. $\frac{11}{12} - \frac{7}{12} = \underline{\hphantom{xx}}$

10. $\frac{7}{8} - \frac{3}{8} = \underline{\hphantom{xx}}$

11. $\frac{4}{7} - \frac{2}{7} = \underline{\hphantom{xx}}$

12. $\frac{14}{16} - \frac{7}{16} = \underline{\hphantom{xx}}$

13. $\frac{18}{20} - \frac{13}{20} = \underline{\hphantom{xx}}$

14. $\frac{13}{15} - \frac{2}{15} = \underline{\hphantom{xx}}$

15. $\frac{5}{6} - \frac{3}{6} = \underline{\hphantom{xx}}$

T $\frac{1}{8}$	P $\frac{5}{24}$	H $\frac{1}{4}$
F $\frac{4}{12}$	E $\frac{2}{7}$	J $\frac{3}{12}$
E $\frac{3}{9}$	O $\frac{2}{9}$	F $\frac{4}{8}$
R $\frac{7}{16}$	O $\frac{2}{8}$	Y $\frac{8}{20}$
Q $\frac{1}{32}$	M $\frac{1}{3}$	S $\frac{5}{20}$
A $\frac{1}{12}$	R $\frac{12}{15}$	S $\frac{3}{5}$
N $\frac{2}{6}$	O $\frac{11}{15}$	

Who helped write the Declaration of Independence?

$\underset{1}{\text{T}}$ $\underline{\hphantom{xx}}_{2}$ $\underline{\hphantom{xx}}_{3}$ $\underline{\hphantom{xx}}_{4}$ $\underline{\hphantom{xx}}_{5}$ $\underline{\hphantom{xx}}_{6}$ $\underline{\hphantom{xx}}_{7}$ $\underline{\hphantom{xx}}_{8}$ $\underline{\hphantom{xx}}_{9}$ $\underline{\hphantom{xx}}_{10}$ $\underline{\hphantom{xx}}_{11}$ $\underline{\hphantom{xx}}_{12}$ $\underline{\hphantom{xx}}_{13}$ $\underline{\hphantom{xx}}_{14}$ $\underline{\hphantom{xx}}_{15}$

Name _____

Equivalent Fractions

Equivalent fractions are two different fractions that represent the same number. **Example:**

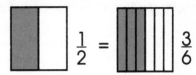

$\frac{1}{2} = \frac{3}{6}$

Directions: Complete these equivalent fractions. Use your fraction pieces from pages 245 and 247.

$\frac{1}{3} = \frac{}{6}$ $\qquad$ $\frac{1}{2} = \frac{}{4}$ $\qquad$ $\frac{3}{4} = \frac{}{8}$ $\qquad$ $\frac{1}{3} = \frac{}{9}$

Directions: Circle the figures that show a fraction equivalent to figure a. Write the fraction for the shaded area under each figure.

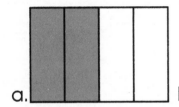   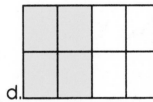

a. _____ b. _____ c. _____ d. _____

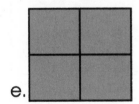 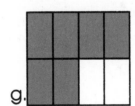 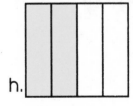

e. _____ f. _____ g. _____ h. _____

To find an equivalent fraction, multiply both parts of the fraction by the same number.

Example: $\frac{2}{3} \times \frac{3}{3} = \frac{6}{9}$

Directions: Find an equivalent fraction.

$\frac{1}{4} = \frac{}{8}$ $\qquad$ $\frac{3}{4} = \frac{}{16}$ $\qquad$ $\frac{4}{5} = \frac{8}{}$ $\qquad$ $\frac{3}{8} = \frac{}{24}$

Name _____

Reducing Fractions

Reducing a fraction means to find the greatest common factor and divide.

Example: 5   factors of 5: 1, 5
15 factors of 15: 1, 3, 5, 15

$5 \div 5 = 1$
$15 \div 5 = 3$

5 is the greatest common factor. Divide both the numerator and denominator by 5.

Directions: Reduce each fraction. Circle the correct answer.

$\frac{2}{4} = \frac{1}{2}, \frac{1}{6}, \frac{1}{8}$ $\frac{3}{9} = \frac{1}{6}, \frac{1}{3}, \frac{3}{6}$ $\frac{5}{10} = \frac{1}{5}, \frac{1}{2}, \frac{5}{6}$ $\frac{4}{12} = \frac{1}{4}, \frac{1}{3}, \frac{2}{3}$ $\frac{10}{15} = \frac{2}{3}, \frac{2}{5}, \frac{2}{7}$

$\frac{12}{14} = \frac{1}{8}, \frac{6}{7}, \frac{3}{5}$ $\frac{3}{24} = \frac{2}{12}, \frac{3}{6}, \frac{1}{8}$ $\frac{1}{11} = \frac{1}{11}, \frac{2}{5}, \frac{3}{4}$ $\frac{11}{22} = \frac{1}{12}, \frac{1}{2}, \frac{2}{5}$

Directions: Find the way home. Color the boxes with fractions equivalent to $\frac{1}{8}$ and $\frac{1}{3}$.

Fractions: Mixed Numbers

A **mixed number** is a number written as a whole number and a fraction, such as $6\frac{5}{8}$.

To change a fraction into a mixed number, divide the denominator (bottom number) into the numerator (top number). Write the remainder over the denominator.

Example:

$$\frac{14}{6} = 2\frac{2}{6} \qquad 6)\overline{14} \quad \begin{array}{r} 2 \ \text{R2} \\ \underline{12} \\ 2 \end{array}$$

To change a mixed number into a fraction, multiply the denominator by the whole number, add the numerator and write it on top of the denominator.

Example:

$$3\frac{1}{7} = \frac{22}{7} \qquad (7 \times 3) + 1 = \frac{22}{7}$$

Directions: Write each fraction as a mixed number. Write each mixed number as a fraction.

$\frac{21}{6} = $ _____ $\frac{24}{5} = $ _____ $\frac{10}{3} = $ _____ $\frac{21}{4} = $ _____

$\frac{11}{6} = $ _____ $\frac{13}{4} = $ _____ $\frac{12}{5} = $ _____ $\frac{10}{9} = $ _____

$4\frac{3}{8} = \dfrac{\square}{8}$ $2\frac{1}{3} = \dfrac{\square}{3}$ $4\frac{3}{5} = \dfrac{\square}{5}$ $3\frac{4}{6} = \dfrac{\square}{6}$

$7\frac{1}{4} = \dfrac{\square}{4}$ $2\frac{3}{5} = \dfrac{\square}{5}$ $7\frac{1}{2} = \dfrac{\square}{2}$ $6\frac{5}{7} = \dfrac{\square}{7}$

$\frac{11}{8} = $ _____ $\frac{21}{4} = $ _____ $\frac{33}{5} = $ _____ $\frac{13}{6} = $ _____

$\frac{23}{7} = $ _____ $8\frac{1}{3} = $ _____ $9\frac{3}{7} = $ _____ $\frac{32}{24} = $ _____

Name _____

Fractions: Adding Mixed Numbers

When adding mixed numbers, add the fractions first, then the whole numbers.

Examples:

$$9\frac{1}{3}$$
$$+3\frac{1}{3}$$
$$\overline{12\frac{2}{3}}$$

$$2\frac{3}{6}$$
$$+1\frac{1}{6}$$
$$\overline{3\frac{4}{6}}$$

Directions: Add the number in the center to the number in each surrounding section.

Name _____

Fractions: Subtracting Mixed Numbers

When subtracting mixed numbers, subtract the fractions first, then the whole numbers.

Directions: Subtract the mixed numbers. The first one is done for you.

$$7\frac{3}{8} - 4\frac{2}{8} = 3\frac{1}{8}$$

$$4\frac{5}{6} - 3\frac{1}{6}$$

$$4\frac{1}{2} - 3$$

$$7\frac{5}{8} - 6\frac{3}{8}$$

$$6\frac{6}{8} - 1\frac{1}{8}$$

$$5\frac{3}{4} - 1\frac{1}{4}$$

$$5\frac{2}{3} - 3\frac{1}{3}$$

$$4\frac{8}{10} - 3\frac{3}{10}$$

$$9\frac{8}{9} - 4\frac{3}{9}$$

$$7\frac{2}{3} - 6\frac{1}{3}$$

$$7\frac{2}{3} - 5$$

$$9\frac{8}{10} - 6\frac{3}{10}$$

$$4\frac{7}{9} - 2$$

$$6\frac{7}{8} - 5\frac{3}{8}$$

$$6\frac{3}{4} - 3\frac{1}{4}$$

$$5\frac{6}{7} - 3\frac{1}{7}$$

$$7\frac{6}{7} - 2\frac{4}{7}$$

Sally needs $1\frac{3}{8}$ yards of cloth to make a dress. She has $4\frac{5}{8}$ yards. How much cloth will be left over? _____

Name _____

Review

Directions: Add or subtract the fractions and mixed numbers. Reduce, if possible.

$$4\frac{7}{8}$$
$$-2\frac{5}{8}$$

$$8\frac{3}{9}$$
$$+2\frac{5}{9}$$

$$3\frac{1}{8}$$
$$+1\frac{3}{8}$$

$$4\frac{5}{6}$$
$$-3\frac{1}{6}$$

$$7\frac{5}{11}$$
$$+3\frac{3}{11}$$

$\frac{4}{12} + \frac{3}{12} =$ _____ $\frac{3}{5} + \frac{1}{5} =$ _____

$\frac{3}{8} - \frac{1}{8} =$ _____ $\frac{3}{9} + \frac{1}{9} =$ _____

$\frac{3}{4} - \frac{2}{4} =$ _____

Directions:
Reduce the fractions.

$\frac{4}{6} =$ _____ $\frac{7}{21} =$ _____

$\frac{9}{12} =$ _____ $\frac{2}{4} =$ _____

$\frac{6}{24} =$ _____ $\frac{8}{32} =$ _____

Directions: Change the mixed numbers to fractions and the fractions to mixed numbers.

$3\frac{1}{3} = \frac{\square}{3}$ $\frac{14}{4} =$ ____ $\frac{26}{6} =$ ____ $3\frac{7}{12} = \frac{\square}{12}$ $\frac{22}{7} =$ ____

Fractions to Decimals

When a figure is divided into 10 equal parts, the parts are called tenths. Tenths can be written two ways—as a fraction or a decimal. A **decimal** is a number with one or more places to the right of a decimal point, such as 6.5 or 2.25. A **decimal point** is the dot between the ones place and the tenths place.

Examples:

ones	tenths
0 .	3

$\frac{3}{10}$ or 0.3 of the square is shaded.

Directions: Write the decimal and fraction for the shaded parts of the following figures. The first one is done for you.

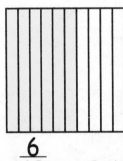

$\frac{6}{10}$ 0.6

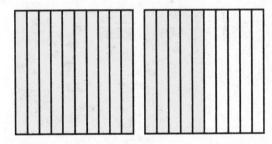

___   ___   ___   ___   ___   ___   ___   ___

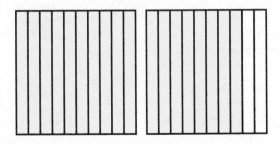
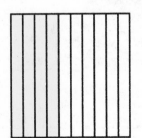
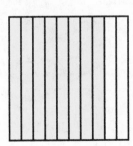

___   ___   ___   ___   ___   ___   ___   ___

Name _____

Decimals

Directions: Add or subtract. Remember to include the decimal point in your answers.

Example:

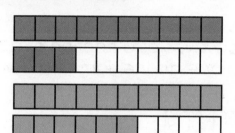

$1\frac{3}{10} = 1.3$

$1\frac{6}{10} = 1.6$

$$\begin{array}{r} 1.3 \\ + 1.6 \\ \hline 2.9 \end{array}$$

$$\begin{array}{r} 8.1 \\ + 1.7 \\ \hline \end{array}$$
$$\begin{array}{r} 4.1 \\ + 6.2 \\ \hline \end{array}$$
$$\begin{array}{r} 0.5 \\ + 1.6 \\ \hline \end{array}$$
$$\begin{array}{r} 7.6 \\ - 6.5 \\ \hline \end{array}$$
$$\begin{array}{r} 7.2 \\ - 2.6 \\ \hline \end{array}$$
$$\begin{array}{r} 1.2 \\ + 5.0 \\ \hline \end{array}$$
$$\begin{array}{r} 8.7 \\ - 3.9 \\ \hline \end{array}$$
$$\begin{array}{r} 6.8 \\ - 3.7 \\ \hline \end{array}$$

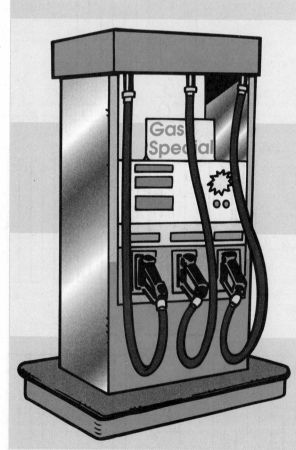

$$\begin{array}{r} 7.8 \\ - 6.8 \\ \hline \end{array}$$
$$\begin{array}{r} 16.5 \\ - 7.3 \\ \hline \end{array}$$
$$\begin{array}{r} 6.4 \\ + 5.3 \\ \hline \end{array}$$
$$\begin{array}{r} 10.0 \\ + 3.5 \\ \hline \end{array}$$

$$\begin{array}{r} 0.42 \\ + 0.35 \\ \hline \end{array}$$
$$\begin{array}{r} 0.98 \\ - 0.87 \\ \hline \end{array}$$
$$\begin{array}{r} 0.78 \\ - 0.13 \\ \hline \end{array}$$
$$\begin{array}{r} 0.83 \\ + 0.12 \\ \hline \end{array}$$

$$\begin{array}{r} 0.95 \\ - 0.14 \\ \hline \end{array}$$
$$\begin{array}{r} 3.23 \\ + 2.48 \\ \hline \end{array}$$
$$\begin{array}{r} 4.68 \\ - 2.65 \\ \hline \end{array}$$
$$\begin{array}{r} 5.86 \\ - 2.73 \\ \hline \end{array}$$

$$\begin{array}{r} 6.98 \\ + 1.40 \\ \hline \end{array}$$
$$\begin{array}{r} 3.27 \\ + 1.82 \\ \hline \end{array}$$
$$\begin{array}{r} 4.65 \\ - 1.32 \\ \hline \end{array}$$
$$\begin{array}{r} 5.97 \\ + 2.77 \\ \hline \end{array}$$

Mr. Martin went on a car trip with his family. Mr. Martin purchased gas 3 times. He bought 6.7 gallons, 7.3 gallons, then 5.8 gallons of gas. How much gas did he purchase in all? _____

Name _____

Decimals: Hundredths

The next smallest decimal unit after a tenth is called a hundredth. One hundredth is one unit of a figure divided into 100 units. Written as a decimal, it is one digit to the right of the tenths place.

Example:

One square divided into hundredths, 34 hundredths are shaded. Write: 0.34.

ones	tenths	hundredths
0 .	3	4

0.34
_____

Directions: Write the decimal for the shaded parts of the following figures.

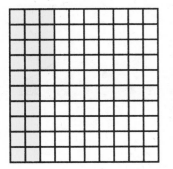
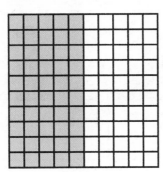
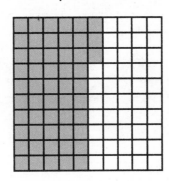
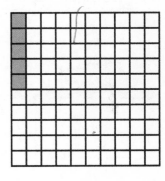

.24   .50   _____   _____

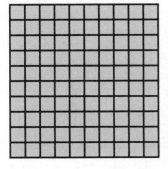
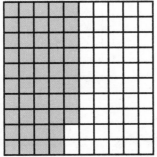
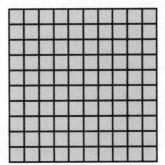
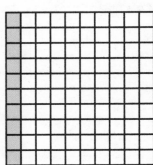

_____   _____

Name _____

Fractions and Decimals

Directions: Compare the fraction to the decimal in each box. Circle the larger number.

Example:

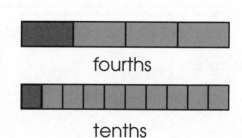

$$\left(\dfrac{1}{4}\right) \quad 0.1$$

fourths

tenths

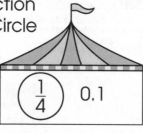
$\dfrac{2}{4} \quad 0.2$

$\dfrac{3}{4} \quad 0.3$

$\dfrac{1}{2} \quad 0.6$

$\dfrac{1}{4} \quad 0.4$

$\dfrac{1}{3} \quad 0.1$

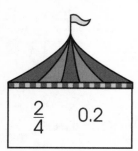
$\dfrac{1}{4} \quad 0.7$

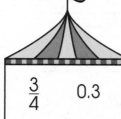
$\dfrac{2}{4} \quad 0.8$

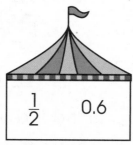
$\dfrac{3}{4} \quad 0.9$

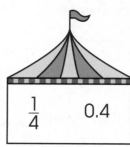
$\dfrac{5}{6} \quad 0.5$

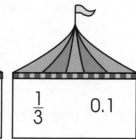
$\dfrac{2}{5} \quad 0.6$

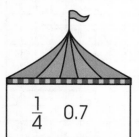
$\dfrac{3}{12} \quad 0.9$

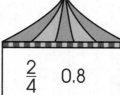
$\dfrac{1}{6} \quad 0.2$

$\dfrac{2}{3} \quad 0.8$

$\dfrac{1}{5} \quad 0.3$

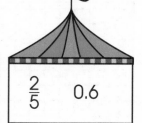
$\dfrac{2}{5} \quad 0.7$

$\dfrac{3}{10} \quad 0.5$

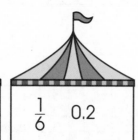
$\dfrac{1}{9} \quad 0.4$

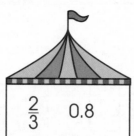
$\dfrac{4}{5} \quad 0.7$

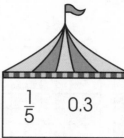
$\dfrac{1}{3} \quad 0.7$

$\dfrac{6}{12} \quad 0.1$

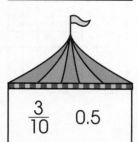

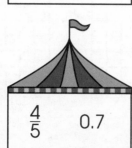

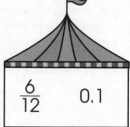

Name _____

Adding and Subtracting Decimals

Directions: Add or subtract the problems.
Then fill in the circle next to the correct answer.

Example:

$$\begin{array}{r} 2.4 \\ + 1.7 \\ \hline \end{array}$$
○ 2.5
○ 3.1
● 4.1

$\begin{array}{r} 2.8 \\ + 3.4 \\ \hline \end{array}$ ○ 5.2 ○ 7.4 ○ 6.2	$\begin{array}{r} 5.7 \\ - 3.8 \\ \hline \end{array}$ ○ 1.9 ○ 2.5 ○ 2.9	$\begin{array}{r} 7.6 \\ + 8.9 \\ \hline \end{array}$ ○ 15.9 ○ 16.5 ○ 17.3
$\begin{array}{r} 16.3 \\ + 9.8 \\ \hline \end{array}$ ○ 25.11 ○ 26.1 ○ 26.01	$\begin{array}{r} 28.6 \\ +43.9 \\ \hline \end{array}$ ○ 73.6 ○ 72.5 ○ 71.9	$\begin{array}{r} 43.9 \\ + 56.5 \\ \hline \end{array}$ ○ 100.4 ○ 107.4 ○ 101.4
$\begin{array}{r} 12.87 \\ - 3.45 \\ \hline \end{array}$ ○ 16.32 ○ 10.31 ○ 9.42	$\begin{array}{r} 47.56 \\ - 33.95 \\ \hline \end{array}$ ○ 13.61 ○ 80.41 ○ 14.61	$\begin{array}{r} 93.6 \\ - 79.8 \\ \hline \end{array}$ ○ 14.8 ○ 15.3 ○ 13.8
$\begin{array}{r} 11.57 \\ +10.64 \\ \hline \end{array}$ ○ 22.21 ○ 1.93 ○ 21.12	$\begin{array}{r} 27.83 \\ -14.94 \\ \hline \end{array}$ ○ 14.09 ○ 12.89 ○ 11.97	$\begin{array}{r} 106.935 \\ - 95.824 \\ \hline \end{array}$ ○ 111.1 ○ 111.11 ○ 11.111

The high-speed train traveled 87.90 miles on day
one, 127.86 miles on day two and 113.41 miles
on day three. How many miles did it travel in all? _____

Measurement: Inches

An **inch** is a unit of length in the standard system equal to $\frac{1}{12}$ of a foot. A ruler is used to measure inches.

This illustration shows a ruler measuring a 4-inch pencil, which can be written as 4" or 4 in.

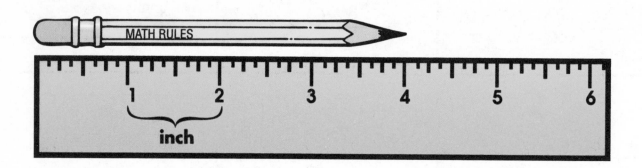

Directions: Use a ruler to measure each object to the nearest inch.

1. The length of your foot _____

2. The width of your hand _____

3. The length of this page _____

4. The width of this page _____

5. The length of a large paper clip _____

6. The length of your toothbrush _____

7. The length of a comb _____

8. The height of a juice glass _____

9. The length of your shoe _____

10. The length of a fork _____

Measurement: Inches

Directions: Use a ruler to measure the width of each foot to the nearest inch.

Name _____

Measurement: Fractions of an Inch

An inch is divided into smaller units, or fractions of an inch.

Example: This stick of gum is 2 ¾ inches long.

Directions: Use a ruler to measure each line to the nearest quarter of an inch. The first one is done for you.

1. $\frac{3}{4}$ inch _____

2. _____ _____

3. _____ _____

4. _____ _____

5. _____ _____

6. _____ _____

7. _____ _____

Name _____

Measurement: Fractions of an Inch

Directions: Use a ruler to measure to the nearest quarter of an inch.

How far did the grasshopper jump?

_____ + _____ + _____ + _____ = _____

What is the total length of the paintbrushes?

_____ + _____ + _____ + _____ + _____ = _____

Name _____

Measurement: Foot, Yard, Mile

Directions: Choose the measure of distance you would use for each object.

1 foot = 12 inches
1 yard = 3 feet
1 mile = 1,760 yards or 5,280 feet

_____ inches _____

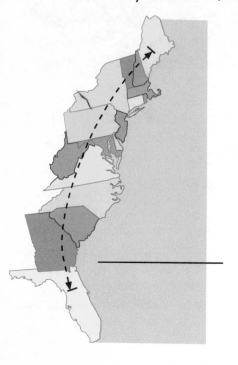

_____

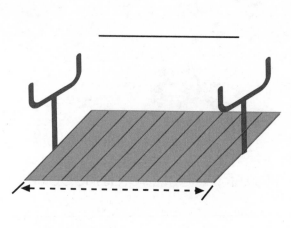

_____

_____

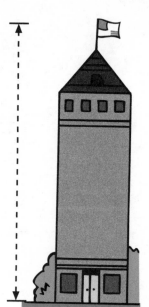

_____

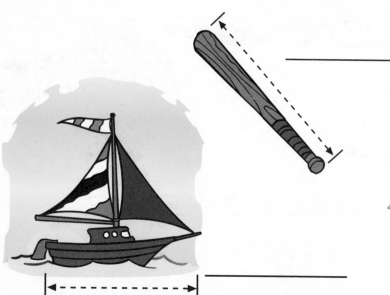

_____

_____

Metric Measurement:
Centimeter, Meter, Kilometer

In the metric system, there are three units of linear measurement: centimeter (cm), meter (m) and kilometer (km).

Centimeters (cm) are used to measure the lengths of small to medium-sized objects. **Meters (m)** measure the lengths of longer objects, such as the width of a swimming pool or height of a tree (100 cm = 1 meter). **Kilometers (km)** measure long distances, such as the distance from Cleveland to Cincinnati or the width of the Atlantic Ocean (1,000 m = 1 km).

Directions: Write whether you would use cm, m or km to measure each object.

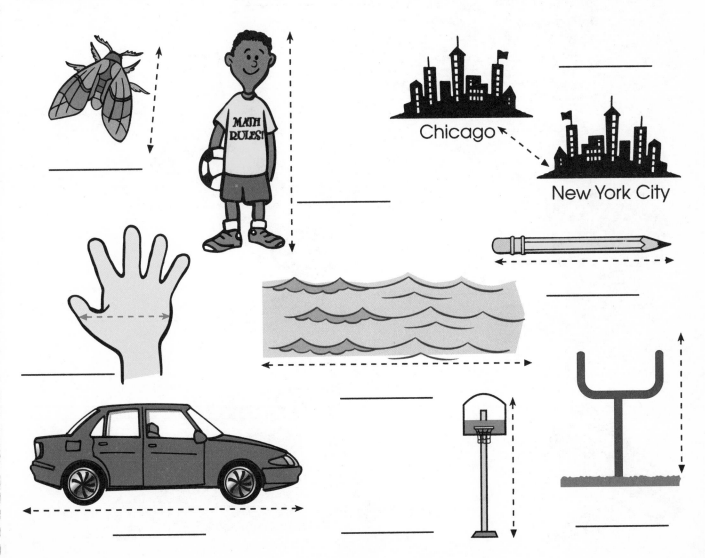

Name _____

Metric Measurement: Centimeter

Directions: Use a centimeter ruler to measure the width of each foot to the nearest centimeter.

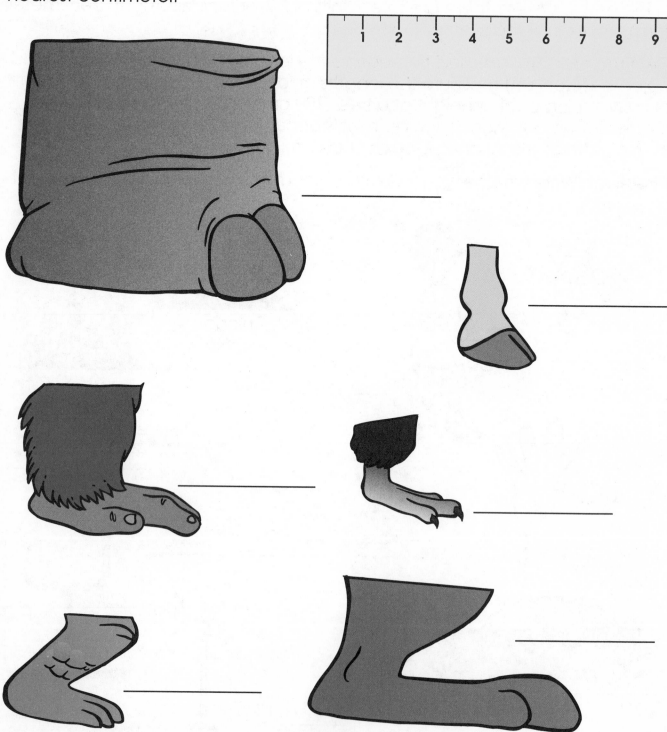

268

Metric Measurement: Meter and Kilometer

A meter is a little longer than a yard—39.37 inches (a yard is 36 inches).
A kilometer is equal to about $\frac{5}{8}$ of a mile.

Directions: Choose the measure of distance you would use for the following.

meter

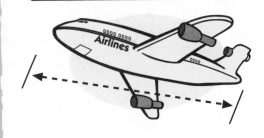

_____

_____

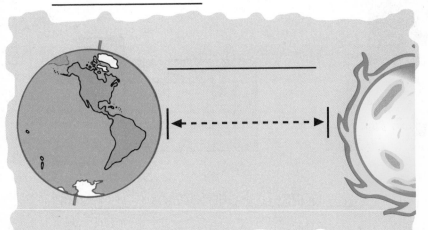

_____

_____

Name _____

Measurement: Perimeter and Area

Perimeter is the distance around a figure. It is found by adding the lengths of the sides. **Area** is the number of square units needed to cover a region. The area is found by adding the number of square units. A unit can be any unit of measure. Most often, inches, feet or yards are used.

Directions: Find the perimeter and area for each figure. The first one is done for you.

☐ = 1 square unit

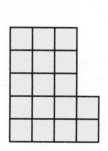

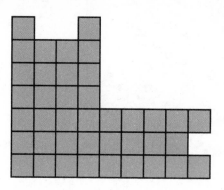

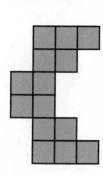

Perimeter = __18__ units

Area = __17__ sq. units

Perimeter = _____ units

Area = _____ sq. units

Perimeter = _____ units

Area = _____ sq. units

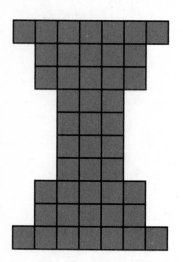

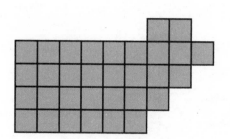

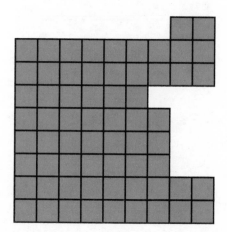

Perimeter = _____ units

Area = _____ sq. units

Perimeter = _____ units

Area = _____ sq. units

Perimeter = _____ units

Area = _____ sq. units

Name _____

Measurement: Perimeter

Perimeter is calculated by adding the lengths of the sides of a figure.

Examples:

6 ft.

2 ft.   2 ft.

2 ft.   2 ft.

6 ft.

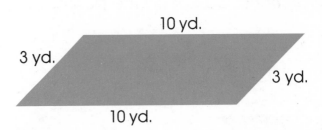

10 yd.

3 yd.   3 yd.

10 yd.

$2 + 2 + 2 + 2 + 6 + 6 = 20$
The perimeter of this hexagon is 20 ft.

$10 + 10 + 3 + 3 = 26$
The perimeter of this parallelogram is 26 yd.

Directions: Find the perimeter of the following figures.

_____
Perimeter

_____
Perimeter

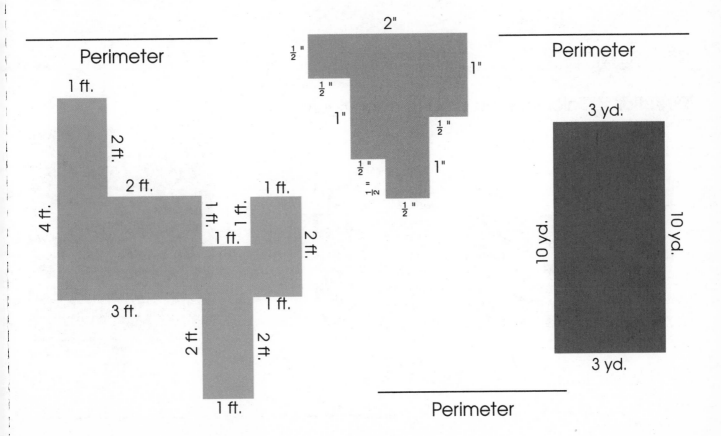

2"

$\frac{1}{2}$"

$\frac{1}{2}$"   1"

1"

$\frac{1}{2}$"

$\frac{1}{2}$"

1"

$\frac{1}{2}$"

$= \frac{1}{2}$

$\frac{1}{2}$"

1 ft.

2 ft.

2 ft.   1 ft.

1 ft. 1 ft.

1 ft.

4 ft.   2 ft.

3 ft.   1 ft.

2 ft.   2 ft.

1 ft.

3 yd.

10 yd.   10 yd.

3 yd.

_____
Perimeter

Name _____

Measurement: Perimeter and Area

Area is also calculated by multiplying the length times the width of a square or rectangular figure. Use the formula: A = l x w.

Directions: Calculate the perimeter of each figure.

2 ft.
2 ft.
2 ft.
2 ft.
2 ft.
2 ft.

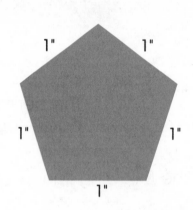

1"   1"
1"   1"
1"

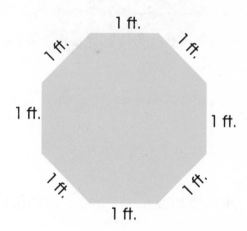

1 ft.
1 ft.   1 ft.
1 ft.   1 ft.
1 ft.   1 ft.
1 ft.

_____   _____   _____

Directions: Calculate the area of each figure.

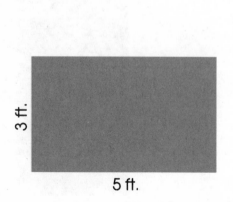

3 ft.
5 ft.

4 yd.
1 yd.

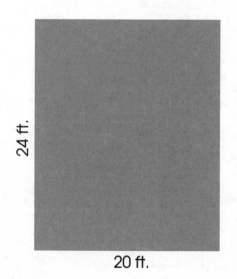

24 ft.
20 ft.

_____   _____   _____

Name _____

Measurement: Volume

Volume is the number of cubic units that fit inside a figure.

Directions: Find the volume of each figure. The first one is done for you.

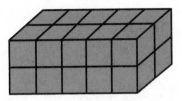

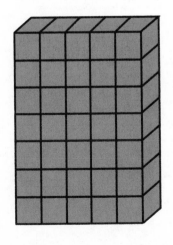

_____**4**_____ cubic units

_____ cubic units

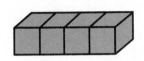

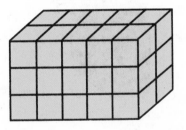

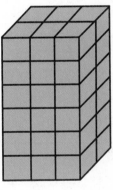

_____ cubic units

_____ cubic units

_____ cubic units

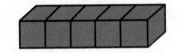

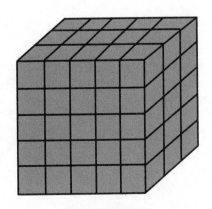

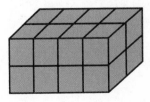

_____ cubic units

_____ cubic units

_____ cubic units

Name _____

Measurement: Volume

The volume of a figure can also be calculated by multiplying the length times the width times the height.
Use the formula: V= l x w x h.

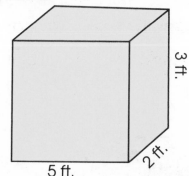

Example:

3 x 5 x 2 = 30 cubic feet

Directions: Find the volume of the following figures. Label your answers in cubic feet, inches or yards. The first one is done for you.

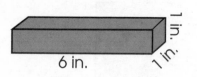

6 in.   1 in.   1 in.

<u>6 cubic inches</u>

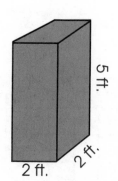

5 ft.   2 ft.   2 ft.

_____

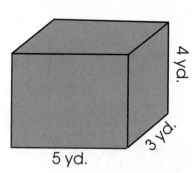

4 yd.   5 yd.   3 yd.

_____

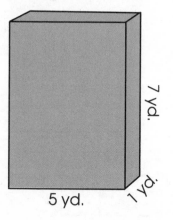

7 yd.   5 yd.   1 yd.

_____

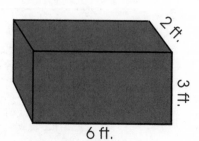

2 ft.   3 ft.   6 ft.

_____

Name _____

Metric Measurement: Perimeter

Directions: Calculate the perimeter of each figure.

Example:

$4 + 5 + 4 + 1 + 2 + 3 + 2 = 21$ meters

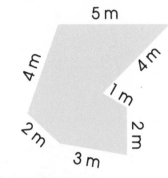

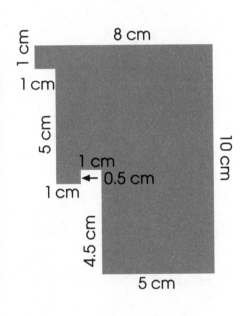

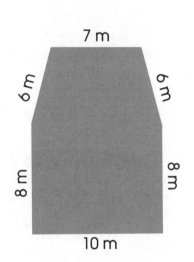

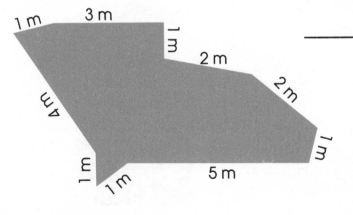

_____

_____

_____

_____

_____

Name _____

Metric Measurement: Area and Volume

Directions: Calculate the area of each figure. Use the formula: A = l x w.

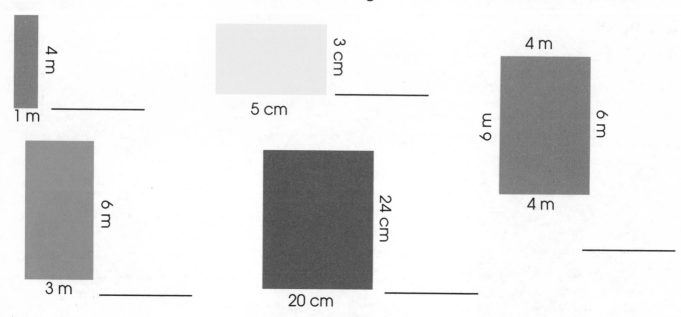

4 m
1 m
_____

3 cm
5 cm
_____

4 m
6 m
6 m
4 m
_____

6 m
3 m
_____

24 cm
20 cm
_____

Directions: Calculate the volume of each figure. Use the formula: V = l x w x h.

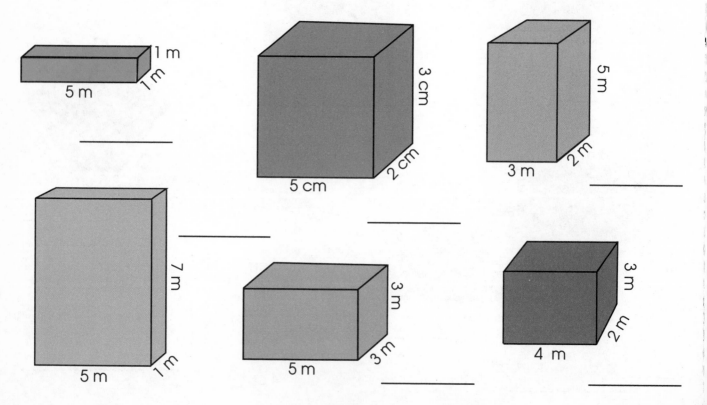

1 m
1 m
5 m
_____

3 cm
5 cm
2 cm
_____

5 m
3 m
2 m
_____

7 m
5 m
1 m
_____

3 m
5 m
3 m
_____

3 m
4 m
2 m
_____

Name _____

Measurement: Ounce, Pound, Ton

The **ounce**, **pound** and **ton** are units in the standard system for measuring weight.

Directions: Choose the measure of weight you would use for each object.

16 ounces = 1 pound
2,000 pounds = 1 ton

ounce   **pound**   **ton**

Example: <u>ounces</u>    _____

 _____    _____

 _____    _____

 _____    _____

Metric Measurement: Gram and Kilogram

Grams and **kilograms** are measurements of weight in the metric system. A gram (g) weighs about $\frac{1}{28}$ of an ounce. A grape or paper clip weighs about one gram. There are 1,000 grams in a kilogram. A kilogram (kg) weighs about 2.2 pounds. A brick weighs about 1 kilogram.

Directions: Choose grams or kilograms to measure the following.

Example: grams
_____   _____

_____   _____

_____   _____

_____   _____

_____   _____

Measurement: Liquid

The **cup**, **pint**, **quart** and **gallon** are units in the standard system for measuring liquids.

Directions: Gather the following materials: 2 dish tubs, one filled with water, sand or rice; measuring cups; pint container; quart container; gallon container. Then answer the questions and complete the chart.

1. Use the cup measure to pour water, sand or rice into the pint container. How many cups did it take?

   _____ cups = 1 pint

2. Use the cup measure to find out how many cups are in a quart and a gallon.

   _____ cups = 1 quart

   _____ cups = 1 gallon

3. Use the pint container to pour water, sand or rice into the quart container. How many pints are in a quart?

   _____ pints = 1 quart

4. How many pints does it take to fill a gallon?

   _____ pints = 1 gallon

5. Use the quart measure to find out how many quarts are in a gallon.

   _____ quarts = 1 gallon

Measurement Chart

_____ cups = 1 pint   _____ pints = 1 quart

_____ cups = 1 quart   _____ pints = 1 gallon

_____ cups = 1 gallon   _____ quarts = 1 gallon

Name _____

Measurement: Cup, Pint, Quart, Gallon

Directions: Circle the number of objects to the right that equal the objects on the left. The first one is done for you.

2 cups = 1 pint
2 pints = 1 quart
4 quarts = 1 gallon

= 1 cup   = 1 pint   = 1 quart   = 1 gallon

Metric Measurement: Milliliter and Liter

Liters and **milliliters** are measurements of liquid in the metric system. A milliliter (mL) equals 0.001 liter or 0.03 fluid ounces. A drop of water equals about 1 milliliter. Liters (L) measure large amounts of liquid. There are 1,000 milliliters in a liter. One liter measures 1.06 quarts. Soft drinks are often sold in 2-liter bottles.

Directions: Choose milliliters or liters to measure these liquids.

Example: _milliliters_

_____

_____

_____

_____

_____

_____

Name _____

Metric Measurement: Weight and Liquid

Directions: Choose grams (g) or kilograms (kg) to weigh the following objects. The first one is done for you.

rhinoceros   **kg**   person _____

dime _____   airplane _____

bucket of wet sand _____   spider _____

eyeglasses _____   pair of scissors _____

toy train engine _____   horse _____

Directions: Choose milliliters (mL) or liters (L) to measure the liquids in the following containers. The first one is done for you.

swimming pool   **L**   baby bottle _____

small juice glass _____   teapot _____

gasoline tank _____   outdoor fountain _____

test tube _____   ink pen _____

washing machine _____   Lake Erie _____

Name _____

Temperature: Fahrenheit

28°F

Fahrenheit is used to measure temperature in the standard system. °**F** stands for degrees Fahrenheit.

72°F

Directions: Use the thermometer to answer these questions.

At what temperature does water boil?   _____

At what temperature does water freeze?   _____

What is normal body temperature?   _____

Is a 100°F day warm, hot or cold?   _____

Is a 0°F day warm, hot or cold?   _____

Which temperature best describes room temperature?
58°F   70°F   80°F   _____

Which temperature best describes a cold winter day?
22°F   38°F   32°F   _____

water
boils
210° F → 210

body
temperature
98.6° F →

water
freezes
32° F →

°F
220
200
190
180
170
160
150
140
130
120
110
100
90
80
70
60
50
40
30
20
10
0
-10
-20

Name _____

Temperature: Celsius

Celsius is used to measure temperature in the metric system. **°C** stands for degrees Celsius.

0°C   30°C

Directions: Use the thermometer to answer these questions.

At what temperature does water boil? _____

At what temperature does water freeze? _____

What is normal body temperature? _____

Is it a hot or cold day when the temperature is 30°C? _____

Is it a hot or cold day when the temperature is 5°C? _____

Which temperature best describes a hot summer day?
5°C 40°C 20°C _____

Which temperature best describes an icy winter day?
0°C 15°C 10°C _____

water boils 100°C →
body temperature 37°C →
water freezes 0°C →

Review

Directions: Find the perimeter and area of each figure.

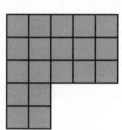  = 1 square unit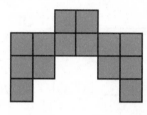

Perimeter = _____ units

Area = _____ sq. units

Perimeter = _____ units

Area = _____ sq. units

Directions: How much does it equal?

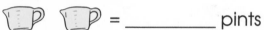 = _____ pints

 = _____ quarts

Directions: Write whether you would use ounce, pound or ton to weigh the following.

 _____

 _____

_____

Directions: Write whether you would use an inch, foot, yard or mile to measure the following.

 _____

 _____

_____

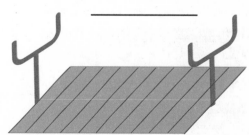

Name _____

Review

Directions: Choose centimeters, meters or kilometers to measure the following.

_____ height of a tree   _____ length of a shoe

_____ distance around Earth   _____ height of a building

_____ length of your yard   _____ distance a plane flies

Directions: Choose grams or kilograms to measure the following.

_____

_____

_____

_____

Directions: Choose liters or milliliters to measure the following.

_____

_____

_____

_____

Name _____

Graphing

A **graph** is a drawing that shows information about changes in numbers.

Directions: Answer the questions by reading the graphs.

Bar Graph

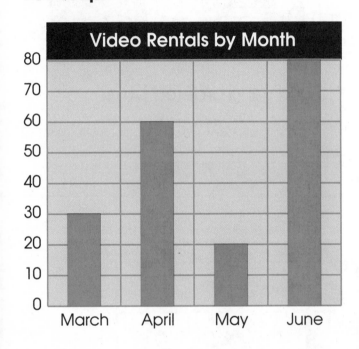

How many videos did the store rent in June?

_____

In which month did the store rent the <u>fewest</u> videos?

_____

How many videos did the store rent for all 4 months?

_____

Line Graph

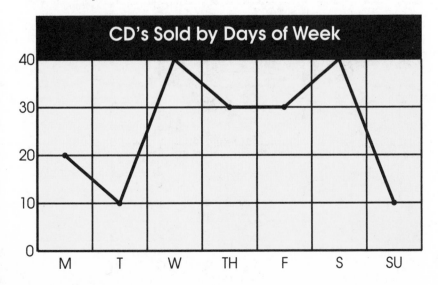

On which days did the store sell the fewest CD's?

_____

How many CD's did the store sell in 1 week?

_____

Ordered Pairs

An **ordered pair** is a pair of numbers
used to locate a point.

Example: (8, 3)

Step 1: Count across to line 8 on the graph.
Step 2: Count up to line 3 on the graph.
Step 3: Draw a dot to mark the spot.

Directions: Map the following spots on the grid using ordered pairs.

(4, 7)   (9, 10)   (2, 1)   (5, 6)   (2, 2)   (1, 5)   (7, 4)   (3, 8)

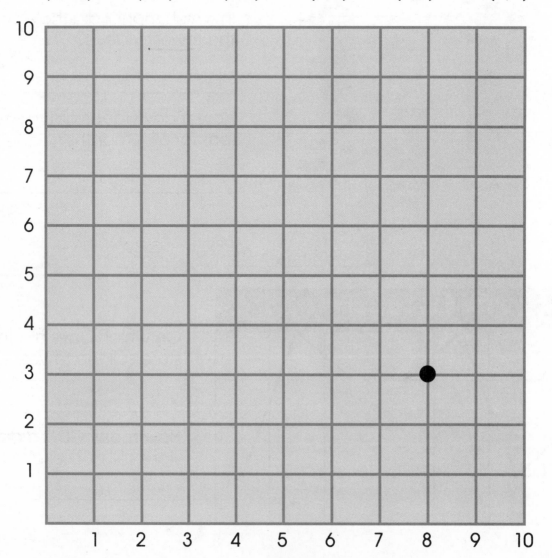

Graphing: Finding Ordered Pairs

Graphs or grids are sometimes used to find the location of objects.

Example: The ice-cream cone is located at point (5,6) on the graph. To find the ice cream's location, follow the line to the bottom of the grid to get the first number — 5. Then go back to the ice cream and follow the grid line to the left for the second number — 6.

Directions: Write the ordered pair for the following objects. The first one is done for you.

book __(4, 8)__   bike _____   suitcase _____   house _____

globe _____   cup _____   triangle _____   airplane _____

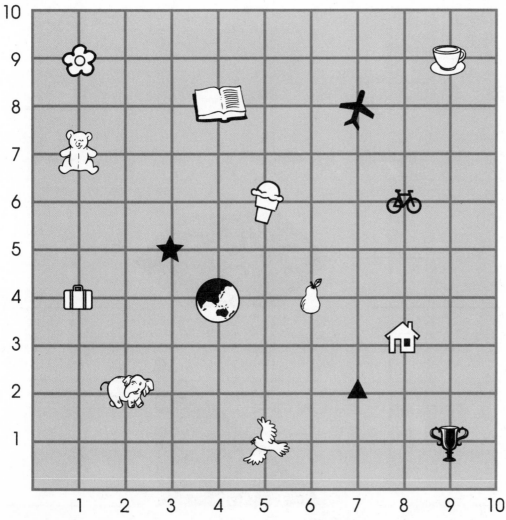

Directions: Identify the objects located at the following points. The first one is done for you.

(9, 1)
___trophy___

(3, 5)
_____

(2, 2)
_____

(6, 4)
_____

(1, 9)
_____

(5, 1)
_____

(1, 7)
_____

Name _____

Geometry: Polygons

A **polygon** is a closed figure with three or more sides.

Examples:

triangle
3 sides

square
4 equal
sides

rectangle
4 sides

pentagon
5 sides

hexagon
6 sides

octagon
8 sides

Directions: Identify the polygons.

 _____

 _____

 _____

 _____

 _____

 _____

Name _____

Geometry: Line, Ray, Segment

A **line segment** has two end points.

A ●————————————● B

Write: ●—● AB

A **line** has no end points and goes on in both directions.

←————●————●————→
     C   D

Write: ←●—●→ CD

A **ray** is part of a line and goes on in one direction. It has one end point.

●————●————————→
E   F

Write: ●—→ EF

Directions: Identify each of the following as a line, line segment or ray.

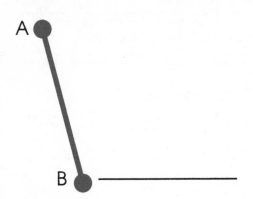

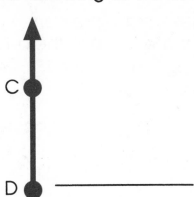

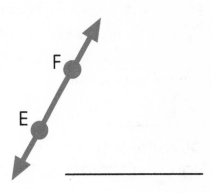

_____   _____   _____

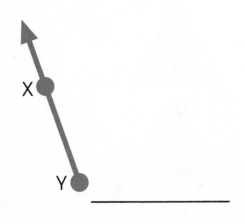

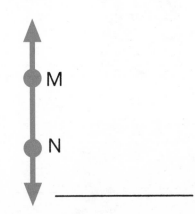

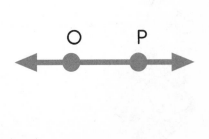

_____   _____   _____

Name _____

Geometry: Angles

The point at which two line segments meet is called an **angle**. There are three types of angles — right, acute and obtuse.

A **right angle** is formed when the two lines meet at 90°.

An **acute angle** is formed when the two lines meet at less than 90°.

An **obtuse angle** is formed when the two lines meet at greater than 90°.

Angles can be measured with a protractor or index card. With a protractor, align the bottom edge of the angle with the bottom of the protractor, with the angle point at the circle of the protractor. Note the direction of the other ray and the number of degrees of the angle.

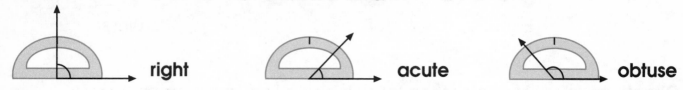

right   acute   obtuse

Place the corner of an index card in the corner of the angle. If the edges line up with the card, it is a right angle. If not, the angle is acute or obtuse.

right   acute   obtuse

Directions: Use a protractor or index card to identify the following angles as right, obtuse or acute.

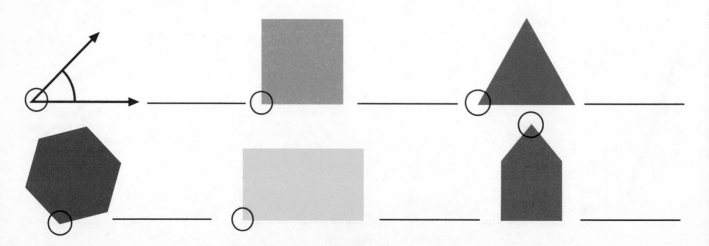

Geometry: Circles

A **circle** is a round figure. It is named by its center. A **radius** is a line segment from the center of a circle to any point on the circle. A **diameter** is a line segment with both end points on the circle. The diameter always passes through the center of the circle.

Directions: Name the radius, diameter and circle.

Example:

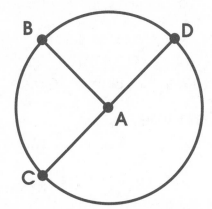

Circle _____A_____

Radius _____AB_____

Diameter _____DC_____

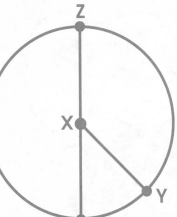

Circle _____

Radius _____

Diameter _____

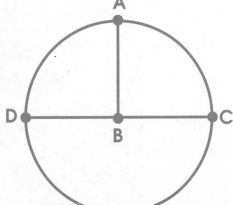

Circle _____

Radius _____

Diameter _____

Review

Directions: Complete the line graph using the information in the box.

Team	Games Played
Red	10
Blue	20
Green	15
Yellow	25

Directions: Draw a line from the figure to its name.

line

square

segment

diameter

octagon

triangle

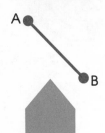

pentagon

Name _____

Number Patterns

Figuring out the secret to a number pattern or code can send you into "thinking overtime."

Directions: Discover the pattern for each set of numbers. Then write the missing numbers.

a) 20, 21, 19, 20, 18, 19, 17, _____ , 16, 17, 15, _____ , _____ , _____ , _____ , _____ .

b) 1, 6, 16, 31, 51, _____ , _____ , 141, _____ , 226.

c) 3, 5, 9, 15, _____ , _____ , 45, _____ , 75.

d) 55, 52, 50, 49, 46, _____ , _____ , _____ , _____ , _____ , 34.

e) 1, 3, 6, 10, 15, 21, _____ , _____ , _____ , 55, 66, 78.

f) 10, 16, 13, 19, 16, _____ , 19, _____ . _____ , 28, _____ .

g) 3, 4, 7, 12, _____ , _____ , 39, _____ , 67, _____ .

h) 100, 90, 95, 85, 90, 80, 85, _____ , _____ , _____ , 75.

Directions: Make up a number pattern of your own. Have a parent, brother or sister figure it out!

_____ , _____ , _____ , _____ , _____ , _____ , _____ , _____ , _____ , _____ .

Directions: Follow the instructions to solve the number puzzler.

Use only these numbers: 2, 4, 5, 7, 8, 11, 13, 14, 16.

Each number may only be used once.

Write even numbers in the squares.

Write odd numbers in the circles.

Each row must add up to 26.

Hint: Work the puzzle in pencil, so you can erase and retry numbers if needed.

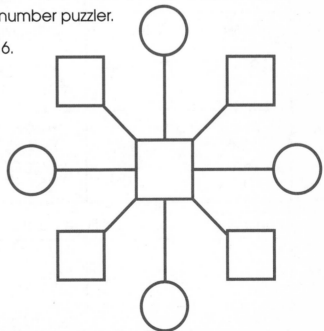

Name _____

Finding Common Attributes

The things that items have in common are called **common attributes**.
Example:

These are Pee-Wees.	These are not Pee-Wees.	Circle the Pee-Wees.
A E I O U	B C M W Z	S ⓞ T ⓤ R ⓔ

When you look at the Pee-Wees, you see what they have in common. They are all vowels. That is their common attribute. The items in the middle box are not Pee-Wees because they are all consonants. In the last box, only the vowels are circled.

Directions: Find the common attributes of the Wobbles, Whimzees, Dwibbles and Zanies. Circle the correct answers.

1.	These are Wobbles.	These are not Wobbles.	Circle the Wobbles.
2.	These are Whimzees.	These are not Whimzees.	Circle the Whimzees.
3.	These are Dwibbles. 48 32 72 56	These are not Dwibbles. 28 54 36 12	Circle the Dwibbles. 16 18 4 24 40
4.	These are Zanies.	These are not Zanies.	Circle the Zanies.

Directions: Write your own attribute puzzle in the boxes.

Name _____

Probability

One thinking skill to get your brain in gear is figuring probability. **Probability** is the likelihood or chance that something will happen. Probability is expressed and written as a ratio.

The probability of tossing heads or tails on a coin is one in two (1:2).

The probability of rolling any number on a die is one in six (1:6).

The probability of getting a red on this spinner is two in four (2:4).

The probability of drawing an ace from a deck of cards is four in fifty-two (4:52).

Directions: Write the probability ratios to answer these questions.

1. There are 26 letters in the alphabet. What is the probability of drawing any letter from a set of alphabet cards?

   _____

2. Five of the 26 alphabet letters are vowels. What is the probability of drawing a vowel from the alphabet cards?

   _____

3. Matt takes 10 shots at the basketball hoop. Six of his shots are baskets. What is the probability of Matt's next shot being a basket?

   _____

4. A box contains 10 marbles: 2 white, 3 green, 1 red, 2 orange and 2 blue. What is the probability of pulling a green marble from the box?

   _____

   A red marble?

   _____

5. What is the probability of pulling a marble that is not blue?

   _____

Name _____

Probability

Directions: Write the probability ratios to answer these questions.

1. Using the spinner shown, what is the probability of spinning a 4? _____

2. Using the spinner show, what is the chance of not spinning a 2? _____

3. Using the spinner shown, what is the probability of spinning a 6, 7 or 3? _____

4. What is the probability of getting heads or tails when you toss a coin? _____

Directions: Toss a coin 20 times and record the outcome of each toss. Then answer the questions.   _____ Heads _____ Tails

5. What was the ratio of heads to tails in the 20 tosses? _____ ____

6. Was the outcome of getting heads or tails in the 20 tosses the same as the probability ratio? _____

7. Why or why not? _____

The probability ratio of getting any number on a cube of dice is 1:6.

Directions: Toss a die 36 times and record how many times it lands on each number. Then answer the questions.

_____ one   _____ two   _____ three   _____ four   _____ five   _____ six

8. What was the ratio for each number on the die?

_____ one   _____ two   _____ three   _____ four   _____ five   _____ six

9. Did any of the numbers have a ratio close to the actual probability ratio? _____

10. What do the outcomes of flipping a coin and tossing a die tell you about the probability of an event happening?

_____

Name _____

Computing

Many people use computers on a daily basis at home, work or school. Computers help us to complete many tasks quickly and efficiently.

The Chinese used a computing device more than 4,000 years ago. It was called an abacus. An **abacus** is a wooden frame with four rows of beads representing ones, tens, hundreds and thousands.

The beads on the bottom half of the abacus are worth one unit. The beads on the top half of the unit are worth five units.

The bottom beads are pushed up to the middle bar of the abacus. The top beads are pushed down to the middle bar of the abacus.

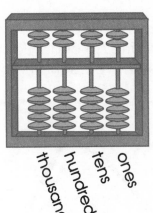

Directions: Determine the number shown on each abacus and write it on the blank. The first one has been done for you.

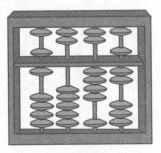

1. __6,047__

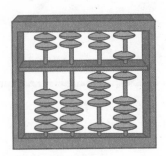

2. _____

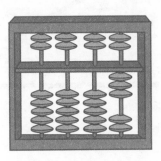

3. _____

4. _____

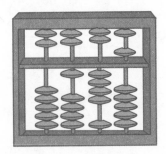

5. _____

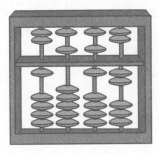

6. _____

Name _____

Problem Solving: A Garden Puzzle

Grace is planting a garden. The garden will be a semi-circle in shape and have two rows. The first row will have three sections and the back row will have six sections. Grace needs to decide how many plants she can put in each section of her garden.

She wants the total number of plants in the back row to be double the total number of plants in front.

Directions: Help Grace finish her garden plan by using the numbers 1, 2, 3, 4, 5, 6, 7, 8 and 9. Each number may only be used once. Three numbers have been written in place for you.

_____ plants   _____ plants

_____ plants   _____ plants

7 plants

1 plant   _____ plants

3 plants   _____ plants

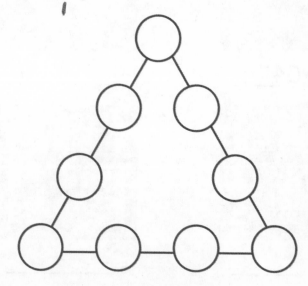

Directions: Arrange the digits 1 through 9 in the circles on the triangle so the numbers on each of the sides add up to 17.

Problem Solving: Sorting Information

When you have two sets of items, they can be grouped in pairs (with one item from each set) in many ways.

Example:

While shopping, Sally bought three pairs of shorts and three blouses. How many different outfits can she make from these items?

To solve, you could draw a picture or make a list:

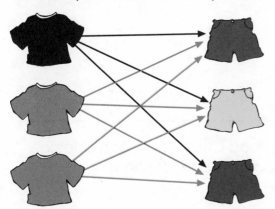

Black shirt — Blue shorts
Black shirt — Yellow shorts
Black shirt — Purple shorts
Red shirt — Blue shorts
Red shirt — Yellow shorts
Red shirt — Purple shorts
Green shirt — Blue shorts
Green shirt — Yellow shorts
Green shirt — Purple shorts

There are nine possible combinations.
3 (shirts) x 3 (shorts) = 9 (outfits)

Directions: Either draw a picture or make a list to solve the problem. Then write the answer.

Sally's mom gave her $37.00 for shopping and lunch. She gave Sally 11 bills—some are ones, some are fives and some are tens.

How many ones, fives and tens does Sally have?

_____ ones _____ fives _____ tens

Name _____

Problem Solving: Sorting Information

Directions: Solve these problems the same way you did on the last page. Then write the answers.

1. Jodie stopped at the Food Court for lunch. She can have a hamburger or hot dog to eat and a soda, milk or lemonade to drink. Make a list or draw a picture to show all possible combinations.

How many lunch possibilities does she have? _____

2. Jodie saw Maria and Dawn sitting on a bench in the Food Court. Jodie can't decide where to sit. Make a list or draw a picture to show all possible combinations of the three girls on the bench.

How many different ways can the three girls sit on the bench? _____

3. After shopping, Jodie can participate in any two of these activities: swimming, crafts, soccer and tennis. Make a list or draw a picture to show all possible combinations of activities Jodie could select.

How many different choices does Jodie have? _____

302

Math

Page 6

Spelling: Short Vowels

Vowels are the letters **a, e, i, o, u** and sometimes **y.** There are five short vowels: ă as in **a**pple, ĕ as in **e**gg and br**ea**th, ĭ as in s**i**ck, ŏ as in t**o**p and ŭ as in **u**p.

Directions: Complete the exercises using words from the box.

blend	insist	health	pump	crop
fact	pinch	pond	hatch	plug

1. Write each word under its vowel sound.

ă	ĕ	ĭ	ŏ	ŭ
fact	blend	insist	pond	pump
hatch	health	pinch	crop	plug

2. Complete these sentences, using a word with the vowel sound given. Use each word from the box only once.

Here's an interesting (ă) __fact__ about your (ĕ) __health__.

Henry was very pleased with his corn (ŏ) __crop__.

The boys enjoyed fishing in the (ŏ) __pond__.

They (ĭ) __insist__ on watching the egg (ă) __hatch__.

(ĕ) __Blend__ in a (ĭ) __pinch__ of salt.

The farmer had to (ŭ) __pump__ water from the lake for his cows to drink.

Did you put the (ŭ) __plug__ in the bathtub this time?

Page 7

Spelling: Short Vowels

Directions: Read the words. After each, write the correct vowel sound. Underline the letter or letters that spell the sound in the word. The first one has been done for you.

	Word	Vowel		Word	Vowel
1.	str<u>u</u>ck	u	9.	br<u>ea</u>th	e
2.	scr<u>a</u>mble	a	10.	<u>e</u>dge	e
3.	str<u>o</u>ng	o	11.	k<u>i</u>ck	i
4.	ch<u>i</u>ll	i	12.	st<u>o</u>p	o
5.	th<u>u</u>d	u	13.	qu<u>i</u>z	i
6.	dr<u>ea</u>d	e	14.	br<u>u</u>sh	u
7.	pl<u>u</u>nge	u	15.	cr<u>a</u>sh	a
8.	m<u>a</u>sk	a	16.	d<u>o</u>dge	o

Directions: List four words (nouns and verbs) with short vowel sounds. Then write two sentences using the words.

Example: Ann, can, hand, Pam
Ann can give Pam a hand.

__Answers will vary.__

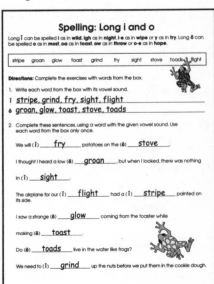

1. __Sentences will vary.__

2. _____

Page 8

Spelling: Long e and a

Long ē can be spelled **ea** as in r**ea**l or **ee** as in d**ee**r. Long ā can be spelled **a** as in **a**pron, **ai** as in p**ai**l, **ay** as in p**ay** or **a-e** as in l**a**k**e**.

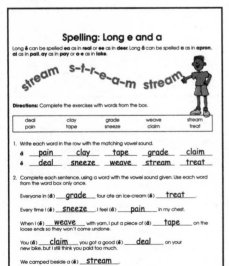
stream s-t-r-e-a-m stream

Directions: Complete the exercises with words from the box.

deal	clay	grade	weave	stream
pain	tape	sneeze	claim	treat

1. Write each word in the row with the matching vowel sound.

ā	pain	clay	tape	grade	claim
ē	deal	sneeze	weave	stream	treat

2. Complete each sentence, using a word with the vowel sound given. Use each word from the word box only once.

Everyone in (ā) __grade__ four ate an ice-cream (ē) __treat__.

Every time I (ē) __sneeze__, I feel (ā) __pain__ in my chest.

When I (ā) __weave__ with yarn, I put a piece of (ā) __tape__ on the loose ends so they won't come undone.

You (ā) __claim__ you got a good (ē) __deal__ on your new bike, but I still think you paid too much.

We camped beside a (ē) __stream__.

We forgot to wrap up our (ā) __clay__ and it dried out.

Page 9

Spelling: Long e and a

When a vowel is long, it sounds the same as its letter name.

Examples: Long ē as in tr**ea**t, **ee**l, compl**e**te.
Long ā as in **a**pe, tr**ai**l, s**ay**, **a**pron.

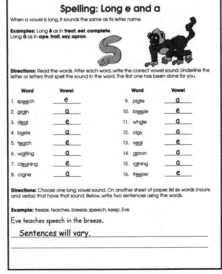

Directions: Read the words. After each word, write the correct vowel sound. Underline the letter or letters that spell the sound in the word. The first one has been done for you.

	Word	Vowel		Word	Vowel
1.	sp<u>ee</u>ch	e	9.	pl<u>a</u>te	a
2.	gr<u>ai</u>n	a	10.	br<u>ee</u>ze	e
3.	d<u>ea</u>l	e	11.	wh<u>a</u>le	a
4.	b<u>a</u>ste	a	12.	cl<u>ay</u>	a
5.	t<u>ea</u>ch	e	13.	v<u>ea</u>l	e
6.	w<u>ai</u>ting	a	14.	<u>a</u>pron	a
7.	cl<u>ea</u>ning	e	15.	r<u>ai</u>ning	a
8.	cr<u>a</u>ne	a	16.	fr<u>ee</u>zer	e

Directions: Choose one long vowel sound. On another sheet of paper, list six words (nouns and verbs) that have that sound. Below, write two sentences using the words.

Example: freeze, teaches, breeze, speech, keep, Eve
Eve teaches speech in the breeze.

__Sentences will vary.__

Page 10

Spelling: Long i and o

Long ī can be spelled **i** as in w**i**ld, **igh** as in n**igh**t, **i-e** as in w**i**p**e** or **y** as in tr**y**. Long ō can be spelled **o** as in m**o**st, **oa** as in t**oa**st, **ow** as in thr**ow** or **o-e** as in h**o**p**e**.

stripe	groan	glow	toast	grind	fry	sight	stove	toads	flight

Directions: Complete the exercises with words from the box.

1. Write each word from the box with its vowel sound.

ī __stripe, grind, fry, sight, flight__
ō __groan, glow, toast, stove, toads__

2. Complete these sentences, using a word with the given vowel sound. Use each word from the box only once.

We will (ī) __fry__ potatoes on the (ō) __stove__.

I thought I heard a low (ō) __groan__, but when I looked, there was nothing in (ī) __sight__.

The airplane for our (ī) __flight__ had a (ī) __stripe__ painted on its side.

I saw a strange (ō) __glow__ coming from the toaster while making (ō) __toast__.

Do (ō) __toads__ live in the water like frogs?

We need to (ī) __grind__ up the nuts before we put them in the cookie dough.

Page 11

Spelling: Long i and o

Directions: Read the words. After each word, write the correct vowel sound. Underline the letter or letters that spell the sound. The first one has been done for you.

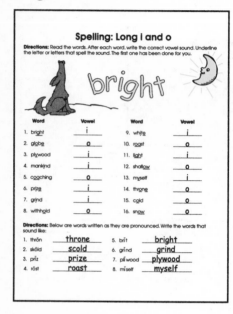

bright

Word	Vowel	Word	Vowel
1. bright	i	9. white	i
2. globe	o	10. roast	o
3. plywood	i	11. light	i
4. mankind	i	12. shallow	o
5. coaching	o	13. myself	i
6. prize	i	14. throne	o
7. grind	i	15. cold	o
8. withhold	o	16. snow	o

Directions: Below are words written as they are pronounced. Write the words that sound like:

1. thrōn	throne	5. brīt	bright
2. skōld	scold	6. grīnd	grind
3. prīz	prize	7. plī'wood	plywood
4. rōst	roast	8. mī'self	myself

Page 12

Spelling: Long u

Long ū can be spelled, **u-e** as in **cube** or **ew** as in **few**. Some sounds are similar in sound to **u** but are not true u sounds, such as the **oo** in **tooth**, the **o-e** in **move** and the **ue** in **blue**.

Directions: Complete each sentence using a word from the box. Do not use the same word more than once.

blew
tune
flute
cute
stew
June
glue

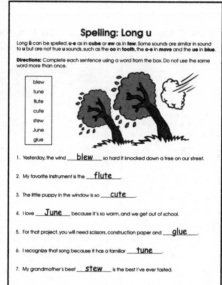

1. Yesterday, the wind **blew** so hard it knocked down a tree on our street.

2. My favorite instrument is the **flute** .

3. The little puppy in the window is so **cute** .

4. I love **June** because it's so warm, and we get out of school.

5. For that project, you will need scissors, construction paper and **glue** .

6. I recognize that song because it has a familiar **tune** .

7. My grandmother's beef **stew** is the best I've ever tasted.

Page 13

Spelling: The k Sound

The **k** sound can be spelled with **k** as in **peek**, **c** as in **cousin**, **ck** as in **sick**, **ch** as in **Chris** and **cc** as in **accuse**. In some words, however, one **c** may be pronounced **k** and the other **s** as in **accident**.

Directions: Answer the questions with words from the box.

Christmas	freckles	command	cork	jacket
accused	castle	stomach	rake	accident

1. Which two words spell **k** with a **k**?
   cork   rake

2. Which two words spell **k** with **ck**?
   freckles   jacket

3. Which two words spell **k** with **ch**?
   Christmas   stomach

4. Which five words spell **k** with **c** or **cc**?
   accused   cork   castle
   command   accident

5. Complete these sentences, using a word with **k** spelled as shown. Use each word from the box only once.

Dad gave Mom a garden (**k**) **rake** for (**ch**) **Christmas** .

There are (**ck**) **freckles** on my face and (**ch**) **stomach** .

The people (**cc**) **accused** her of taking a (**ck**) **jacket** .

The police took (**c**) **command** after the (**cc**) **accident** .

The model of the (**c**) **castle** was made out of

(**c and k**) **cork** .

Page 14

Spelling: The f Sound

The **f** sound can be spelled with **f** as in **fun**, **gh** as in **laugh** and **ph** as in **phone**.

Directions: Answer the questions with words from the box.

fuss	paragraph	phone	friendship	freedom
defend	flood	alphabet	rough	laughter

1. Which three words spell **f** with **ph**?
   paragraph   phone   alphabet

2. Which two words spell **f** with **gh**?
   rough   laughter

3. Which five words spell **f** with an **f**?
   fuss   defend   flood
   friendship   freedom

4. Complete these sentences, using a word with **f** spelled as shown. Use each word from the box only once.

I don't know why my teacher makes so much (**f**) **fuss** over writing a (**ph**) **paragraph** .

A (**f**) **friendship** can help you through (**gh**) **rough** times.

The soldiers will (**f**) **defend** our (**f**) **freedom** .

Can you say the (**ph**) **alphabet** backwards?

When I answered the (**ph**) **phone** , all I could hear was (**gh**) **laughter** .

If it keeps raining, we'll have a (**f**) **flood** .

Page 15

Spelling: The s Sound

The **s** sound can be spelled with **s** as in **super**, **ss** as in **assign**, **c** as in **city**, **ce** as in **fence** or **sc** as in **scene**. In some words, though, **sc** is pronounced **sk**, as in **scare**.

Directions: Answer the questions using words from the box.

exciting	medicine	lettuce	peace	scissors
slice	scientist	sauce	bracelet	distance

1. Which five words spell **s** with an **s** or **ss**?
   slice   sauce   distance
   scissors   scientist

2. Which two words spell **s** with just a **c**?
   exciting   medicine

3. Which six words spell **s** with a **ce**?
   slice   sauce   bracelet
   lettuce   peace   distance

4. Which two words spell **s** with **sc**?
   scientist   scissors

5. Complete these sentences, using a word with **s** spelled as shown. Use each word from the box only once.

My (**ce**) **bracelet** fell off my wrist into the tomato (**s and ce**) **sauce** (**s and ce**)

My salad was just a (**s and ce**) **slice** of (**ce**) **lettuce**

It was (**c**) **exciting** to see the lions, even though they were a long (**s and ce**) **distance** away.

The (**sc and s**) **scientist** invented a new (**c**) **medicine**

If I lend you my (**sc**) **scissors** , will you leave me in (**ce**) **peace** ?

Page 16

Spelling: Syllables

A **syllable** is a word—or part of a word—with only one vowel sound. Some words have just one syllable, such as **eat**, **dog** and **house**. Some words have two syllables, such as **in-sist** and **be-fore**. Some words have three syllables, such as **re-mem-ber**; four syllables, such as **un-der-stand-ing**; or more. Often words are easier to spell if you know how many syllables they have.

Syl-la-bles

Directions: Write the number of syllables in each word below.

Word	Syllables	Word	Syllables
1. amphibian	4	11. want	1
2. liter	2	12. communication	5
3. guild	1	13. pedestrian	4
4. chill	1	14. kilo	2
5. vegetarian	5	15. autumn	2
6. comedian	4	16. dinosaur	3
7. warm	1	17. grammar	2
8. piano	3	18. dry	1
9. barbarian	4	19. solar	2
10. chef	1	20. wild	1

Directions: Next to each number, write words with the same number of syllables.

1 ____
2 ____ Answers will vary.
3 ____
4 ____
5 ____

Page 17

Spelling: Syllables

Directions: Write each word from the box next to the number that shows how many syllables it has.

fuss	paragraph	phone	friendship	freedom
defend	flood	alphabet	rough	laughter

One: fuss flood phone rough
Two: defend friendship freedom laughter
Three: paragraph alphabet

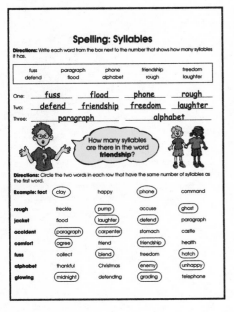

How many syllables are there in the word **friendship**?

Directions: Circle the two words in each row that have the same number of syllables as the first word.

Example: fact (clay) happy (phone) command

rough	freckle	(pump)	accuse	(ghost)
jacket	flood	(laughter)	(defend)	paragraph
accident	(paragraph)	(carpenter)	stomach	castle
comfort	(agree)	friend	(friendship)	health
fuss	collect	(blend)	freedom	(hatch)
alphabet	thankful	Christmas	(enemy)	(unhappy)
glowing	(midnight)	defending	(grading)	telephone

Page 18

Vocabulary: Synonyms

A **synonym** is a word that means the same, or nearly the same, as another word.
Example: quick and **fast**

Directions: Draw lines to match the words in Column A with their synonyms in Column B.

Column A	Column B
plain	unusual
career	vocation
rare	disappear
vanish	greedy
beautiful	finish
selfish	simple
complete	lovely

Directions: Choose a word from Column A or Column B to complete each sentence below.
Sample answers:
1. Dad was very excited when he discovered the **rare/unusual** coin for sale on the display counter.
2. My dog is a real magician; he can **vanish/disappear** into thin air when he sees me getting his bath ready!
3. Many of my classmates joined the discussion about **career/vocation** choices we had considered.
4. "You will need to **finish/complete** your report on ancient Greece before you sign up for computer time," said Mr. Rastetter.
5. Your **beautiful/lovely** painting will be on display in the art show.

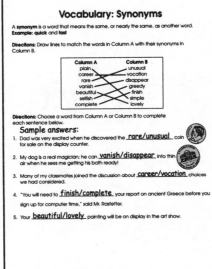

Page 19

Vocabulary: Synonyms

tired	greedy	easy	rough	minute	melted	friend	smart

Directions: For each sentence, choose a word from the box that is a synonym for the bold word. Write the synonym above the word.

1. Boy, this road is really **bumpy**! → rough
2. The operator said politely, "One **moment**, please." → minute
3. My parents are usually **exhausted** when they get home from work. → tired
4. "Don't be so **selfish**! Can't you share with us?" asked Rob. → greedy
5. That puzzle was actually quite **simple**. → easy
6. "Who's your **buddy**?" Dad asked as we walked onto the porch. → friend
7. When it comes to animals, my Uncle Steve is quite **intelligent**. → smart
8. The frozen treat **thawed** while I stood in line for the bus. → melted

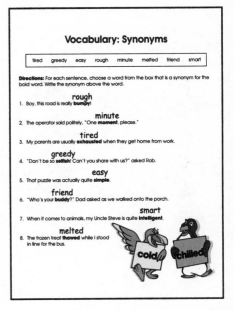

cold chilled

Page 20

Vocabulary: Antonyms

An **antonym** is a word that means the opposite of another word.
Example: difficult and **easy**

Directions: Choose words from the box to complete the crossword puzzle.

friend	vanish	quit	safety	liquids	scatter	help	noisy

ACROSS:
2. Opposite of **gather**
3. Opposite of **enemy**
4. Opposite of **prevent**
6. Opposite of **begin**
7. Opposite of **silent**

DOWN:
1. Opposite of **appear**
2. Opposite of **danger**
5. Opposite of **solids**

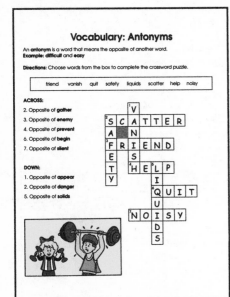

Page 21

Vocabulary: Antonyms

Directions: Each bold word below has an antonym in the box. Use these words to write new sentences. The first one is done for you.

friend	vanish	quit	safety	liquids	help	scatter	worse

1. I'll help you **gather** all the papers on the lawn.
   The strong winds will scatter the leaves.
2. The fourth graders were learning about the many **solids** in their classroom.
   Answer should include "liquids."
3. "It's time to **begin** our lesson on the continents," said Ms. Haynes.
   Answer should include "quit."
4. "That's strange. The stapler decided to **appear** all of a sudden," said Mr. Jonson.
   Answer should include "vanish."
5. The doctor said this new medicine should **prevent** colds.
   Answer should include "help."
6. "She is our **enemy**, boys, we can't let her in our clubhouse!" cried Paul.
   Answer should include "friend."
7. I'm certain that dark cave is full of **danger**!
   Answer should include "safety."
8. Give me a chance to make the situation **better**.
   Answer should include "worse."

Page 22

Vocabulary: Homophones

Homophones are two words that sound the same, have different meanings and are usually spelled differently.
Example: write and **right**

Directions: Write the correct homophone in each sentence below.

weight — how heavy something is
wait — to be patient

threw — tossed
through — passing between

steal — to take something that doesn't belong to you
steel — a heavy metal

1. The bands marched **through** the streets lined with many cheering people.
2. **Wait** for me by the flagpole.
3. One of our strict rules at school is: Never **steal** from another person.
4. Could you estimate the **weight** of this bowling ball?
5. The bleachers have **steel** rods on both ends and in the middle.
6. He walked in the door and **threw** his jacket down.

Page 23

Vocabulary: Homophones

Directions: Write the correct homophone in each sentence below.

cent — a coin having the value of one penny
scent — odor or aroma

chews — grinds with the teeth
choose — to select

course — the path along which something moves
coarse — rough in texture

heard — received sounds in the ear
herd — a group of animals

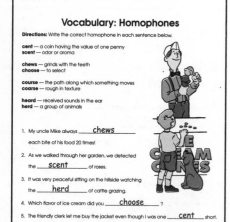

1. My uncle Mike always __chews__ each bite of his food 20 times!

2. As we walked through her garden, we detected the __scent__ of roses.

3. It was very peaceful sitting on the hillside watching the __herd__ of cattle grazing.

4. Which flavor of ice cream did you __choose__ ?

5. The friendly clerk let me buy the jacket even though I was one __cent__ short.

6. You will need __coarse__ sandpaper to make the wood smoother.

Page 24

Vocabulary: Prefixes

A **prefix** is a syllable at the beginning of a word that changes its meaning.

Directions: Add a prefix to the beginning of each word in the box to make a word with the meaning given in each sentence below. The first one is done for you.

PREFIX	MEANING
bi	two or twice
en	to make
in	within
mis	wrong
non	not or without
pre	before
re	again
un	not

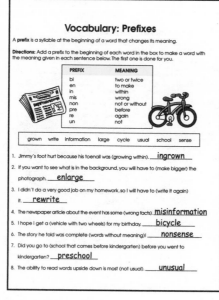

grown   write   information   large   cycle   usual   school   sense

1. Jimmy's foot hurt because his toenail was (growing within). __ingrown__

2. If you want to see what is in the background, you will have to (make bigger) the photograph. __enlarge__

3. I didn't do a very good job on my homework, so I will have to (write it again) it. __rewrite__

4. The newspaper article about the event has some (wrong facts). __misinformation__

5. I hope I get a (vehicle with two wheels) for my birthday. __bicycle__

6. The story he told was complete (words without meaning)! __nonsense__

7. Did you go to (school that comes before kindergarten) before you went to kindergarten? __preschool__

8. The ability to read words upside down is most (not usual). __unusual__

Page 25

Vocabulary: Prefixes

Directions: Circle the correct word for each sentence.

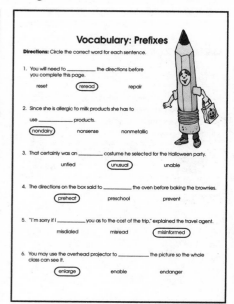

1. You will need to _____ the directions before you complete this page.
   reset   (reread)   repair

2. Since she is allergic to milk products she has to use _____ products.
   (nondairy)   nonsense   nonmetallic

3. That certainly was an _____ costume he selected for the Halloween party.
   untied   (unusual)   unable

4. The directions on the box said to _____ the oven before baking the brownies.
   (preheat)   preschool   prevent

5. "I'm sorry if I _____ you as to the cost of the trip," explained the travel agent.
   misdialed   misread   (misinformed)

6. You may use the overhead projector to _____ the picture so the whole class can see it.
   (enlarge)   enable   endanger

Page 26

Vocabulary: Suffixes

A **suffix** is a syllable at the end of a word that changes its meaning. most cases, when adding a suffix that begins with a vowel, drop the final **e** of the root wo. For example, **fame** becomes **famous**. Also, change a final y in the root word to i bet adding any suffix except **ing**. For example, **silly** becomes **silliness**.

Directions: Add a suffix to the end of each word in the box to make a wor. the meaning given (in parentheses) in each sentence below. The first one is don for you.

SUFFIX	MEANING
ful	full of
ity	quality or degree
ive	have or tend to be
less	without or lacking
able	able to be
ness	state of
ment	act of
or	person that does something
ward	in the direction of

effect   like   thought   pay   beauty   thank   back   act   happy

1. Mike was (full of thanks) for a hot meal. __thankful__

2. I was (without thinking) for forgetting your birthday. __thoughtless__

3. The mouse trap we put out doesn't seem to be (have an effect). __effective__

4. In spring, the flower garden is (full of beauty). __beautiful__

5. Sally is such a (able to be liked) girl! __likable__

6. Tim fell over (in the direction of the back) because he wasn't watching where he was going. __backward__

7. Jill's wedding day was one of great (the state of being happy). __happiness__

8. The (person who performs) was very good in the play. __actor__

9. I have to make a (act of paying) for the stereo I bought. __payment__

Page 27

Vocabulary: Suffixes

Directions: Read the story. Choose the correct word from the box to complete the sentences.

beautiful   colorful   payment
breakable   careful   backward
careless   director   agreement
basement   forward   firmness

Colleen and Marj carried the boxes down to the __basement__ apartment. "Be __careful__ with those," cautioned Colleen's mother. "All the things in that box are __breakable__." As soon as the two girls helped carry all the boxes from the moving van down the stairs, they would be able to go to school for the play tryouts. That was the __agreement__ made with Colleen's mother earlier that day.

"It won't do any good to get __careless__ with your work. Just keep at it and the job will be done quickly," she spoke with a __firmness__ in her voice.

"It's hard to see where I'm going when I have to walk __backward__," groaned M   "Can we switch places with the next box?"

   een agreed to switch places, but they soon discovered that the last two boxes were   weight. Each girl had her own box to carry, so each of them got to walk looking fo __forward__. "These are so light," remarked Marj. "What's in them?"

"These   e the __beautiful__ __colorful__ hats I was telling you about. We ca   ke them to the play tryouts with us," answered Colleen. "I bet we'll impress the __director__. Even if we don't get parts in the play, I bet our hats will!"

Colleen's moth   nded each of the girls a 5-dollar bill. "I really appreciate your help. Will this be enough?"

"Thanks, Mom. You   " Colleen shouted as the girls ran down the sidewalk.

Page 28

Reading Skills: Classifying

Classifying is placing similar things into categories.

Directions: Classify each group by crossing out the word that does not belong.

1. factory   hotel   lodge   ~~pattern~~

2. ~~Thursday~~   September   December   October

3. cottage   hut   ca~~rpenter~~   castle

4. cupboard   or~~chard~~   refrigerator   stove

5. Christmas   Thanksgiving   Easter   s~~pring~~

6. brass   copper   ~~clay~~   tin

7. stomach   br~~eathe~~   liver   brain

8. teacher   mother   dentist   ~~nurse~~

9. m~~arket~~   faucet   bathtub   sink

10. basement   attic   kitchen   neigh~~borhood~~

Page 29

Reading Skills: Classifying

Directions: Complete each idea by crossing out the word or phrase that does not belong.

1. If the main idea is **things that are green,** I don't need:

~~the sun~~   apples   grass   leaves in summer

2. If the idea is **musical instruments,** I don't need a:

piano   trombone   ~~baseball~~   tuba

3. If the idea is **months of the year,** I don't need:

~~Friday~~   January   July   October

4. If the idea is **colors on the U.S. flag,** I don't need:

white   blue   ~~black~~   red

5. If the idea is **types of weather,** I don't need:

sleet   stormy   ~~roses~~   sunny

6. If the idea is **fruits,** I don't need:

kiwi   orange   ~~spinach~~   banana

7. If the idea is **U.S. presidents,** I don't need:

Lincoln   ~~Jordan~~   Washington   Adams

8. If the idea is **flowers,** I don't need:

~~rose~~   daisy   tulip   daffodil

9. If the idea is **sports,** I don't need:

~~pears~~   soccer   wrestling   baseball

Page 30

Reading Skills: Analogies

An **analogy** indicates how different items go together or are similar in some way.

Examples:
Petal is to **flower** as **leaf** is to **tree.**
Book is to **library** as **food** is to **grocery.**

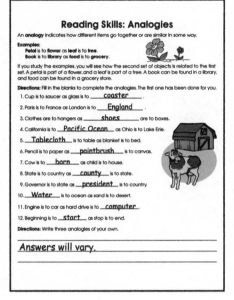

If you study the examples, you will see how the second set of objects is related to the first set. A petal is part of a flower, and a leaf is part of a tree. A book can be found in a library, and food can be found in a grocery store.

Directions: Fill in the blanks to complete the analogies. The first one has been done for you.

1. Cup is to saucer as glass is to ___coaster___.

2. Paris is to France as London is to ___England___.

3. Clothes are to hangers as ___shoes___ are to boxes.

4. California is to ___Pacific Ocean___ as Ohio is to Lake Erie.

5. ___Tablecloth___ is to table as blanket is to bed.

6. Pencil is to paper as ___paintbrush___ is to canvas.

7. Cow is to ___barn___ as child is to house.

8. State is to country as ___county___ is to state.

9. Governor is to state as ___president___ is to country.

10. ___Water___ is to ocean as sand is to desert.

11. Engine is to car as hard drive is to ___computer___.

12. Beginning is to ___start___ as stop is to end.

Directions: Write three analogies of your own.

___Answers will vary.___

Page 31

Reading Skills: Analogies

Directions: Write a word from the box to complete the following analogies.

fence	club	glove	saw	father
blanket	dish	rug	snow	ten
compass	hat	brake	finger	blue

1. Racket is to tennis as ___club___ is to golf.

2. Glass is to drink as ___dish___ is to eat.

3. Wheel is to steer as ___brake___ is to stop.

4. Roof is to house as ___rug___ is to floor.

5. Rain is to storm as ___snow___ is to blizzard.

6. Clock is to time as ___compass___ is to directions.

7. Lid is to pan as ___hat___ is to head.

8. Hammer is to pound as ___saw___ is to cut.

9. Mother is to daughter as ___father___ is to son.

10. Shoe is to foot as ___glove___ is to hand.

11. Five is to ten as ___ten___ is to twenty.

12. Shade is to lamp as ___blanket___ is to bed.

13. Toe is to foot as ___finger___ is to hand.

14. Frame is to picture as ___fence___ is to yard.

15. Green is to grass as ___blue___ is to sky.

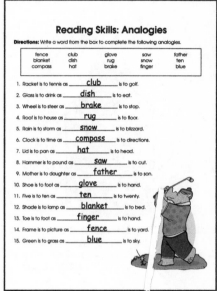

Page 32

Following Directions: Maps

Directions: Follow the directions below to reach a "mystery" location on the map.
1. Begin at home.
2. Drive east on River Road.
3. Turn south on Broadway.
4. Drive to Central Street and turn west.
5. When you get to City Street, turn south.
6. Turn east on Main Street and drive one block to Park Avenue; turn north.
7. At Central Street turn east, then turn southeast on Through Way.
8. Drive to the end of Through Way. Your "mystery" location is to the east.

You are at the ___school___.

Can you write an easier way to get back home?

___

| Answers will vary. |

Page 33

Following Directions: Recipes

Sequencing is putting items or events in logical order.

Directions: Read the recipe. Then number the steps in order for making brownies.

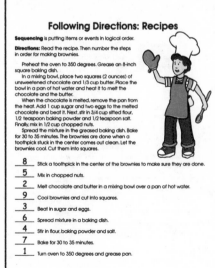

Preheat the oven to 350 degrees. Grease an 8-inch square baking dish.

In a mixing bowl, place two squares (2 ounces) of unsweetened chocolate and 1/3 cup butter. Place the bowl in a pan of hot water and heat it to melt the chocolate and the butter.

When the chocolate is melted, remove the pan from the heat. Add 1 cup sugar and two eggs to the melted chocolate and beat it. Next, stir in 3/4 cup sifted flour, 1/2 teaspoon baking powder and 1/2 teaspoon salt. Finally, mix in 1/2 cup chopped nuts.

Spread the mixture in the greased baking dish. Bake for 30 to 35 minutes. The brownies are done when a toothpick stuck in the center comes out clean. Let the brownies cool. Cut them into squares.

__8__ Stick a toothpick in the center of the brownies to make sure they are done.

__5__ Mix in chopped nuts.

__2__ Melt chocolate and butter in a mixing bowl over a pan of hot water.

__9__ Cool brownies and cut into squares.

__3__ Beat in sugar and eggs.

__6__ Spread mixture in a baking dish.

__4__ Stir in flour, baking powder and salt.

__7__ Bake for 30 to 35 minutes.

__1__ Turn oven to 350 degrees and grease pan.

Page 34

Reading Skills: Bus Schedules

Schedules are important to our daily lives. Your parents' jobs, school, even watching television—all are based on schedules. When you travel, you probably follow a schedule, too. Most forms of public transportation, such as subways, buses and trains, run on schedules. These "timetables" tell passengers when they will leave each stop or station.

Directions: Use the following city bus schedule to answer the questions.

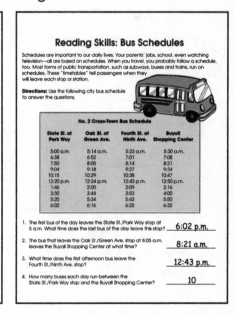

No. 2 Cross-Town Bus Schedule			
State St. at Park Way	**Oak St. at Green Ave.**	**Fourth St. at Ninth Ave.**	**Buyall Shopping Center**
5:00 a.m.	5:14 a.m.	5:23 a.m.	5:30 a.m.
6:38	6:52	7:01	7:08
7:50	8:05	8:14	8:21
9:04	9:18	9:27	9:34
10:15	10:29	10:38	10:47
12:20 p.m.	12:34 p.m.	12:43 p.m.	12:50 p.m.
1:46	2:00	2:09	2:16
3:30	3:44	3:53	4:00
5:20	5:34	5:43	5:50
6:02	6:16	6:25	6:32

1. The first bus of the day leaves the State St./Park Way stop at 5 a.m. What time does the last bus of the day leave this stop? ___6:02 p.m.___

2. The bus that leaves the Oak St./Green Ave. stop at 8:05 a.m. leaves the Buyall Shopping Center at what time? ___8:21 a.m.___

3. What time does the first afternoon bus leave the Fourth St./Ninth Ave. stop? ___12:43 p.m.___

4. How many buses each day run between the State St./Park Way stop and the Buyall Shopping Center? ___10___

Page 35

Reading Skills: Labels

Directions: You should never take any medicine without your parents' permission, but it is good to know how to read the label of a medicine bottle. Read the label to answer the questions.

Children's Cold Relief
Sneezing and Runny Nose Formula

For relief of runny nose and sneezing due to common cold, hay fever or other allergies.

Dosage:
Children under 2 years, only as directed by a physician.

Children 2 to 6 years old, 1 teaspoon.

Children 6 to 11 years old, 2 teaspoons.

All doses may be repeated every 4 to 6 hours. Do not give more than four doses every day.

Warning: May cause dizziness in some. Do not give to children with heart disease. Keep this and all medicines out of reach of children.

1. How much medicine should a 5-year-old take? __1 teaspoon__
2. How often can this medicine be taken? __every 4 to 6 hours__
3. How do you know how much medicine to give a 1-year-old? __ask a physician__
4. Who should not take this medicine? __children with heart disease__

Page 36

Reading Skills: Advertisements

Directions: Use the following newspaper ad to answer the questions.

New-Look Fashions

Final Week!
Spring Suit Sale

Buy one suit at the regular price and get a second one for only $50!

Suits: From $75 to $150

New-Look Fashions
5290 Main Street

Hours: Monday–Friday 10–7; Saturday 10–6;
Closed Sunday

1. What is the regular price for a suit? __$75 to $150__
2. If you buy one suit at the regular price, what is the price for a second one? __$50__
3. What day is the store closed? __Sunday__
4. What hours is the store open on Wednesday? __between 10 a.m. and 7 p.m.__
5. When is the sale? __this week__

Page 37

Reading Skills: Facts and Opinions

Facts are statements or events that have happened and can be proven to be true.

Example: George Washington was the first president of the United States.
This statement is a fact. It can be proven to be true by researching the history of our country.

Opinions are statements that express how someone thinks or feels.

Example: George Washington was the greatest president the United States has ever had. This statement is an opinion. Many people agree that George Washington was a great president, but not everyone agrees he was the greatest president. In some people's opinion, Abraham Lincoln was our greatest president.

Directions: Read each sentence. Write F for fact or O for opinion.

__F__ 1. There is three feet of snow on the ground.
__O__ 2. A lot of snow makes the winter enjoyable.
__O__ 3. Chris has a better swing set than Mary.
__F__ 4. Both Chris and Mary have swing sets.
__F__ 5. California is a state.
__O__ 6. California is the best state in the west.

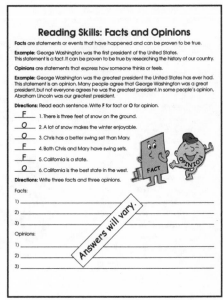

Directions: Write three facts and three opinions.

Facts:
1) _____
2) _____
3) _____

Opinions:
1) _____
2) _____
3) _____

Answers will vary.

Page 38

Reading Skills: Facts and Opinions

Directions: Write **F** before the facts and **O** before the opinions.

__F__ 1. Our school football team has a winning season this year.
__O__ 2. Mom's spaghetti is the best in the world!
__O__ 3. Autumn is the nicest season of the year.
__F__ 4. Mrs. Burns took her class on a field trip last Thursday.
__F__ 5. The library always puts 30 books in our classroom book collection.
__O__ 6. They should put only books about horses in the collection.
__O__ 7. Our new art teacher is very strict.
__O__ 8. Everyone should keep take-home papers in a folder so they don't have to look for them when it is time to go home.
__F__ 9. The bus to the mall goes right by her house at 7:45 a.m.
__O__ 10. Our new superintendent, Mr. Willeke, is very nice.

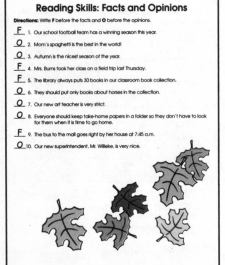

Page 39

Reading Skills: Context Clues

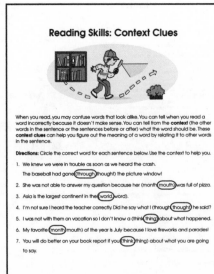

When you read, you may confuse words that look alike. You can tell when you read a word incorrectly because it doesn't make sense. You can tell from the **context** (the other words in the sentence or the sentences before or after) what the word should be. These **context clues** can help you figure out the meaning of a word by relating it to other words in the sentence.

Directions: Circle the correct word for each sentence below. Use the context to help you.

1. We knew we were in trouble as soon as we heard the crash.
   The baseball had gone (**through**/thought) the picture window!
2. She was not able to answer my question because her (month/**mouth**) was full of pizza.
3. Asia is the largest continent in the (**world**/word).
4. I'm not sure I heard the teacher correctly. Did he say what I (through/**thought**) he said?
5. I was not with them on vacation so I don't know a (think/**thing**) about what happened.
6. My favorite (month/**mouth**) of the year is July because I love fireworks and parades!
7. You will do better on your book report if you (**think**/thing) about what you are going to say.

Page 40

Reading Skills: Context Clues

Directions: Read each sentence carefully and circle the word that makes sense.

1. We didn't (except/**expect**) you to arrive so early.
2. "I can't hear a (**word**/world) you are saying. Wait until I turn down the stereo," said Val.
3. I couldn't sleep last night because of the (**noise**/nose) from the apartment below us.
4. Did Peggy say (weather/**whether**) or not we needed our binoculars for the game?
5. He broke his (noise/**nose**) when he fell off the bicycle.
6. All the students (**except**/expect) the four in the front row are excused to leave.
7. The teacher said we should have good (whether/**weather**) for our field trip.

Context Clues

Directions: Choose a word pair from the sentences above. Write two sentences of your own.

1. _____
2. _____

Answers will vary.

Page 41

Reading Skills: Context Clues

Directions: Use context clues to help you choose the correct word for each sentence below.

designs	studying	collection

Our fourth-grade class will be **studying** castles for the next four weeks. Mrs. Oswalt will be helping with our study. She plans to share her **collection** of castle models with the class. We are all looking forward to our morning in the sand at the school's volleyball court. We all get to try our own **designs** to see how they work.

breath	excited	quietly

Michelle was very **excited** the other day when she came into the classroom. We all noticed that she had trouble sitting **quietly** in her seat until it was her turn to share with us. When her turn finally came, she took a deep **breath** and told us that her mom was going to have a baby!

responsibility	chooses	messages

Each week, our teacher **chooses** classroom helpers. They get to be part of the Job Squad. Some helpers have the **responsibility** of watering the plants. Everyone's favorite job is when they get to take **messages** to the office or to another teacher's room.

Page 42

Reading Skills: Sequencing

Directions: Read each set of events. Then number them in the correct order.

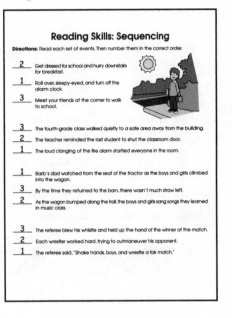

2 Get dressed for school and hurry downstairs for breakfast.
1 Roll over, sleepy-eyed, and turn off the alarm clock.
3 Meet your friends at the corner to walk to school.

3 The fourth-grade class walked quietly to a safe area away from the building.
2 The teacher reminded the last student to shut the classroom door.
1 The loud clanging of the fire alarm startled everyone in the room.

1 Barb's dad watched from the seat of the tractor as the boys and girls climbed into the wagon.
3 By the time they returned to the barn, there wasn't much straw left.
2 As the wagon bumped along the trail, the boys and girls sang songs they learned in music class.

3 The referee blew his whistle and held up the hand of the winner of the match.
2 Each wrestler worked hard, trying to outmaneuver his opponent.
1 The referee said, "Shake hands, boys, and wrestle a fair match."

Page 43

Reading Skills: Sequencing

Directions: In each group below, one event in the sequence is missing. Write the correct sentence from the box where it belongs.

- Paul put his bait on the hook and cast out into the pond.
- "Sorry," he said, "but the TV repairman can't get here until Friday."
- Everyone pitched in and helped.
- Corey put the ladder up against the trunk of the tree.

1. "All the housework has to be done before anyone goes to the game," said Mom.
2. **Everyone pitched in and helped.**
3. We all agreed that "many hands make light work."

1. **Paul put his bait on the hook and cast out into the pond.**
2. It wasn't long until he felt a tug on the line, and we watched the bobber go under.
3. He was the only one to go home with something other than bait!

1. The little girl cried as she stood looking up into the maple tree.
2. Between her tears, she managed to say, "My kitten is up in the tree and can't get down."
3. **Corey put the ladder up against the trunk of the tree.**

1. Dad hung up the phone and turned to look at us.
2. **"Sorry," he said, "but the TV repairman can't get here until Friday."**
3. "This would be a good time to get out those old board games in the hall closet," he said.

Page 44

Reading Skills: Main Idea in Sentences

The **main idea** is the most important idea, or main point, in a sentence, paragraph or story.

Directions: Circle the main idea for each sentence.

1. Emily knew she would be late if she watched the end of the TV show.
   a. Emily likes watching TV.
   b. Emily is always running late.
   c. If Emily didn't leave, she would be late.

2. The dog was too strong and pulled Jason across the park on his leash.
   a. The dog is stronger than Jason.
   b. Jason is not very strong.
   c. Jason took the dog for a walk.

3. Jennifer took the book home so she could read it over and over.
   a. Jennifer loves to read.
   b. Jennifer loves the book.
   c. Jennifer is a good reader.

4. Jerome threw the baseball so hard it broke the window.
   a. Jerome throws baseballs very hard.
   b. Jerome was mad at the window.
   c. Jerome can't throw very straight.

5. Lori came home and decided to clean the kitchen for her parents.
   a. Lori is a very nice person.
   b. Lori did a favor for her parents.
   c. Lori likes to cook.

6. It was raining so hard that it was hard to see the road through the windshield.
   a. It always rains hard in April.
   b. The rain blurred our vision.
   c. It's hard to drive in the rain.

Page 45

Reading Skills: Main Idea in Paragraphs

Directions: Read each paragraph below. Then circle the sentence that tells the main idea.

It looked as if our class field day would have to be cancelled due to the weather. We tried not to show our disappointment, but Mr. Wade knew that it was hard to keep our minds on the math lesson. We noticed that even he had been sneaking glances out the window. All morning the classroom had been buzzing with plans. Each team met to plan team strategies for winning the events. Then, it happened! Clouds began to cover the sky, and soon the thunder and lightning confirmed what we were afraid of—field day was cancelled. Mr. Wade explained that we could still keep our same teams. We could put all of our plans into motion, but we would have to get busy and come up with some inside games and competitions. I guess the day would not be a total disaster!

a. Many storms occur in the late afternoon.
b. Our class field day had to be cancelled due to the weather.
c. Each team came up with its own strategies.

Allison and Emma had to work quietly and quickly to get Mom's birthday cake baked before she got home from work. Each of the girls had certain jobs to do—Allison set the oven temperature and got the cake pans prepared, while Emma got out all the ingredients. As they stirred and mixed, the two girls talked about the surprise party Dad had planned for Mom. Even Dad didn't know that the girls were baking this special cake. The cake was delicious. "It shows you what teamwork can do!" said the girls in unison.

a. Dad worked with the girls to bake the cake.
b. Mom's favorite frosting is chocolate cream.
c. Allison and Emma baked a birthday cake for Mom.

Page 46

Main Idea: Busy Beavers

Directions: Read about busy beavers. Then answer the questions.

Has anyone ever told you that you are as busy as a beaver? If they have, then they mean that you are very busy. Beavers swim easily in streams, picking up rocks and sticks to build their dams. They gnaw at trees with their big front teeth to cut them down. Then they use parts of the trees to build their houses.

Beavers are clever builders. They know exactly what they need to build their beaver dams. They use mud from the stream to make their dams stay together. They use their tails to pat down the mud.

Beavers put a snug room at the top of their dams for their babies. They store their food underwater. Beavers eat the bark from the trees that they cut down!

1. What is the main idea of the first paragraph? __Beavers are very busy.__

2. What is the main idea of the second paragraph? __Beavers are clever builders.__

3. What is the main idea of the third paragraph? __Beavers' homes provide a snug place for their babies and a place to store food.__

4. What do beavers use for their dams? __sticks, rocks, trees and mud__

5. What parts of their bodies do beavers use to build their homes? __They use their teeth to cut down trees and their tails to pat down mud.__

Page 47

Main Idea: Bats

Directions: Read about bats. Then answer the questions.

Bats are unusual animals. Even though they fly, they are not birds. A bat's body is covered with fur. Its wings are made of skin. Bats do not have any feathers.

Bats are the only mammals that fly. A mammal is an animal that has hair and feeds its babies with its own milk. Humans are mammals, too. Mother bats have one or two babies each spring. Baby bats hang onto their mothers until they learn to fly by themselves.

Bats can be many different colors. Most are brown, but some are black, orange, gray or even green.

Even though many people do not like bats, bats don't usually bother people. Only vampire bats, which live in hot jungles, are very dangerous. Bats in the United States help people. Every year they eat billions and billions of harmful insects! Some bats also eat fruit or pollen from flowers.

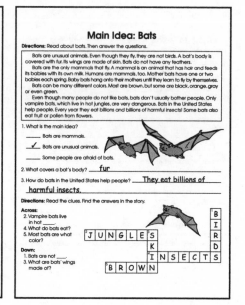

1. What is the main idea?
___ Bats are mammals.
_✓_ Bats are unusual animals.
___ Some people are afraid of bats.

2. What covers a bat's body? __fur__

3. How do bats in the United States help people? __They eat billions of harmful insects.__

Directions: Read the clues. Find the answers in the story.

Across:
2. Vampire bats live in hot ____.
4. What do bats eat?
5. Most bats are what color?

Down:
1. Bats are not ____.
3. What are bats' wings made of?

Crossword:
J U N G L E S / B I R D / S K I N / I N S E C T S / B R O W N

Page 48

Recognizing Details: Blind Bats

Directions: Read about bats. Then answer the questions.

Bats sleep all day because they cannot see well in the bright sunlight. They hang upside down in dark places such as barns, caves or hollow trees. As soon as darkness begins to fall, bats wake up. They fly around easily and quickly at night.

Bats make sounds that help them fly, since they cannot see well. People cannot hear these sounds. When bats make sounds, the sounds hit objects in front of them and bounce back at them. Bats can tell if something is in their way because there is an echo. Some people say this is like a radar system!

There are many different kinds of bats. Some bats fly all night, while others fly only in the evening or the early morning.

Most bats eat mosquitoes and moths, but there are some bats that will catch fish swimming in water and eat them. Still other kinds of bats eat birds or mice. Bats that live in very hot areas eat only some parts of flowers.

Bats that live in cold areas of the country sometimes sleep all winter. That means they hibernate. Other bats that live in cold areas fly to warmer places for the winter. We call this migration.

1. Who cannot hear the sounds bats make? __people__

2. Why do bats sleep all day? __They cannot see well in bright sunlight.__

3. When do bats eat? __at night__

4. Where do bats that eat only parts of flowers live? __in very hot areas__

5. Why do bats make sounds? __to tell if something is in their way__

6. What does **hibernate** mean? __to sleep all winter__

7. What is the main idea of this selection? __Bats are active at night because they cannot see well in bright sunlight.__

8. Do you think a bat would make a good pet? Why or why not? __Answers will vary.__

Page 51

Reading Skills: Sequencing

Directions: Reread the story, if necessary. Then choose an important event from the beginning, middle and end of the story, and write it below.

Beginning:

Middle: Answers will vary.

End:

Directions: Number these story events in the order in which they happened.

_4_ Paul moaned, "Oh, no! I left my lunch on the table at home!"

_1_ Megan watched as the bus stopped at Emily's house to pick up Emily and her little sister.

_5_ Miss Haynes sent Paul to the cafeteria with a note explaining the problem.

_3_ The teacher said they had some business to take care of before they could leave on the trip.

_6_ Paul quickly returned with a sack lunch packed by the cafeteria helpers.

_2_ Megan told Emily, "I see you remembered your sack lunch."

_7_ The fourth graders finally loaded onto the bus for the field trip.

Page 52

Reading Skills: Recalling Details

Directions: Answer the questions below about "Class Field Trip."

1. Who were the two adult helpers that would be going on the trip with Miss Haynes' class? __Ms. Diehl and Mrs. Denes__

2. The students in Miss Haynes' class were excited about the field trip for different reasons. What were the three different reasons mentioned in the story?
a. __They got to ride the bus.__
b. __They enjoyed learning about their town's history.__
c. __They got a day out of school.__

3. What business did Miss Haynes need to take care of before the class could leave on its trip? __Check attendance and pass out name tags.__

Directions: Write the letter of the definition beside the word it defines. If you need help, use a dictionary or check the context of the story.

a. sat down, not very gently
b. easy to understand; without doubt
c. family members that lived in the past, such as grandparents
d. in a favorable way

_C_ ancestors
_D_ fortunately
_A_ plopped
_B_ obviously

Page 54

Comprehension: "The Princess and the Pea"

Fairy tales are short stories written for children involving magical characters.

Directions: Read the story. Then answer the questions.

Once there was a prince who wanted to get married. The catch was, he had to marry a *real* princess. The Prince knew that real princesses were few and far between. When they heard he was looking for a bride, many young women came to the palace. All claimed to be real princesses.

"Hmmm," thought the Prince. "I must think of a way to sort out the real princesses from the fake ones. I will ask the Queen for advice."

Luckily, since he was a prince, the Queen was also his mother. So of course she had her son's best interests at heart. "A real princess is very delicate," said the Queen. "She must sleep on a mattress as soft as a cloud. If there is even a small lump, she will not be able to sleep."

"Why not?" asked the Prince. He was a nice man but not as smart as his mother.

"Because she is so delicate!" said the Queen impatiently. "Let's figure out a way to test her. Better still, let me figure out a test. You go down and pick a girl to try out my plan."

The Prince went down to the lobby of the castle. A very pretty but humble-looking girl caught his eye. He brought her back to his mother, who welcomed her.

"Please be our guest at the castle tonight," said the Queen. "Tomorrow we will talk with you about whether you are a real princess."

The pretty but humble girl was shown to her room. In it was a pile of five mattresses, all fluffy and clean. "A princess is delicate," said the Queen. "Sweet dreams!"

The girl climbed to the top of the pile and laid down, but she could not sleep. She tossed and turned and was quite cross the next morning.

"I found this under the fourth mattress when I got up this morning," she said. She handed a small green pea to the Queen. "No wonder I couldn't sleep!"

The Queen clapped her hands. The Prince looked confused. "A real princess is delicate. If this pea I put under the mattress kept you awake, you are definitely a princess."

"Of course I am," said the Princess. "Now may I please take a nap?"

1. Why does the Prince worry about finding a bride? __His bride must be a real princess and real princesses are hard to find.__

2. According to the Queen, how can the Prince tell who is a real princess? __A real princess is very delicate.__

3. Who hides something under the girl's mattress? __the Queen__

Page 55

Comprehension: "The Princess and the Pea"

Directions: Review the story "The Princess and the Pea." Then answer the questions.

1. Why does the Prince need a test to see who is a real princess?
__Many young women wanted to marry him, but the Prince could only marry a "real" princess.__

2. Why does the Princess have trouble sleeping? __There was a pea under her mattress.__

3. In this story, the Queen puts a small pea under a pile of mattresses to see if the girl is delicate. What else could be done to test a princess for delicacy?

The story does not tell whether or not the Prince ~~married~~ and live happily ever after, only that the Princess ~~took~~ a nap.

Directions: Write a new ending to the ~~story~~.
4. What do you think happens aft~~er~~?

Answers will vary.

Page 56

Comprehension: "The Frog Prince"

Directions: Read the story "The Frog Prince." Then answer the questions.

Once upon a time, there lived a beautiful princess who liked to play alone in the woods. One day, as she was playing with her golden ball, it rolled into a lake. The water was so deep she could not see the ball. The Princess was very sad. She cried out, "I would give anything to have my golden ball back!"

Suddenly, a large ugly frog popped out of the water. "Anything?" he croaked. The Princess looked at him with distaste. "Yes," she said, "I would give anything."

"I will get your golden ball," said the frog. "In return, you must take me back to the castle. You must let me live with you and eat from your golden plate."

"Whatever you want," said the Princess. She thought the frog was very ugly, but she wanted her golden ball.

The frog dove down and brought the ball to the Princess. She put the frog in her pocket and took him home. "He is ugly," the Princess said. "But a promise is a promise. And a princess always keeps her word."

The Princess changed her clothes and forgot all about the frog. That evening, she heard a tapping at her door. She ran to the door to open it and a handsome prince stepped in.

"Who are you?" asked the Princess.

"I am the prince you rescued at the lake," said the handsome Prince. "I was turned into a frog one hundred years ago today by a wicked lady. Because they value keeping their promises, only a beautiful princess could break the spell. You are a little forgetful, but you did keep your word!"

Can you guess what happened next? Of course, they were married and lived happily ever after.

1. What does the frog ask the Princess to promise? __to take him back to the castle, let him live with her and eat from her golden plate__

2. Where does the Princess put the frog when she leaves the lake? __in her pocket__

3. Why could only a princess break the spell? __Because they always keep their promises.__

Page 57

Comprehension: "The Frog Prince"

Directions: Review the story "The Frog Prince." Then answer the questions.

1. What does the Princess lose in the lake? __a golden ball__

2. How does she get it back? __A frog dove to the bottom of the lake and got it for her in return for a promise from the Princess.__

3. How does the frog turn back into a prince? __The spell is broken when the Princess keeps her word.__

4. What phrases are used to begin and end this story? __"once upon a time" and "happily ever after"__

5. Are these words used frequently to begin and end fairy tales? __yes__

There is more than one version of most fairy tales. In another version of this story, the Princess has to kiss the frog in order for him to change back into a prince.

Directions: Write your answers.

6. What do you think would happen in a story ~~if the~~ Princess kisses the frog, but he remains a ~~frog?~~

7. What kinds of problems ~~might there b~~e with a bossy frog in the castle? Brainstorm ideas and write them ~~down.~~

8. Rewrite the ~~story "Th~~e Frog Prince" so that the frog remains a frog and does not tur~~n~~ into a handsom~~e prin~~ce. Continue your story on another sheet of paper.

Answers will vary.

Page 58

Main Idea: "The Hare and the Tortoise"

The story of "The Hare and the Tortoise" is called a **fable**. Fables are usually short stories. As you read this story and the other fables on the next few pages, look for two characteristics the fables have in common.

Directions: Read the fable "The Hare and the Tortoise." Then answer the questions.

One day the hare and the tortoise were talking. Or rather, the hare was bragging and the tortoise was listening.

"I am faster than the wind," bragged the hare. "I feel sorry for you because you are so slow! Why, you are the slowest fellow I have ever seen."

"Do you think so?" asked the tortoise with a smile. "I will race you to that big tree across the field."

Slowly, he lifted a leg. Slowly, he pointed toward the tree.

"Ha!" scoffed the hare. "You must be kidding! You will most certainly be the loser! But, if you insist, we will race."

The tortoise nodded politely. "I'll be off," he said. Slowly and steadily, the tortoise moved across the field.

The hare stood back and laughed. "How sad that he should compete with me!" he said. His chest puffed up with pride. "I will take a little nap while the poor old tortoise lumbers along. When I wake up, he will still be only halfway across the field."

The tortoise kept on, slow and steady, across the field. Some time later, the hare awoke. He discovered that while he slept, the tortoise had won the race.

1. What is the main idea? (Check one.)
____ Tortoises are faster than hares.
____ Hares need more sleep than tortoises.
__✓__ Slow and steady wins the race.

2. The hare brags that he is faster than what? (Check one.)
____ a bullet
____ a greyhound
__✓__ the wind

3. Who is modest, the tortoise or the hare? __the tortoise__

Page 59

Cause and Effect: "The Hare and the Tortoise"

Another important skill in reading is recognizing cause and effect. The **cause** is the reason something happens. The **effect** is what happens or the situation that results from the cause. In the story, the hare falling asleep is a cause. It causes the hare to lose the race. Losing the race is the effect.

Directions: Identify the underlined words or phrases by writing **cause** or **effect** in the blanks.

1. The hare and tortoise had a race because the hare bragged about being faster. — **effect**

2. The tortoise won the race because he continued on, slowly, but steadily. — **cause**

Directions: Review the fable "The Hare and the Tortoise." Then answer the questions.

1. Who are the two main characters? **hare and tortoise**

2. Where does the story take place? **in a field with trees**

3. What lessons can be learned from this story? **slow and steady wins the race, people shouldn't brag**

4. The lesson that is learned at the end of a fable has a special name. What is that special name? **moral**

5. Why did the tortoise want to race the hare? **to prove that he could beat the hare**

6. How do you think the hare felt at the end of the story? _Answers will vary._

7. How do you think the tortoise felt at the e... _Answers will vary._

Page 60

Sequencing: "The Fox and the Crow"

Directions: Read the fable "The Fox and the Crow." Then number the events in order.

Once upon a time, a crow found a piece of cheese on the ground. "Aha!" he said to himself. "This dropped from a workman's sandwich. It will make a fine lunch for me."

The crow picked up the cheese in his beak. He flew to a tree to eat it. Just as he began to chew it, a fox trotted by.

"Hello, crow!" he said slyly, for he wanted the cheese. The fox knew if the crow answered, the cheese would fall from its mouth. Then the fox would have cheese for lunch!

The crow just nodded.

"It's a wonderful day, isn't it?" asked the fox.

The crow nodded again and held onto the cheese.

"You are the most beautiful bird I have ever seen," added the fox.

The crow spread his feathers. Everyone likes a compliment. Still, the crow held firmly to the cheese.

"There is something I have heard," said the fox, "and I wonder if it is true. I heard that you sing more sweetly than any of the other birds."

The crow was eager to show off his talents. He opened his beak to sing. The cheese dropped to the ground.

"I said you were beautiful," said the fox as he ran away with the cheese. "I did not say you were smart!"

7 The crow drops the cheese.

3 The crow flies to a tree with the cheese.

5 The fox tells the crow he is beautiful.

8 The fox runs off with the cheese.

1 A workman loses the cheese from his sandwich.

4 The fox comes along.

6 The fox tells the crow he has heard that crows sing beautifully.

2 The crow picks up the cheese.

Page 61

Predicting: "The Fox and the Crow"

Directions: Review the fable "The Fox and the Crow." Then answer the questions.

1. With what words does the story begin? **"Once upon a time"**

2. What other type of story often begins with these same words? **fairy tales**

3. Although it is not stated, where do you think the story takes place? **in a woods or forest**

4. How does the fox get what he wants from the crow? **The fox appealed to the crow's vanity by saying he heard that crows sing beautifully.**

5. How is the crow in this story like the hare in the last fable? **They are both proud, and when they bragged and tried to show off, they lost.**

Predicting is telling or guessing what you think might happen in a story or situation based on what you already know.

Directions: Write predictions to answer these questions.

6. Based on what you read, what do you think the crow will do the next time he finds a piece of cheese? _Answers will vary._

7. What do you think the fox... wants to trick the crow? _Answers will vary._

Page 62

Following Directions: "The Boy Who Cried Wolf"

Directions: Read the fable "The Boy Who Cried Wolf." Then complete the puzzle.

Once there was a shepherd boy who tended his sheep alone. Sheep are gentle animals. They are easy to take care of. The boy grew bored.

"I can't stand another minute alone with these sheep," he said crossly. He knew only one thing would bring people quickly to him. If he cried, "Wolf!" the men in the village would run up the mountain. They would come to help save the sheep from the wolf.

"Wolf!" he yelled loudly, and he blew on his horn.

Quick as a wink, a dozen men came running. When they realized it was a joke, they were very angry. The boy promised never to do it again. But a week later, he grew bored and cried, "Wolf!" again. Again, the men ran to him. This time they were very, very angry.

Soon afterwards, a wolf really came. The boy was scared. "Wolf!" he cried. "Wolf! Wolf! Wolf!"

He blew his horn, but no one came, and the wolf ate all his sheep.

Crossword puzzle:
M O U N T A I N (with V cross), S C (A T E), G E N T L E, E, R, E, D

Across:
2. This is where the boy tends sheep.
4. When no one came, the wolf ____ all the sheep.
5. Sheep are ____ and easy to take care of.

Down:
1. The people who come are from here.
2. At first, when the boy cries, "Wolf!" the ____ come running.
3. When a wolf really comes, this is how the boy feels.

Page 63

Cause and Effect: "The Boy Who Cried Wolf"

Directions: Identify the underlined words as a cause or an effect.

1. The boy cries wolf because he is bored. — **effect**

2. The boy blows his horn and the men come running. — **effect**

3. No one comes, and the wolf eats all the sheep. — **effect**

Directions: Answer the questions.

4. What lesson can be learned from this story? **Sample answer: Always tell the truth.**

5. How is this story like the two other fables you read?

6. Is the boy in the story more like the fox o...

Answers will vary.

Page 64

Reading Comprehension: Paul Bunyan

There is a certain kind of fable called a "tall tale." In these stories, each storyteller tries to "top" the other. The stories get more and more unbelievable. A popular hero of American tall tales is Paul Bunyan—a giant of a man. Here are some of the stories that have been told about him.

Even as a baby, Paul was very big. One night, he rolled over in his sleep and knocked down a mile of trees. Of course, Paul's father wanted to find some way to keep Paul from getting hurt in his sleep and to keep him from knocking down all the forests. So he cut down some tall trees and made a boat for Paul to use as a cradle. He tied a long rope to the boat and let it drift out a little way into the sea to rock Paul to sleep.

One night, Paul had trouble sleeping. He kept turning over in his bed. Each time he turned, the cradle rocked. And each time the cradle rocked, it sent up waves as big as buildings. The waves got bigger and bigger until the people on the land were afraid they would all be drowned. They told Paul's parents that Paul was a danger to the whole state! So Paul and his parents had to move away.

After that, Paul didn't get into much trouble when he was growing up. His father taught him some very important lessons, such as, "If there are any towns or farms in your way, be sure to step around them!"

Directions: Answer these questions about Paul Bunyan.

1. What kind of fable is the story of Paul Bunyan? **tall tale**

2. What did Paul's father make for Paul to use as a cradle? **boat**

3. What happened when Paul rolled over in his cradle? **He made waves as big as buildings.**

4. What did Paul's father tell Paul to do to towns and farms that were in his way? **Step around them!**

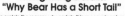

Page 65

Reading Comprehension: Paul Bunyan

When Paul Bunyan grew up, he was taller than other men—by about 50 feet or so! Because of his size, he could do almost anything. One of the things he did best was to cut down trees and turn them into lumber. With only four strokes of his axe, he could cut off all the branches and bark. After he turned all the trees for miles into these tall square posts, he tied a long rope to an axe head. Then he yelled, "T-I-M-B-E-R-R-R!" and swung the rope around in a huge circle. With every swing, 100 trees fell to the ground.

One cold winter day, Paul found a huge blue ox stuck in the snow. It was nearly frozen. Although it was only a baby, even Paul could hardly lift it. Paul took the ox home and cared for it. He named it Babe, and they became best friends. Babe was a big help to Paul when he was cutting down trees.

When Babe was full grown, it was hard to tell how big he was. There were no scales big enough to weigh him. Paul once measured the distance between Babe's eyes. It was the length of 42 axe handles!

Once Paul and Babe were working with other men to cut lumber. The job was very hard because the road was so long and winding. It was said that the road was so crooked that men starting home for camp would meet themselves coming back! Well, Paul hitched Babe to the end of that crooked road. He pulled so hard that his eyes nearly turned red. There was a loud snap. The first curve came out of the road and Babe pulled harder. Finally the whole road started to move. Babe pulled it completely straight!

Directions: Answer these questions about Paul Bunyan and Babe.

1. What was Paul Bunyan particularly good at doing? __Cutting down trees__
2. What did Paul find in the snow? __a huge blue ox__
3. How big was the distance between Babe's eyes? __42 axe handles__
4. What did Babe do to the crooked road? __He pulled it completely straight.__

Page 66

Sequencing: Kanati's Son

A **legend** is a story or group of stories handed down through generations. Legends are usually about an actual person.

Directions: Read about Kanati's son. Then number the events in order.

This legend is told by a tribe called the Cherokee (chair-oh-key).

Long ago, soon after the world was made, a hunter and his wife lived on a big mountain with their son. The father's name was Kanati (kah-na-tee), which means "lucky hunter." The mother's name was Selu (see-loo), which means "corn." No one remembers the son's name.

The little boy used to play alone by the river each day. One day, elders of the tribe told the boy's parents they had heard two children playing. Since their boy was the only child around, the parents were puzzled. They told their son what the elders said.

"I do have a playmate," the boy said. "He comes out of the water. He says he is the brother that mother threw in the river."

Then Selu knew what had happened.

"He is formed from the blood of the animals I washed in the river," she told Kanati. "After you kill them, I wash them in the river before I cook them."

Here is what Kanati told his boy: "Tomorrow when the other boy comes, wrestle with him. Hold him to the ground and call for us."

The boy did as his parents told him. When he called, they came running and grabbed the wild boy. They took him home and tried to tame him. The boy grew up with magic powers. The Cherokee called this "adawehi" (ad-da-we-hi). He was always getting into mischief! But he saved himself with his magic.

__5__ Selu and Kanati try to tame the boy from the river.

__3__ The little boy tells Selu and Kanati about the other boy.

__2__ The little boy's parents are puzzled.

__6__ The new boy grows up with magic powers.

__1__ The elders tell Selu and Kanati they heard two children playing.

__4__ The little boy wrestles his new playmate to the ground.

Page 67

Recognizing Details: "Why Bear Has a Short Tail"

Some stories try to explain the reasons why certain things occur in nature.

Directions: Read the legend "Why Bear Has a Short Tail." Then answer the questions.

Long ago, Bear had a long tail like Fox. One winter day, Bear met Fox coming out of the woods. Fox was carrying a long string of fish. He had stolen the fish, but that is not what he told Bear.

"Where did you get those fish?" asked Bear, rubbing his paws together. Bear loved fish. It was his favorite food.

"I was out fishing and caught them," replied Fox.

Bear did not know how to fish. He had only tasted fish that others gave him. He was eager to learn to catch his own.

"Please Fox, will you tell me how to fish?" asked Bear.

So, the mean old Fox said to Bear, "Cut a hole in the ice and stick your tail in the hole. It will get cold, but soon the fish will begin to bite. When you can stand it no longer, pull your tail out. It will be covered with fish!"

"Will it hurt?" asked Bear, patting his tail.

"It will hurt some," admitted Fox. "But the longer you leave your tail in the water, the more fish you will catch."

Bear did as Fox told him. He loved fish, so he left his tail in the icy water a very, very long time. The ice froze around Bear's tail. When he pulled free, his tail remained stuck in the ice. That is why bears today have short tails.

1. How does Fox get his string of fish? __He stole it.__
2. What does Fox tell Bear to do? __to put his tail in a hole in the ice to catch fish__
3. Why does Bear do as Fox told him? __He loves to eat fish but doesn't know how to catch them.__
4. How many fish does Bear catch? __none__
5. What happens when Bear tries to pull his tail out? __His tail remains stuck in the ice.__

Page 68

Recognizing Details: "Why Bear Has a Short Tail"

Directions: Review the legend "Why Bear Has a Short Tail." Then answer the questions.

1. When Bear asks Fox where he got his fish, is Fox truthful in his response? Why or why not? __No. Fox lies to trick Bear.__

2. Why does Bear want to know how to fish? __He loves to eat fish. It is his favorite food.__

3. In reality, are bears able to catch their own fish? How? __Yes, with their paws.__

4. Is Bear very smart to believe Fox? Why or why not? __No. Bear should have known Fox was sly and tricky.__

5. How would you have told Bear to catch his own fish? __Answers will vary.__

6. What is one word you would use to describe Fox? __sly, tricky, crafty__
   Explain your answer. __Answers will vary.__

7. What is one word you would use to describe Bear? __silly, trusting__
   Explain your answer. __Answers will vary.__

8. Is this story realistic? __No.__

9. Could it have really happened? Explain your answer. __Answers will vary.__

Page 69

Predicting: "How the Donkey Got Long Ears"

Directions: Write your predictions to answer these questions.

1. How do you think animals got their names?

2. Why would it be confusing if anim[...] __Answers will vary.__

Directions: Read the legend "How the Donkey Got Long Ears." Then answer the questions.

In the beginning when the world was young, animals had no names. It was very confusing! A woman would say, "Tell the thingamajig to bring in the paper." The man would say, "What thingamajig?" She was talking about the dog, of course, but the man didn't know that.

Together, they decided to name the animals on their farm. First, they named their pet thingamajig Dog. They named the pink thingamajig that oinked Pig. They named the red thingamajig that crowed Rooster. They named the white thingamajig that laid eggs Hen. They named the little yellow thingamajigs that cheeped Chicks. They named the big brown thingamajig they rode Horse.

Then they came to another thingamajig. It looked like Horse, but was smaller. It would be confusing to call the smaller thingamajig Horse, they decided.

"Let's name it Donkey," said the woman. So they did.

Soon all the animals knew their names. All but Donkey, that is. Donkey kept forgetting.

"What kind of a thingamajig am I again?" he would ask the man.

"You are Donkey!" the man would answer. Each time Donkey forgot, the man tugged on Donkey's ears to help him remember.

Soon, however, Donkey would forget his name again.

"Uh, what's my name?" he would ask the woman.

She would answer, "Donkey! Donkey! Donkey!" and pull his ears out each time. She was a clever woman but not very patient.

At first, the man and woman did not notice that Donkey's ears grew longer each time they were pulled. Donkey was patient but not very clever. It took him a long time to learn his name. By the time he remembered his name was Donkey, his ears were much longer than Horse's ears. That is why donkeys have long ears.

3. What words could you use to describe Donkey? __forgetful, patient__
   Explain your choice. __Answers will vary.__

Page 70

Comprehension: "How the Donkey Got Long Ears"

Directions: Review the legend "How the Donkey Got Long Ears." Then answer the questions.

1. What do the man and woman call the animals before they have names? __thingamajigs__

2. Why do they decide to name the animals? __because it was too confusing when they didn't have names__

3. What is the first animal they name? __Dog__

4. Besides being impatient, what else is the woman? __clever__

5. What do the people do each time they reminded Donkey of his name? __They tugged on his ears.__

6. Which thingamajigs are yellow? __Chicks__

7. Which thingamajig is pink? __Pig__

8. What is the thingamajig they ride? __Horse__

9. Why don't they call the donkey Horse? __Donkey is smaller.__

Directions: Imagine that you are the one who gets to name the animals. Write names for these new "animals."

10. A thingamajig with yellow spots that swims

11. A thingamajig with large ears, a short tail and [...]

12. A thingamajig with purple [...] __Answers will vary.__

13. A thingamajig [...]

Page 71

Following Directions: Early Native Americans

Directions: Read about the early Native Americans. Then work the puzzle.

There were about 300 Native American tribes in North America when the first white settlers came to New England in the 1500s. These Native Americans loved and respected the earth. They hunted buffalo on the plains. They fished in the clear rivers. They planted corn and beans on the rich land. They gathered roots and herbs. Before the white settlers drove them out, the Native Americans were masters of the land and all its riches.

The Native Americans grew crops, hunted for food, made clothing and built their homes from what they found on the land in the area where they lived. That is why each tribe of Native Americans was different. Some Native Americans lived in special tents called tepees. Some lived in adobe pueblos. Some lived in simple huts called hogans.

Across:
2. Native American homes made of adobe
3. Native Americans hunted this animal.
4. Tents some Native Americans lived in

Down:
1. Huts some Native Americans lived in
4. There were this many hundred tribes of Native Americans when settlers came.
5. All the tribes loved the _____.

Crossword answers:
- 2 across: PUEBLOS
- 3 across: BUFFALO
- 4 across: TEPEES
- 1 down: HOGANS
- 4 down: THREE
- 5 down: EARTH

Page 72

Comprehension: The Pueblo People

Directions: Read about the Pueblo people. Then answer the questions.

Long ago, Native Americans occupied all the land that is now Arizona, New Mexico, Utah and parts of California and Colorado. Twenty-five different tribes lived in this southwestern area. Several of the tribes lived in villages called pueblos. The Hopi (hope-ee) Indians lived in pueblos. So did the Zuñi (zoo-nee) and the Laguna (lah-goon-nah). These and other tribes who lived in villages were called the "Pueblo people."

When it was time for the Pueblo people to plant crops, everyone helped. The men kept the weeds pulled. Native Americans prayed for rain to make their crops grow. As part of their worship, they also had special dances called rain dances. When it was time for harvest, the women helped.

The land was bountiful to the Pueblo people. They grew many different crops. They planted beans, squash and 19 different kinds of corn. They gathered wild nuts and berries. They hunted for deer and rabbits. They also traded with other tribes for things they could not grow or hunt.

The Pueblo people lived in unusual houses. Their homes were made of adobe brick. Adobe is a type of mud. They shaped the mud into bricks, dried them, then built with them. Many adobe homes exist today in the Southwest.

The adobe homes of long ago had no doors. The Pueblo people entered through a type of trapdoor at the top. The homes were three or four stories high. The ground floor had no windows and was used for storage. These adobe homes were clustered around a central plaza. Each village had several clusters of homes. Villages also had two or three clubhouses where people could gather for celebrations. Each village also had places for worship.

1. What were the five states where the Pueblo people lived? _Arizona, Utah New Mexico, California, Colorado_

2. What were three crops the Pueblo people grew? _beans, squash, corn_

3. The early pueblo houses had no
☐ yards. ☐ windows. ☑ doors.

Page 73

Recognizing Details: The Pueblo People

"At the edge of the world
It grows light.
The trees stand shining."
(Pueblo poem)

Directions: Read more about the Pueblo people. Then answer the questions.

The Pueblo people were peaceful. They loved nature, and they seldom fought in wars. When they did fight, it was to protect their people or their land. Their dances, too, were gentle. The Pueblo people danced to ask the gods to bring rain or sunshine. Sometimes they asked the gods to help the women have children.

Some Native Americans wore masks when they danced. The masks were called kachinas (ka-chee-nas). They represented the faces of dead ancestors. (Ancestors are all the family members who have lived and died before.)

The Pueblo people were talented at crafts. The men of many tribes made beautiful jewelry. The women made pottery and painted it with beautiful colors. They traded some of the things they made with people from other tribes.

Both boys and girls needed their parents' permission to marry. After they married, they were given a room next to the bride's mother. If the marriage did not work out, sometimes the groom moved back home again.

1. Among the Pueblo people, who made jewelry? _the men_
2. Who made pottery? _the women_
3. What did some of the Pueblo people wear when they danced? _masks called kachinas_
4. Why did the Pueblo people dance for the gods? _to ask the gods for rain or sunshine or help with childbirth_
5. Where did newly married couples live? _in a room next to the bride's mother_
6. Why would a man move back home after marriage? _He would move out if the marriage did not work out._

Page 74

Recognizing Details: The Pueblo People

Directions: Review what you learned about the Pueblo people. Then answer the questions.

1. How many different tribes lived in the Southwestern part of the United States? _25_
2. The article specifically names three of the Pueblo tribes. Where could you find the names of the other Pueblo tribes?
reference sources like encyclopedias or the Internet

3. How did the Pueblo people build their adobe homes? _They shaped mud into bricks, dried them, then built with them._

4. How did the location and climate affect their lifestyle? _Location and climate affected what they wore, what crops they grew, the animals they hunted and materials used for building homes._

5. How were the jobs of the men and women of a Pueblo tribe alike? _Both helped care for crops._

6. How were their jobs different? _Men made jewelry. Women made pottery._

7. How do the responsibilities of the Pueblo men and women discussed differ from those of men and women today?
Answers will vary.

Page 75

Comprehension: A California Tribe

Directions: Read about the Yuma. Then answer the questions.

California was home to many Native Americans. The weather was warm, and food was plentiful. California was an ideal place to live.

One California tribe that made good use of the land was the Yuma. The Yuma farmed and gathered roots and berries. They harvested dozens of wild plants. They gathered acorns, ground them up and used them in cooking. The Yuma mixed acorns with flour and water to make a kind of oatmeal. They fished in California's rich waters. They hunted deer and small game. The Yuma made the most of what Mother Nature offered.

The Yuma lived in huts. The roofs were made of dirt. The walls were made of grass. Some Yuma lived together in big round buildings made with poles and woven grasses. As many as 50 people lived in these large homes.

Like other tribes, the Yuma made crafts. Their woven baskets were especially beautiful. The women also wove cradles, hats, bowls and other useful items for the tribe.

When it was time to marry, a boy's parents chose a 15-year-old girl for him. The girl was a Yuma, too, but from another village. Except for the chief, each man took only one wife.

When a Yuma died, a big ceremony was held. The Yuma had great respect for death. After someone died, his or her name was never spoken again.

1. What were two reasons why California was an ideal place to live?
The weather was warm and food was plentiful.

2. What did the Yuma use acorns for? _They ground them up and used them for cooking._

3. What was a beautiful craft made by the Yuma? _woven baskets_
4. How old was a Yuma bride? _15_
5. What types of homes did the Yuma live in? _dirt and grass huts_
6. How did the Yuma feel about death? _They had great respect for death._

Page 76

Recognizing Details: The Yuma

Directions: Review what you read about the Yuma. Write the answers.

1. How did the Yuma make good use of the land?
They farmed and gathered roots, acorns and berries. They fished and hunted.

2. How were the Yuma like the Pueblo people? _Both hunted deer and small game, farmed, gathered berries and made crafts._

3. How were they different? _The Yuma fished, made baskets and lived in huts. The Pueblos made pottery and jewelry and lived in adobe homes._

4. Why did the Yuma have homes different than those of the Pueblo tribes? _Answers should indicate differences in natural materials available due to different climates._

5. When it was time for a young Yuma man to marry, his parents selected a fifteen-year-old bride for him from another tribe. Do you think this is a good idea? Why or why not?

6. Why do you suppose the Yuma _____ person's name after he/she died?

7. Do you think this _____ thing to do? Explain your answer.

Answers will vary.

Page 77

Following Directions: Sailor Native Americans

Directions: Read about the Sailor Native Americans of Puget Sound. Then work the puzzle.

Three tribes lived on Puget (pew-jit) Sound in Washington state. They made their living from the sea. People later called them the "Sailor" Indians.

These Native Americans fished for salmon. They trapped the salmon in large baskets. Sometimes they used large nets. The sea was filled with fish. Their nets rarely came up empty. The Sailor Native Americans also gathered roots and berries. They hunted deer, black bear and ducks.

Their homes were amazing! They built big wooden buildings without nails. They did not use saws to cut the wood. The walls and roofs were tied together. Each building had different homes inside. As many as 50 families lived in each big building.

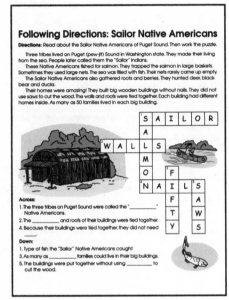

Across:
1. The three tribes on Puget Sound were called the "_____" Native Americans.
2. The _____ and roofs of their buildings were tied together.
4. Because their buildings were tied together, they did not need _____.

Down:
1. Type of fish the "Sailor" Native Americans caught
3. As many as _____ families could live in their big buildings.
5. The buildings were put together without using _____ to cut the wood.

Crossword answers: SAILOR, WALLS, SALMON, NAILS, FIFTY, SAWS

Page 78

Following Directions: Sailor Native Americans

Directions: Review what you read about the Sailor Native Americans. Write your answers.

1. How were the housing arrangements of the Puget Sound Native Americans similar to those of the Yuma?
   Many families lived together in large buildings.

2. How was the diet of the Sailor Native Americans like those of the Yuma and Pueblo?
   All three hunted and gathered berries.

3. How was it different? Yumas and Pueblos grew their own crops.

4. The Sailor Native Americans made a living from the sea, and their nets were rarely empty. What type of transportation do you think these Native Americans used to get their nets to the sea?
   canoes, boats or rafts

5. Where could you find more information on this group of Native Americans to check your answer?
   reference sources like encyclopedias and the Internet

6. Verify your answer. Were you correct? Answers will vary.

7. Who do you think performed the many tasks in the Sailor village? Write men, women, boys and/or girls for your answers.
   Built homes? _____ ? _____
   Fished? _____ _____ and berries? _____
   Hunted game? _____ Made fishing nets? _____

   Answers will vary.

8. The homes of the Sailor Native Americans could be compared to what type of modern dwelling?
   apartment buildings or condos

Page 79

Reading Comprehension: Hummingbirds

Hummingbirds are very small birds. This tiny bird is quite an acrobat. Only a few birds, such as kingfishers and sunbirds, can hover, which means to stay in one place in the air. But no other bird can match the flying skills of the hummingbird. The hummingbird can hover, fly backward and fly upside down!

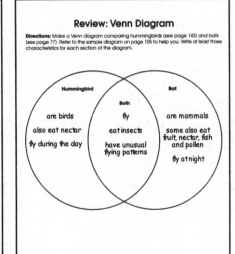

Hummingbirds got their name because their wings move very quickly when they fly. This causes a humming sound. Their wings move so fast that you can't see them at all. This takes a lot of energy. These little birds must have food about every 20 minutes to have enough strength to fly. Their favorite foods are insects and nectar. Nectar is the sweet water deep inside a flower. Hummingbirds use their long, thin bills to drink from flowers. When a hummingbird sips nectar, it hovers in front of a flower. It never touches the flower with its wings or feet.

Besides being the best at flying, the hummingbird is also one of the prettiest birds. Of all the birds in the world, the hummingbird's colors are among the brightest. Some are bright green with red and white markings. Some are purple. One kind of hummingbird can change its color from reddish-brown to purple to red!

The hummingbird's nest is special, too. It looks like a tiny cup. The inside of the nest is very soft. This is because one of the things the mother bird uses to build the nest is the silk from a spider's web.

Directions: Answer these questions about hummingbirds.

1. How did hummingbirds get their name? Because their wings move very quickly when they fly, and it causes a humming sound.

2. What does *hover* mean? to hang in the air

3. How often do hummingbirds need to eat? every 20 minutes

4. Name two things that hummingbirds eat. insects and nectar

5. What is one of the things a mother hummingbird uses to build her nest?
   silk from a spider's web

Page 80

Reading Comprehension: Bats

Bats are the only mammals that can fly. They have wings made of thin skin stretched between long fingers. Bats can fly amazing distances. Some small bats have been known to fly more than 25 miles in one night.

Most bats eat insects or fruit. But some eat only fish, others only blood and still others the nectar and pollen of flowers that bloom at night. Bats are active only at night. They sleep during the day in caves or other dark places. At rest, they always hang with their heads down.

You may have heard the expression "blind as a bat." But bats are not blind. They don't, however, use their eyes to guide their flight or to find the insects they eat. A bat makes a high-pitched squeak, then waits for the echo to return to it. This echo tells it how far away an object is. This is often called the bat's sonar system. Using this system, a bat can fly through a dark cave without bumping into anything. Hundreds of bats can fly about in the dark without ever running into each other. They do not get confused by the squeaks of the other bats. They always recognize their own echoes.

Directions: Answer these questions about bats.

1. Bats are the only mammals that
   □ eat insects. ☒ fly. □ live in caves.

2. Most bats eat
   □ plants. □ other animals. ☒ fruits and insects.

3. Bats always sleep
   ☒ with their heads down. □ lying down. □ during the night.

4. Bats are blind.   True   (False)

5. Bats use a built-in sonar system to guide them.   (True)   False

6. Bats are confused by the squeaks of other bats.   True   (False)

Page 81

Review: Venn Diagram

Directions: Make a Venn diagram comparing hummingbirds (see page 143) and bats (see page 77). Refer to the sample diagram on page 105 to help you. Write at least three characteristics for each section of the diagram.

Hummingbird
are birds
also eat nectar
fly during the day

Both
fly
eat insects
have unusual flying patterns

Bat
are mammals
some also eat fruit, nectar, fish and pollen
fly at night

Page 82

Recognizing Details: Giraffes

Directions: Read about giraffes. Then answer the questions.

Giraffes are tall, beautiful, graceful animals that live in Africa. When they are grown, male giraffes are about 18 feet tall. Adult females are about 14 feet tall.

Giraffes are not fat animals, but because they are so big, they weigh a lot. The average male weighs 2,800 pounds. Females weigh about 400 pounds less. Giraffes reach their full height when they are four years old. They continue to gain weight until they are about eight years old.

If you have ever seen giraffes, you know their necks and legs are very long. They are not awkward, though! Giraffes can move very quickly. They like to jump over fences and streams. They do this gracefully. They do not trip over their long legs.

If they are frightened, they can run 35 miles an hour. When giraffes gallop, all four feet are sometimes off the ground! Usually, young and old giraffes pace along at about 10 miles an hour.

Giraffes are strong. They can use their back legs as weapons. A lion can run faster than a giraffe, but a giraffe can kill a lion with one quick kick from its back legs.

Giraffes do not look scary. Their long eyelashes make them look gentle. They usually have a curious look on their faces. Many people think they are cute. Do you?

1. What is the weight of a full-grown male giraffe? 2,800 pounds
2. What is the weight of an adult female? 2,400 pounds
3. When does a giraffe run 35 miles an hour? when it is frightened
4. What do giraffes use as weapons? their back legs
5. For how long do giraffes continue to gain weight?
   until they are 8 years old
6. When do giraffes reach their full height?
   when they are 4 years old
7. Use a dictionary. What does *gallop* mean?
   to run quickly; to run at full speed

Page 83

Comprehension: More About Giraffes

Directions: Read more about giraffes. Then answer the questions.

Most people don't notice, but giraffes have different patterns of spots. Certain species of giraffes have small spots. Other species have large spots. Some species have spots that are very regular. You can tell where one spot ends and another begins. Other species have spots that are kind of blotchy. This means the spots are not set off from each other as clearly. There are many other kinds of spot patterns. The pattern of a giraffe's spots is called "markings." No two giraffes have exactly the same markings.

There is one very rare type of giraffe. It is totally black! Have you ever seen one? This kind of giraffe is called a melanistic (mel-an-iss-tick) giraffe. The name comes from the word "melanin," which is the substance in cells that gives them color. Giraffes' spots help them blend in with their surroundings. A black giraffe would not blend in well with tree trunks and leaves. Maybe that is why they are so rare.

Being able to blend with surroundings helps animals survive. If a lion can't see a giraffe, he certainly can't eat it. This is called "protective coloration." The animal's color helps protect it.

Another protection giraffes have is their keen eyesight. Their large eyes are on the sides of their heads. Giraffes see anything that moves. They can see another animal a mile away! It is very hard to sneak up on a giraffe. Those who try usually get a quick kick with a powerful back leg.

1. What are markings? __the pattern of an animal's spots__

2. How far away can a giraffe see another animal? __one mile__

3. Where are a giraffe's eyes? __on the sides of its head__

4. What is protective colorat __being able to blend into the surroundings__

5. What color is the very rare type of giraffe? __black__

6. How do giraffes protect themselves? __They kick with their back legs.__

7. How many kinds of spot patterns do giraffes have? ☐ two ☐ four ☑ many

8. Use a dictionary. What does **species** mean? __a group of animals closely related and capable of breeding with others in the same species__

Page 84

Following Directions: Puzzling Out Giraffes

Directions: Review what you read about giraffes. Read more about giraffes below. Then work the puzzle.

Have you noticed that giraffes have a curious look? That is because they are always paying attention. Their lives depend upon it! Giraffes cannot save themselves from a lion if they don't see it. Giraffes look around a lot. Even when they are chewing their food, they are checking to see if danger is near.

By nature, giraffes are gentle. They do not attack unless they are in danger. A giraffe will lower its head when it is angry. It will open its nostrils and its mouth. Then watch out!

Across:
2. How a giraffe feels when it lowers its head and opens its nose and mouth
4. Giraffes look this way because they are always paying attention.
6. By nature, giraffes are _____.
7. The continent where giraffes live
9. Another name for a black giraffe is _____.

Down:
1. The patterns of a giraffe's spots
3. An animal's ability to blend with surroundings is called protective _____.
5. _____ means a certain kind of animal.
8. Giraffes' eyes are so keen they can see another animal a mile _____.
10. Are giraffes often mean?

Page 85

Recognizing Details: Giraffes

Directions: Review what you learned about giraffes. Then answer the questions.

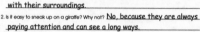

1. How are a giraffe's spots helpful? __They help them blend in with their surroundings.__

2. Is it easy to sneak up on a giraffe? Why not? __No, because they are always paying attention and can see a long ways.__

3. What makes a giraffe look so gentle? __They have long eyelashes.__

4. How do you know when a giraffe is angry? __It will lower its head and open its nostrils and mouth.__

5. Do you think a giraffe in a zoo is as observant as a giraffe in the wilds of Africa? Why or why not? __Answers will vary.__

6. Do you think giraffes have any other enemies besides lions? __Yes__
What animals might they be? __Answers may include: hyenas, cheetahs__

7. Why do you suppose giraffes grow so large? __Answers will vary.__

8. Use a dictionary. What does **habitat** mean? Describe the giraffe's natural habitat. __Habitat is a place where an animal lives in its natural state. Giraffes live on open grassy plains and sometimes near trees.__

Page 86

Comprehension: Wild Horses

Directions: Read about wild horses. Then answer the questions.

Have you ever heard of a car called a Mustang? It is named after a type of wild horse.

In the 1600s, the Spanish explorers who came to North America brought horses with them. Some of these horses escaped onto the prairies and plains. Their numbers quickly grew, and they roamed in herds. They ran free and ate grass on the prairie.

Later, when the West was settled, people needed horses. They captured wild ones. This was not easy to do. Wild horses could run very fast. They did not want to be captured! Some men made their living by capturing wild horses, taming them and selling them. These men were called "mustangers." Can you guess why?

After cars were invented, people did not need as many horses. Not as many mustangers were needed to catch them. More and more wild horses roamed the western prairies. In 1925, about a million mustangs were running loose.

The government was worried that the herds would eat too much grass. Ranchers who owned big herds of cattle complained that their animals didn't have enough to eat because the mustangs ate all the grass. Permission was given to ranchers and others to kill many of the horses. Thousands were killed and sold to companies that made them into pet food.

Now, wild horses live in only 12 states. The largest herds are in California, New Mexico, Oregon, Wyoming and Nevada. Most people who live in these states never see wild horses. The herds live away from people in the distant plains and mountains. They are safer there.

1. What is one type of wild horse called? __a mustang__

2. What were men called who captured wild horses? __mustangers__

3. About how many wild horses were running free in the U.S. in 1925? __one million__

4. The wild mustangs were killed and turned into ☐ cars. ☑ pet food. ☐ lunch meat.

5. The largest herds of wild horses are now in:
☑ Oregon. ☐ Ohio. ☑ New Mexico. ☑ Wyoming.
☑ California. ☑ Nevada. ☐ Kansas. ☐ Arkansas.

Page 87

Main Idea: More About Wild Horses

Directions: Read more about wild horses. Then answer the questions.

Have you noticed that in any large group, one person seems to be the leader? This is true for wild horses, too. The leader of a band of wild horses is a stallion. Stallions are adult male horses.

The stallion's job is important. He watches out for danger. If a bear or other animal comes close, he lets out a warning cry. This helps keep the other horses safe. Sometimes they all run away together. Other times, the stallion protects the other horses. He shows his teeth. He rears up on his back legs. Often, he scares the other animal away. Then the horses can safely continue eating grass.

Much of the grass on the prairies is gone now. Wild horses must move around a lot to find new grass. They spend about half their time eating and looking for food. If they cannot find prairie grass, wild horses will eat tree bark. They will eat flowers. If they can't find these either, wild horses will eat anything that grows!

Wild horses also need plenty of water. It is often hot in the places where they roam. At least twice a day, they find streams and take long, long drinks. Like people, wild horses lose water when they sweat. They run and sweat a lot in hot weather. To survive, they need as much water as they can get.

Wild horses also use water another way. When they find deep water, they wade into it. It feels good! It cools their skin.

1. What is the main idea? (Check one.)

___ Wild horses need plenty of water.

_✓_ Wild horses move in bands protected by a stallion.

___ Wild horses eat grass.

2. What are two reasons why wild horses need water? __to drink and to cool their skin__

3. Why do wild horses move around so much? __to find new grass__

4. What do wild horses most like to eat? __prairie grass__

5. What do wild horses spend half their time doing? __eating and looking for food__

Page 88

Recognizing Details: Wild Horses

Directions: Review what you read about wild horses. Then answer the questions.

1. How did horses come to North America and become wild? __Spanish explorers brought them. Some escaped and became wild.__

2. Why is it so difficult to capture, tame and train wild horses? __Wild horses can run very fast and do not want to be captured.__

3. Do you think it was right of the government to allo____ g of wild horses?
Explain your answer. _____ *Answers will vary.*

4. Do you think the remaining ____ protected?
Explain your answer. _____

5. What is the role of the lead stallion in a wild horse herd? __to watch out for danger and protect the herd__

6. What are some things wild horses have in common with giraffes? _____ *Answers will vary.*

7. What do you think will happe____ prairie lands continue to disappear as a result of developm____ sses? _____

Page 90

Writing: Sentences

A **sentence** is a group of words that expresses a complete thought.

Directions: Write **S** by each group of words that is a sentence and **NS** by those that are not a complete sentence.

Examples:

NS A pinch of salt in the soup.

S Grandmother was fond of her flower garden.

S 1. Tigers blend in with their surroundings.

NS 2. Our crop of vegetables for this summer.

S 3. Don't forget to put the plug in the sink.

NS 4. Usually older people in good health.

NS 5. Fond of lying in the sun for hours.

S 6. Will ducks hatch a swan egg?

S 7. I hope he won't insist on coming with us.

S 8. Regular exercise will pump up your muscles.

NS 9. A fact printed in all the newspapers.

S 10. Did you pinch the baby?

S 11. Plug the hole with your finger.

NS 12. A new teacher today in health class.

S 13. I insist on giving you some of my candy.

NS 14. A blend of peanut butter and honey.

NS 15. As many facts as possible in your report.

Page 91

Kinds of Sentences: Statements and Questions

A **statement** tells some kind of information. It is followed by a period (.).

Examples: It is a rainy day. We are going to the beach next summer.

A **question** asks for a specific piece of information. It is followed by a question mark (?).

Examples: What is the weather like today? When are you going to the beach?

Directions: Write whether each sentence is a statement or question. The first one has been done for you.

1. Jamie went for a walk at the zoo. _statement_
2. The leaves turn bright colors in the fall. _statement_
3. When does the Easter Bunny arrive? _question_
4. Madeleine went to the new art school. _statement_
5. Is school over at 3:30? _question_
6. Grandma and Grandpa are moving. _statement_
7. Anthony went home. _statement_
8. Did Mary go to Amy's house? _question_
9. Who went to work late? _question_
10. Ms. McDaniel is a good teacher. _statement_

Directions: Write two statements and two questions below.

Statements:

_____

Questions: _Answers will vary._

_____

Page 92

Kinds of Sentences: Commands and Exclamations

A **command** tells someone to do something. It is followed by a period (.).

Examples: Get your math book. Do your homework.

An **exclamation** shows strong feeling or excitement. It is followed by an exclamation mark (!).

Examples: Watch out for that car! Oh, no! There's a snake!

Directions: Write whether each sentence is a command or exclamation. The first one has been done for you.

1. Please clean your room. _command_
2. Wow! Those fireworks are beautiful! _exclamation_
3. Come to dinner now. _command_
4. Color the sky and water blue. _command_
5. Trim the paper carefully. _command_
6. Hurry, here comes the bus! _exclamation_
7. Isn't that a lovely picture! _exclamation_
8. Time to stop playing and clean up. _command_
9. Brush your teeth before bedtime. _command_
10. Wash your hands before you eat! _exclamation_

Directions: Write two commands and two exclamations below.

Commands:

Exclamations: _Answers will vary._

Page 93

Sentences: Subjects

The **subject** of a sentence tells you who or what the sentence is about. A subject is either a common noun, a proper noun or a pronoun.

Examples: Sue went to the store.

Sue is the subject of the sentence.

The tired boys and girls walked home slowly.
The tired boys and girls is the subject of the sentence.

Directions: Underline the subject of each sentence. The first one has been done for you.

1. The birthday cake was pink and white.
2. Anthony celebrated his fourth birthday.
3. The tower of building blocks fell over.
4. On Saturday, our family will go to a movie.
5. The busy editor was writing sentences.
6. Seven children painted pictures.
7. Two happy dolphins played cheerfully on the surf.
8. A sand crab buried itself in the dunes.
9. Blue waves ran peacefully ashore.
10. Sleepily, she went to bed.

Directions: Write a subject for each sentence.

1. Chocolate-chip ice cream was melting in the...
2. _____ ran do...
3. _____ ...me.
4. _____ ...
5. _____ ...r a beautiful dress.
6. _____ hopped, skipped and jumped all the way home.
7. _____ wrote a long letter.
8. _____ moved to Paris, France.

Answers will vary.

Page 94

Sentences: Predicates

The **predicate** of a sentence tells what the subject is doing. The predicate contains the action, linking and/or helping verb.

Examples: Sue went to the store.

Went to the store is the predicate.

The tired boys and girls walked home slowly.
Walked home slowly is the predicate.

Hint: When identifying the predicate, look for the verb. The verb is usually the first word of the predicate.

Directions: Underline the predicate in each sentence with two lines. The first one has been done for you.

1. The choir sang joyfully.
2. Their song had both high and low notes.
3. Sal played the piano while they sang.
4. This Sunday the orchestra will have a concert in the park.
5. John is working hard on his homework.
6. He will write a report on electricity.
7. The report will tell about Ben Franklin's kite experiment.
8. Jackie, Mary and Amy played on the swings.
9. They also climbed the rope ladder.
10. Before the girls went home, they slid down the slide.

Directions: Write a predicate for each sentence.

1. Sam and Libby _____
2. At school, the children _____
3. The football team _____
4. Seven silly serpents _____
5. At the zoo, the animals _____

Answers will vary.

Page 95

Subjects and Predicates

The **subject** tells who or what the sentence is about. The **predicate** tells what the subject does, did, is doing or will do. A complete sentence must have a subject and a predicate.

Examples:

Subject	Predicate
Sharon	writes to her grandmother every week.
The horse	ran around the track quickly.
My mom's car	is bright green.
Denise	will be here after lunch.

Directions: Circle the subject of each sentence. Underline the predicate.

1. (My sister) is a very happy person.
2. (I) wish we had more holidays in the year.
3. (Laura) is one of the nicest girls in our class.
4. (John) is fun to have as a friend.
5. (The rain) nearly ruined our picnic!
6. (My birthday present) was exactly what I wanted.
7. (Your bicycle) is parked beside my skateboard.
8. (The printer) will need to be filled with paper before you use it.
9. (Six dogs) chased my cat home yesterday!
10. (Anthony) likes to read anything he can get his hands on.
11. (Twelve students) signed up for the dance committee.
12. (Your teacher) seems to be a reasonable person.

Page 96

Subjects and Predicates

Directions: Write subjects to complete the following sentences.

1. _____ went to school last Wednesday.
2. _____ did not under___ ___ke.
3. _____ one could sleep a wink.
4. _____ felt unhappy when the ball game was rained out.
5. _____ wonder what happened at the end of the book.
6. _____ jumped for joy when she won the contest.

Answers will vary.

Directions: Write predicates to complete the following sentences.

7. Everyone _____
8. Dogs _____
9. I _____
10. Justin _____
11. Jokes _____
12. Twelve people _____

Answers will vary.

Page 97

Compound Subjects

A **compound subject** is a subject with two parts joined by the word **and** or another conjunction. Compound subjects share the same predicate.

Example:

Her shoes were covered with mud. Her ankles were covered with mud, too.
Compound subject: Her shoes and ankles were covered with mud.
The predicate in both sentences is **were covered with mud.**

Directions: Combine each pair of sentences into one sentence with a compound subject.

1. Bill sneezed. Kassie sneezed.
   Bill and Kassie sneezed.
2. Kristin made cookies. Joey made cookies.
   Kristin and Joey made cookies.
3. Fruit flies are insects. Ladybugs are insects.
   Fruit flies and ladybugs are insects.
4. The girls are planning a dance. The boys are planning a dance.
   The girls and boys are planning a dance.
5. Our dog ran after the ducks. Our cat ran after the ducks.
   Our dog and cat ran after the ducks.
6. Joshua got lost in the parking lot. Daniel got lost in the parking lot.
   Joshua and Daniel got lost in the parking lot.

Page 98

Compound Subjects

If sentences do not share the same predicate, they cannot be combined to write a sentence with a compound subject.

Example: Mary laughed at the story.
Tanya laughed at the television show.

Directions: Combine the pairs of sentences that share the same predicate. Write new sentences with compound subjects.

1. Pete loves swimming. Jake loves swimming.
   Pete and Jake love swimming.
2. A bee stung Elizabeth. A hornet stung Elizabeth.
   A bee and a hornet stung Elizabeth.
3. Sharon is smiling. Susan is frowning.
   _____
4. The boys have great suntans. The girls have great suntans.
   The boys and girls have great suntans.
5. Six squirrels chased the kitten. Ten dogs chased the kitten.
   Six squirrels and ten dogs chased the kitten.
6. The trees were covered with insects. The roads were covered with ice.
   _____

Page 99

Compound Predicates

A **compound predicate** is a predicate with two parts joined by the word **and** or another conjunction. Compound predicates share the same subject.

Example: The baby grabbed the ball. The baby threw the ball.
Compound predicate: The baby grabbed the ball and threw it.
The subject in both sentences is **the baby.**

Directions: Combine each pair of sentences into one sentence to make a compound predicate.

1. Leah jumped on her bike. Leah rode around the block.
   Leah jumped on her bike and rode around the block.
2. Father rolled out the pie crust. Father put the pie crust in the pan.
   Father rolled out the pie crust and put it in the pan.
3. Anthony slipped on the snow. Anthony nearly fell down.
   Anthony slipped on the snow and nearly fell down.
4. My friend lives in a green house. My friend rides a red bicycle.
   My friend lives in a green house and rides a red bicycle.
5. I opened the magazine. I began to read it quietly.
   I opened the magazine and began to read it quietly.
6. My father bought a new plaid shirt. My father wore his new red tie.
   My father bought a new plaid shirt and wore his new red tie.

Page 100

Compound Predicates

Directions: Combine the pairs of sentences that share the same subject. Write new sentences with compound predicates.

1. Jenny picked a bouquet of flowers. Jenny put the flowers in a vase.
   Jenny picked a bouquet of flowers and put them in a vase.
2. I really enjoy ice cream. She really enjoys ice cream.
   _____
3. Everyone had a great time at the pep rally. Then everyone went out for a pizza.
   Everyone had a a great time at the pep rally, then went out for pizza.
4. Cassandra built a model airplane. She painted the airplane bright yellow.
   Cassandra built a model airplane and painted it bright yellow.
5. Her brother was really a hard person to get to know. Her sister was very shy, too.
   _____

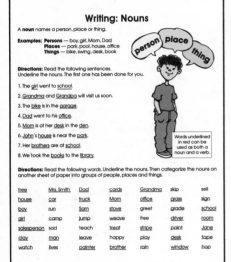

Page 101

Writing: Nouns

A **noun** names a person, place or thing.

Examples: Persons — boy, girl, Mom, Dad
Places — park, pool, house, office
Things — bike, swing, desk, book

Directions: Read the following sentences. Underline the nouns. The first one has been done for you.

1. The girl went to school.
2. Grandma and Grandpa will visit us soon.
3. The bike is in the garage.
4. Dad went to his office.
5. Mom is at her desk in the den.
6. John's house is near the park.
7. Her brothers are at school.
8. We took the books to the library.

Words underlined in red can be used as both a noun and a verb.

Directions: Read the following words. Underline the nouns. Then categorize the nouns on another sheet of paper into groups of people, places and things.

tree	Mrs. Smith	Dad	cards	Grandma	skip	sell
house	car	truck	Mom	office	grass	sign
boy	run	Sam	stove	greet	grade	school
girl	camp	jump	weave	free	driver	room
salesperson	sad	teach	treat	stripe	paint	Jane
clay	man	leave	happy	play	desk	tape
watch	lives	painter	brother	rain	window	hop

Page 102

Nouns

Directions: Write nouns that name persons.

1. Could you please give this report to my _____ ?
2. The _____ works many long hours to plant crops.
3. I had to help my little _____ when he wrecked his bike yesterday.

Directions: Write nouns that name places.

4. I always keep my library books on top of the _____ so I can find them.
5. We enjoyed watching the kites fly _____ .
6. Dad built a _____ to keep us warm.

Directions: Write nouns that name things.

7. The little _____ purred softly as I held it.
8. Wouldn't you think a _____ would get tired of carrying its house around all day?
9. The _____ scurried into its hole with the piece of cheese.
10. I can tell by the writing that this _____ is mine.
11. Look at the _____ I made in art.
12. His _____ blew away because of the strong wind.

Answers will vary.

Page 103

Writing: Common and Proper Nouns

Common nouns name general people, places and things.

Examples: boy, girl, cat, dog, park, city, building

Proper nouns name specific persons, places and things.

Examples: John, Mary, Fluffy, Rover, Central Park, Chicago, Empire State Building

Proper nouns begin with capital letters.

Directions: Read the following nouns. On the blanks, indicate whether the nouns are common or proper. The first two have been done for you.

1. New York City	proper		9. Dr. DiCarlo	proper	
2. house	common		10. man	common	
3. car	common		11. Rock River	proper	
4. Ohio	proper		12. building	common	
5. river	common		13. lawyer	common	
6. Rocky Mountains	proper		14. Grand Canyon	proper	
7. Mrs. Jones	proper		15. city	common	
8. nurse	common		16. state	common	

On another sheet of paper, write proper nouns for the above common nouns.

Answers will vary.

Directions: Read the following sentences. Underline the common nouns. Circle the proper nouns.

1. Mary's birthday is Friday, October 7.
2. She likes having her birthday in a fall month.
3. Her friends will meet her at the Video Arcade for a party.
4. Ms. McCarthy and Mr. Landry will help with the birthday party games.
5. Mary's friends will play video games all afternoon.
6. Amy and John will bring refreshments and games to the party.

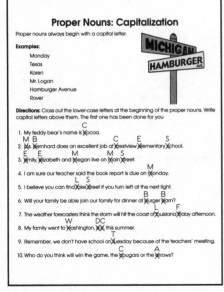

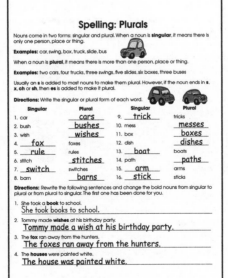

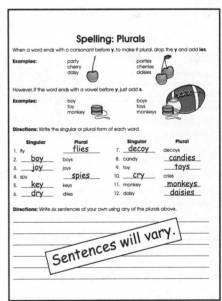

Page 104

Proper Nouns: Capitalization

Proper nouns always begin with a capital letter.

Examples:

Monday
Texas
Karen
Mr. Logan
Hamburger Avenue
Rover

Directions: Cross out the lower-case letters at the beginning of the proper nouns. Write capital letters above them. The first one has been done for you.

1. My teddy bear's name is C̶ocoa.
2. M̶s. B̶ernhard does an excellent job at C̶restview E̶lementary S̶chool.
3. E̶mily, E̶lizabeth and M̶egan live on M̶ain S̶treet.
4. I am sure our teacher said the book report is due on M̶onday.
5. I believe you can find L̶ake S̶treet if you turn left at the next light.
6. Will your family be able join our family for dinner at B̶urger B̶arn?
7. The weather forecasters think the storm will hit the coast of L̶ouisiana F̶riday afternoon.
8. My family went to W̶ashington, D̶C this summer.
9. Remember, we don't have school on T̶uesday because of the teachers' meeting.
10. Who do you think will win the game, the C̶ougars or the A̶rrows?

Page 105

Spelling: Plurals

Nouns come in two forms: singular and plural. When a noun is **singular**, it means there is only one person, place or thing.

Examples: car, swing, box, truck, slide, bus

When a noun is **plural**, it means there is more than one person, place or thing.

Examples: two cars, four trucks, three swings, five slides, six boxes, three buses

Usually an **s** is added to most nouns to make them plural. However, if the noun ends in **s**, **x**, **ch** or **sh**, then **es** is added to make it plural.

Directions: Write the singular or plural form of each word.

	Singular	Plural		Singular	Plural
1.	car	cars	9.	trick	tricks
2.	bush	bushes	10.	mess	messes
3.	wish	wishes	11.	box	boxes
4.	fox	foxes	12.	dish	dishes
5.	rule	rules	13.	boat	boats
6.	stitch	stitches	14.	path	paths
7.	switch	switches	15.	arm	arms
8.	barn	barns	16.	stick	sticks

Directions: Rewrite the following sentences and change the bold nouns from singular to plural or from plural to singular. The first one has been done for you.

1. She took a **book** to school.
   She took books to school.
2. Tommy made **wishes** at his birthday party.
   Tommy made a wish at his birthday party.
3. The **fox** ran away from the hunters.
   The foxes ran away from the hunters.
4. The **houses** were painted white.
   The house was painted white.

Page 106

Spelling: Plurals

When a word ends with a consonant before **y**, to make it plural, drop the **y** and add **ies**.

Examples:

party — parties
cherry — cherries
daisy — daisies

However, if the word ends with a vowel before **y**, just add **s**.

Examples:

boy — boys
toy — toys
monkey — monkeys

Directions: Write the singular or plural form of each word.

	Singular	Plural		Singular	Plural
1.	fly	flies	7.	decoy	decoys
2.	boy	boys	8.	candy	candies
3.	joy	joys	9.	toy	toys
4.	spy	spies	10.	cry	cries
5.	key	keys	11.	monkey	monkeys
6.	dry	dries	12.	daisy	daisies

Directions: Write six sentences of your own using any of the plurals above.

Sentences will vary.

Page 107

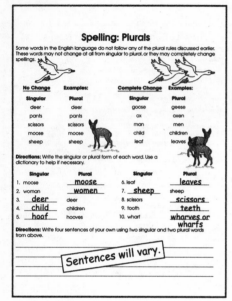

Spelling: Plurals

Some words in the English language do not follow any of the plural rules discussed earlier. These words may not change at all from singular to plural, or they may completely change spellings.

No Change	Examples:		Complete Change	Examples:	
Singular	**Plural**		**Singular**	**Plural**	
deer	deer		goose	geese	
pants	pants		ox	oxen	
scissors	scissors		man	men	
moose	moose		child	children	
sheep	sheep		leaf	leaves	

Directions: Write the singular or plural form of each word. Use a dictionary to help if necessary.

	Singular	Plural		Singular	Plural
1.	moose	**moose**	6.	leaf	**leaves**
2.	woman	**women**	7.	**sheep**	sheep
3.	**deer**	deer	8.	scissors	**scissors**
4.	**child**	children	9.	tooth	**teeth**
5.	**hoof**	hooves	10.	wharf	**wharves or wharfs**

Directions: Write four sentences of your own using two singular and two plural words from above.

Sentences will vary.

Page 108

Pronouns

A **pronoun** is a word that takes the place of a noun in a sentence.

Examples:

I, my, mine, me
we, our, ours, us
you, your, yours
he, his, him
she, her, hers
it, its
they, their, theirs, them

Directions: Underline the pronouns in each sentence.

1. Bring <u>them</u> to <u>us</u> as soon as <u>you</u> are finished.
2. <u>She</u> has been <u>my</u> best friend for many years.
3. <u>They</u> should be here soon.
4. <u>We</u> enjoyed <u>our</u> trip to the Mustard Museum.
5. Would <u>you</u> be able to help <u>us</u> with the project on Saturday?
6. <u>Our</u> homeroom teacher will not be here tomorrow.
7. <u>My</u> uncle said that <u>he</u> will be leaving soon for Australia.
8. Hurry! Could <u>you</u> please open the door for <u>him</u>?
9. <u>She</u> dropped <u>her</u> gloves when <u>she</u> got off the bus.
10. <u>I</u> can't figure out who the mystery writer is today.

Page 109

Writing: Verbs

Verbs are the action words in a sentence. There are three kinds of verbs: action verbs, linking verbs and helping verbs.

An **action verb** tells the action of a sentence.

Examples: run, hop, skip, sleep, jump, talk, snore
Michael **ran** to the store. Ran is the action verb.

A **linking verb** joins the subject and predicate of a sentence.

Examples: am, is, are, was, were
Michael **was** at the store. Was is the linking verb.

A **helping verb** is used with an action verb to "help" the action of the sentence.

Examples: am, is, are, was, were
Matthew **was** helping Michael. **Was** helps the action verb **helping**.

Directions: Read the following sentences. Underline the verbs. Above each, write **A** for action verb, **L** for linking verb and **H** for helping verb. The first one has been done for you.

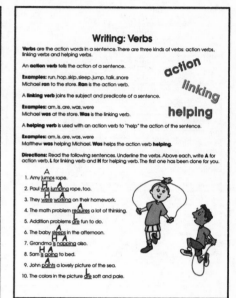

1. Amy <u>jumps</u> rope. (A)
2. Paul <u>was jumping</u> rope, too. (H A)
3. They <u>were working</u> on their homework. (H A)
4. The math problem <u>requires</u> a lot of thinking. (A)
5. Addition problems <u>are</u> fun to do. (L)
6. The baby <u>sleeps</u> in the afternoon. (A)
7. Grandma <u>is napping</u> also. (H A)
8. Sam <u>is going</u> to bed. (H A)
9. John <u>paints</u> a lovely picture of the sea. (A)
10. The colors in the picture <u>are</u> soft and pale. (L)

Page 110

Writing: Verb Tense

Not only do verbs tell the action of a sentence but they also tell when the action takes place. This is called the **verb tense**. There are three verb tenses: past, present and future.

Present-tense verbs tell what is happening now.

Example: Jane **spells** words with long vowel sounds.

Past-tense verbs tell about action that has already happened. Past-tense verbs are usually formed by adding **ed** to the verb.

Example: stay — stayed
John **stayed** home yesterday.

Past-tense verbs can also be made by adding helping verbs **was** or **were** before the verb and adding **ing** to the verb.

Example: talk — was talking
Sally **was talking** to her mom.

Future-tense verbs tell what will happen in the future. Future-tense verbs are made by putting the word **will** before the verb.

Example: paint — will paint
Susie and Sherry **will paint** the house.

Directions: Read the following verbs. Write whether the verb tense is past, present or future.

	Verb	Tense		Verb	Tense
1.	watches	**present**	8.	writes	**present**
2.	wanted	**past**	9.	vaulted	**past**
3.	will eat	**future**	10.	were sleeping	**past**
4.	was squawking	**past**	11.	will sing	**future**
5.	yawns	**present**	12.	is speaking	**present**
6.	crawled	**past**	13.	will cook	**future**
7.	will hunt	**future**	14.	likes	**present**

Page 111

Verbs: Present, Past and Future Tense

Directions: Read the following sentences. Write **PRES** if the sentence is in present tense. Write **PAST** if the sentence is in past tense. Write **FUT** if the sentence is in future tense. The first one has been done for you.

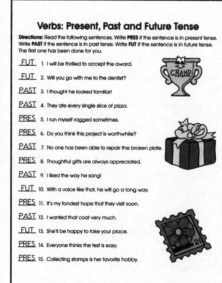

FUT 1. I will be thrilled to accept the award.
FUT 2. Will you go with me to the dentist?
PAST 3. I thought he looked familiar.
PAST 4. They ate every single slice of pizza.
PRES 5. I run myself ragged sometimes.
PRES 6. Do you think this project is worthwhile?
PAST 7. No one has been able to repair the broken plate.
PRES 8. Thoughtful gifts are always appreciated.
PAST 9. I liked the way he sang!
FUT 10. With a voice like that, he will go a long way.
PRES 11. It's my fondest hope that they visit soon.
PAST 12. I wanted that coat very much.
FUT 13. She'll be happy to take your place.
PRES 14. Everyone thinks the test is easy.
PRES 15. Collecting stamps is her favorite hobby.

Page 112

Writing: Using ing Verbs

Remember, use **is** and **are** when describing happening right now. Use **was** and **were** when describing something that already happened.

Directions: Use the verb in bold to complete each sentence. Add ing to the verb and use **is**, **are**, **was** or **were**.

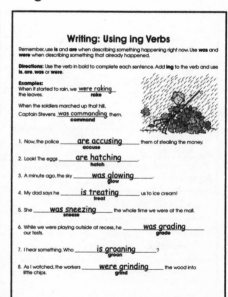

Examples:
When it started to rain, we **were raking** the leaves. (rake)

When the soldiers marched up that hill, Captain Stevens **was commanding** them. (command)

1. Now, the police **are accusing** them of stealing the money. (accuse)
2. Look! The eggs **are hatching** . (hatch)
3. A minute ago, the sky **was glowing** . (glow)
4. My dad says he **is treating** us to ice cream! (treat)
5. She **was sneezing** the whole time we were at the mall. (sneeze)
6. While we were playing outside at recess, he **was grading** our tests. (grade)
7. I hear something. Who **is groaning** ? (groan)
8. As I watched, the workers **were grinding** the wood into little chips. (grind)

Page 113

Writing: Present-Tense Verbs

Directions: Write two sentences for each verb below. Tell about something that is happening now and write the verb as both simple present tense and present tense with a helping verb.

Example: run

Mia runs to the store.   Mia is running to the store.

1. hatch

2. check

3. spell

4. blend

5. lick

6. cry

7. write

8. dream

Sentences will vary.

Page 114

Writing: Verb Tense

Directions: Read the following sentences. Underline the verbs. Above each verb, write whether it is past, present or future tense.

1. The crowd was booing the referee. — past
2. Sally will compete on the balance beam. — future
3. Matt marches with the band. — present
4. Nick is marching, too. — present
5. The geese swooped down to the pond. — past
6. Dad will fly home tomorrow. — future
7. They were looking for a new book. — past
8. Presently, they are going to the garden. — present
9. The children will pick the ripe vegetables. — future
10. Grandmother canned the green beans. — past

Directions: Write six sentences of your own using the correct verb tense.

Past tense:

Present tense:

Future tense:

Sentences will vary.

past   future   present

Page 115

Adding "ed" to Make Verbs Past Tense

To make many verbs past tense, add **ed**.

Examples:
cook + ed = cooked   wish + ed = wished   play + ed = played

When a verb ends in a **silent e**, drop the **e** and add **ed**.

Examples:
hope + ed = hoped   hate + ed = hated

When a verb ends in **y** after a consonant, change the **y** to **i** and add **ed**.

Examples:
hurry + ed = hurried   marry + ed = married

When a verb ends in a single consonant after a single short vowel, double the final consonant before adding **ed**.

Examples:
stop + ed = stopped   hop + ed = hopped

Directions: Write the past tense of the verb correctly. The first one has been done for you.

1. call	called	11. reply	replied
2. copy	copied	12. top	topped
3. frown	frowned	13. clean	cleaned
4. smile	smiled	14. scream	screamed
5. live	lived	15. clap	clapped
6. talk	talked	16. mop	mopped
7. name	named	17. soap	soaped
8. list	listed	18. choke	choked
9. spy	spied	19. scurry	scurried
10. phone	phoned	20. drop	dropped

Page 116

Writing: Past-Tense Verbs

To write about something that already happened, you can add **ed** to the verb.

Example: Yesterday, we **talked**.
You can also use **was** and **were** and add **ing** to the verb.

Example: Yesterday, we **were talking**.
When a verb ends with **e**, you usually drop the **e** before adding **ing**.

Examples: grade — was grading   weave — were weaving
tape — was taping   sneeze — were sneezing

Directions: Write two sentences for each verb below. Tell about something that has already happened and write the verb both ways. (Watch the spelling of the verbs that end with **e**.)

Example: stream

The rain streamed down the window.
The rain was streaming down the window.

1. grade

2. tape

3. weave

4. sneeze

Sentences will vary.

Page 117

Irregular Verbs: Past Tense

Irregular verbs change completely in the past tense. Unlike regular verbs, past-tense forms of irregular verbs are not formed by adding **ed**.

Example: The past tense of **go** is **went**.

Other verbs change some letters to form the past tense.
Example: The past tense of **break** is **broke**.

A **helping verb** helps to tell about the past. **Has**, **have** and **had** are helping verbs used with action verbs to show the action occurred in the past. The past-tense form of the irregular verb sometimes changes when a helping verb is added.

Present Tense Irregular Verb	Past Tense Irregular Verb	Past Tense Irregular Verb With Helper
go	went	have/has/had gone
see	saw	have/has/had seen
do	did	have/has/had done
bring	brought	have/has/had brought
sing	sang	have/has/had sung
drive	drove	have/has/had driven
swim	swam	have/has/had swum
sleep	slept	have/has/had slept

Directions: Choose four words from the chart. Write one sentence using the past-tense form of the verb without a helping verb. Write another sentence using the past-tense form with a helping verb.

1.

2.

3.

4.

Sentences will vary.

Page 118

The Irregular Verb "Be"

Be is an irregular verb. The present-tense forms of **be** are **be**, **am**, **is** and **are**. The past-tense forms of **be** are **was** and **were**.

Directions: Write the correct form of **be** in the blanks. The first one has been done for you.

1. I **am** so happy for you!
2. Jared **was** unfriendly yesterday.
3. English can **be** a lot of fun to learn.
4. They **are** among the nicest people I know.
5. They **were** late yesterday.
6. She promises she **is** going to arrive on time.
7. I **am** nervous right now about the test.
8. If you **are** satisfied now, so am I.
9. He **was** as nice to me last week as I had hoped.
10. He can **be** very gracious.
11. Would you **be** offended if I moved your desk?
12. He **was** watching at the window for me yesterday.

Page 119

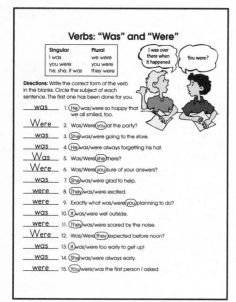

Verbs: "Was" and "Were"

Singular	Plural
I was	we were
you were	you were
he, she, it was	they were

I was over there when it happened.

You were?

Directions: Write the correct form of the verb in the blanks. Circle the subject of each sentence. The first one has been done for you.

was	1. (He) was/were so happy that we all smiled, too.
Were	2. Was/Were (you) at the party?
was	3. (She) was/were going to the store.
was	4. (He) was/were always forgetting his hat.
Was	5. Was/Were (she) there?
Were	6. Was/Were (you) sure of your answers?
was	7. (She) was/were glad to help.
were	8. (They) was/were excited.
were	9. Exactly what was/were (you) planning to do?
was	10. (It) was/were wet outside.
were	11. (They) was/were scared by the noise.
Were	12. Was/Were (they) expected before noon?
was	13. (It) was/were too early to get up!
was	14. (She) was/were always early.
were	15. (You) were/was the first person I asked.

Page 120

Verbs: "Went" and "Gone"

The word **went** is used without a helping verb.

Examples:

Correct: Susan **went** to the store.
Incorrect: Susan **has went** to the store.

Gone is used with a helping verb.

Examples:

Correct: Susan **has gone** to the store.
Incorrect: Susan **gone** to the store.

Directions: Write **C** in the blank if the verb is used correctly. Draw an **X** in the blank if the verb is not used correctly.

C	1. She has gone to my school since last year.
C	2. Has he been gone a long time?
X	3. He has went to the same class all year.
X	4. I have went to that doctor since I was born.
C	5. She is long gone!
C	6. Who among us has not gone to get a drink yet?
C	7. The class has gone on three field trips this year.
C	8. The class went on three field trips this year.
X	9. Who has not went to the board with the right answer?
X	10. We have not went on our vacation yet.
C	11. Who is went for the pizza?
C	12. The train has been gone for 2 hours.
C	13. The family had gone to the movies.
X	14. Have you went to visit the new bookstore?
C	15. He has gone on and on about how smart you are!

Page 121

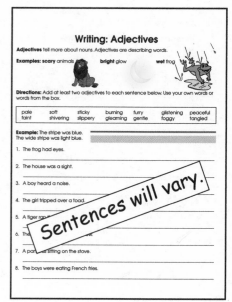

Writing: Adjectives

Adjectives tell more about nouns. Adjectives are describing words.

Examples: scary animals **bright** glow **wet** frog

Directions: Add at least two adjectives to each sentence below. Use your own words or words from the box.

pale	soft	sticky	burning	furry	glistening	peaceful
faint	shivering	slippery	gleaming	gentle	foggy	tangled

Example: The stripe was blue.
The wide stripe was light blue.

1. The frog had eyes.

2. The house was a sight.

3. A boy heard a noise.

4. The girl tripped over a toad.

5. A tiger ran ...

6. The ...

7. A pan ... sitting on the stove.

8. The boys were eating French fries.

Sentences will vary.

Page 122

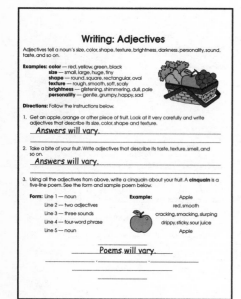

Writing: Adjectives

Adjectives tell a noun's size, color, shape, texture, brightness, darkness, personality, sound, taste, and so on.

Examples: color — red, yellow, green, black
size — small, large, huge, tiny
shape — round, square, rectangular, oval
texture — rough, smooth, soft, scaly
brightness — glistening, shimmering, dull, pale
personality — gentle, grumpy, happy, sad

Directions: Follow the instructions below.

1. Get an apple, orange or other piece of fruit. Look at it very carefully and write adjectives that describe its size, color, shape and texture.
   Answers will vary.

2. Take a bite of your fruit. Write adjectives that describe its taste, texture, smell, and so on.
   Answers will vary.

3. Using all the adjectives from above, write a cinquain about your fruit. A **cinquain** is a five-line poem. See the form and sample poem below.

Form:	Line 1 — noun	Example	Apple
	Line 2 — two adjectives		red, smooth
	Line 3 — three sounds		cracking, smacking, slurping
	Line 4 — four-word phrase		drippy, sticky, sour juice
	Line 5 — noun		Apple

Poems will vary.

Page 123

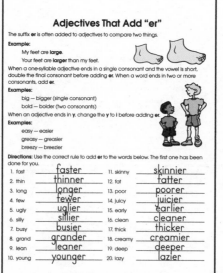

Adjectives That Add "er"

The suffix **er** is often added to adjectives to compare two things.

Example:

My feet are **large**.
Your feet are **larger** than my feet.

When a one-syllable adjective ends in a single consonant and the vowel is short, double the final consonant before adding **er**. When a word ends in two or more consonants, add **er**.

Examples:

big — bigger (single consonant)
bold — bolder (two consonants)

When an adjective ends in **y**, change the **y** to **i** before adding **er**.

Examples:

easy — easier
greasy — greasier
breezy — breezier

Directions: Use the correct rule to add **er** to the words below. The first one has been done for you.

1. fast	faster	11. skinny	skinnier
2. thin	thinner	12. fat	fatter
3. long	longer	13. poor	poorer
4. few	fewer	14. juicy	juicier
5. ugly	uglier	15. early	earlier
6. silly	sillier	16. clean	cleaner
7. busy	busier	17. thick	thicker
8. grand	grander	18. creamy	creamier
9. lean	leaner	19. deep	deeper
10. young	younger	20. lazy	lazier

Page 124

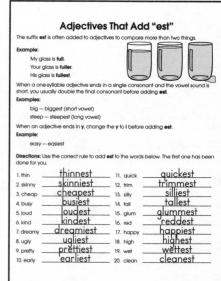

Adjectives That Add "est"

The suffix **est** is often added to adjectives to compare more than two things.

Example:

My glass is **full**.
Your glass is **fuller**.
His glass is **fullest**.

When a one-syllable adjective ends in a single consonant and the vowel sound is short, you usually double the final consonant before adding **est**.

Examples:

big — biggest (short vowel)
steep — steepest (long vowel)

When an adjective ends in **y**, change the **y** to **i** before adding **est**.

Example:

easy — easiest

Directions: Use the correct rule to add **est** to the words below. The first one has been done for you.

1. thin	thinnest	11. quick	quickest
2. skinny	skinniest	12. trim	trimmest
3. cheap	cheapest	13. silly	silliest
4. busy	busiest	14. tall	tallest
5. loud	loudest	15. glum	glummest
6. kind	kindest	16. red	reddest
7. dreamy	dreamiest	17. happy	happiest
8. ugly	ugliest	18. high	highest
9. pretty	prettiest	19. wet	wettest
10. early	earliest	20. clean	cleanest

Page 125

Adjectives Preceded by "More"

Most adjectives of two or more syllables are preceded by the word **more** as a way to show comparison between two things.

Examples:

Correct: intelligent, more intelligent
Incorrect: intelligenter
Correct: famous, more famous
Incorrect: famouser

Directions: Write **more** before the adjectives that fit the rule. Draw an X in the blanks of the adjectives that do not fit the rule. To test yourself, say the words aloud using **more** and adding **er** to hear which way sounds correct. The first two have been done for you.

X	1. cheap	more	11. awful
more	2. beautiful	more	12. delicious
X	3. quick	more	13. embarrassing
more	4. terrible	X	14. nice
more	5. difficult	more	15. often
more	6. interesting	X	16. hard
X	7. polite	more	17. valuable
X	8. cute	X	18. close
X	9. dark	X	19. fast
X	10. sad	more	20. important

Page 126

Adjectives Using "er" or "More"

Directions: Add the word or words needed in each sentence. The first one has been done for you.

1. I thought the book was **more interesting** than the movie. (interesting)

2. Do you want to carry this box? It is **lighter** than the one you have now. (light)

3. I noticed you are moving **slower** this morning. Does your ankle still bother you? (slow)

4. Thomas Edison is probably **more famous** for his invention of the electric light bulb than the phonograph. (famous)

5. She stuck out her lower lip and whined, "Your ice-cream cone is **bigger** than mine!" (big)

6. Mom said my room was **cleaner** than it has been in a long time. (clean)

Page 127

Adjectives Preceded by "Most"

Most adjectives of two or more syllables are preceded by the word **most** as a way to show comparison between more than two things.

Examples:

Correct: intelligent, most intelligent
Incorrect: intelligentest
Correct: famous, most famous
Incorrect: famousest

Directions: Read the following groups of sentences. In the last sentence for each group, write the adjective preceded by **most**. The first one has been done for you.

1. My uncle is intelligent.
   My aunt is more intelligent.
   My cousin is the **most intelligent**.

2. I am thankful.
   My brother is more thankful.
   My parents are the **most thankful**.

3. Your sister is polite.
   Your brother is more polite.
   You are the **most polite**.

4. The blouse was expensive.
   The sweater was more expensive.
   The coat was the **most expensive**.

5. The class was fortunate.
   The teacher was more fortunate.
   The principal was the **most fortunate**.

6. The cookies were delicious.
   The cake was even more delicious.
   The brownies were the **most delicious**.

7. That painting is elaborate.
   The sculpture is more elaborate.
   The finger painting is the **most elaborate**.

Page 128

Adjectives Using "est" or "Most"

Directions: Add the word or words needed to complete each sentence. The first one has been done for you.

1. The star over there is the **brightest** of all! (bright)

2. "I believe this is the **most delightful** time I have ever had," said Mackenzie. (delightful)

3. That game was the **most exciting** one of the whole year! (exciting)

4. I think this tree has the **greenest** leaves. (green)

5. We will need the **sharpest** knife you have to cut the face for the jack-o-lantern. (sharp)

6. Everyone agreed that your chocolate chip cookies were the **most delicious** of all. (delicious)

Page 129

Writing: Adverbs

Like adjectives, **adverbs** are describing words. They describe verbs. Adverbs tell how, when or where action takes place.

Examples: How | **When** | **Where**
slowly | yesterday | here
gracefully | today | there
swiftly | tomorrow | everywhere
quickly | soon

How? When? Where?

Hint: To identify an adverb, locate the verb, then ask yourself if there are any words that tell how, when or where action takes place.

Directions: Read the following sentences. Underline the adverbs, then write whether they tell how, when or where. The first one has been done for you.

1. At the end of the day, the children ran <u>quickly</u> home from school. — **how**
2. They will have a spelling test <u>tomorrow</u>. — **when**
3. <u>Slowly</u>, the children filed to their seats. — **how**
4. The teacher sat <u>here</u> at her desk. — **where**
5. She will pass the tests back <u>later</u>. — **when**
6. The students received their grades <u>happily</u>. — **how**

Directions: Write four sentences of your own using any of the adverbs above.

Sentences will vary.

Page 130

Adverbs

Adverbs are words that tell when, where or how.

Adverbs of time tell when.

Example:

The train left yesterday.

Yesterday is an adverb of time. It tells when the train left.

Adverbs of place tell where.

Example:

The girl walked away.

Away is an adverb of place. It tells where the girl walked.

Adverbs of manner tell how.

Example:

The boy walked quickly.

Quickly is an adverb of manner. It tells how the boy walked.

Directions: Write the adverb for each sentence in the first blank. In the second blank, write whether it is an adverb of time, place or manner. The first one has been done for you.

1. The family ate downstairs.	downstairs	place
2. The relatives laughed loudly.	loudly	manner
3. We will finish tomorrow.	tomorrow	time
4. The snowstorm will stop soon.	soon	time
5. She sings beautifully!	beautifully	manner
6. The baby slept soundly.	soundly	manner
7. The elevator stopped suddenly.	suddenly	manner
8. Does the plane leave today?	today	time
9. The phone call came yesterday.	yesterday	time
10. She ran outside.	outside	place

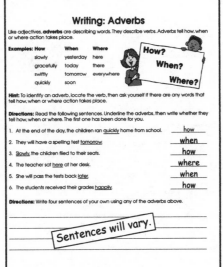

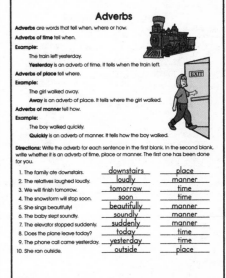

Page 131

Adverbs of Time

Directions: Choose a word or group of words from the box to complete each sentence. Make sure the adverb you choose makes sense with the rest of the sentence.

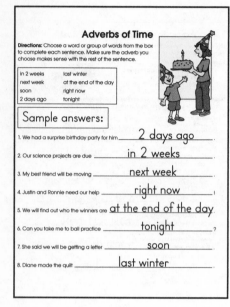

in 2 weeks	last winter
next week	at the end of the day
soon	right now
2 days ago	tonight

Sample answers:

1. We had a surprise birthday party for him ___2 days ago___

2. Our science projects are due ___in 2 weeks___

3. My best friend will be moving ___next week___

4. Justin and Ronnie need our help ___right now___ !

5. We will find out who the winners are ___at the end of the day___

6. Can you take me to ball practice ___tonight___ ?

7. She said we will be getting a letter ___soon___

8. Diane made the quilt ___last winter___

Page 132

Adverbs of Place

Directions: Choose one word from the box to complete each sentence. Make sure the adverb you choose makes sense with the rest of the sentence.

| inside | upstairs | below | everywhere |
| home | somewhere | outside | there |

Sample answers:

1. Each child took a new library book ___home___

2. We looked ___everywhere___ for his jacket.

3. We will have recess ___inside___ because it is raining.

4. From the top of the mountain we could see the village far ___below___ .

5. My sister and I share a bedroom ___upstairs___

6. The teacher warned the children, "You must play with the ball ___outside___

7. Mother said, "I know that recipe is ___somewhere___ in this file box!"

8. You can put the chair ___there___

Page 133

Adverbs of Manner

Directions: Choose a word from the box to complete each sentence. Make sure the adverb you choose makes sense with the rest of the sentence. One word will be used twice.

| quickly | carefully | loudly | easily | carelessly | slowly |

Sample answers:

1. The scouts crossed the old bridge ___carefully___

2. We watched the turtle move ___slowly___ across the yard.

3. Everyone completed the math test ___quickly___

4. The quarterback scampered ___easily___ down the sideline.

5. The mother ___carefully___ cleaned the child's sore knee.

6. The fire was caused by someone ___carelessly___ tossing a match.

7. The alarm rang ___loudly___ while we were eating.

Page 134

Adjectives and Adverbs

Directions: Write **ADJ** on the line if the bold word is an adjective. Write **ADV** if the bold word is an adverb. The first one has been done for you.

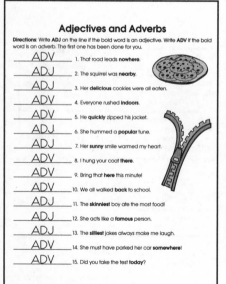

ADV — 1. That road leads **nowhere**.

ADJ — 2. The squirrel was **nearby**.

ADJ — 3. Her **delicious** cookies were all eaten.

ADV — 4. Everyone rushed **indoors**.

ADV — 5. He **quickly** zipped his jacket.

ADJ — 6. She hummed a **popular** tune.

ADJ — 7. Her **sunny** smile warmed my heart.

ADV — 8. I hung your coat **there**.

ADV — 9. Bring that **here** this minute!

ADV — 10. We all walked **back** to school.

ADJ — 11. The **skinniest** boy ate the most food!

ADJ — 12. She acts like a **famous** person.

ADJ — 13. The **silliest** jokes always make me laugh.

ADV — 14. She must have parked her car **somewhere**!

ADV — 15. Did you take the test **today**?

Page 135

Writing: Using Conjunctions

Conjunctions are joining words that can be used to combine sentences. Words such as **and**, **but**, **or**, **when** and **after** are conjunctions.

Examples:
Sally went to the mall. She went to the movies.
Sally went to the mall, and she went to the movies.

We can have our vacation at home. We can vacation at the beach.
We can have our vacation at home, or we can vacation at the beach.

Mary fell on the playground. She did not hurt herself.
Mary fell on the playground, but she did not hurt herself.

Note: The conjunctions **after** or **when** are usually placed at the beginning of the sentence.

Example: Marge went to the store. She went to the gas station.
After Marge went to the store, she went to the gas station.

Directions: Combine the following sentences using a conjunction.

Sample answers:
1. Peter fell down the steps. He broke his foot. (and)
   Peter fell down the steps, and he broke his foot.
2. I visited New York. I would like to see Chicago. (but)
   I visited New York, but I would like to see Chicago.
3. Amy can edit books. She can write stories. (or)
   Amy can edit books, or she can write stories.
4. He played in the barn. John started to sneeze. (when)
   When John played in the barn, he started to sneeze.
5. The team won the playoffs. They went to the championships. (after)
   After the team won the playoffs, they went to the championships.

Directions: Write three sentences of your own using the conjunctions **and**, **but**, **or**, **when** or **after**.

___

Sentences will vary.

Page 136

"And," "But," "Or"

Directions: Write **and**, **but** or **or** to complete the sentences.

1. I thought we might try that new hamburger place, ___but___ Mom wants to eat at the Spaghetti Shop.

2. We could stay home, ___or___ would you rather go to the game?

3. She went right home after school, ___but___ he stopped at the store.

4. Mother held the piece of paneling, ___and___ Father nailed it in place.

5. She babysat last weekend, ___and___ her big sister went with her.

6. She likes raisins in her oatmeal, ___but___ I would rather have mine with brown sugar.

7. She was planning on coming over tomorrow, ___but___ I asked her if she could wait until the weekend.

8. Tomato soup with crackers sounds good to me, ___or___ would you rather have vegetable beef soup?

Page 137

"Because" and "So"

Directions: Write **because** or **so** to complete the sentences.

1. She cleaned the paint brushes ___so___ they would be ready in the morning.

2. Father called home complaining of a sore throat ___so___ Mom stopped by the pharmacy.

3. His bus will be running late ___because___ it has a flat tire.

4. We all worked together ___so___ we could get the job done sooner.

5. We took a variety of sandwiches on the picnic ___because___ we knew not everyone liked cheese and olives with mayonnaise.

6. All the school children were sent home ___because___ the electricity went off at school.

7. My brother wants us to meet his girlfriend ___so___ she will be coming to dinner with us on Friday.

8. He forgot to take his umbrella along this morning ___so___ now his clothes are very wet.

Page 138

"When" and "After"

Directions: Write **when** or **after** to complete the sentences.

Answers may vary.

1. I knew we were in trouble ___when___ I heard the thunder in the distance.

2. We carried the baskets of cherries to the car ___after___ we were finished picking them.

3. Mother took off her apron ___after___ I reminded her that our dinner guests would be here any minute.

4. I wondered if we would have school tomorrow ___after___ I noticed the snow begin to fall.

5. The boys and girls all clapped ___when___ the magician pulled the colored scarves out of his sleeve.

6. I was startled ___when___ the phone rang so late last night.

7. You will need to get the film developed ___after___ you have taken all the pictures.

8. The children began to run ___when___ the snake started to move!

Page 139

Conjunctions

Directions: Choose the best conjunction from the box to combine the pairs of sentences. Then rewrite the sentences.

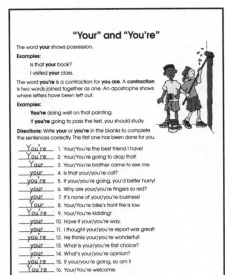

| and | but | or | because | when | after | so |

Answers may vary:

1. I like Leah. I like Ben.
I like Leah and Ben.

2. Should I eat the orange? Should I eat the apple?
Should I eat the orange or the apple?

3. You will get a reward. You turned in the lost item.
You will get a reward because you turned in the lost item.

4. I really mean what I say! You had better listen!
I really mean what I say, and you had better listen!

5. I like you. You're nice, friendly, helpful and kind.
I like you because you're nice, friendly, helpful and kind.

6. You can have dessert. You ate all your peas.
You can have dessert because you ate all your peas.

7. I like your shirt better. You should decide for yourself.
I like your shirt better, but you should decide for yourself.

8. We walked out of the building. We heard the fire alarm.
We walked out of the building after we heard the fire alarm.

9. I like to sing folk songs. I like to play the guitar.
I like to sing folk songs, and I like to play the guitar.

Page 140

"Good" and "Well"

Use the word **good** to describe a noun. Good is an adjective.

Example: She is a **good** teacher.

Use the word **well** to tell or ask how something is done or to describe someone's health. Well is an adverb. It describes a verb.

Example: She is not feeling **well**.

Directions: Write **good** or **well** in the blanks to complete the sentences correctly. The first one has been done for you.

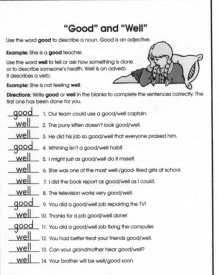

good 1. Our team could use a good/well captain.
well 2. The puny kitten doesn't look good/well.
well 3. He did his job so good/well that everyone praised him.
good 4. Whining isn't a good/well habit.
well 5. I might just as good/well do it myself.
well 6. She was one of the most well-/good- liked girls at school.
well 7. I did the book report as good/well as I could.
well 8. The television works very good/well.
good 9. You did a good/well job repairing the TV!
well 10. Thanks for a job good/well done!
good 11. You did a good/well job fixing the computer.
well 12. You had better treat your friends good/well.
well 13. Can your grandmother hear good/well?
well 14. Your brother will be well/good soon.

Page 141

"Your" and "You're"

The word **your** shows possession.

Examples:
Is that **your** book?
I visited **your** class.

The word **you're** is a contraction for **you are**. A **contraction** is two words joined together as one. An apostrophe shows where letters have been left out.

Examples:
You're doing well on that painting.
If **you're** going to pass the test, you should study.

Directions: Write **your** or **you're** in the blanks to complete the sentences correctly. The first one has been done for you.

You're 1. Your/You're the best friend I have!
You're 2. Your/You're going to drop that!
Your 3. Your/You're brother came to see me.
your 4. Is that your/you're cat?
you're 5. If your/you're going, you'd better hurry!
your 6. Why are your/you're fingers so red?
your 7. It's none of your/you're business!
Your 8. Your/You're bike's front tire is low.
You're 9. Your/You're kidding!
your 10. Have it your/you're way.
your 11. I thought your/you're report was great!
you're 12. He thinks your/you're wonderful!
your 13. What is your/you're first choice?
your 14. What's your/you're opinion?
you're 15. If your/you're going, so am I!
You're 16. Your/You're welcome.

Page 142

"Its" and "It's"

The word **its** shows ownership.

Examples:
Its leaves have all turned red.
Its paw was injured.

The word **it's** is a contraction for **it is**.

Examples:
It's better to be early than late.
It's not fair!

Directions: Write **its** or **it's** to complete the sentences correctly. The first one has been done for you.

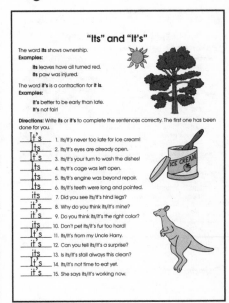

It's 1. Its/It's never too late for ice cream!
It's 2. Its/It's eyes are already open.
It's 3. Its/It's your turn to wash the dishes!
Its 4. Its/It's cage was left open.
Its 5. Its/It's engine was beyond repair.
Its 6. Its/It's teeth were long and pointed.
its 7. Did you see its/it's hind legs?
it's 8. Why do you think its/it's mine?
It's 9. Do you think its/it's the right color?
Its 10. Don't pet its/it's fur too hard!
It's 11. Its/It's from my Uncle Harry.
It's 12. Can you tell its/it's a surprise?
its 13. Is its/it's stall always this clean?
It's 14. Its/It's not time to eat yet.
it's 15. She says its/it's working now.

GRADE 4

Page 143

"Can" and "May"

The word **can** means am able to or to be able to.

Examples:
    I **can** do that for you.
    Can you do that for me?

The word **may** means be allowed to or permitted to. May is used to ask or give permission. **May** can also mean **might** or **perhaps**.

Examples:
    May I be excused?
    You **may** sit here.

Directions: Write **can** or **may** in the blanks to complete the sentences correctly. The first one has been done for you.

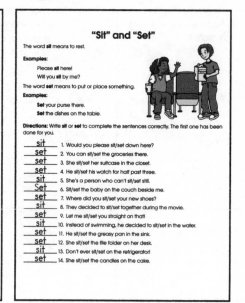

1. **May** Can/May I help you?
2. **can** He's smart. He can/may do it himself.
3. **may** When can/may I have my dessert?
4. **can** I can/may tell you exactly what she said.
5. **can** He can/may speak French fluently.
6. **may** You can/may use my pencil.
7. **may** I can/may be allowed to attend the concert.
8. **can** It's bright. I can/may see you!
9. **May** Can/May my friend stay for dinner?
10. **may** You can/may leave when your report is finished.
11. **can** I can/may see your point!
12. **can** She can/may dance well.
13. **Can** Can/May you hear the dog barking?
14. **Can** Can/May you help me button this sweater?
15. **may** Mother, can/may I go to the movies?

Page 144

"Sit" and "Set"

The word **sit** means to rest.

Examples:
    Please **sit** here!
    Will you **sit** by me?

The word **set** means to put or place something.

Examples:
    Set your purse there.
    Set the dishes on the table.

Directions: Write **sit** or **set** to complete the sentences correctly. The first one has been done for you.

1. **sit** Would you please sit/set down here?
2. **set** You can sit/set the groceries there.
3. **set** She sit/set her suitcase in the closet.
4. **set** He sit/set his watch for half past three.
5. **sit** She's a person who can't sit/set still.
6. **Set** Sit/Set the baby on the couch beside me.
7. **set** Where did you sit/set your new shoes?
8. **sit** They decided to sit/set together during the movie.
9. **set** Let me sit/set you straight on that!
10. **sit** Instead of swimming, he decided to sit/set in the water.
11. **set** He sit/set the greasy pan in the sink.
12. **set** She sit/set the file folder on her desk.
13. **sit** Don't ever sit/set on the refrigerator!
14. **set** She sit/set the candles on the cake.

Page 145

"They're," "Their," "There"

The word **they're** is a contraction for **they are**.

Examples:
    They're our very best friends!
    Ask them if **they're** coming over tomorrow.

The word **their** shows ownership.

Examples:
    Their dog is friendly.
    It's **their** bicycle.

The word **there** shows place or direction.

Examples:
    Look over **there**.
    There it is.

Directions: Write **they're**, **their** or **there** to complete the sentences correctly. The first one has been done for you.

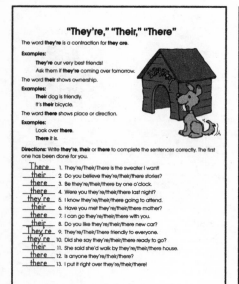

1. **There** They're/Their/There is the sweater I want!
2. **their** Do you believe they're/their/there stories?
3. **there** Be they're/their/there by one o'clock.
4. **there** Were you they're/their/there last night?
5. **they're** I know they're/their/there going to attend.
6. **their** Have you met they're/their/there mother?
7. **there** I can go they're/their/there with you.
8. **their** Do you like they're/their/there new car?
9. **They're** They're/Their/There friendly to everyone.
10. **they're** Did she say they're/their/there ready to go?
11. **their** She said she'd walk by they're/their/there house.
12. **there** Is anyone they're/their/there?
13. **there** I put it right over they're/their/there!

Page 146

"This" and "These"

The word **this** is an adjective that refers to things that are near. **This** always describes a singular noun. Singular means one.

Example:
    I'll buy **this** coat.
    (Coat is singular.)

The word **these** is also an adjective that refers to things that are near. **These** always describes a plural noun. A plural refers to more than one thing.

Example:
    I will buy **these** flowers.
    (Flowers is a plural noun.)

Directions: Write **this** or **these** to complete the sentences correctly. The first one has been done for you.

1. **these** I will take this/these cookies with me.
2. **these** Do you want this/these seeds?
3. **these** Did you try this/these nuts?
4. **this** Do it this/these way!
5. **this** What do you know about this/these situation?
6. **these** Did you open this/these doors?
7. **this** Did you open this/these window?
8. **these** What is the meaning of this/these letters?
9. **these** Will you carry this/these books for me?
10. **These** This/These pans are hot!
11. **this** Do you think this/these light is too bright?
12. **these** Are this/these boots yours?
13. **this** Do you like this/these rainy weather?

Page 148

Capital Letters and Periods

The first letter of a person's first, last and middle name is always capitalized.

Example: Elizabeth Jane Marks is my best friend.

The first letter of a person's title is always capitalized. If the title is abbreviated, the title is followed by a period.

Examples: Her mother is Dr. Susan Jones Marks.
Ms. Jessica Joseph was a visitor.

Directions: Write **C** if the sentence is punctuated and capitalized correctly. Draw an **X** if the sentence is not punctuated and capitalized correctly. The first one has been done for you.

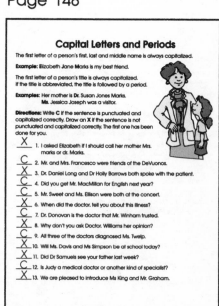

1. **X** I asked Elizabeth if I should call her mother Mrs. marks or dr. Marks.
2. **C** Mr. and Mrs. Francesco were friends of the DeVuonos.
3. **X** Dr. Daniel Long and Dr Holly Barrows both spoke with the patient.
4. **C** Did you get Mr. MacMillan for English next year?
5. **C** Mr. Sweet and Ms. Ellison were both at the concert.
6. **X** When did the doctor, tell you about this illness?
7. **C** Dr. Donovan is the doctor that Mr. Winham trusted.
8. **X** Why don't you ask Doctor. Williams her opinion?
9. **C** All three of the doctors diagnosed Ms. Twelp.
10. **X** Will Ms. Davis and Ms Simpson be at school today?
11. **X** Did Dr Samuels see your father last week?
12. **C** Is Judy a medical doctor or another kind of specialist?
13. **X** We are pleased to introduce Ms King and Mr. Graham.

Total Basic Skills Grade 4   326   Answer Key

Page 149

Punctuation: Commas

Use a comma to separate the number of the day of a month and the year. Do not use a comma to separate the month and year if no day is given.

Examples:

June 14, 1999
June 1999

Use a comma after **yes** or **no** when it is the first word in a sentence.

Examples:

Yes, I will do it right now.
No, I don't want any.

Directions: Write **C** if the sentence is punctuated correctly. Draw an **X** if the sentence is not punctuated correctly. The first one has been done for you.

C 1. No, I don't plan to attend.
C 2. I told them, oh yes, I would go.
C 3. Her birthday is March 13, 1995.
X 4. He was born in May, 1997.
C 5. Yes, of course I like you!
X 6. No I will not be there.
X 7. They left for vacation on February, 14.
C 8. No, today is Monday.
C 9. The program was first shown on August 12, 1991.
X 10. In September, 2007 how old will you be?
X 11. He turned 12 years old on November, 13.
C 12. I said no, I will not come no matter what!
C 13. Yes, she is a friend of mine.
C 14. His birthday is June 12, 1992, and mine is June 12, 1993.
X 15. No I would not like more dessert.

Page 150

Punctuation: Commas

Use a comma to separate words in a series. A comma is used after each word in a series but is not needed before the last word. Both ways are correct. In your own writing, be consistent about which style you use.

Examples:

We ate apples, oranges, and pears.
We ate apples, oranges and pears.

Always use a comma between the name of a city and a state.

Example:

She lives in Fresno, California.
He lives in Wilmington, Delaware.

Directions: Write **C** if the sentence is punctuated correctly. Draw an **X** if the sentence is not punctuated correctly. The first one has been done for you.

X 1. She ordered shoes, dresses and shirts to be sent to her home in Oakland California.
C 2. No one knew her pets' names were Fido, Spot and Tiger.
X 3. He likes green beans lima beans, and corn on the cob.
C 4. Typing paper, pens and pencils are all needed for school.
C 5. Send your letters to her in College Park, Maryland.
X 6. Orlando Florida is the home of Disney World.
C 7. Mickey, Minnie, Goofy and Daisy are all favorites of mine.
C 8. Send your letter to her in Reno, Nevada.
X 9. Before he lived in New York, City he lived in San Diego, California.
C 10. She mailed postcards, and letters to him in Lexington, Kentucky.
X 11. Teacups, saucers, napkins, and silverware were piled high.
C 12. Can someone give me a ride to Indianapolis, Indiana?
X 13. He took a train a car, then a boat to visit his old friend.
X 14. Why can't I go to Disney World to see Mickey, and Minnie?

Page 151

Book Titles

All words in the title of a book are underlined. Underlined words also mean italics.

Examples:

The Hunt for Red October was a best-seller!
(The Hunt for Red October)

Have you read Lost in Space? (Lost in Space)

Directions: Underline the book titles in these sentences. The first one has been done for you.

1. The Dinosaur Poster Book is for eight year olds.
2. Have you read Lion Dancer by Kate Waters?
3. Baby Dinosaurs and Giant Dinosaurs were both written by Peter Dodson.
4. Have you heard of the book That's What Friends Are For by Carol Adorjan?
5. J.B. Stamper wrote a book called The Totally Terrific Valentine Party Book.
6. The teacher read Almost Ten and a Half aloud to our class.
7. Marrying Off Mom is about a girl who tries to get her widowed mother to start dating.
8. The Snow and The Fire are the second and third books by author Caroline Cooney.
9. The title sounds silly, but Goofbang Value Daze really is the name of a book!
10. A book about space exploration is The Day We Walked on the Moon by George Sullivan.
11. Alice and the Birthday Giant tells about a giant who came to a girl's birthday party.
12. A book about a girl who is sad about her father's death is called Rachel and the Upside Down Heart by Eileen Douglas.
13. Two books about baseball are Baseball Bloopers and Oddball Baseball.
14. Katharine Ross wrote Teenage Mutant Ninja Turtles: The Movie Storybook.

Page 152

Book Titles

Capitalize the first and last word of book titles. Capitalize all other words of book titles except short prepositions, such as **of**, **at** and **in**; conjunctions, such as **and**, **or** and **but**; and articles, such as **a**, **an** and **the**.

Examples:

Have you read War and Peace?
Pippi Longstocking in Moscow is her favorite book.

Directions: Underline the book titles. Circle the words that should be capitalized. The first one has been done for you.

1. murder in the blue room by Elliot Roosevelt
2. growing up in a divided society by Sandra Burnham
3. the corn king and the spring queen by Naomi Mitchison
4. new kids on the block by Grace Catalano
5. best friends don't tell lies by Linda Barr
6. turn your kid into a computer genius by Carole Gerber
7. 50 simple things you can do to save the earth by Earth Works Press
8. garfield goes to waist by Jim Davis
9. the hunt for red october by Tom Clancy
10. fall into darkness by Christopher Pike
11. oh the places you'll go by Dr. Seuss
12. amy the dancing bear by Carly Simon
13. the great waldo search by Martin Handford
14. the time and space of uncle albert by Russel Stannard
15. true stories about abraham lincoln by Ruth Gross

Page 153

Punctuation: Quotation Marks

Use quotation marks (" ") before and after the exact words of a speaker.

Examples:

I asked Aunt Martha, "How do you feel?"
"I feel awful," Aunt Martha replied.

Do not put quotation marks around words that report what the speaker said.

Examples:

Aunt Martha said she felt awful.
I asked Aunt Martha how she felt.

Directions: Write **C** if the sentence is punctuated correctly. Draw an **X** if the sentence is not punctuated correctly. The first one has been done for you.

C 1. "I want it right now!" she demanded angrily.
X 2. "Do you want it now? I asked."
X 3. She said "she felt better" now.
C 4. Her exact words were, "I feel much better now!"
C 5. "I am so thrilled to be here!" he shouted.
C 6. "Yes, I will attend," she replied.
X 7. Elizabeth said "she was unhappy."
C 8. "I'm unhappy," Elizabeth reported.
C 9. "Did you know her mother?" I asked.
X 10. I asked "whether you knew her mother."
C 11. I wondered, "What will dessert be?"
C 12. "Which will it be, salt or pepper?" the waiter asked.
C 13. "No, I don't know the answer!" he snapped.
X 14. He said "yes he'd take her on the trip."
X 15. Be patient, he said. "It will soon be over."

Page 154

Punctuation: Quotation Marks

Use quotation marks around the titles of songs and poems.

Examples:

Have you heard "Still Cruising" by the Beach Boys?
"Ode To a Nightingale" is a famous poem.

Directions: Write **C** if the sentence is punctuated correctly. Draw an **X** if the sentence is not punctuated correctly. The first one has been done for you.

C 1. Do you know "My Bonnie Lies Over the Ocean"?
X 2. We sang The Stars and Stripes Forever" at school.
C 3. Her favorite song is "The Eensy Weensy Spider."
X 4. Turn the music up when "A Hard Day's "Night comes on!
C 5. "Yesterday" was one of Paul McCartney's most famous songs.
C 6. "Mary Had a Little Lamb" is a very silly poem!
C 7. A song everyone knows is "Happy Birthday."
C 8. "Swing Low, Sweet Chariot" was first sung by slaves.
X 9. Do you know the words to Home on "the Range"?
C 10. "Hiawatha" is a poem many older people had to memorize.
X 11. "Happy Days Are Here Again! is an upbeat tune.
C 12. Frankie Valli and the Four Seasons sang "Sherry."
X 13. The words to "Rain, Rain" Go Away are easy to learn.
C 14. A slow song I know is called "Summertime."
C 15. Little children like to hear "The Night Before Christmas."

Page 155

Proofreading

Proofreading means searching for and correcting errors by carefully reading and rereading what has been written. Use the proofreading marks below when correcting your writing or someone else's.

To insert a word or a punctuation mark that has been left out, use this mark: ∧
It is called a caret.

Example: We⌃to the dance together. *went*

To show that a letter should be capitalized, put three lines under it.

Example: Mrs. jones drove us to school.

To show that a capital letter should be small or lowercase, draw a diagonal line through it.

Example: Mrs. Jones Ɗrove us to school.

To show that a word is spelled incorrectly, draw a horizontal line through it and write the correct spelling above it.

Example: The wolros is an amazing animal. *walrus*

Directions: Proofread the two paragraphs using the proofreading marks you learned. The author's last name, Towne, is spelled correctly.

The Modern ark
My book report is on the modern ark by Cecilia Fitzsimmons. The book tells abut 80 of worlds endangered animals. The book has an ark and animals inside for kids put together.

Their House
there-house is a great book! The arthor's name is Mary Towne. they're house tells about a girl name Molly. Molly's family bys an old house from some people named warren. Then there-big problems begin!

Page 156

Proofreading

Directions: Proofread the sentences. Write C if the sentence has no errors. Draw an X if the sentence contains missing words or other errors. The first one has been done for you.

C 1. The new Ship Wreck Museum in Key West is exciting!

X 2. Another thing I liked was the litehouse.

C 3. Do you remember Hemingway's address in Key West?

X 4. The Key West semetery is on 21 acres of ground.

X 5. Ponce de eon discovered Key West.

C 6. The cemetery in Key West is on Francis Street.

X 7. My favorete tombstone was the sailor's.

C 8. His wife wrote the words on it. Remember?

X 9. The words said, "at least I know where to find him now!"

C 10. That sailor must have been away at sea all the time.

X 11. The troley ride around Key West is very interesting.

X 12. Do you why it is called Key West?

C 13. Can you imagine a lighthouse in the middle of your town?

X 14. It's interesting to no that Key West is our southernmost city.

C 15. Besides Harry Truman and Hemingway, did other famous people live there?

Page 157

Proofreading

Directions: Proofread the paragraphs, using the proofreading marks you learned. There are seven capitalization errors, three missing words and eleven errors in spelling or word usage.

Key West
key West has been tropical paradise ever since Ponce de Leon first saw the set of islands called the keys in 1513. Two famus streets in Key West are named duval and whitehead. You will find the city semetery cemetery on Francis Street. The tombstones are funny!

The message on one is, "I told you I was sick!" On sailor's tombstone is this message from his widow: "At least know lease I ne where to find him now."

The cemetery is on 21 acres in the middle of town.

The most famous home in key west is that of the author, Ernest Hemingway. Hemingway's home was there at 907 whitehead Street. He lived there for 30 years.

Page 158

Proofreading

Directions: Read more about Key West. Proofread and correct the errors. There are eight errors in capitalization, seven misspelled words and three missing words.

More About Key West
a good way to lern more about key West is to ride the trolley. Key West has a great troley system. the trolley will take on a tour of the salt ponds. You can also see three red brick forts. The trolley tour goes by a 110-foot high lighthouse. It is in the middle of it! It is also the southernmost city in the United States.

If you have time, the new Ship Wreck Museum. Key west was also the hom of former president Harry truman. During his presidency, Truman spent many vacations on key west.

Page 159

Run-On Sentences

A **run-on sentence** occurs when two or more sentences are joined together without punctuation.

Examples:

Run-on sentence: I lost my way once did you?
Two sentences with correct punctuation: I lost my way once. Did you?
Run-on sentence: I found the recipe it was not hard to follow.
Two sentences with correct punctuation: I found the recipe. It was not hard to follow.

Directions: Rewrite the run-on sentences correctly with periods, exclamation points and question marks. The first one has been done for you.

1. Did you take my umbrella I can't find it anywhere!
Did you take my umbrella? I can't find it anywhere!

2. How can you stand that noise I can't!
How can you stand that noise? I can't!

3. The cookies are gone I see only crumbs.
The cookies are gone. I see only crumbs.

4. The dogs were barking they were hungry.
The dogs were barking. They were hungry.

5. She is quite ill please call a doctor immediately!
She is quite ill. Please call a doctor immediately!

6. The clouds came up we knew the storm would hit soon.
The clouds came up. We knew the storm would hit soon.

7. You weren't home he stopped by this morning.
You weren't home. He stopped by this morning.

Page 160

Writing: Punctuation

Directions: In the paragraphs below, use periods, question marks or exclamation marks to show where one sentence ends and the next begins. Circle the first letter of each new sentence to show the capital.

Example: my sister accused me of not helping her rake the leaves, that's silly. I helped at least a hundred times.

1. I always tie on my fishing line, when it moves up and down, I know a fish is there, after waiting a minute or two, I pull up the fish, it's fun!

2. I tried putting lemon juice on my freckles to make them go away, did you ever do that? it didn't work, my skin just got sticky, now, I'm slowly getting used to my freckles.

3. once, I had an accident on my bike, I was on my way home from school, what do you think happened? my wheel slipped in the loose dirt at the side of the road, my bike slid into the road.

4. one night, I dreamed I lived in a castle, in my dream, I was the king or maybe the queen, everyone listened to my commands, then Mom woke me up for school. I tried commanding her to let me sleep, it didn't work!

5. what's your favorite holiday? Christmas is mine, for months before Christmas, I save my money, so I can give a present to everyone in my family, last year, I gave my big sister earrings, they cost me five dollars!

6. my dad does exercises every night to make his stomach flat, he says he doesn't want to grow old, I think it's too late, don't tell him I said that!

Total Basic Skills Grade 4

328

Answer Key

GRADE
4

Page 161

Writing: Putting Ideas Together

Directions: Make each pair of sentences into one sentence. (You may have to change the verbs for some sentences—from **is** to **are**, for example.)

Example: Our house was flooded. Our car was flooded.

Our house and car were flooded.

1. Kenny sees a glow.   Carrie sees a glow.
   Kenny and Carrie see a glow.
2. Our new stove came today.   Our new refrigerator came today.
   Our new stove and refrigerator came today.
3. The pond is full of toads.   The field is full of toads.
   The pond and field are full of toads.
4. Stripes are on the flag.   Stars are on the flag.
   Stripes and stars are on the flag.
5. The ducks took flight.   The geese took flight.
   The ducks and geese took flight.
6. Joe reads stories.   Dana reads stories.
   Joe and Dana read stories.
7. French fries will make you fat.   Milkshakes will make you fat.
   French fries and milkshakes will make you fat.
8. Justine heard someone groan.   Kevin heard someone groan.
   Justine and Kevin heard someone groan.

Page 162

Writing: Putting Ideas Together

Directions: Write each pair of sentences as one sentence.

Example: Jim will deal the cards one at a time. Jim will give four cards to everyone.

Jim will deal the cards one at a time and give four cards to everyone.

1. Amy won the contest.   Amy claimed the prize.
   Amy won the contest and claimed the prize.
2. We need to find the scissors.   We need to buy some tape.
   We need to find the scissors and buy some tape.
3. The stream runs through the woods.   The stream empties into the East River.
   The stream runs through the woods and empties into the East River.
4. Katie tripped on the steps.   Katie has a pain in her left foot.
   Katie tripped on the steps and has a pain in her left foot.
5. Grandpa took me to the store.   Grandpa bought me a treat.
   Grandpa took me to the store and bought me a treat.
6. Charity ran 2 miles.   She walked 1 mile to cool down afterwards.
   Charity ran 2 miles and walked 1 mile to cool down afterwards.

Page 163

Writing: Using Fewer Words

Writing can be more interesting when fewer words are used. Combining sentences is easy when the subjects are the same. Notice how the comma is used.

Example: Sally woke up. Sally ate breakfast. Sally brushed her teeth.

Sally woke up, ate breakfast and brushed her teeth.

Combining sentences with more than one subject is a little more complicated. Notice how commas are used to "set off" information.

Examples: Jane went to the store. Spot is my dog.

Jane went to the store with Sally, her sister.

Eddie likes to play with cars. Eddie is my younger brother.

Eddie, my younger brother, likes to play with cars.

Directions: Write each pair of sentences as one sentence.

1. Jerry played soccer after school. He played with his best friend, Tom.
   Jerry played soccer after school with his best friend, Tom.
2. Spot likes to chase cats. Spot is my dog.
   Spot, my dog, likes to chase cats.
3. Lori and Janice both love ice cream. Janice is Lori's cousin.
   Lori and Janice, Lori's cousin, both like ice cream.
4. Jayna is my cousin. Jayna helped me move into my new apartment.
   Jayna, my cousin, helped me move into my new apartment.
5. Romeo is a big tomcat. Romeo loves to hunt mice.
   Romeo, a big tomcat, loves to hunt mice.

Page 164

Combining Sentences

Some simple sentences can be easily combined into one sentence.

Examples:

Simple sentences: The bird sang. The bird was tiny. The bird was in the tree.
Combined sentence: The tiny bird sang in the tree.

Directions: Combine each set of simple sentences into one sentence. The first one has been done for you.

1. The big girls laughed. They were friendly. They helped the little girls.
   The big, friendly girls laughed as they helped the little girls.

2. The dog was hungry. The dog whimpered. The dog looked at its bowl.

3. Be quiet now. I want you to listen. You listen to my joke!

4. I lost my

5. I see my mother. My mother is walking. My mother is walking down the street.

6. Do you like ice cream? Do you like hot dogs? Do you like mustard?

7. Tell me you'll do it! Tell me you will! Tell me right now!

Answers may vary.

Page 165

Combining Sentences in Paragraph Form

A **paragraph** is a group of sentences that share the same idea.

Directions: Rewrite the paragraph by combining the simple sentences into larger sentences.

Jason awoke early. He threw off his covers. He ran to his window. He looked outside. He saw snow. It was white and fluffy. Jason thought of something. He thought of his sled. His sled was in the garage. He quickly ate breakfast. He dressed warmly. He got his sled. He went outside. He went to play in the snow.

Jason awoke early and threw off his covers. He ran to his window and looked outside. He saw white and fluffy snow. Jason thought of his sled in the garage. He quickly ate breakfast and dressed warmly. He got his sled and went outside to play in the snow.

Answer may vary.

Page 166

Nouns and Pronouns

To make a story or report more interesting, pronouns can be substituted for "overused" nouns.

Example:

Mother made the beds. Then Mother started the laundry.

The noun **Mother** is used in both sentences. The pronoun **she** could be used in place of **Mother** the second time to make the second sentence more interesting.

Directions: Cross out nouns when they appear a second and/or third time. Write a pronoun that could be used instead. The first one has been done for you.

we 1. My friends and I like to go ice skating in the winter. My friends and I usually fall down a lot, but my friends and I have fun!

they 2. All the children in the fourth-grade class next to us must have been having a party. All the children were very loud. All the children were happy it was Friday.

he 3. I try to help my father with work around the house on the weekends. My father works many hours during the week and would not be able to get everything done.

they 4. Can I share my birthday treat with the secretary and the principal? The secretary and the principal could probably use a snack right now!

him 5. I know Mr. Jones needs a copy of this history report. Please take it to Mr. Jones when you finish.

Page 167

Nouns and Pronouns

Directions: Cross out nouns when they appear a second and/or third time. Write a pronoun that could be used instead.

___it___ 1. The merry-go-round is one of my favorite rides at the county fair. I ride the ~~merry-go-round~~ so many times that I sometimes get sick.

___we___ 2. My parents and I are planning a 2-week vacation next year. ~~My parents and I~~ will be driving across the country to see the Grand Canyon. ~~My parents and I~~ hope to have a great time.

___he/she___ 3. The new art teacher brought many ideas from the city school where ~~the art teacher~~ worked before.

___them___ 4. Green beans, corn and potatoes are my favorite vegetables. I could eat ~~green beans, corn and potatoes~~ for every meal. I especially like ~~green beans, corn and potatoes~~ in stew.

___it___ 5. I think I left my pen in the library when I was looking up reference materials earlier today. Did you find ~~my pen~~ when you cleaned?

___she___ 6. My grandmother makes very good apple pie. ~~My grandmother~~ said I could learn how to make one the next time we visit.

___us___ 7. My brothers and I could take care of your pets while you are away if you show ~~my brothers and me~~ what you want done.

Page 168

Pronoun Referents

A **pronoun referent** is the noun or nouns a pronoun refers to.

Example:
Green beans, corn and potatoes are my favorite vegetables. I could eat them for every meal.
The pronoun **them** refers to the nouns green beans, corn and potatoes.

Directions: Find the pronoun in each sentence, and write it in the blank below. Underline the word or words the pronoun refers to. The first one has been done for you.

1. The fruit trees look so beautiful in the spring when they are covered with blossoms.
___they___

2. Tori is a high school cheerleader. She spends many hours at practice.
___she___

3. The football must have been slippery because of the rain. The quarterback could not hold on to it.
___it___

4. Aunt Donna needs a babysitter for her three year old tonight.
___her___

5. The art projects are on the table. Could you please put them on the top shelf along the wall?
___them___

Page 169

Pronoun Referents

Directions: Find the pronoun in each sentence, and write it in the blank below. Underline the word or words the pronoun refers to.

1. Did Aaron see the movie _Titanic_? Jay thought it was a very good movie.
___it___

2. Maysie can help you with the spelling words now, Tasha.
___you___

3. The new tennis coach said to call him after 6:00 tonight.
___him___

4. Jim, John and Jason called to say they would be later than planned.
___they___

5. Mrs. Burns enjoyed the cake her class had for the surprise party.
___her___

6. The children are waiting outside. Ask Josh to take the pinwheels out to them.
___them___

7. Mrs. Taylor said to go on ahead because she will be late.
___she___

8. The whole team must sit on the bus until the driver gives us permission to get off.
___us___

9. Dad said the umbrella did a poor job of keeping the rain off him.
___him___

10. The umbrella was blowing around too much. That's probably why it didn't do a good job.
___it___

Page 170

Writing: Topic Sentences

A **paragraph** is a group of sentences that tells about one main idea. A **topic sentence** tells the main idea of a paragraph.

Many topic sentences come first in the paragraph. The topic sentence in the paragraph below is underlined. Do you see how it tells the reader what the whole paragraph is about?

<u>Friendships can make you happy or make you sad.</u> You feel happy to do things and go places with your friends. You get to know each other so well that you can almost read each others' minds. But friendships can be sad when your friend moves away—or decides to be best friends with someone else.

Directions: Underline the topic sentence in the paragraph below.

<u>We have two rules about using the phone at our house.</u> Our whole family agreed on them. The first rule is not to talk longer than 10 minutes. The second rule is to take good messages if you answer the phone for someone else.

Directions: After you read the paragraph below, write a topic sentence for it.

<u>There are many ways you can earn money.</u>

For one thing, you could ask your neighbors if they need any help. They might be willing to pay you for walking their dog or mowing their grass or weeding their garden. Maybe your older brothers or sisters would pay you to do some of their chores. You also could ask your parents if there's an extra job you could do around the house to make money.

Directions: Write a topic sentence for a paragraph on each of these subjects.

Homework: _____

Television: ____

Sentences will vary.

Page 171

Writing: Supporting Sentences

Supporting sentences provide details about the topic sentence of a paragraph.

Directions: In the paragraph below, underline the topic sentence. Then cross out the supporting sentence that does not belong in the paragraph.

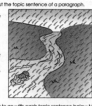

<u>One spring it started to rain and didn't stop for 2 weeks.</u> All the rivers flooded. Some people living near the rivers had to leave their homes. Farmers couldn't plant their crops because the fields were so wet. ~~Plants need water to grow.~~ The sky was dark and gloomy all the time.

Directions: Write three supporting sentences to go with each topic sentence below. Make sure each supporting sentence stays on the same subject as the topic sentence.

Not everyone should have a pet.
_____

I like to go on field trips with my class.
_____

Sentences will vary.

I've ____ want to be when I get older.

Page 172

Writing: Topic Sentences and Supporting Details

Directions: For each topic below, write a topic sentence and four supporting details.

Example:
Playing with friends: (topic sentence) <u>Playing with my friends can be lots of fun.</u>
(details)
1. We like to ride our bikes together.
2. We play fun games like "dress up" and "animal hospital."
3. Sometimes, we swing on the swings or slide down the slides on our swingsets.
4. We like to pretend we are having tea with our stuffed animals.

Recess at school: _____

Summer vacation: _____

Brothers or ____

Answers will vary.

Page 173

Writing: Paragraphs

Each paragraph should have one main idea. If you have a lot of ideas, you need to write several paragraphs.

Directions: Read the ideas below and number them:
1. If the idea tells about Jill herself.
2. If the idea tells what she did.
3. If the idea tells why she did it.

__2__ found a bird caught in a kite string

__2 or 1__ plays outside a lot

__1__ in grade four at Center School

__3__ knew the bird was wild

__2__ untangled the bird

__1__ likes pets

__3__ wouldn't want to live in a cage

__2__ gave the bird its freedom

Now, use the ideas to write three paragraphs. Use your own paper if necessary. Write paragraph 1 about Jill. Write paragraph 2 about what she did. Write paragraph 3 about why she did it.

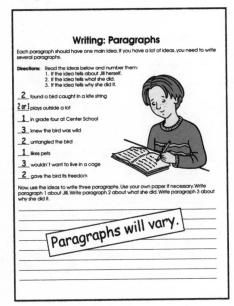

Paragraphs will vary.

Page 174

Writing: Paragraphs

When you have many good ideas about a subject, you need to organize your writing into more than one paragraph. It is easy to organize your thoughts about a topic if you use a "cluster of ideas" chart.

Example:

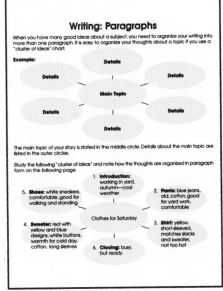

Details — Details — Details — Details — Main Topic — Details — Details

The main topic of your story is stated in the middle circle. Details about the main topic are listed in the outer circles.

Study the following "cluster of ideas" and note how the thoughts are organized in paragraph form on the following page.

1. **Introduction:** working in yard, autumn—cool weather

5. **Shoes:** white sneakers, comfortable, good for walking and standing

2. **Pants:** blue jeans, old, cotton, good for yard work, comfortable

Clothes for Saturday

4. **Sweater:** red with yellow and blue designs, white buttons, warmth for cold day, cotton, long sleeves

3. **Shirt:** yellow, short-sleeved, matches slacks and sweater, not too hot

6. **Closing:** busy, but ready

Page 175

Writing: Paragraphs

Once your ideas are "clustered," go back and decide which ideas should be the first, second, third, and so on. These numbers will be the order of the paragraph in the finished story.

Directions: Read the story paragraphs below.

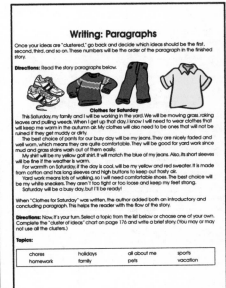

Clothes for Saturday

This Saturday, my family and I will be working in the yard. We will be mowing grass, raking leaves and pulling weeds. When I get up that day, I know I will need to wear clothes that will keep me warm in the autumn air. My clothes will also need to be ones that will not be ruined if they get muddy or dirty.

The best choice of pants for our busy day will be my jeans. They are nicely faded and well worn, which means they are quite comfortable. They will be good for yard work since mud and grass stains wash out of them easily.

My shirt will be my yellow golf shirt. It will match the blue of my jeans. Also, its short sleeves will be fine if the weather is warm.

For warmth on Saturday, if the day is cool, will be my yellow and red sweater. It is made from cotton and has long sleeves and high buttons to keep out frosty air.

Yard work means lots of walking, so I will need comfortable shoes. The best choice will be my white sneakers. They aren't too tight or too loose and keep my feet strong.

Saturday will be a busy day, but I'll be ready!

When "Clothes for Saturday" was written, the author added both an introductory and concluding paragraph. This helps the reader with the flow of the story.

Directions: Now, it's your turn. Select a topic from the list below or choose one of your own. Complete the "cluster of ideas" chart on page 176 and write a brief story. (You may or may not use all the clusters.)

Topics:

chores	holidays	all about me	sports
homework	family	pets	vacation

Page 176

Writing: Cluster of Ideas

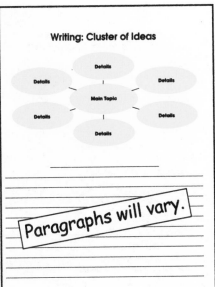

Details — Details — Details — Details — Main Topic — Details — Details

Paragraphs will vary.

Page 177

Taking Notes

Taking notes effectively can help you in many ways with schoolwork. It will help you better understand and remember what you read and hear. It will also help you keep track of important facts needed for reports, essays and tests.

Each person develops his/her own way of taking notes. While developing your style, keep in mind the following:
- Write notes in short phrases instead of whole sentences.
- Abbreviate words to save time.
  Examples: pres for president & **&** for and
- If you use the same name often in your notes, use initials.
  Examples: GW for George Washington **AL** for Abraham Lincoln.
- Be brief, but make sure you understand what you write.
- Number your notes, so you can understand where each note starts and stops.
- When taking notes from a long article or book, write down one or two important points per paragraph or chapter.

Directions: Reread the article "Bats" on page 80. As you read the first three paragraphs, fill in the note-taking format below with your notes.

Title of Article or Story __Floating in Space__

Notes may include: Important Points

Paragraph 1 __life different in space & on Earth;__
__no gravity in space__

Paragraph 2 __astros have suction cup shoes;__
__astros zip themselves into sleeping bags on the wall__

Paragraph 3 __astros have to squirt to drink bottles &__
__containers of water__

Page 178

Taking Notes

Directions: Use this guide for taking notes on the articles in the next two pages. Set up your own paper in a similar way, or make several photocopies, for note-taking on future pages.

Penguins Are Unusual Birds
(Title)

Paragraph or Chapter numbers   Important Points

1 _____

2 _____

3 _____

Notes will vary.

From Grapes to Raisins
(Title)

Paragraph or Chapter numbers   Important Points

1 _____

2 _____

3 _____

Notes will vary.

Page 179

Taking Notes: Penguins Are Unusual Birds

Directions: Use a sheet of paper to cover up the story about penguins. Then read the questions.

1. Why are penguins unusual?

2. Do penguins swim?

3. Where do penguins live?

4. Do penguins lay eggs like other birds?

Directions: Read about penguins. While reading, make notes on the note-taking sheet on the previous page.

> Penguins may be the most unusual birds. They cannot fly, but they can swim very fast through ice-cold water. They can dive deep into the water, and they can jump high out of it. Sometimes they make their nests out of rocks instead of twigs and grass. Some penguins live in very cold parts of the world. Others live in warmer climates. All penguins live south of the equator.
> Unlike other birds, penguins lay only one egg at a time. Right after a mother penguin lays her egg, she waddles back to the ocean. The father penguin holds the egg on his feet, covering it with part of his stomach to keep it warm. When the egg is ready to hatch, the mother penguin returns. Then the father penguin takes a turn looking for food.
> When a penguin swims, its white belly and dark back help it hide from enemies. From under the water, predators cannot see it. From on top of the water, large birds cannot see it either. This is how the penguin stays safe!

Directions: Use your notes to complete these sentences.

1. Penguins cannot fly, but ___they can swim fast___

2. Penguins can dive deep and ___jump high out of the water___

3. Penguins lay only ___one egg at a time___

4. Father penguins keep the egg ___warm___

5. Mother penguins return when the egg ___is ready to hatch___

Page 180

Taking Notes: From Grapes to Raisins

Directions: Use a piece of paper to cover up the story about how grapes become raisins. Then read the questions.

1. How do grapes become raisins?

2. What happens after the grapes become raisins?

3. Why are raisins brown?

4. In what countries do grapes grow?

Directions: Read about how grapes become raisins. While reading, make notes on the note-taking sheet on page 25.

> Grapes grow well in places that have lots of sun. In the United States, California is a big producer of grapes and raisins. When grapes are plump and round, they can be picked from their vines to be made into raisins. After the grapes are picked, they are put on big wooden or paper trays. They sit in the sun for many days.
> Slowly, the grapes begin to dry and turn into wrinkled raisins. The sun causes them to change colors. Grapes turn brown as they become raisins. Machines take off the stems. Then the raisins are washed. After being dried again, they are put into boxes.
> Some places use machines to make raisins dry faster. The grapes are put into ovens that have hot air blowing around inside. These ovens make the grapes shrivel and dry. Raisins are made in many countries that grow grapes. Besides the United States, countries such as Greece, Turkey, Iran, Spain and Australia produce a lot of raisins.

Directions: Use your notes to answer the four questions at the top of the page. Write your answers on the lines below.

1. ___After the grapes are picked, they are put on wooden or paper trays to dry in the sun for many days.___

2. ___When the grapes become raisins, machines take off the stems. The raisins are washed and dried. Then they are put into boxes.___

3. ___As the sun dries the raisins, they turn brown.___

4. ___United States, Greece, Turkey, Iran, Spain, Australia___

Page 181

Taking Notes: Graham Crackers

Directions: Use your notes to cover up the story about Graham crackers. Then read the questions.

1. Where did Graham crackers come from?

2. Who invented Graham crackers?

3. What are Graham crackers made of?

4. Why were Graham crackers made?

Directions: Read about Graham crackers. While reading, make notes on another sheet of paper.

> Graham crackers were invented around 1830. A minister named Sylvester Graham wanted people to eat healthier foods. He did not think that people should eat meat or white bread. He wanted people to eat more fruits and vegetables and wheat breads that were brown instead of white.
> Graham crackers were named after Sylvester Graham. He liked them because they were made of whole-wheat flour. There are many other kinds of crackers, but not all of them are as good for you as Graham crackers. Graham crackers are still considered a healthy snack!

Directions: Use your notes to answer the four questions at the top of the page. Write your answers on the lines below.

1. ___Graham crackers were invented by Sylvester Graham around 1830.___

2. ___Sylvester Graham, a minister___

3. ___They are made of whole-wheat flour.___

4. ___Sylvester Graham wanted people to eat healthier foods.___

Page 182

Compare and Contrast

To **compare** means to look for ways two items are alike. To **contrast** means to look for ways two items are different.

Directions: Use the Venn diagram to compare and contrast penguins (page 304) with most birds where you live.

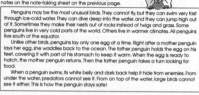

Penguins only | Other Birds only

Penguins / Other Birds

Venn diagram

cannot fly
swim fast
nests of rocks
1 egg at a time

make nests
lay eggs
parents get food for the babies
parents sit on egg

fly
don't swim
nest of twigs & grass
several eggs at a time

Penguins | Other birds

Sample answers:

To write a comparison paragraph, begin with a topic sentence which states your main idea. Write sentences that provide supporting details. End your paragraph with a conclusion sentence. A conclusion sentence often restates the topic sentence.

Directions: Use the information from your Venn diagram to write a short comparison paragraph.

___Although they are birds, penguins are different from the birds in my neighborhood. Penguins don't fly—but they do swim. These unusual birds make their nests out of rocks, and only have one egg at a time. Penguins, however, are the same as other birds in some ways. They do sit on their eggs and get food for their babies like other birds do. Penguins are certainly a different kind of bird!___

Page 183

Outlining

Outlines are plans that help you organize your thoughts. If you are writing an essay, an outline helps you decide what to write. An outline should similar to this:

```
I. First main idea
   A. A smaller idea
      1. An example
      2. An example
II. Second main idea
   A. A smaller idea
   B. Another smaller idea
III. Third main idea
   A. A smaller idea
   B. Another smaller idea
      1. An example
```

```
I. Planting a garden
   A. Choosing seeds
      1. Tomatoes
      2. Lettuce
II. Taking care of the garden
   A. Pulling the weeds
   B. Watering the garden
III. Harvesting
   A. Are they ripe?
   B. How to pick them
      1. Pick only the tomato off the vine
```

Directions: Use the outline for planting a garden to answer the questions.

1. What are the three main ideas?

1) ___Planting a garden___
2) ___Taking care of the garden___
3) ___Harvesting___

2. What are the two smaller ideas listed under "Taking care of the garden"?

1) ___Pulling the weeds___
2) ___Watering the garden___

3. What are the smaller ideas listed under "Harvesting"?

1) ___Are they ripe?___
2) ___How to pick them___

4. What is listed under the smaller idea "How to pick them"?

___Pick only the tomato off the vine.___

Page 184

Outlining: Building a Tree House

Directions: Study the sample outline for building a house. Then use words and phrases from the box to fill in the missing parts of the outline on how to build a tree house.

```
I. Find land
   A. On a hill
   B. By a lake
   C. In the city
II. Gather materials
   A. Buy wood
   B. Buy nails
   C. Buy tools
      1. Hammer
      2. Screwdriver
      3. Drill
      4. Saw
III. Build the house
   A. Who will use the tools?
   B. Who will carry the wood?
```

> Collect wood scraps
> Who will hold the boards?
> Who will use the hammer?
> Gather tools
> Can we climb it easily?
> How will we get things off the ground?

```
I. Find a tree
   A. Is it sturdy?
   B. Can we climb it easily?
II. Gather supplies
   A. Collect wood scraps
   B. Gather tools
      1. Hammer and nails
      2. Saw
III. Build the tree house
   A. Who will hold the boards?
   B. Who will use the hammer?
   C. How will we get things off the ground?
```

Page 185

Outlining: Finishing the Tree House

Directions: Use words and phrases from the box to fill in the missing parts of the outline of what to do once your tree house is built.

Sisters and brothers	When can they visit?
Parents	Spray paint
Tables	Choose a kind of paint
Chairs	Who can visit?

I. Painting the tree house

  A. Choose a color of paint

  B. <u>Choose a kind of paint</u>

    1. Cans of paint

    2. <u>Spray paint</u>

II. Putting furniture in the tree house

  A. <u>Tables</u>

  B. <u>Chairs</u>

III. Making a visitors' policy

  A. <u>Who can visit?</u>

    1. Friends

    2. <u>Sisters and brothers</u>

    3. <u>Parents</u>

  B. <u>When can they visit?</u>

Page 186

Outlining: The *Mayflower's* Voyage

Directions: Read about the *Mayflower*. Then complete the outline for an essay.

The *Mayflower* left England in 1620. It carried 101 passengers. Some of those passengers were called Pilgrims. Pilgrims were people who had wandered from country to country looking for a place to make their home.

It took 66 days to cross the Atlantic Ocean. The ship was crowded. There were some accidents on board. The *Mayflower* landed at the tip of Cape Cod in Massachusetts. Several men searched the area to find the best place to start a colony. They finally settled on Plymouth.

The Pilgrims lived on the *Mayflower* through the winter. The *Mayflower* returned to England in April 1621. None of the Pilgrims went back with it.

Sample answers:

I. The *Mayflower* leaves England

  A. <u>101 passengers</u>

  B. <u>Some people were Pilgrims</u>

II. The journey

  A. <u>Took 66 days</u>

  B. <u>Crowded</u>

  C. <u>Some accidents</u>

III. Landing in America

  A. <u>Landed at Cape Cod, MA</u>

  B. <u>Pilgrims settled in Plymouth</u>

Page 187

Outlining: The First Thanksgiving

Directions: Read about the first Thanksgiving. Then complete the outline.

The Pilgrims arrived at Plymouth Rock just as winter set in. Many people died that winter from cold and hunger. The following spring, the Pilgrims started planting vegetable gardens. A Native American named Squanto helped them. They planted peas, wheat, beans, corn and pumpkins.

When fall came, the Pilgrims were so glad to have enough food that they invited the Native Americans to share their first Thanksgiving. In addition to food from their garden, they also shared wild geese that they had killed and other food like sweet potatoes and fresh berries.

Sample answers:

I. The first winter

  A. <u>Came right away</u>

  B. <u>Many people died</u>

II. Spring

  A. <u>Befriended Squanto</u>

  B. <u>Squanto helped them plant gardens</u>

III. Fall

  A. <u>Had enough food from their gardens</u>

  B. <u>Had a Thanksgiving dinner</u>

    1. <u>Invited Native Americans</u>

    2. <u>Ate harvest from garden</u>

    3. <u>Ate wild geese</u>

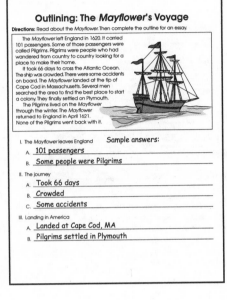

Page 188

Using an Outline to Write an Essay

Outlines help you organize information and notes into a manageable form. Outlines also help you prepare to write reports and essays by keeping your thoughts in a logical order or sequence. Once you have a good outline, converting it to paragraph form is easy.

To convert an outline to an essay, add your own words to expand the words and phrases in the outline into sentence form. Information from the first main topic becomes the first paragraph.

I. Painting the tree house
  A. Choose a color of paint
  B. Choose a kind of paint
    1. Cans of paint
    2. Spray paint

Information from the second and third main topics become the second and third paragraphs of the essay.

II. Putting furniture in the tree house
  A. Tables
  B. Chairs
III. Making a visitors' policy
  A. Who can visit?
    1. Friends
    2. Sisters and brothers
    3. Parents
  B. When can they visit?

To write an essay, remember to indent each paragraph, begin each paragraph with a topic sentence and include supporting details.

Directions: Read the beginning of the essay. Then finish it on another sheet of paper using your own words and information from the outline.

Finishing Touches

Finishing a tree house takes a lot of thought and planning. First, it needs to be painted. The paint will help protect the wood from rain and snow. The best kind of paint for finishing the wood would be in cans. It would brush on easily, smoothly and quickly. Green would be a great color for the tree house because it would blend in with the green leaves of the trees.

> Essays will vary.

Page 189

Summarizing: Writing an Autobiography

When you **summarize** an article, book or speech, you are simply writing a shorter article that contains only the main points. This shorter article of main points is called a **summary**.

To prepare for writing a summary of your life, you would begin with an outline. Since a summary is a brief account of main points, you will not be able to include every detail of your life. Your summary should include only basic facts.

I. Yourself
  A. Name
  B. Age and grade in school
    1. Subjects you like in school
    2. Subjects you do not like in school
  C. Looks
    1. Eye color
    2. Hair color
    3. Other features
II. Your family
  A. Parents
  B. Brothers/sisters
  C. Pets
III. Hobbies and interests
  A. Sports
  B. Clubs

Directions: Follow the format above to write an outline about your life. Feel free to add more main ideas, smaller ideas or examples.

Outline should follow format.

Page 190

Summarizing: Writing an Autobiography

A summary of your life would include when you were born, who your parents are, other members of your family, your age and your grade in school. Details like your favorite joke, today's weather or how much homework you had yesterday would not be included in a summary.

Directions: Use the information from your outline to write a summary of your life.

Summaries will vary.

Page 191

Summarizing: The North Pole

Directions: Read about the North Pole. Then use the main points of the article to write a paragraph summarizing conditions at the North Pole.

At the North Pole, the sun does not shine for half of the year. It stays dark outside for six months, but for the other six months of the year, the sun does not set. It is light through the night.

The North Pole is as far north as you can go. If you traveled north to the North Pole and kept going, you would start going south. You could call the North Pole the top of the Earth.

The average temperature at the North Pole is -9 degrees Fahrenheit. That is not any colder than many places in the United States get in the winter. In fact, some places get much colder than that, but at the North Pole, it stays very cold for a very long time.

The cold winds that blow off the Arctic Ocean make the North Pole a very cold place most of the time. In the summer when the sun is shining all day and all night, the temperature can rise to 38 degrees Fahrenheit in places that are sheltered from the wind. But that is still very cold.

The Arctic Ocean is at the North Pole. The area surrounding the North Pole is called the Arctic Region. Some of Canada, Alaska, Greenland, Russia and Scandinavia are in the Arctic Region. These places get very cold in the long, dark winters, too!

The main points of this article are:
1. At the North Pole, the sun is never out in the winter. It is always out in the summer.
2. The North Pole is very cold all year.
3. Winds from the Arctic Ocean make the North Pole stay very cold. The Arctic Ocean surrounds the North Pole.
4. There is some land in the Arctic Region.

Paragraph should include main points listed.

Page 192

Summarizing: Settler Children

Directions: Read about settler children. Then complete the list of main points at the end of the article.

In the 1700s and 1800s, many children from other countries came with their parents to America. In the beginning, they had no time to go to school. They had to help their families work in the fields, care for the animals and clean the house. They also helped care for their younger brothers and sisters.

Sometimes settler children helped build houses and schools. Usually, these early school buildings were just one room. There was only one teacher for all the children. Settler children were very happy when they could attend school.

Because settler children worked so much, they had little time to play. There were not many things settler children could do just for fun. One pastime was gardening. Weeding their gardens taught them how to be orderly. Children sometimes made gifts out of the things they grew.

The settlers also encouraged their children to sing. Each one was expected to play at least one musical instrument. Parents wanted their children to walk, ride horses, visit friends and relatives and read nonfiction books.

Most settler children did not have many toys. The toys they owned were made by their parents and grandparents. The children made up games with string, like "cat's cradle." They also made things out of wood, such as seesaws. Settler children did not have all the toys we have today, but they managed to have fun anyway!

The main points of this article are:
1. Settler children worked hard.
2. Settler children had many jobs.
3. **Settler children liked school.**
4. **Settler children had little time to play.**
5. **Settler children had few toys.**

Directions: Use the main points to write a summary of this article on a separate sheet of paper.

Page 193

Library Skills: Call Numbers

The **call number** of a book tells where it can be found among nonfiction books.

Information is presented differently on the title, subject and author card for the same book. A computer listing for this book would look quite similar.

Author card
567.91 VanCleave, Janice
V278   Dinosaurs for Every Kid
        John Wiley & Sons, Inc., 1994

Subject card
567.91 DINOSAURS
V278   VanCleave, Janice
        Dinosaurs for Every Kid
        John Wiley & Sons, Inc. 1994

Title card
567.91 Dinosaurs for Every Kid
V278   VanCleave, Janice
        John Wiley & Sons, Inc., 1994

Directions: Answer the questions about what is shown on these cards.

1. What is written at the top of the subject card?
Dinosaurs (the subject)

2. What is written at the top of the title card?
Dinosaurs for Every Kid (the title)

3. What is written at the top of the author card?
VanCleave, Janice (the author) and the call number

4. Why do libraries have three different kinds of listings for the same book?
to make it easier to find

5. What is the number listed at the top left of each card? **the call number**

6. What other information is on the cards? **John Wiley & Sons, Inc.**
1944 (name of publisher and date of publication)

Page 194

Library Skills: The Dewey Decimal System

Using a library catalog helps you find the books you want. All nonfiction books—except biographies and autobiographies—are filed according to their call number. **Nonfiction books** are books based on facts. **Biographies** are true books that tell about people's lives. **Autobiographies** are books that people write about their own lives.

The call numbers are part of the **Dewey Decimal System.** Each listing in a library catalog will include a book's call number.

Example:
918.8 Bringle, Mary
B85e   Eskimos
       F. Watts, 1973

All libraries using the **Dewey Decimal System** follow the same system for filing books. The system divides all nonfiction books into 10 main groups, each represented by numbers.

0-099	General works (libraries, computers, etc.)
100-199	Philosophy
200-299	Religion
300-399	Social Sciences
400-499	Language
500-599	Pure Science (math, astronomy, chemistry, etc.)
600-699	Applied Science (medicine, engineering, etc.)
700-799	Arts and Recreation
800-899	Literature
900-999	History

Each book is given a specific call number. A book about ghosts could be 133.1.

This is where some subjects fall in the Dewey Decimal System.

Pets	630	Maps	910	Cathedrals	236	Dinosaurs	560
Baseball	796	Monsters	791	Trees	580	Presidents	920
Butterflies	595	Mummies	390	Space	620	Cooking	640

Directions: Write the Dewey Decimal number for the following books.

560	Animals of Long Ago	**920**	Our American Presidents
580	City Leaves, City Trees	**390**	Mummies Made in Egypt
640	Easy Microwave Cooking for Kids	**791**	Real-Life Monsters
620	To Space and Back	**236**	Great Churches in Europe
796	Amazing Baseball Teams	**910**	The Children's Atlas

Page 195

Library Skills

Some books in a library are not filed by the Dewey Decimal System. Those books include biographies, autobiographies and fiction. Biographies and autobiographies may be filed together in the 920s or be assigned a call number by subject.

Fiction books are stories that someone has made up. They are filed in alphabetical order by the author's last name in the fiction section of the library.

Directions: For each title, write **B** if it is a biography, **A** if it is an autobiography or **F** if it is fiction. Then circle the titles that would not be filed by the Dewey Decimal System.

F — (Tales of a Fourth Grade Nothing)
B — The Real Tom Thumb
F — (Ramona the Pest)
A — Bill Peet: An Autobiography
B — Abraham Lincoln
F — (Charlotte's Web)
A — The King and I
A — My Life With Chimpanzees
F — (Sara Plain and Tall)
B — Michael Jordan, Basketball's Soaring Star
B — The First Book of Presidents
B — The Helen Keller Story

Page 196

Putting Library Skills to Use

You can improve your library skills by using them at your local library.

Directions: While at the library, follow the instructions and answer the questions.

1. Use the library catalog to find a book about dinosaurs. What is its title?

2. What is the call number for that book?

3. Who is the author of that book?

4. Go to the shelf and look for the book. Did you find it?

Answers will vary.

5. Use the library catalog to find the author of the book, Mummies Made in Egypt. Who wrote it?
Aliki

6. Use the library catalog to find other books by that author. What are the names of four other books by that author? **Answers may include:**
My Hands
Feelings
Jack and Jake
Dinosaur Bones

7. Use the library catalog to find a book written by Judy Blume with the word "fudge" in the title. What is its title?
Superfudge or **Fudgemania**

8. What is the library's most recent book by Ezra Jack Keats?
Answers will vary based on selection available.

Page 197

Encyclopedia Skills

Encyclopedias are sets of books that provide information about different subjects. If you want to know when cars were first made or who invented the phonograph, you could find the information in an encyclopedia.

Encyclopedias come in sets of books and on computer CD's. They contain many facts, illustrations, maps, graphs and tables. Encyclopedias are **reference books** found in the reference section of the library.

Each subject listed in an encyclopedia is called an **entry**. Entries are organized alphabetically.

Some good encyclopedias for students are *World Book Encyclopedia, Compton's Encyclopedia* and *Children's Britannica*.

Specialty encyclopedias, like the *McGraw-Hill Encyclopedia of Science and Technology*, contain information on one particular subject.

Directions: Number these encyclopedia entries in alphabetical order. The first one has been done for you.

4	deep-sea diving	9	Little League
5	deer	10	Little Rock
6	Florida	11	metric system
12	natural fiber	14	United Nations
3	Death Valley	13	poison oak
7	flour	1	Air Force
8	Gretzky, Wayne	2	Carter, Jimmy

Page 198

Encyclopedia Skills: Using the Index

The **index** of an encyclopedia contains an alphabetical listing of all entries. To find information about a subject, decide on the best word to describe the subject. If you want to know about ducks, look up the word "duck" in the index. If you're really interested in learning about mallard ducks, then look under "mallard ducks." The index shows the page number and volume where the information is located.

Look at the index entry below about Neil Armstrong. Most index entries also tell you when a person lived and died and give a short description of the person.

ARMSTRONG, NEIL   United States astronaut, b. 1930
   Commander of *Gemini 8*, 1966; first man to walk on the Moon, July 1969
   References in
      Astronaut: illus. 2:56
      Space travel 17:214

Neil Armstrong is listed under "Astronaut" and "Space travel." You can find information about him in both articles. The first entry shows there is an illustration (illus.) of Neil Armstrong in volume 2 on page 56 (2:56).

If Neil Armstrong were listed in a separate article in the encyclopedia, the index would look something like this:

main article Armstrong, Neil
2:48

Directions: Answer these questions about using an encyclopedia index.

1. According to the index listing for Neil Armstrong, when was he born? __1930__

2. According to the index listing, who was Neil Armstrong? __commander of__
__Gemini 8 and first man to walk on the Moon__

3. When did he walk on the Moon? __July 1969__

4. What are the titles of the two articles containing information about Neil Armstrong?
__Astronaut__   __Space travel__

5. Where would you find the article on Space travel?
Volume number __17__, page number __214__.

Page 200

Place Value

Place value is the value of a digit, or numeral, shown by where it is in the number. For example, in 1,234, 1 has the place value of thousands, 2 is hundreds, 3 is tens and 4 is ones.

Directions: Write the numbers in the correct boxes to find how far the car has traveled.

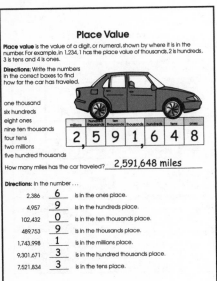

one thousand
six hundreds
eight ones
nine ten thousands
four tens
two millions
five hundred thousands

millions	hundred thousands	ten thousands	thousands	hundreds	tens	ones
2,	5	9	1,	6	4	8

How many miles has the car traveled? __2,591,648 miles__

Directions: In the number . . .

2,386	6	is in the ones place.
4,957	9	is in the hundreds place.
102,432	0	is in the ten thousands place.
489,753	9	is in the thousands place.
1,743,998	1	is in the millions place.
9,301,671	3	is in the hundred thousands place.
7,521,834	3	is in the tens place.

Page 201

Place Value: Standard Form

For this activity, you will need a number spinner or number cube.

Directions: Roll the cube or spin the spinner the same number of times as there are spaces in each place value box. The first number rolled or spun goes in the ones place, the second number in the tens place, and so on.

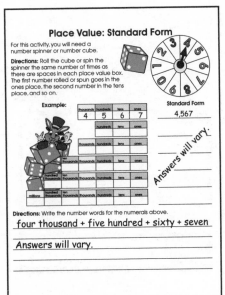

Example:

thousands	hundreds	tens	ones
4	5	6	7

Standard Form
4,567

hundreds	tens	ones

thousands	hundreds	tens	ones

Answers will vary.

hundred thousands	ten thousands	thousands	hundreds	tens	ones

millions	hundred thousands	ten thousands	thousands	hundreds	tens	ones

Directions: Write the number words for the numerals above.

__four thousand + five hundred + sixty + seven__

__Answers will vary.__

Page 202

Place Value: Expanded Notation and Standard Form

Directions: Use the number cube or spinner to create numbers for the place value boxes below. Then write the number in expanded notation and standard form.

Example:

thousands	hundreds	tens	ones
8	6	2	4

Standard Form __8,624__
Expanded Notation __8,000 + 600 + 20 + 4__

thousands	hundreds	tens	ones

Standard Form _____
Expanded Notation _____

ten thousands	thousands	hundreds	tens	ones

Standard Form _____
Expanded Notation _____

hundred thousands	ten thousands	thousands	hundreds	tens	ones

Standard Form _____
Expanded Notation _____

Answers will vary.

Directions: Write the value of the 4 in each number below.

742,521	4 ten thousands (40,000)
456	4 hundreds (400)
1,234,567	4 thousands (4,000)
65,504	4 ones (4)
937,641	4 tens (40)

Page 203

Add 'Em Up!

Addition is "putting together" or adding two or more numbers to find the sum.

Directions: Add the following problems as quickly and as accurately as you can.

3 +2 = **5**	6 +4 = **10**	5 +4 = **9**	2 +9 = **11**		
6 +2 = **8**	4 +1 = **5**	9 +6 = **15**	7 +6 = **13**	8 +7 = **15**	8 +9 = **17**
9 +4 = **13**	1 +8 = **9**	4 +7 = **11**	7 +9 = **16**	5 +6 = **11**	5 +3 = **8**
		6 +6 = **12**	8 +8 = **16**	7 +7 = **14**	4 +4 = **8**
		2 +8 = **10**	5 +2 = **7**	3 +6 = **9**	5 +8 = **13**

How quickly did you complete this page? **Answers will vary.**

Page 204

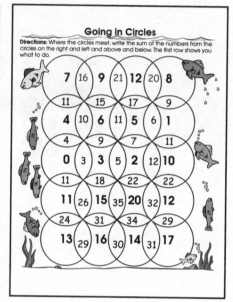

Going in Circles

Directions: Where the circles meet, write the sum of the numbers from the circles on the right and left and above and below. The first row shows you what to do.

Row 1: 7 (16) 9 (21) 12 (20) 8
11 15 17 9
Row 2: 4 (10) 6 (11) 5 (6) 1
4 9 7 11
Row 3: 0 (3) 3 (5) 2 (12) 10
11 18 22 22
Row 4: 11 (26) 15 (35) 20 (32) 12
24 31 34 29
Row 5: 13 (29) 16 (30) 14 (31) 17

Page 206

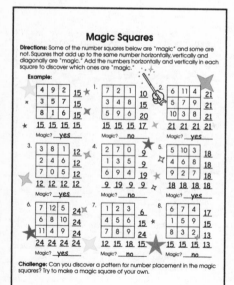

Magic Squares

Directions: Some of the number squares below are "magic" and some are not. Squares that add up to the same number horizontally, vertically and diagonally are "magic." Add the numbers horizontally and vertically in each square to discover which ones are "magic."

Example:

4	9	2	15
3	5	7	15
8	1	6	15
15	15	15	15

Magic? **yes**

1. | 7 | 2 | 1 | 10 |
3	4	8	15
5	9	6	20
15	15	15	17
Magic? **no**

2. | 6 | 11 | 4 | 21 |
5	7	9	21
10	3	8	21
21	21	21	21
Magic? **yes**

3. | 3 | 8 | 1 | 12 |
2	4	6	12
7	0	5	12
12	12	12	12
Magic? **yes**

4. | 2 | 7 | 0 | 9 |
1	3	5	9
6	4	9	19
9	19	9	9
Magic? **no**

5. | 5 | 10 | 3 | 18 |
4	6	8	18
9	2	7	18
18	18	18	18
Magic? **yes**

6. | 7 | 12 | 5 | 24 |
6	8	10	24
11	4	9	24
24	24	24	24
Magic? **yes**

7. | 1 | 2 | 3 | 6 |
4	5	6	15
7	8	9	24
12	15	18	15
Magic? **no**

8. | 6 | 7 | 4 | 17 |
1	5	9	15
8	3	2	13
15	15	15	13
Magic? **no**

Challenge: Can you discover a pattern for number placement in the magic squares? Try to make a magic square of your own.

Page 207

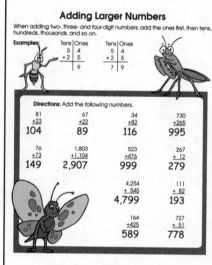

Adding Larger Numbers

When adding two-, three- and four-digit numbers, add the ones first, then tens, hundreds, thousands, and so on.

Examples:

	Tens	Ones
	5	4
+2		5
		9

	Tens	Ones
	5	4
+2		5
	7	9

Directions: Add the following numbers.

81 +23 = **104**	67 +22 = **89**	34 +82 = **116**	730 +265 = **995**
76 +73 = **149**	1,803 +1,104 = **2,907**	523 +476 = **999**	267 + 12 = **279**
		4,254 + 545 = **4,799**	111 + 82 = **193**
		164 +425 = **589**	727 + 51 = **778**

Page 208

Addition: Regrouping

Regrouping uses 10 ones to form one 10, 10 tens to form one hundred, one 10 and 5 ones to form 15, and so on.

Directions: Add using regrouping. Color in all the boxes with a 5 in the answer to help the dog find its way home.

63 +22 = **85**	5,268 4,910 +1,683 = **11,861**	248 +463 = **711**	291 +543 = **834**	2,934 + 112 = **3,046**
1,736 +5,367 = **7,103**	2,946 +7,384 = **10,330**	3,245 1,239 + 981 = **5,465**	738 +692 = **1,430**	896 +728 = **1,624**	594 +738 = **1,332**
2,603 +5,004 = **7,607**	4,507 + 289 = **4,796**	1,483 +6,753 = **8,236**	1,258 +6,301 = **7,559**	27 469 +6,002 = **6,498**	4,637 +7,531 = **12,168**
782 + 65 = **847**	485 +276 = **761**	3,421 +8,064 = **11,485**			
48 93 +26 = **167**	90 263 +864 = **1,217**	362 453 +800 = **1,615**			

Page 209

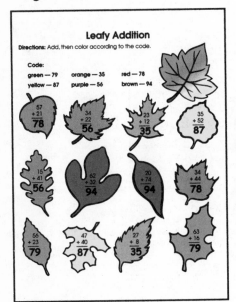

Leafy Addition

Directions: Add, then color according to the code.

Code:
green — 79   orange — 35   red — 78
yellow — 87   purple — 56   brown — 94

57 + 21 = **78**
34 + 22 = **56**
23 + 12 = **35**
35 + 52 = **87**

15 + 41 = **56**
62 + 32 = **94**
20 + 74 = **94**
34 + 44 = **78**

56 + 23 = **79**
47 + 40 = **87**
27 + 8 = **35**
63 + 16 = **79**

Page 210

Subtraction

Subtraction is "taking away" or subtracting one number from another.

Directions: Complete the following problems as quickly and as accurately as you can.

18 − 9 = **9**   13 − 6 = **7**   12 − 5 = **7**   17 − 8 = **9**   16 − 8 = **8**

12 − 5 = **7**   10 − 4 = **6**   5 − 3 = **2**   14 − 6 = **8**   15 − 9 = **6**

9 − 5 = **4**   8 − 3 = **5**   6 − 2 = **4**   5 − 4 = **1**   10 − 7 = **3**

11 − 4 = **7**   12 − 8 = **4**   16 − 9 = **7**   11 − 8 = **3**   10 − 10 = **0**

How quickly did you complete this page? _____

Page 211

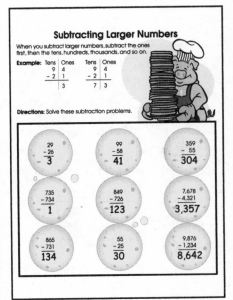

Subtracting Larger Numbers

When you subtract larger numbers, subtract the ones first, then the tens, hundreds, thousands, and so on.

Example:

Tens	Ones
9	4
− 2	1
	3

Tens	Ones
9	4
− 2	1
7	3

Directions: Solve these subtraction problems.

29 − 26 = **3**   99 − 58 = **41**   359 − 55 = **304**

735 − 734 = **1**   849 − 726 = **123**   7,678 − 4,321 = **3,357**

865 − 731 = **134**   55 − 25 = **30**   9,876 − 1,234 = **8,642**

Page 212

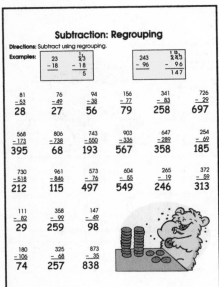

Subtraction: Regrouping

Directions: Subtract using regrouping.

Examples:

23 − 18 = **5**   243 − 96 = **147**

81 − 53 = **28**   76 − 49 = **27**   94 − 38 = **56**   156 − 77 = **79**   341 − 83 = **258**   726 − 29 = **697**

568 − 173 = **395**   806 − 738 = **68**   743 − 550 = **193**   903 − 336 = **567**   647 − 289 = **358**   254 − 69 = **185**

730 − 518 = **212**   961 − 846 = **115**   573 − 76 = **497**   604 − 55 = **549**   265 − 19 = **246**   372 − 59 = **313**

111 − 82 = **29**   358 − 99 = **259**   147 − 49 = **98**

180 − 106 = **74**   325 − 68 = **257**   873 − 35 = **838**

Page 213

Addition and Subtraction

Directions: Add or subtract, using regrouping when needed.

32 + 68 + 43 = **143**   183 + 246 + 89 = **518**   456 + 398 + 597 = **1,451**   643 − 377 = **266**

1,563 − 941 = **622**   3,586 + 4,218 = **7,804**   8,711 − 4,937 = **3,774**   9,361 − 7,452 = **1,909**

5,734 + 6,298 = **12,032**   293 + 431 + 93 = **817**   743 − 529 = **214**   849 + 250 + 82 = **1,181**

1,227 + 2,431 + 5,792 = **9,450**   9,117 − 3,828 = **5,289**

68 + 93 + 146 = **307**   73 + 246 + 1,579 = **1,898**

43 + 745 − 29 = **759**   128 + 403 + 2,571 = **3,102**

156 + 627 + 541 = **1,324**   97 + 51 + 37 + 79 = **264**

Tom walks 389 steps from his house to the video store. It is 149 steps to Elm Street. It is 52 steps from Maple Street to the video store. How many steps is it from Elm Street to Maple Street? **188 steps**

Page 214

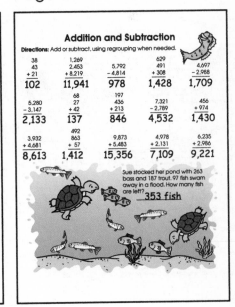

Addition and Subtraction

Directions: Add or subtract, using regrouping when needed.

38 + 43 + 21 = **102**   1,269 + 2,453 + 8,219 = **11,941**   5,792 − 4,814 = **978**   491 + 308 = **1,428**   4,697 − 2,988 = **1,709**

5,280 − 3,147 = **2,133**   68 + 27 + 42 = **137**   197 + 436 + 213 = **846**   7,321 − 2,789 = **4,532**   456 + 974 = **1,430**

3,932 + 4,681 = **8,613**   492 + 863 + 57 = **1,412**   9,873 + 5,483 = **15,356**   4,978 + 2,131 = **7,109**   6,235 + 2,986 = **9,221**

Sue stocked her pond with 263 bass and 187 trout. 97 fish swam away in a flood. How many fish are left? **353 fish**

Page 215

Rounding: Tens

Rounding a number means expressing it to the nearest ten, hundred, thousand, and so on. Knowing how to round numbers makes estimating sums, differences and products easier. When rounding to the nearest ten, the key number is in the ones place. If the ones digit is 5 or larger, round up to the next highest ten. If the ones digit is 4 or less, round down to the nearest ten.

Examples:
• Round 81 to the nearest ten.
• 1 is the key digit.
• If it is less than 5, round down.
• Answer: 80
• Round 246 to the nearest ten.
• 6 is the key digit.
• If it is more than 5, round up.
• Answer: 250

Directions: Round these numbers to the nearest ten.

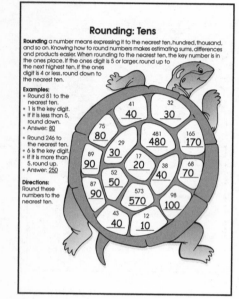

41 **40**   32 **30**
75 **80**   481 **480**   165 **170**
89 **90**   29 **30**   17 **20**   38 **40**   68 **70**
87 **90**   52 **50**   573 **570**   98 **100**
43 **40**   12 **10**

Page 216

Rounding: Hundreds and Thousands

When rounding to the nearest hundred, the key number is in the tens place. If the tens digit is 5 or larger, round up to nearest hundred. If the tens digit is 4 or less, round down to the nearest hundred.

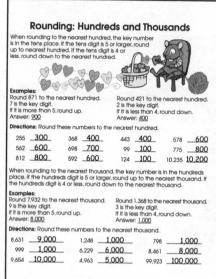

Examples:
Round 871 to the nearest hundred.
7 is the key digit.
If it is more than 5, round up.
Answer: 900

Round 421 to the nearest hundred.
2 is the key digit.
If it is less than 4, round down.
Answer: 400

Directions: Round these numbers to the nearest hundred.

255 **300**   368 **400**   443 **400**   578 **600**
562 **600**   698 **700**   99 **100**   775 **800**
812 **800**   592 **600**   124 **100**   10,235 **10,200**

When rounding to the nearest thousand, the key number is in the hundreds place. If the hundreds digit is 5 or larger, round up to the nearest thousand. If the hundreds digit is 4 or less, round down to the nearest thousand.

Examples:
Round 7,932 to the nearest thousand.
9 is the key digit.
If it is more than 5, round up.
Answer: 8,000

Round 1,368 to the nearest thousand.
3 is the key digit.
If it is less than 4, round down.
Answer: 1,000

Directions: Round these numbers to the nearest thousand.

8,631 **9,000**   1,248 **1,000**   798 **1,000**
999 **1,000**   6,229 **6,000**   8,461 **8,000**
9,654 **10,000**   4,963 **5,000**   99,923 **100,000**

Page 217

Rounding

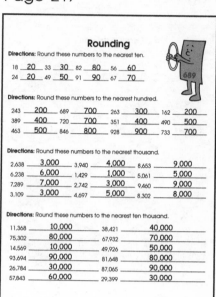

Directions: Round these numbers to the nearest ten.

18 **20**   33 **30**   82 **80**   56 **60**
24 **20**   49 **50**   91 **90**   67 **70**

Directions: Round these numbers to the nearest hundred.

243 **200**   689 **700**   263 **300**   162 **200**
389 **400**   720 **700**   351 **400**   490 **500**
463 **500**   846 **800**   928 **900**   733 **700**

Directions: Round these numbers to the nearest thousand.

2,638 **3,000**   3,940 **4,000**   8,653 **9,000**
6,238 **6,000**   1,429 **1,000**   5,061 **5,000**
7,289 **7,000**   2,742 **3,000**   9,460 **9,000**
3,109 **3,000**   4,697 **5,000**   8,302 **8,000**

Directions: Round these numbers to the nearest ten thousand.

11,368 **10,000**   38,421 **40,000**
75,302 **80,000**   67,932 **70,000**
14,569 **10,000**   49,926 **50,000**
93,694 **90,000**   81,648 **80,000**
26,784 **30,000**   87,065 **90,000**
57,843 **60,000**   29,399 **30,000**

Page 218

Estimating

Estimating is used for certain mathematical calculations. For example, to figure the cost of several items, round their prices to the nearest dollar, then add up the approximate cost. A store clerk, on the other hand, needs to know the exact prices in order to charge the correct amount. To estimate to the nearest hundred, round up numbers over 50. **Example:** 251 is rounded up to 300. Round down numbers less than 50. **Example:** 128 is rounded down to 100.

Directions: In the following situations, write whether an exact or estimated answer should be used.

Example:
You make a deposit in your bank account. Do you want an estimated total or an exact total?   **Exact**

1. Your family just ate dinner at a restaurant. Your parents are trying to calculate the tip for your server. Should they estimate by rounding or use exact numbers?   **Estimate**

2. You are at the store buying candy, and you want to know if you have enough money to pay for it. Should you estimate or use exact numbers?   **Estimate**

3. Some friends are planning a trip from New York City to Washington, D.C. They need to know about how far they will travel in miles. Should they estimate or use exact numbers?   **Estimate**

4. You plan a trip to the zoo. Beforehand, you call the zoo for the price of admission. Should the person at the zoo tell you an estimated or exact price?   **Exact**

5. The teacher is grading your papers. Should your scores be exact or estimated?   **Exact**

Page 219

Estimating

To **estimate** means to give an approximate, rather than an exact, answer. To find an estimated sum or difference, round the numbers of the problem, then add or subtract. If the number has 5 ones or more, round up to the nearest ten. If the number has 4 ones or less, round down to the nearest ten.

Directions: Round the numbers to the nearest ten, hundred or thousand. Then add or subtract.

Examples:

Ten		Hundred		Thousand	
74 → 70		352 → 400		7,681 → 8,000	
+ 39 → + 40		− 164 → − 200		+ 4,321 → + 4,000	
110		200		12,000	

64 → 60	
− 25 → − 30	
30	

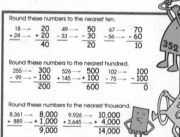

Round these numbers to the nearest ten.

18 → **20**   49 → **50**   67 → **70**
+ 24 → + **20**   − 33 → − **30**   − 56 → − **60**
40   **20**   **10**

Round these numbers to the nearest hundred.

255 → **300**   526 → **500**   102 → **100**
− 99 → − **100**   + 145 → + **100**   − 75 → − **100**
200   **600**   **0**

Round these numbers to the nearest thousand.

8,361 → **8,000**   9,926 → **10,000**
+ 889 → + **1,000**   + 3,645 → + **4,000**
9,000   **14,000**

Page 220

Estimating

Directions: Round the numbers to the nearest hundred. Then solve the problems.

Example:
Jack and Alex were playing a computer game. Jack scored 428 points. Alex scored 132. About how many more points did Jack score than Alex?

Round Jack's 428 points down to the nearest hundred, 400.

Round Alex's 132 points down to 100.

400
− 100
estimate   **300**

258 → 300	493 → 500	837 → 800
+ 117 → +100	+ 114 → + 100	− 252 → − 300
375 = **400**	**600**	500

928 → 900	700 → 700	319 → 300
− 437 → − 400	− 491 → − 500	+ 630 → + 600
500	**200**	**900**

332 → 300	493 → 500	1,356 → 1,400
+ 567 → + 600	− 162 → − 200	+ 2,941 → + 2,900
900	**300**	**4,300**

GRADE 4

Page 221

Skip Counting

Skip counting is a quick way to count by skipping numbers. For example, when you skip count by 2's, you count 2, 4, 6, 8, and so on. You can skip count by many different numbers such as 2's, 4's, 5's, 10's and 100's.

The illustration below shows skip counting by 2's to 14.

Directions: Use the number line to help you skip count by 2's from 0 to 20.

0, **2**, **4**, **6**, 8, **10**, **12**, 14, **16**, **18**, **20**

Directions: Skip count by 3's by filling in the rocks across the pond.

3, **6**, 9, **12**, **15**, 18, **21**

Page 222

Multiples

A **multiple** is the product of a specific number and any other number. For example, the multiples of 2 are 2 (2 x 1), 4 (2 x 2), 6, 8, 10, 12, and so on.

Directions: Write the missing multiples.

Example: Count by 5's.

5, 10, 15, 20, 25, 30, 35. These are multiples of 5.

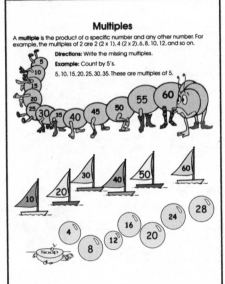

5, **10**, **15**, **20**, **25**, **30**, 35, 40, 45, 50, **55**, **60**

10, **20**, 30, 40, **50**, 60

4, **8**, **12**, 16, **20**, 24, 28

Page 223

Review

Directions: Add or subtract using regrouping.

67		732		
93	5,029	801	2,467	8,453
+ 48	– 3,068	+ 18	+ 3,184	– 6,087
208	**1,961**	**1,551**	**5,651**	**2,366**

5,792	7,489	463	3,567	6,342
– 3,889	+ 5,938	– 209	– 2,394	+ 959
1,903	**13,427**	**254**	**1,173**	**7,301**

Directions: Write the numbers in the boxes. In the blanks, write the numbers in standard form.

millions	hundred thousands	ten thousands	thousands	hundreds	tens	ones	
8	4	0	0	9	5	2	8,400,952

eight millions, four hundred thousands, zero ten thousands, zero thousands, nine hundreds, five tens, two ones

hundred thousands	ten thousands	thousands	hundreds	tens	ones	
5	3	5	0	4	1	535,041

five hundred thousands, three ten thousands, five thousands, zero hundreds, four tens, one one

Directions: Write the missing multiples in the blanks.

6, 12, 18, **24**, 30, **36**   3, **6**, **9**, 12, 15

4, **8**, 12, 16, **20**, 24   **5**, 10, 15, **20**, **25**

Page 224

Multiplication

Multiplication is a short way to find the sum of adding the same number a certain amount of times, such as 7 x 4 = 28 instead of 7 + 7 + 7 + 7 = 28.

Directions: Multiply as quickly and as accurately as you can.

4	7	0	7	9	1	6
x7	x6	x8	x2	x5	x5	x4
28	**42**	**0**	**14**	**45**	**5**	**24**

8	7	4	9	8	6	9
x3	x1	x2	x6	x5	x7	x8
24	**7**	**8**	**54**	**40**	**42**	**72**

3	7	3	5	9	7	9
x5	x8	x9	x6	x9	x5	x4
15	**56**	**27**	**30**	**81**	**35**	**36**

3	2	8	7
x6	x8	x6	x7
18	**16**	**48**	**49**

0	3	5
x7	x3	x9
0	**9**	**45**

How quickly did you complete this page? **Answers will vary.**

Page 225

Fact Factory

Factors are the numbers multiplied together in a multiplication problem. The **product** is the answer.

Directions: Write the missing factors or products.

X	5
1	5
5	25
4	20
6	30
3	15
2	10
7	35
9	45

X	9
8	72
3	27
4	36
9	81
6	54
7	63
2	18
1	9

X	7
2	14
5	35
6	42
8	56
7	49
4	28
3	21
0	0

X	3
7	21
4	12
6	18
1	3
3	9
2	6
5	15
8	24

X	1
1	1
12	12
10	10
3	3
5	5
7	7
6	6
4	4

X	8
9	72
8	64
4	32
5	40
6	48
7	56
3	24
2	16

X	2
12	24
1	2
11	22
2	4
10	20
3	6
9	18
4	8

X	4
2	8
4	16
6	24
8	32
1	4
3	12
5	20
7	28

X	6
7	42
6	36
5	30
4	24
3	18
2	12
1	6
0	0

X	10
2	20
3	30
4	40
5	50
6	60
7	70
8	80
9	90

X	11
4	44
7	77
9	99
10	110
3	33
5	55
6	66
8	88

X	12
1	12
2	24
3	36
4	48
5	60
6	72
7	84
8	96

Page 226

Multiplication: Tens, Hundreds, Thousands

When multiplying a number by 10, the answer is the number with a 0. It is like counting by tens.

Examples:

10	10	10	10	10	10
x 1	x 2	x 3	x 4	x 5	x 6
10	**20**	**30**	**40**	**50**	**60**

When multiplying a number by 100, the answer is the number with two 0's. When multiplying by 1,000, the answer is the number with three 0's.

Examples:

100	100	100	1,000	1,000	1,000
x 1	x 2	x 3	x 1	x 2	x 3
100	**200**	**300**	**1,000**	**2,000**	**3,000**

4	400	8	800	7	700
x 2	x 2	x 3	x 3	x 5	x 5
8	**800**	**24**	**2,400**	**35**	**3,500**

Directions: Multiply.

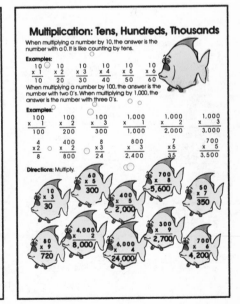

10 x 3 = **30**
60 x 5 = **300**
700 x 8 = **5,600**
50 x 7 = **350**
400 x 5 = **2,000**
80 x 9 = **720**
4,000 x 2 = **8,000**
6,000 x 4 = **24,000**
300 x 9 = **2,700**
700 x 6 = **4,200**

Page 227

Multiplication: One-Digit Numbers Times Two-Digit Numbers

Follow the steps for multiplying a one-digit number by a two-digit number using regrouping.

Example: Step 1: Multiply the ones. Regroup.
Step 2: Multiply the tens. Add two tens.

Directions: Multiply.

| 27 ×3 = 81 | 63 ×4 = 252 | 52 ×5 = 260 | 91 ×9 = 819 | 45 ×7 = 315 | 75 ×2 = 150 |

| 64 ×5 = 320 | 76 ×3 = 228 | 93 ×6 = 558 | 87 ×4 = 348 | 66 ×7 = 462 | 38 ×2 = 76 |

| 47 ×8 = 376 | 64 ×9 = 576 | 51 ×8 = 408 | 99 ×3 = 297 |

| 13 ×7 = 91 | 32 ×4 = 128 | 25 ×8 = 200 | 15 ×7 = 105 |

The chickens on the Smith farm produce 48 dozen eggs each day. How many dozen eggs do they produce in 7 days? **336**

Page 228

Multiplication: Two-Digit Numbers Times Two-Digit Numbers

Follow the steps for multiplying a two-digit number by a two-digit number using regrouping.

Example: Step 1: Multiply the ones. Regroup.
Step 2: Multiply the tens. Regroup. Add.

Directions: Multiply.

| 12 ×55 = 660 | 27 ×15 = 405 | 65 ×27 = 1,755 | 19 ×39 = 741 | 99 ×13 = 1,287 | 35 ×14 = 490 |

| 43 ×26 = 1,118 | 38 ×17 = 646 | 53 ×86 = 4,558 | 47 ×72 = 3,384 | 57 ×62 = 3,534 | 48 ×33 = 1,584 |

| 27 ×54 = 1,458 | 93 ×45 = 4,185 | 64 ×16 = 1,024 | 53 ×23 = 1,219 |

The Jones farm has 24 cows that each produce 52 quarts of milk a day. How many quarts are produced each day altogether? **1,248 quarts**

Page 229

Multiplication: Two-Digit Numbers Times Three-Digit Numbers

Follow the steps for multiplying a two-digit number by a three-digit number using regrouping.

Example: Step 1: Multiply the ones. Regroup.
Step 2: Multiply the tens. Regroup. Add.

Directions: Multiply.

| 261 ×36 = 9,396 | 434 ×48 = 20,832 | 357 ×75 = 26,775 |

| 231 ×46 = 10,626 | 754 ×65 = 49,010 | 614 ×59 = 36,226 |

| 549 ×89 = 48,861 | 372 ×94 = 34,968 | 458 ×85 = 38,930 | 368 ×98 = 36,064 |

At the Douglas berry farm, workers pick 378 baskets of peaches each day. Each basket holds 65 peaches. How many peaches are picked each day? **24,570**

Page 230

Multiplication: Two-Digit Numbers Times Two- and Three-Digit Numbers

Directions: Multiply.

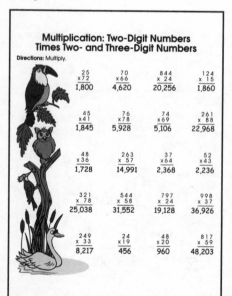

| 25 ×72 = 1,800 | 70 ×66 = 4,620 | 844 ×24 = 20,256 | 124 ×15 = 1,860 |

| 45 ×41 = 1,845 | 76 ×78 = 5,928 | 74 ×69 = 5,106 | 261 ×88 = 22,968 |

| 48 ×36 = 1,728 | 263 ×57 = 14,991 | 37 ×64 = 2,368 | 52 ×43 = 2,236 |

| 321 ×78 = 25,038 | 544 ×58 = 31,552 | 797 ×24 = 19,128 | 998 ×37 = 36,926 |

| 249 ×33 = 8,217 | 24 ×19 = 456 | 48 ×20 = 960 | 817 ×59 = 48,203 |

Page 231

Multiplication: Three-Digit Numbers Times Three-Digit Numbers

Directions: Multiply. Regroup when needed.

Example: 563 ×248 = 139,624

Hint: When multiplying by the tens, start writing the number in the tens place. When multiplying by the hundreds, start in the hundreds place.

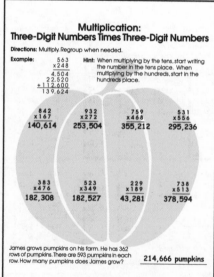

| 842 ×167 = 140,614 | 932 ×272 = 253,504 | 759 ×468 = 355,212 | 531 ×556 = 295,236 |

| 383 ×476 = 182,308 | 523 ×349 = 182,527 | 229 ×189 = 43,281 | 738 ×513 = 378,594 |

James grows pumpkins on his farm. He has 362 rows of pumpkins. There are 593 pumpkins in each row. How many pumpkins does James grow? **214,666 pumpkins**

Page 232

Multiplication Drill

Directions: Multiply.

| 134 ×22 = 2,948 | 48 ×66 = 3,168 | 876 ×13 = 11,388 | 432 ×64 = 27,648 |

| 68 ×11 = 748 | 5,478 ×8 = 43,824 | 248 ×61 = 15,128 | 6,897 ×6 = 41,382 |

| 82 ×4 = 328 | 6,798 ×5 = 33,990 | 79 ×86 = 6,794 | 694 ×38 = 26,372 |

Directions: Color the picture by matching each number with its paintbrush.

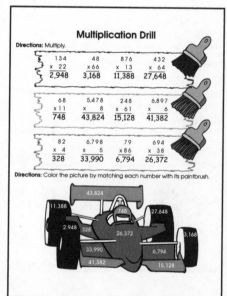

GRADE 4

Page 233

Division

Division is a way to find out how many times one number is contained in another number. For example, 28 ÷ 7 = 4 means that there are 4 groups of 7 in 28.

Division problems can be written two ways: 36 ÷ 6 = 6 or 6)36

These are the parts of a division problem: dividend → 36 ÷ 6 = 6 ← quotient
divisor

quotient → 6)36
divisor → 6)36 ← dividend

Directions: Divide.

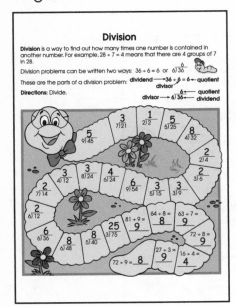

Page 234

Division With Remainders

Sometimes groups of objects or numbers cannot be divided into equal groups. The **remainder** is the number left over in the quotient of a division problem. The remainder must be smaller than the divisor.

Example:

Divide 18 butterflies into groups of 5. You have 3 equal groups, with 3 butterflies left over.

18 ÷ 5 = 3 R3

Directions: Divide. Some problems may have remainders.

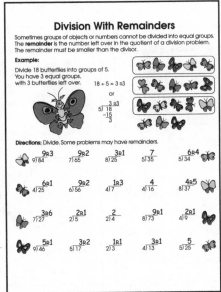

Page 235

Division: Larger Numbers

Follow the steps for dividing larger numbers.

Example: **Step 1:** Divide the tens first. **Step 2:** Divide the ones next.

Directions: Divide.

In some larger numbers, the divisor goes into the first two digits of the dividend.

Example:

Directions: Divide.

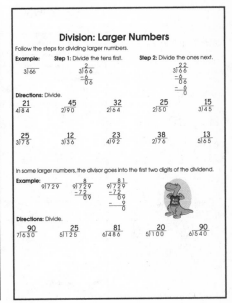

Page 236

Division

Directions: Divide.

The music store has 491 CD's. The store sells 8 CD's a day. How many days will it take to sell all of the CD's?   61R3 → 62 days

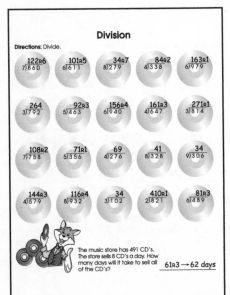

Page 237

Division: Checking the Answers

To check a division problem, multiply the quotient by the divisor. Add the remainder. The answer will be the dividend.

Example:
quotient → 58 R1
divisor → 3)175
dividend
  -15
   25
  -24
    1 ← remainder

58 ← quotient
x 3 ← divisor
174
+ 1 ← remainder
175 ← dividend

Directions: Divide each problem, then draw a line from the division problem to the correct checking problem.

The toy factory puts 7 robot dogs in each box. The factory has 256 robot dogs. How many boxes will they need?

36R4 → 37 boxes

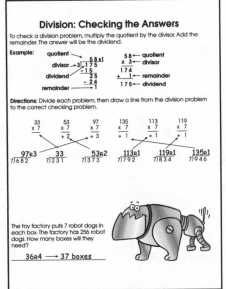

Page 238

Division: Checking the Answers

Directions: Divide, then check your answers.

Example:

Divide	Check		Divide	Check

The bookstore puts 53 books on a shelf. How many shelves will it need for 1,590 books?   30 shelves

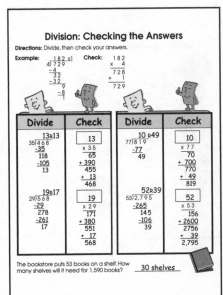

Page 239

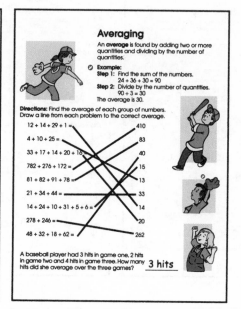

Division: Two-Digit Divisors

Directions: Divide. Then check each answer on another sheet of paper by multiplying it by the divisor and adding the remainder.

Example:

```
      2              21 R4
12)256         12)256
   -24            -24
     1             16
                  -12
                    1
```

Check:
```
   21
 x 12
   42
  210
  252
 +  4
  256
```

32R16 27)880	11R22 81)913	12R10 65)790	16R2 42)674	12R19 67)823
13R41 72)977	13R41 54)743	19R8 45)863	18 24)432	20R12 18)372
6R7 28)175	10R48 49)538	12R12 77)936	16R11 37)603	13R16 63)835

The Allen farm has 882 chickens. The chickens are kept in 21 coops. How many chickens are there in each coop? **42 chickens**

Page 240

Averaging

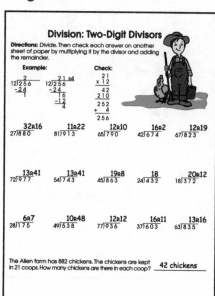

An **average** is found by adding two or more quantities and dividing by the number of quantities.

Example:
Step 1: Find the sum of the numbers.
$24 + 36 + 30 = 90$
Step 2: Divide by the number of quantities.
$90 \div 3 = 30$
The average is 30.

Directions: Find the average of each group of numbers. Draw a line from each problem to the correct average.

$12 + 14 + 29 + 1 =$	410
$4 + 10 + 25 =$	83
$33 + 17 + 14 + 20 + 16 =$	40
$782 + 276 + 172 =$	15
$81 + 82 + 91 + 78 =$	13
$21 + 34 + 44 =$	33
$14 + 24 + 10 + 31 + 5 + 6 =$	14
$278 + 246 =$	20
$48 + 32 + 18 + 62 =$	262

A baseball player had 3 hits in game one, 2 hits in game two and 4 hits in game three. How many hits did she average over the three games? **3 hits**

Page 241

Averaging

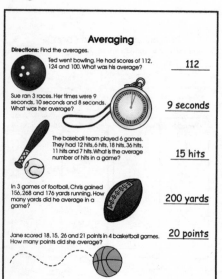

Directions: Find the averages.

Ted went bowling. He had scores of 112, 124 and 100. What was his average? **112**

Sue ran 3 races. Her times were 9 seconds, 10 seconds and 8 seconds. What was her average? **9 seconds**

The baseball team played 6 games. They had 12 hits, 6 hits, 18 hits, 36 hits, 11 hits and 7 hits. What is the average number of hits in a game? **15 hits**

In 3 games of football, Chris gained 156, 268 and 176 yards running. How many yards did he average in a game? **200 yards**

Jane scored 18, 15, 26 and 21 points in 4 basketball games. How many points did she average? **20 points**

Page 242

Review

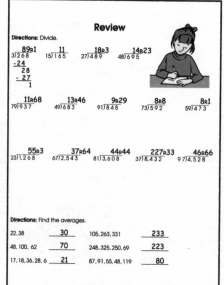

Directions: Divide.

```
   89R1
3)268
  -24
   28
  -27
    1
```

11 15)165	18R3 27)489	14R23 48)695	
11R68 79)937	13R46 49)683	9R29 91)848	8R8 73)592
8R1 59)473			
55R3 23)1,268	37R64 67)2,543	44R44 81)3,608	227R33 37)8,432
46R66 97)4,528			

Directions: Find the averages.

22, 38	**30**	105, 263, 331	**233**
48, 100, 62	**70**	248, 325, 250, 69	**223**
17, 18, 36, 28, 6	**21**	87, 91, 55, 48, 119	**80**

Page 244

Fractions

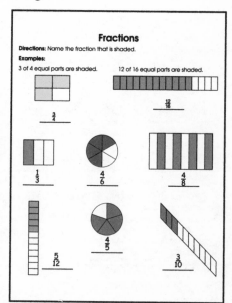

Directions: Name the fraction that is shaded.

Examples:

3 of 4 equal parts are shaded.

$\frac{3}{4}$

12 of 16 equal parts are shaded.

$\frac{12}{16}$

$\frac{1}{3}$ $\frac{4}{6}$ $\frac{4}{8}$

$\frac{5}{12}$ $\frac{4}{5}$ $\frac{3}{10}$

GRADE 4

Page 249

Fractions: Addition

When adding fractions with the same denominator, the denominator stays the same. Add only the numerators.

Example: $\frac{numerator}{denominator}$ $\frac{1}{8} + \frac{2}{8} = \frac{3}{8}$

Directions: Add the fractions on the flowers. Begin in the center of each flower and add each petal. The first one is done for you.

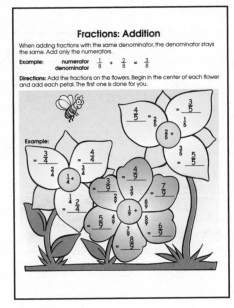

Page 250

Fractions: Subtraction

When subtracting fractions with the same denominator, the denominator stays the same. Subtract only the numerators.

Directions: Solve the problems, working from left to right. As you find each answer, copy the letter from the key into the numbered blanks. The answer is the name of a famous American. The first one is done for you.

1. $\frac{3}{8} - \frac{2}{8} = \frac{1}{8}$

2. $\frac{2}{4} - \frac{1}{4} = \frac{1}{4}$

3. $\frac{5}{9} - \frac{3}{9} = \frac{2}{9}$

4. $\frac{2}{3} - \frac{1}{3} = \frac{1}{3}$

5. $\frac{8}{12} - \frac{7}{12} = \frac{1}{12}$

6. $\frac{4}{5} - \frac{1}{5} = \frac{3}{5}$

7. $\frac{6}{12} - \frac{3}{12} = \frac{3}{12}$

8. $\frac{4}{9} - \frac{1}{9} = \frac{3}{9}$

9. $\frac{11}{12} - \frac{7}{12} = \frac{4}{12}$

10. $\frac{7}{8} - \frac{3}{8} = \frac{4}{8}$

11. $\frac{4}{7} - \frac{2}{7} = \frac{2}{7}$

12. $\frac{14}{16} - \frac{7}{16} = \frac{7}{16}$

13. $\frac{18}{20} - \frac{13}{20} = \frac{5}{20}$

14. $\frac{13}{15} - \frac{2}{15} = \frac{11}{15}$

15. $\frac{5}{6} - \frac{3}{6} = \frac{2}{6}$

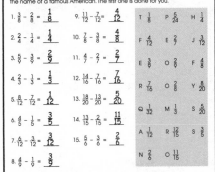

Who helped write the Declaration of Independence?

T H O M A S   J E F F E R S O N

Page 251

Equivalent Fractions

Equivalent fractions are two different fractions that represent the same number. **Example:** $\frac{1}{2}$ $\frac{3}{6}$

Directions: Complete these equivalent fractions.

$\frac{1}{3} = \frac{2}{6}$ $\frac{1}{2} = \frac{2}{4}$ $\frac{3}{4} = \frac{6}{8}$ $\frac{1}{3} = \frac{3}{9}$

Directions: Circle the figures that show a fraction equivalent to figure a. Write the fraction for the shaded area under each figure.

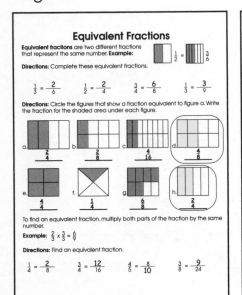

a. $\frac{2}{4}$ b. $\frac{4}{16}$ c. $\frac{4}{8}$ d. $\frac{4}{8}$

e. $\frac{4}{4}$ f. $\frac{1}{4}$ g. $\frac{6}{8}$ h. $\frac{2}{4}$

To find an equivalent fraction, multiply both parts of the fraction by the same number.

Example: $\frac{2}{3} \times \frac{3}{3} = \frac{6}{9}$

Directions: Find an equivalent fraction.

$\frac{1}{4} = \frac{2}{8}$ $\frac{3}{4} = \frac{12}{16}$ $\frac{4}{5} = \frac{8}{10}$ $\frac{3}{8} = \frac{9}{24}$

Page 252

Reducing Fractions

Reducing a fraction means to find the greatest common factor and divide.

Example: $\frac{5}{15}$ factors of 5: 1, 5   5 is the greatest common factor.
factors of 15: 1, 3, 5, 15   Divide both the numerator and denominator by 5.

$5 \div 5 = 1$
$15 \div 5 = 3$

Directions: Reduce each fraction. Circle the correct answer.

$\frac{2}{4}$ ($\frac{1}{2}$) $\frac{1}{6}$, $\frac{1}{8}$ $\frac{3}{6}$ = ($\frac{1}{3}$) $\frac{3}{8}$ $\frac{5}{10}$ = $\frac{1}{5}$ ($\frac{1}{2}$) $\frac{1}{6}$ $\frac{4}{12}$ = ($\frac{1}{3}$) $\frac{1}{4}$, $\frac{2}{5}$ $\frac{10}{15}$ = $\frac{3}{2}$ ($\frac{2}{3}$) $\frac{2}{5}$

$\frac{12}{14}$ = ($\frac{6}{7}$) $\frac{9}{8}$ $\frac{3}{24}$ = ($\frac{1}{8}$) $\frac{1}{2}$, $\frac{1}{6}$ $\frac{1}{11}$ = $\frac{1}{11}$ ($\frac{1}{11}$) $\frac{5}{3}$, $\frac{4}{2}$ $\frac{11}{22}$ = ($\frac{1}{2}$) $\frac{2}{3}$, $\frac{2}{5}$

Directions: Find the way home. Color the boxes with fractions equivalent to $\frac{1}{3}$ and $\frac{1}{2}$.

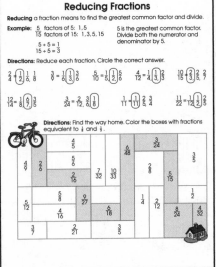

Page 253

Fractions: Mixed Numbers

A **mixed number** is a number written as a whole number and a fraction, such as $6\frac{1}{3}$.

To change a fraction into a mixed number, divide the denominator (bottom number) into the numerator (top number). Write the remainder over the denominator.

Example: $\frac{14}{6} = 2\frac{2}{6}$ $6\overline{)14}$ $\frac{12}{2}$

To change a mixed number into a fraction, multiply the denominator by the whole number, add the numerator and write it on top of the denominator.

Example: $3\frac{1}{7} = \frac{22}{7}$ $(7 \times 3) + 1 = \frac{22}{7}$

Directions: Write each fraction as a mixed number. Write each mixed number as a fraction.

$\frac{21}{6} = 3\frac{3}{6}$ $\frac{24}{5} = 4\frac{4}{5}$ $\frac{10}{3} = 3\frac{1}{3}$ $\frac{21}{4} = 5\frac{1}{4}$

$\frac{11}{6} = 1\frac{5}{6}$ $\frac{13}{4} = 3\frac{1}{4}$ $\frac{12}{5} = 2\frac{2}{5}$ $\frac{10}{9} = 1\frac{1}{9}$

$4\frac{3}{8} = \frac{35}{8}$ $2\frac{1}{3} = \frac{7}{3}$ $4\frac{3}{5} = \frac{23}{5}$ $3\frac{4}{6} = \frac{22}{6}$

$7\frac{1}{4} = \frac{29}{4}$ $2\frac{3}{5} = \frac{13}{5}$ $7\frac{1}{2} = \frac{15}{2}$ $6\frac{5}{7} = \frac{47}{7}$

$\frac{11}{8} = 1\frac{3}{8}$ $\frac{21}{4} = 5\frac{1}{4}$ $\frac{33}{5} = 6\frac{3}{5}$ $\frac{13}{6} = 2\frac{1}{6}$

$\frac{23}{7} = 3\frac{2}{7}$ $8\frac{1}{3} = \frac{25}{3}$ $9\frac{3}{7} = \frac{66}{7}$ $\frac{32}{24} = 1\frac{8}{24}$

Page 254

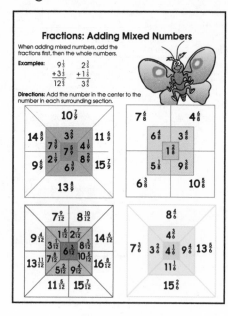

Fractions: Adding Mixed Numbers

When adding mixed numbers, add the fractions first, then the whole numbers.

Examples:
$9\frac{1}{3}$ $2\frac{2}{5}$
$+3\frac{1}{3}$ $+1\frac{1}{5}$
$\overline{12\frac{2}{3}}$ $\overline{3\frac{3}{5}}$

Directions: Add the number in the center to the number in each surrounding section.

Page 255

Fractions: Subtracting Mixed Numbers

When subtracting mixed numbers, subtract the fractions first, then the whole numbers.

Directions: Subtract the mixed numbers. The first one is done for you.

$7\frac{3}{8}$ $-4\frac{2}{8}$ $\overline{3\frac{1}{8}}$	$4\frac{5}{6}$ $-3\frac{1}{6}$ $\overline{1\frac{4}{6}}$	$4\frac{1}{2}$ -3 $\overline{1\frac{1}{2}}$	$7\frac{8}{8}$ $-6\frac{3}{8}$ $\overline{1\frac{2}{8}}$	$6\frac{6}{8}$ $-1\frac{1}{8}$ $\overline{5\frac{5}{8}}$	$5\frac{3}{4}$ $-1\frac{2}{4}$ $\overline{4\frac{2}{4}}$
$5\frac{2}{3}$ $-3\frac{1}{3}$ $\overline{2\frac{1}{3}}$	$4\frac{10}{10}$ $-3\frac{9}{10}$ $\overline{1\frac{1}{10}}$	$9\frac{3}{8}$ $-4\frac{3}{8}$ $\overline{5\frac{5}{8}}$	$7\frac{2}{3}$ $-6\frac{1}{3}$ $\overline{1\frac{1}{3}}$	$7\frac{2}{3}$ -5 $\overline{2\frac{2}{3}}$	$9\frac{8}{10}$ $-6\frac{3}{10}$ $\overline{3\frac{5}{10}}$
$4\frac{7}{9}$ -2 $\overline{2\frac{7}{9}}$	$6\frac{7}{8}$ $-5\frac{3}{8}$ $\overline{1\frac{4}{8}}$	$6\frac{3}{4}$ $-3\frac{1}{4}$ $\overline{3\frac{2}{4}}$	$5\frac{5}{7}$ $-3\frac{3}{7}$ $\overline{2\frac{2}{7}}$	$7\frac{9}{7}$ $-2\frac{4}{7}$ $\overline{5\frac{5}{7}}$	

Sally needs $1\frac{6}{8}$ yards of cloth to make a dress. She has $4\frac{8}{8}$ yards. How much cloth will be left over? $3\frac{2}{8}$

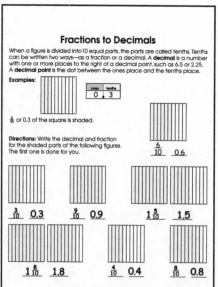

Page 256

Review

Directions: Add or subtract the fractions and mixed numbers. Reduce, if possible.

$4\frac{3}{4}$ $8\frac{3}{8}$ $3\frac{1}{8}$ $4\frac{5}{8}$ $7\frac{4}{11}$
$-2\frac{1}{4}$ $+2\frac{5}{8}$ $+1\frac{3}{8}$ $-3\frac{1}{8}$ $+3\frac{4}{11}$
$2\frac{2}{4}=2\frac{1}{4}$ $10\frac{8}{8}$ $4\frac{4}{8}=4\frac{1}{2}$ $1\frac{4}{8}=1\frac{3}{8}$ $10\frac{8}{11}$

$\frac{4}{12}+\frac{3}{12}=\frac{7}{12}$ $\frac{3}{5}+\frac{1}{5}=\frac{4}{5}$

$\frac{3}{8}-\frac{1}{8}=\frac{2}{8}=\frac{1}{4}$ $\frac{3}{9}+\frac{1}{9}=\frac{4}{9}$

$\frac{3}{4}-\frac{2}{4}=\frac{1}{4}$

Directions: Reduce the fractions.

$\frac{4}{6}=\frac{2}{3}$ $\frac{7}{21}=\frac{1}{3}$

$\frac{9}{12}=\frac{3}{4}$ $\frac{2}{4}=\frac{1}{2}$

$\frac{6}{24}=\frac{1}{4}$ $\frac{8}{32}=\frac{1}{4}$

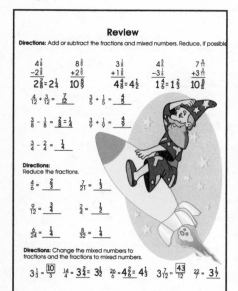

Directions: Change the mixed numbers to fractions and the fractions to mixed numbers.

$3\frac{1}{3}=\frac{10}{3}$ $\frac{14}{4}=3\frac{2}{4}=3\frac{1}{2}$ $\frac{26}{6}=4\frac{2}{6}=4\frac{1}{3}$ $3\frac{7}{12}=\frac{43}{12}$ $\frac{22}{6}=3\frac{1}{6}$

Page 257

Fractions to Decimals

When a figure is divided into 10 equal parts, the parts are called tenths. Tenths can be written two ways—as a fraction or a decimal. A **decimal** is a number with one or more places to the right of a decimal point, such as 6.5 or 2.25. A **decimal point** is the dot between the ones place and the tenths place.

Examples:

ones	tenths
0	3

$\frac{3}{10}$ or 0.3 of the square is shaded.

Directions: Write the decimal and fraction for the shaded parts of the following figures. The first one is done for you.

$\frac{6}{10}$ 0.6

$\frac{3}{10}$ 0.3 $\frac{9}{10}$ 0.9 $1\frac{5}{10}$ 1.5

$1\frac{8}{10}$ 1.8 $\frac{4}{10}$ 0.4 $\frac{8}{10}$ 0.8

Page 258

Decimals

Directions: Add or subtract. Remember to include the decimal point in your answers.

$1\frac{3}{10}=1.3$

Example: $\frac{1.3}{+1.6}$ $\overline{2.9}$

$1\frac{6}{10}=1.6$

8.1 +1.7 **9.8**	4.1 +6.2 **10.3**	0.5 +1.6 **2.1**	7.6 -6.5 **1.1**	7.2 -2.6 **4.6**	1.2 +5.0 **6.2**	8.7 -3.9 **4.8**	6.8 -3.7 **3.1**
			7.8 -6.8 **1.0**	16.5 -7.3 **9.2**	6.4 +5.3 **11.7**	10.0 +3.5 **13.5**	
			0.42 +0.35 **0.77**	0.98 -0.87 **0.11**	0.78 -0.13 **0.65**	0.83 +0.12 **0.95**	
			0.95 -0.14 **0.81**	3.23 +2.48 **5.71**	4.68 -2.65 **2.03**	5.86 -2.73 **3.13**	
			6.98 +1.40 **8.38**	3.27 +1.82 **5.09**	4.65 -1.32 **3.33**	5.97 +2.77 **8.74**	

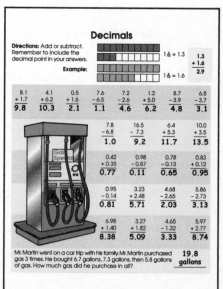

Mr. Martin went on a car trip with his family. Mr. Martin purchased gas 3 times. He bought 6.7 gallons, 7.3 gallons, then 5.8 gallons of gas. How much gas did he purchase in all? **19.8 gallons**

Page 259

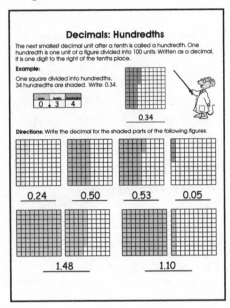

Decimals: Hundredths

The next smallest decimal unit after a tenth is called a hundredth. One hundredth is one unit of a figure divided into 100 units. Written as a decimal, it is one digit to the right of the tenths place.

Example:

One square divided into hundredths, 34 hundredths are shaded. Write: 0.34.

ones	tenths	hundredths
0	3	4

0.34

Directions: Write the decimal for the shaded parts of the following figures.

0.24   0.50   0.53   0.05

1.48   1.10

Page 260

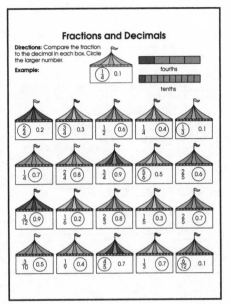

Fractions and Decimals

Directions: Compare the fraction to the decimal in each box. Circle the larger number.

Example: 1/4 0.1 fourths tenths

(2/4) 0.2   3/4 (0.3)   1/2 (0.6)   1/4 (0.4)   1/3 (0.1)

1/4 (0.7)   2/4 (0.8)   3/4 (0.9)   5/6 (0.5)   3/5 (0.6)

3/12 (0.9)   1/6 (0.2)   2/3 (0.8)   1/5 (0.3)   2/5 (0.7)

3/10 (0.5)   1/9 (0.4)   4/5 0.7   1/3 (0.7)   6/12 0.1

Page 261

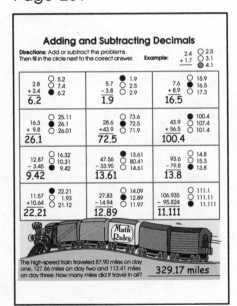

Adding and Subtracting Decimals

Directions: Add or subtract the problems. Then fill in the circle next to the correct answer.   **Example:** 2.4 + 1.7 = ● 4.1

2.8 + 3.4 = **6.2** ● 6.2
5.7 − 3.8 = **1.9** ● 1.9
7.6 + 8.9 = **16.5** ● 16.5

16.3 + 9.8 = **26.1** ● 26.1
28.6 + 43.9 = **72.5** ● 72.5
43.9 + 56.5 = **100.4** ● 100.4

12.87 − 3.45 = **9.42** ● 9.42
47.56 − 33.95 = **13.61** ● 13.61
93.6 − 79.8 = **13.8** ● 13.8

11.57 + 10.64 = **22.21** ● 22.21
27.83 − 14.94 = **12.89** ● 12.89
106.935 − 95.824 = **11.111** ● 11.111

The high-speed train traveled 87.90 miles on day one, 127.86 miles on day two and 113.41 miles on day three. How many miles did it travel in all? **329.17 miles**

Page 262

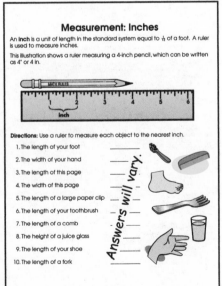

Measurement: Inches

An **inch** is a unit of length in the standard system equal to 1/12 of a foot. A ruler is used to measure inches.

This illustration shows a ruler measuring a 4-inch pencil, which can be written as 4" or 4 in.

Directions: Use a ruler to measure each object to the nearest inch.

Answers will vary.
1. The length of your foot
2. The width of your hand
3. The length of this page
4. The width of this page
5. The length of a large paper clip
6. The length of your toothbrush
7. The length of a comb
8. The height of a juice glass
9. The length of your shoe
10. The length of a fork

Page 263

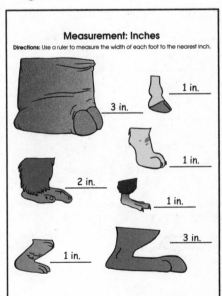

Measurement: Inches

Directions: Use a ruler to measure the width of each foot to the nearest inch.

3 in.   1 in.   1 in.   2 in.   1 in.   1 in.   3 in.

Page 264

Measurement: Fractions of an Inch

An inch is divided into smaller units, or fractions of an inch.

Example: This stick of gum is 2¾ inches long.

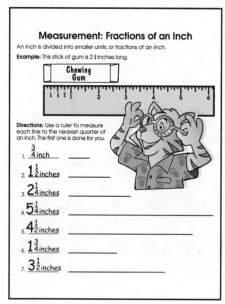

Directions: Use a ruler to measure each line to the nearest quarter of an inch. The first one is done for you.

1. $\frac{3}{4}$ inch _____
2. $1\frac{1}{2}$ inches _____
3. $2\frac{1}{4}$ inches _____
4. $5\frac{1}{4}$ inches _____
5. $4\frac{1}{2}$ inches _____
6. $1\frac{3}{4}$ inches _____
7. $3\frac{1}{2}$ inches _____

Page 265

Measurement: Fractions of an Inch

Directions: Use a ruler to measure to the nearest quarter of an inch.

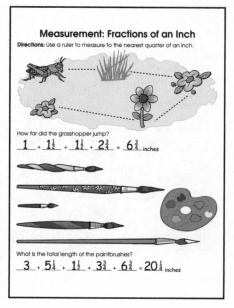

How far did the grasshopper jump?

$1 + 1\frac{1}{2} + 1\frac{1}{2} + 2\frac{3}{4} = 6\frac{3}{4}$ inches

What is the total length of the paintbrushes?

$3 + 5\frac{1}{4} + 1\frac{1}{2} + 3\frac{3}{4} + 6\frac{3}{4} = 20\frac{1}{4}$ inches

Page 266

Measurement: Foot, Yard, Mile

Directions: Choose the measure of distance you would use for each object.

1 foot = 12 inches
1 yard = 3 feet
1 mile = 1,760 yards or 5,280 feet

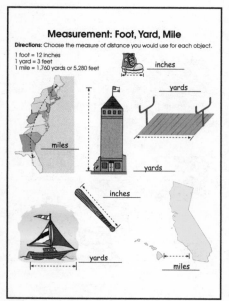

inches

yards

miles

yards

inches

yards

miles

Page 267

Metric Measurement: Centimeter, Meter, Kilometer

In the metric system, there are three units of linear measurement: centimeter (cm), meter (m) and kilometer (km).

Centimeters (cm) are used to measure the lengths of small to medium-sized objects. **Meters (m)** measure the lengths of longer objects, such as the width of a swimming pool or height of a tree (100 cm = 1 meter). **Kilometers (km)** measure long distances, such as the distance from Cleveland to Cincinnati or the width of the Atlantic Ocean (1,000 m = 1 km).

Directions: Write whether you would use cm, m or km to measure each object.

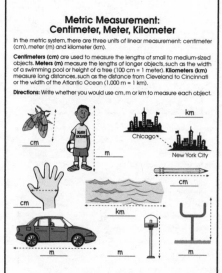

cm

km

Chicago

New York City

m

cm

cm

km

m

m

m

Page 268

Metric Measurement: Centimeter

Directions: Use a centimeter ruler to measure the width of each foot to the nearest centimeter.

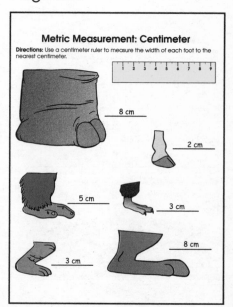

8 cm

2 cm

5 cm

3 cm

8 cm

3 cm

Page 269

Metric Measurement: Meter and Kilometer

A meter is a little longer than a yard—39.37 inches (a yard is 36 inches). A kilometer is equal to about ⅝ of a mile.

Directions: Choose the measure of distance you would use for the following.

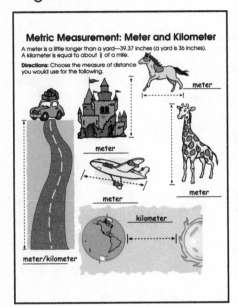

meter

meter

meter

meter

meter

kilometer

meter/kilometer

Page 270

Measurement: Perimeter and Area

Perimeter is the distance around a figure. It is found by adding the lengths of the sides. **Area** is the number of square units needed to cover a region. The area is found by adding the number of square units. A unit can be any unit of measure. Most often, inches, feet or yards are used.

Directions: Find the perimeter and area for each figure. The first one is done for you. ☐ = 1 square unit

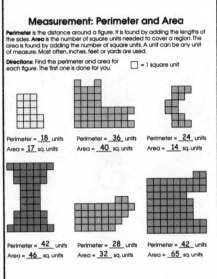

Perimeter = __18__ units
Area = __17__ sq. units

Perimeter = __36__ units
Area = __40__ sq. units

Perimeter = __24__ units
Area = __14__ sq. units

Perimeter = __42__ units
Area = __46__ sq. units

Perimeter = __28__ units
Area = __32__ sq. units

Perimeter = __42__ units
Area = __65__ sq. units

Page 271

Measurement: Perimeter

Perimeter is calculated by adding the lengths of the sides of a figure.

Examples:

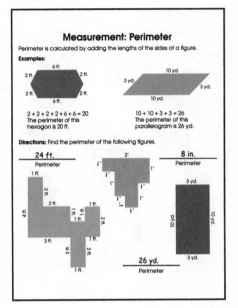

2 + 2 + 2 + 2 + 6 + 6 = 20
The perimeter of this hexagon is 20 ft.

10 + 10 + 3 + 3 = 26
The perimeter of this parallelogram is 26 yd.

Directions: Find the perimeter of the following figures.

__24 ft.__
Perimeter

__8 in.__
Perimeter

__26 yd.__
Perimeter

Page 272

Measurement: Perimeter and Area

Area is also calculated by multiplying the length times the width of a square or rectangular figure. Use the formula: A = l x w.

Directions: Calculate the perimeter of each figure.

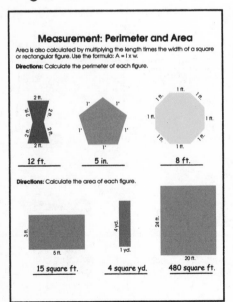

__12 ft.__

__5 in.__

__8 ft.__

Directions: Calculate the area of each figure.

__15 square ft.__

__4 square yd.__

__480 square ft.__

Page 273

Measurement: Volume

Volume is the number of cubic units that fit inside a figure.

Directions: Find the volume of each figure. The first one is done for you.

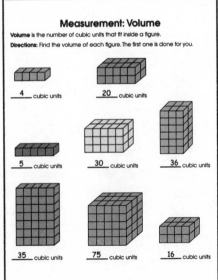

__4__ cubic units

__20__ cubic units

__5__ cubic units

__30__ cubic units

__36__ cubic units

__35__ cubic units

__75__ cubic units

__16__ cubic units

Page 274

Measurement: Volume

The volume of a figure can also be calculated by multiplying the length times the width times the height.
Use the formula: V= l x w x h.

Example:

3 x 5 x 2 = 30 cubic feet

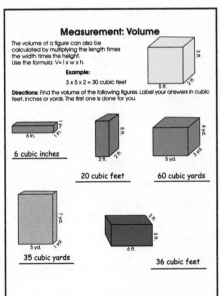

Directions: Find the volume of the following figures. Label your answers in cubic feet, inches or yards. The first one is done for you.

6 cubic inches

20 cubic feet

60 cubic yards

35 cubic yards

36 cubic feet

GRADE 4

Page 275

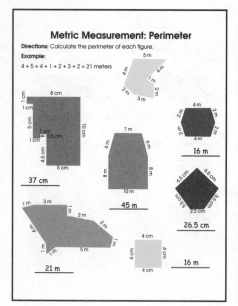

Metric Measurement: Perimeter

Directions: Calculate the perimeter of each figure.

Example:

$4 + 5 + 4 + 1 + 2 + 3 + 2 = 21$ meters

37 cm

45 m

21 m

16 m

26.5 cm

16 m

Page 276

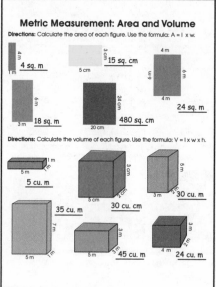

Metric Measurement: Area and Volume

Directions: Calculate the area of each figure. Use the formula: A = l x w.

4 sq. m

15 sq. cm

24 sq. m

18 sq. m

480 sq. cm

Directions: Calculate the volume of each figure. Use the formula: V = l x w x h.

5 cu. m

30 cu. cm

30 cu. m

35 cu. m

45 cu. m

24 cu. m

Page 277

Measurement: Ounce, Pound, Ton

The **ounce, pound** and **ton** are units in the standard system for measuring weight.

Directions: Choose the measure of weight you would use for each object.

16 ounces = 1 pound
2,000 pounds = 1 ton

ounce   pound   ton

Example: ounces   tons/pounds

pounds   ounces

ounces/pounds   tons

tons   ounces/pounds

Page 278

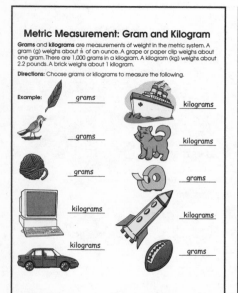

Metric Measurement: Gram and Kilogram

Grams and **kilograms** are measurements of weight in the metric system. A gram (g) weighs about ⅕ of an ounce. A grape or paper clip weighs about one gram. There are 1,000 grams in a kilogram. A kilogram (kg) weighs about 2.2 pounds. A brick weighs about 1 kilogram.

Directions: Choose grams or kilograms to measure the following.

Example: grams   kilograms

grams   kilograms

grams   grams

kilograms   kilograms

kilograms   grams

Page 279

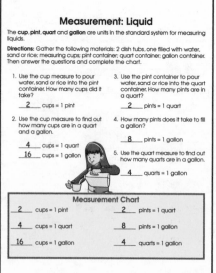

Measurement: Liquid

The **cup, pint, quart** and **gallon** are units in the standard system for measuring liquids.

Directions: Gather the following materials: 2 dish tubs, one filled with water, sand or rice; measuring cups; pint container; quart container; gallon container. Then answer the questions and complete the chart.

1. Use the cup measure to pour water, sand or rice into the pint container. How many cups did it take?

   __2__ cups = 1 pint

2. Use the cup measure to find out how many cups are in a quart and a gallon.

   __4__ cups = 1 quart
   __16__ cups = 1 gallon

3. Use the pint container to pour water, sand or rice into the quart container. How many pints are in a quart?

   __2__ pints = 1 quart

4. How many pints does it take to fill a gallon?

   __8__ pints = 1 gallon

5. Use the quart measure to find out how many quarts are in a gallon.

   __4__ quarts = 1 gallon

Measurement Chart	
__2__ cups = 1 pint	__2__ pints = 1 quart
__4__ cups = 1 quart	__8__ pints = 1 gallon
__16__ cups = 1 gallon	__4__ quarts = 1 gallon

Page 280

Measurement: Cup, Pint, Quart, Gallon

Directions: Circle the number of objects to the right that equal the objects on the left. The first one is done for you.

2 cups = 1 pint
2 pints = 1 quart
4 quarts = 1 gallon

= 1 cup   = 1 pint   = 1 quart   = 1 gallon

Page 281

Metric Measurement: Milliliter and Liter

Liters and **milliliters** are measurements of liquid in the metric system. A milliliter (mL) equals 0.001 liter or 0.03 fluid ounces. A drop of water equals about 1 milliliter. Liters (L) measure large amounts of liquid. There are 1,000 milliliters in a liter. One liter measures 1.06 quarts. Soft drinks are often sold in 2-liter bottles.

Directions: Choose milliliters or liters to measure these liquids.

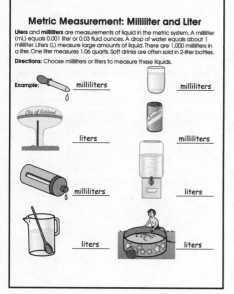

Example: **milliliters**   **milliliters**

liters   **milliliters**

milliliters   **liters**

liters   **liters**

Page 282

Metric Measurement: Weight and Liquid

Directions: Choose grams (g) or kilograms (kg) to weigh the following objects. The first one is done for you.

rhinoceros	kg	person	kg
dime	g	airplane	kg
bucket of wet sand	kg	spider	g
eyeglasses	g	pair of scissors	g
toy train engine	g	horse	kg

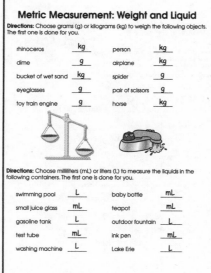

Directions: Choose milliliters (mL) or liters (L) to measure the liquids in the following containers. The first one is done for you.

swimming pool	L	baby bottle	mL
small juice glass	mL	teapot	mL
gasoline tank	L	outdoor fountain	L
test tube	mL	ink pen	mL
washing machine	L	Lake Erie	L

Page 283

Temperature: Fahrenheit

Fahrenheit is used to measure temperature in the standard system. °F stands for degrees Fahrenheit.

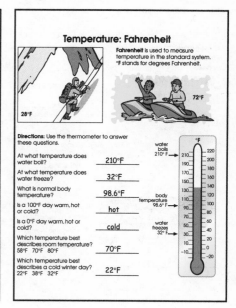

28°F   72°F

Directions: Use the thermometer to answer these questions.

At what temperature does water boil?	210°F
At what temperature does water freeze?	32°F
What is normal body temperature?	98.6°F
Is a 100°F day warm, hot or cold?	hot
Is a 0°F day warm, hot or cold?	cold
Which temperature best describes room temperature? 58°F 70°F 80°F	70°F
Which temperature best describes a cold winter day? 22°F 38°F 32°F	22°F

water boils 210°F → 210
body temperature 98.6°F
water freezes 32°F

Page 284

Temperature: Celsius

Celsius is used to measure temperature in the metric system. °C stands for degrees Celsius.

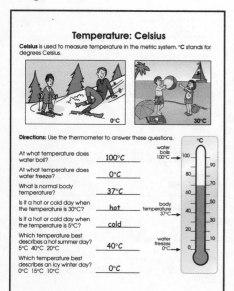

0°C   30°C

Directions: Use the thermometer to answer these questions.

At what temperature does water boil?	100°C
At what temperature does water freeze?	0°C
What is normal body temperature?	37°C
Is it a hot or cold day when the temperature is 30°C?	hot
Is it a hot or cold day when the temperature is 5°C?	cold
Which temperature best describes a hot summer day? 5°C 40°C 20°C	40°C
Which temperature best describes an icy winter day? 0°C 15°C 10°C	0°C

water boils 100°C → 100
body temperature 37°C
water freezes 0°C

Page 285

Review

Directions: Find the perimeter and area of each figure.

☐ = 1 square unit

Perimeter = **20** units
Area = **19** sq. units

Perimeter = **24** units
Area = **14** sq. units

Directions: How much does it equal?

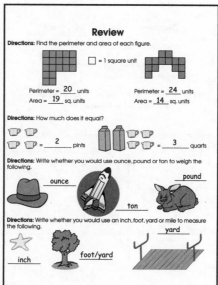 = **2** pints

= **3** quarts

Directions: Write whether you would use ounce, pound or ton to weigh the following.

ounce   **pound**

ton

Directions: Write whether you would use an inch, foot, yard or mile to measure the following.

inch   **foot/yard**   **yard**

Page 286

Review

Directions: Choose centimeters, meters or kilometers to measure the following.

meters height of a tree   **centimeters** length of a shoe
kilometers distance around Earth   **meters** height of a building
meters length of your yard   **kilometers** distance a plane flies

Directions: Choose grams or kilograms to measure the following.

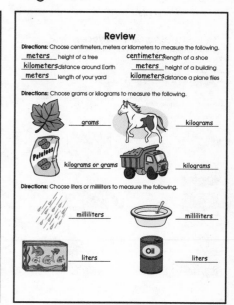

grams   **kilograms**

kilograms or grams   **kilograms**

Directions: Choose liters or milliliters to measure the following.

milliliters   **milliliters**

liters   **liters**

Page 287

Graphing

A **graph** is a drawing that shows information about changes in numbers.

Directions: Answer the questions by reading the graphs.

Bar Graph

Video Rentals by Month

How many videos did the store rent in June?

80 videos

In which month did the store rent the fewest videos?

May

How many videos did the store rent for all 4 months?

190 videos

Line Graph

CD's Sold by Days of Week

On which days did the store sell the fewest CD's?

Tuesday and Sunday

How many CD's did the store sell in 1 week?

_180 CD's_

Page 288

Ordered Pairs

An **ordered pair** is a pair of numbers used to locate a point.

Example: (8, 3)

Step 1: Count across to line 8 on the graph.
Step 2: Count up to line 3 on the graph.
Step 3: Draw a dot to mark the spot.

Directions: Map the following spots on the grid using ordered pairs.

(4, 7)　(9, 10)　(2, 1)　(5, 6)　(2, 2)　(1, 5)　(7, 4)　(3, 8)

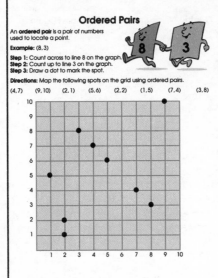

Page 289

Graphing: Finding Ordered Pairs

Graphs or grids are sometimes used to find the location of objects.

Example: The ice-cream cone is located at point (5, 6) on the graph. To find the ice cream's location, follow the line to the bottom of the grid to get the first number — 5. Then go back to the ice cream and follow the grid line to the left for the second number — 6.

Directions: Write the ordered pair for the following objects. The first one is done for you.

book **(4, 8)**　bike **(8, 6)**　suitcase **(1, 4)**　house **(8, 3)**
globe **(4, 4)**　cup **(9, 9)**　triangle **(7, 2)**　airplane **(7, 8)**

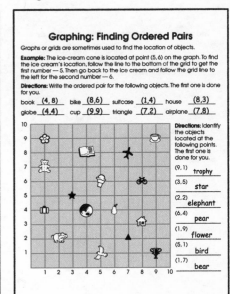

Directions: Identify the objects located at the following points. The first one is done for you.

(9, 1) _trophy_
(3, 5) _star_
(2, 2) _elephant_
(6, 4) _pear_
(1, 9) _flower_
(5, 1) _bird_
(1, 7) _bear_

Page 290

Geometry: Polygons

A **polygon** is a closed figure with three or more sides.

Examples:

triangle 3 sides　square 4 equal sides　rectangle 4 sides　pentagon 5 sides　hexagon 6 sides　octagon 8 sides

Directions: Identify the polygons.

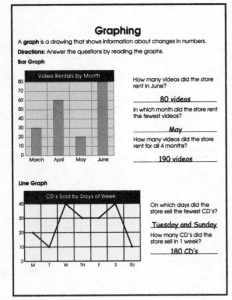

octagon　_rectangle_

square　_hexagon_

pentagon　_triangle_

Page 291

Geometry: Line, Ray, Segment

A **line segment** has two end points.
Write: AB

A **line** has no end points and goes on in both directions.
Write: CD

A **ray** is part of a line and goes on in one direction. It has one end point.
Write: EF

Directions: Identify each of the following as a line, line segment or ray.

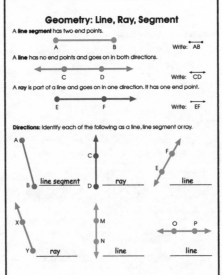

line segment　_ray_　_line_

ray　_line_　_line_

Page 292

Geometry: Angles

The point at which two line segments meet is called an **angle**. There are three types of angles — right, acute and obtuse.

A **right angle** is formed when the two lines meet at 90°.
An **acute angle** is formed when the two lines meet at less than 90°.
An **obtuse angle** is formed when the two lines meet at greater than 90°.

Angles can be measured with a protractor or index card. With a protractor, align the bottom edge of the angle with the bottom of the protractor, with the angle point at the circle of the protractor. Note the direction of the other ray and the number of degrees of the angle.

right　acute　obtuse

Place the corner of an index card in the corner of the angle. If the edges line up with the card, it is a right angle. If not, the angle is acute or obtuse.

right　acute　obtuse

Directions: Use a protractor or index card to identify the following angles as right, obtuse or acute.

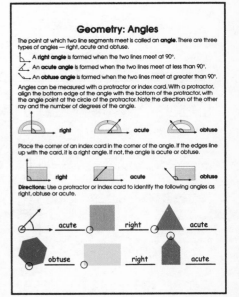

acute　_right_　_acute_

obtuse　_right_　_acute_

Page 293

Geometry: Circles

A **circle** is a round figure. It is named by its center. A **radius** is a line segment from the center of a circle to any point on the circle. A **diameter** is a line segment with both end points on the circle. The diameter always passes through the center of the circle.

Directions: Name the radius, diameter and circle.

Example:

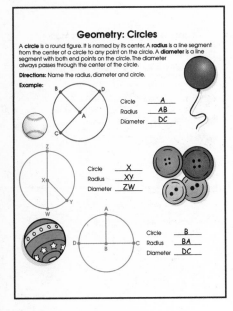

Circle	A
Radius	AB
Diameter	DC

Circle	X
Radius	XY
Diameter	ZW

Circle	B
Radius	BA
Diameter	DC

Page 294

Review

Directions: Complete the line graph using the information in the box.

Team	Games Played
Red	10
Blue	20
Green	15
Yellow	25

Directions: Draw a line from the figure to its name.

- line
- square
- segment
- diameter
- octagon
- triangle
- pentagon

Page 295

Number Patterns

Figuring out the secret to a number pattern or code can send you into "thinking overtime."

Directions: Discover the pattern for each set of numbers. Then write the missing numbers.

a) 20, 21, 19, 20, 18, 19, 17, **18**, 16, 17, 15, **16**, **14**, **15**, **13**, **14**.

b) 1, 6, 16, 31, 51, **76**, **106**, 141, **181**, 226.

c) 3, 5, 9, 15, **23**, **33**, 45, **59**, 75.

d) 55, 52, 50, 49, 46, **44**, **43**, 40, **38**, **37**, 34.

e) 1, 3, 6, 10, 15, 21, **28**, **36**, **45**, 55, 66, 78.

f) 10, 16, 13, 19, 16, **22**, 19, **25**, **22**, 28, **25**.

g) 3, 4, 7, 12, **19**, **28**, 39, **52**, 67, **84**.

h) 100, 90, 95, 85, 90, 80, 85, **75**, **80**, **70**, 75.

Directions: Make up a number pattern of your own. Have a parent, brother or sister figure it out!

Patterns will vary.

Directions: Follow the instructions to solve the number puzzler.

Use only these numbers: 2, 4, 5, 7, 8, 11, 13, 14, 16.

Each number may only be used once.

Write even numbers in the squares.

Write odd numbers in the circles.

Each row must add up to 26.

Hint: Work the puzzle in pencil, so you can erase and retry numbers if needed.

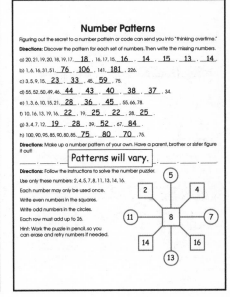

Page 296

Finding Common Attributes

The things that items have in common are called **common attributes**.

Example:

These are Pee-Wees.	These are not Pee-Wees.	Circle the Pee-Wees
A E I O U	B C M W Z	S O T U R E

When you look at the Pee-Wees, you see what they have in common. They are all vowels. That is their common attribute. The items in the middle box are not Pee-Wees because they are all consonants. In the last box, only the vowels are circled.

Directions: Find the common attributes of the Wobbles, Whimzees, Dwibbles and Zanies. Circle the correct answers.

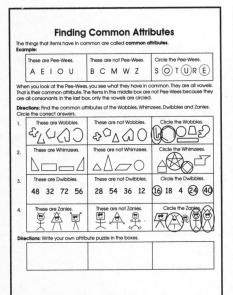

1. These are Wobbles. / These are not Wobbles. / Circle the Wobbles

2. These are Whimzees. / These are not Whimzees. / Circle the Whimzees

3. These are Dwibbles. 48 32 72 56 / These are not Dwibbles. 28 54 36 12 / Circle the Dwibbles 16 18 4 24 40

4. These are Zanies. / These are not Zanies. / Circle the Zanies

Directions: Write your own attribute puzzle in the boxes.

Page 297

Probability

Another thinking skill to get your brain in gear is figuring probability. **Probability** is the likelihood or chance that something will happen. Probability is expressed and written as a ratio.

The probability of tossing heads or tails on a coin is one in two (1:2).

The probability of rolling any number on a die is one in six (1:6).

The probability of getting a red on this spinner is two in four (2:4).

The probability of drawing an ace from a deck of cards is four in fifty-two (4:52).

Directions: Write the probability ratios to answer these questions.

1. There are 26 letters in the alphabet. What is the probability of drawing any letter from a set of alphabet cards? **1:26**

2. Five of the 26 alphabet letters are vowels. What is the probability of drawing a vowel from the alphabet cards? **5:26**

3. Matt takes 10 shots at the basketball hoop. Six of his shots are baskets. What is the probability of Matt's next shot being a basket? **6:10**

4. A box contains 10 marbles: 2 white, 3 green, 1 red, 2 orange and 2 blue. What is the probability of pulling a green marble from the box? **3:10**
   A red marble? **1:10**

5. What is the probability of pulling a marble that is not blue? **8:10**

Page 298

Probability

Directions: Write the probability ratios to answer these questions.

1. Using the spinner shown, what is the probability of spinning a 4? **1:8**

2. Using the spinner show, what is the chance of not spinning a 2? **7:8**

3. Using the spinner shown, what is the probability of getting a 6 in three spins? **3:8**

4. What is the probability of getting heads or tails when you toss a coin? **1:2**

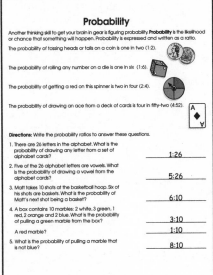

Directions: Toss a coin 20 times and record the outcome of each toss. Then answer the questions.

Heads _____ Tails _____

5. What was the ratio of heads to tails in the 20 tosses?

6. Was the outcome of getting heads or tails in the 20 tosses the same as the probability?

7. Why or why not?

The probability ratio of _____ of dice is 1:6.

Directions: T___ ___ many times it lands ___ ___ questions.

_____ three _____ four _____ five _____ six

8. What ___ ___ of each number on the die?
   one _____ three _____ four _____ five _____ six

9. Did any of the numbers have a ratio close to the actual probability ratio? _____

10. What do the outcomes of flipping a coin and tossing a die tell you about the probability of an event happening?

Answers will vary.

Page 299

Computing

Many people use computers on a daily basis at home, work or school. Computers help us to complete many tasks quickly and efficiently.

The Chinese used a computing device more than 4,000 years ago. It was called an abacus. An **abacus** is a wooden frame with four rows of beads representing ones, tens, hundreds and thousands.

The beads on the bottom half of the abacus are worth one unit. The beads on the top half of the unit are worth five units.

The bottom beads are pushed up to the middle bar of the abacus. The top beads are pushed down to the middle bar of the abacus.

Directions: Determine the number shown on each abacus and write it on the blank. The first one has been done for you.

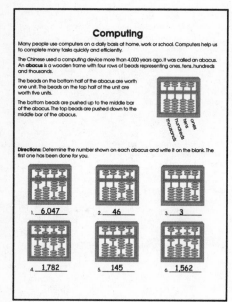

1. 6,047   2. 46   3. 3

4. 1,782   5. 145   6. 1,562

Page 300

Problem Solving: A Garden Puzzle

Grace is planting a garden. The garden will be a semi-circle in shape and have two rows. The first row will have three sections and the back row will have six sections. Grace needs to decide how many plants she can put in each section of her garden.

She wants the total number of plants in the back row to be double the total number of plants in front.

Directions: Help Grace finish her garden plan by using the numbers 1, 2, 3, 4, 5, 6, 7, 8 and 9. Each number may only be used once. Three numbers have been written in place for you.

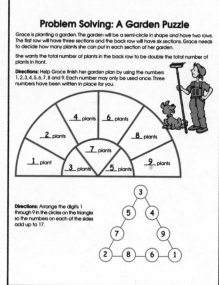

4 plants   6 plants

2 plants   8 plants

1 plant   7 plants   9 plants

3 plants   5 plants

Directions: Arrange the digits 1 through 9 in the circles on the triangle so the numbers on each of the sides add up to 17.

```
        3
      5   4
    7       9
  2   8   6   1
```

Page 301

Problem Solving: Sorting Information

When you have two sets of items, they can be grouped in pairs (with one item from each set) in many ways.

Example:
While shopping, Sally bought three pairs of shorts and three blouses. How many different outfits can she make from these items?

To solve, you could draw a picture or make a list:

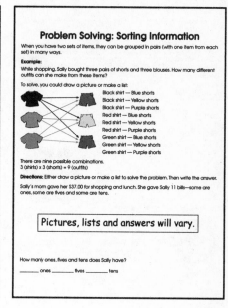

Black shirt — Blue shorts
Black shirt — Yellow shorts
Black shirt — Purple shorts
Red shirt — Blue shorts
Red shirt — Yellow shorts
Red shirt — Purple shorts
Green shirt — Blue shorts
Green shirt — Yellow shorts
Green shirt — Purple shorts

There are nine possible combinations.
3 (shirts) x 3 (shorts) = 9 (outfits)

Directions: Either draw a picture or make a list to solve the problem. Then write the answer.

Sally's mom gave her $37.00 for shopping and lunch. She gave Sally 11 bills—some are ones, some are fives and some are tens.

> Pictures, lists and answers will vary.

How many ones, fives and tens does Sally have?
_____ ones _____ fives _____ tens

Page 302

Problem Solving: Sorting Information

Directions: Solve these problems the same way you did on the last page. Then write the answers.

1. Jodie stopped at the Food Court for lunch. She can have a hamburger or hot dog to eat and a soda, milk or lemonade to drink. Make a list or draw a picture to show all possible combinations.

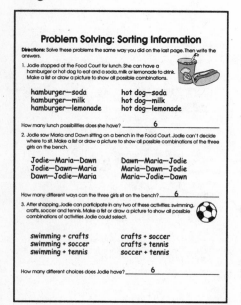

hamburger—soda   hot dog—soda
hamburger—milk   hot dog—milk
hamburger—lemonade   hot dog—lemonade

How many lunch possibilities does she have? _____ 6

2. Jodie saw Maria and Dawn sitting on a bench in the Food Court. Jodie can't decide where to sit. Make a list or draw a picture to show all possible combinations of the three girls on the bench.

Jodie—Maria—Dawn   Dawn—Maria—Jodie
Jodie—Dawn—Maria   Maria—Dawn—Jodie
Dawn—Jodie—Maria   Maria—Jodie—Dawn

How many different ways can the three girls sit on the bench? _____ 6

3. After shopping, Jodie can participate in any two of these activities: swimming, crafts, soccer and tennis. Make a list or draw a picture to show all possible combinations of activities Jodie could select.

swimming + crafts   crafts + soccer
swimming + soccer   crafts + tennis
swimming + tennis   soccer + tennis

How many different choices does Jodie have? _____ 6